Frommer's®

W9-BLU-492

Santa Fe, Taos & Albuquerque

13th Edition

by Lesley S. King

WILEY

Wiley Publishing, Inc.

Published by:

WILEY PUBLISHING, INC.

111 River St.

Hoboken, NJ 07030-5774

ISBN 978-0-470-64376-1 (paper); ISBN 978-0-470-94627-5 (ebk); ISBN 978-0-470-94628-2 (ebk);
ISBN 978-0-470-94629-9 (ebk)

Editor: Billy Fox
Production Editor: Jonathan Scott
Cartographer: Guy Ruggiero
Photo Editor: Richard Fox
Production by Wiley Indianapolis Composition Services
Santa Fe photo credits:
Front cover: Chile ristras, Santa Fe, New Mexico ©Dave G. Houser / Alamy Images
Back cover: Skier doing a "helicopter" from a cliff in Taos Ski Valley. ©Christian Aslund / Lonely Planet
Images

For information on our other products and services or to obtain technical support, please contact our
Customer Care Department within the U.S. at 877/762-2974, outside the U.S. at 317/572-3993 or fax
317/572-4002.

Wiley also publishes its books in a variety of electronic formats. Some content that appears in print may
not be available in electronic formats.

Manufactured in the United States of America

5   4   3   2   1

CONTENTS

16 ALBUQUERQUE 238

17 FAST FACTS 293

Index 298

LIST OF MAPS

ACKNOWLEDGMENTS

My sincere thanks go to Allison Rand, who helped research this book. The assistance of the many tourism agencies, hotel and restaurant owners and managers, and attractions' public-relations people was invaluable, as was the support of my family, friends, and editor, Billy Fox.

—Lesley S. King

ABOUT THE AUTHOR

Lesley S. King grew up on a ranch in northern New Mexico, not far from where she currently lives. She's a freelance writer and photographer and a columnist for *New Mexico* magazine. Formerly managing editor for *The Santa Fean,* she has written for the *New York Times,* United Airline's *Hemispheres* magazine, and *Audubon,* among other publications. She is the author of *Frommer's New Mexico, Frommer's Great Outdoor Guide to Arizona & New Mexico,* and *New Mexico For Dummies.* She's also the coauthor of *Frommer's American Southwest.* Her newest book, released in 2007, is *King of the Road.*

HOW TO CONTACT US

In researching this book, we discovered many wonderful places—hotels, restaurants, shops, and more. We're sure you'll find others. Please tell us about them, so we can share the information with your fellow travelers in upcoming editions. If you were disappointed with a recommendation, we'd love to know that, too. Please write to:

Frommer's Santa Fe, Taos & Albuquerque, 13th Edition
Wiley Publishing, Inc. • 111 River St. • Hoboken, NJ 07030-5774
frommersfeedback@wiley.com

AN ADDITIONAL NOTE

Please be advised that travel information is subject to change at any time—and this is especially true of prices. We therefore suggest that you write or call ahead for confirmation when making your travel plans. The authors, editors, and publisher cannot be held responsible for the experiences of readers while traveling. Your safety is important to us, however, so we encourage you to stay alert and be aware of your surroundings. Keep a close eye on cameras, purses, and wallets, all favorite targets of thieves and pickpockets.

FROMMER'S STAR RATINGS, ICONS & ABBREVIATIONS

Every hotel, restaurant, and attraction listing in this guide has been ranked for quality, value, service, amenities, and special features using a star rating system. In country, state, and regional guides, we also rate towns and regions to help you narrow down your choices and budget your time accordingly. Hotels and restaurants are rated on a scale of zero (recommended) to three stars (exceptional). Attractions, shopping, nightlife, towns, and regions are rated according to the following scale: zero stars (recommended), one star (highly recommended), two stars (very highly recommended), and three stars (must-see).

In addition to the star-rating system, we also use seven feature icons that point you to the great deals, in-the-know advice, and unique experiences that separate travelers from tourists. Throughout the book, look for:

special finds—those places only insiders know about

fun facts—details that make travelers more informed and their trips more fun

kids—best bets for kids and advice for the whole family

special moments—those experiences that memories are made of

overrated—places or experiences not worth your time or money

insider tips—great ways to save time and money

great values—where to get the best deals

The following abbreviations are used for credit cards:

AE	American Express	DISC	Discover	V	Visa
DC	Diners Club	MC	MasterCard		

TRAVEL RESOURCES AT FROMMERS.COM

Frommer's travel resources don't end with this guide. Frommer's website, www.frommers.com, has travel information on more than 4,000 destinations. We update features regularly, giving you access to the most current trip-planning information and the best airfare, lodging, and car-rental bargains. You can also listen to podcasts, connect with other Frommers.com members through our active-reader forums, share your travel photos, read blogs from guidebook editors and fellow travelers, and much more.

THE BEST OF NORTHERN NEW MEXICO

New Mexico's Pueblo tribes have one character who stands out among many as a symbol of the spirit of this state: the fun-maker, called by a variety of names, most notably Koshare. Within the Native American dances, this black-and-white-striped character has many powers. He can cure some diseases, make rain fall, and increase fertility. Above all, the irreverent joker exposes our deepest foibles.

As you travel throughout northern New Mexico, you may see evidence of the Koshare-like powers in the land's magical beauty and in the tender relationships between cultures. This place has witnessed immense geologic upheavals, from volcanic explosions to cataclysmic ground shifts. It has seen tragedy in the clash among Spanish, Native American, and Anglo cultures. And yet, with its Koshare nature, it has transformed those experiences into immeasurable richness. Today, it is a land of stunning expanses, immense cultural diversity, and creativity—a place where people very much pursue their own paths.

The center of the region is **Santa Fe,** a hip, artsy city that wears its 400-year-old mores on its sleeve. Not far away is upstart **Taos,** the little arts town and ski center of just 5,000 people that lies wedged between the 13,000-foot **Sangre de Cristo Mountains** and the 700-foot-deep **Rio Grande Gorge. Albuquerque** is the big city, New Mexico style, where people from all over the state come to trade. Not far from these three cities are the 19 settlements and numerous ruins of the Native American Pueblo culture, an incredible testament to the resilience of a proud people. And through it all weave the **Manzano, Sandia, Sangre de Cristo,** and **Jemez mountains,** multimillion-year-old reminders of the recent arrival of humans in this vast and unique landscape.

From skiing to art galleries, you have a wealth of choices in front of you when planning a trip to northern New Mexico. To help you get started, here are some of my favorite things to do, places to stay, and places to eat in and around Santa Fe, Taos, and Albuquerque.

THE best NORTHERN NEW MEXICO EXPERIENCES

o **Northern New Mexican Enchiladas:** There are few things more New Mexican than the enchilada. You can order red or green chile, or "Christmas"—half and half. Sauces are rich, seasoned with *ajo* (garlic) and oregano. New Mexican cuisine isn't smothered in cheese and sour cream, so the flavors of the chiles, corn, and meats can really be savored. Enchiladas often are served with *frijoles* (beans), *posole* (hominy), and *sopaipillas* (fried bread). See "Eating & Drinking in Northern New Mexico," in chapter 2.

o **High Road to Taos:** This spectacular 80-mile route into the mountains between Santa Fe and Taos takes you through red painted deserts, villages bordered by apple and peach orchards, and the foothills of 13,000-foot peaks. You can stop in Cordova, known for its woodcarvers, or Chimayo, known for its weavers. At the fabled **Santuario de Chimayo,** you can rub healing dust between your fingers. See "Along the High Road to Taos," in chapter 11.

o **Santa Fe Opera** (© **800/280-4654;** www.santafeopera.org): One of the finest opera companies in the United States has called Santa Fe home for a half-century. Performances are held during the summer months in a hilltop, open-air amphitheater. See p. 151.

o **Museum of International Folk Art,** 706 Camino Lejo (© **505/476-1200;** www.moifa.org): Santa Fe's perpetually expanding collection of folk art is the largest in the world, with thousands of objects from more than 100 countries. You'll find an amazing array of imaginative works, ranging from Hispanic folk art *santos* (carved saints) to Indonesian textiles and African sculptures. See p. 117.

o **Albuquerque International Balloon Fiesta** (© **505/821-1000;** www.balloonfiesta.com): The world's largest balloon rally assembles some 600 colorful balloons and includes races and contests. Highlights are the mass ascension at sunrise and the special shapes rodeo, in which balloons in all sorts of whimsical forms, from liquor bottles to cows, rise into the sky. See "Northern New Mexico Calendar of Events," in chapter 3.

o **María Benitez Teatro Flamenco,** Institute for Spanish Arts (© **505/470-7828;** www.mariabenitez.com): A native New Mexican, María Benitez was trained in Spain, where she returns each year to find dancers and prepare her show. Now she teaches a group of young dancers that performs at the Lodge at Santa Fe from mid-July to mid-August on Sundays at 2pm. See p. 153.

o **Taos Pueblo,** Veterans Highway, Taos Pueblo (© **575/758-1028;** www.taospueblo.com): Possibly the original home of pueblo-style architecture, this bold structure, where 200 residents still live much as their ancestors did a thousand years ago, is awe inspiring. Rooms built of mud are poetically stacked to echo the shape of Taos Mountain behind them. As you explore the pueblo, you can visit the residents' studios, munch on bread baked in an *horno* (a beehive-shaped oven), and wander past the fascinating ruins of the old church and cemetery. See p. 214.

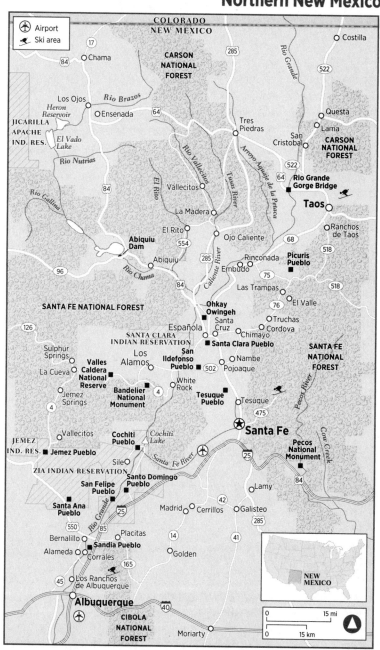

THE best SPLURGE HOTELS

- **Bishop's Lodge Ranch Resort & Spa,** Bishop's Lodge Road, Santa Fe (© **505/983-6377;** www.bishopslodge.com): More than a century ago, Bishop Jean-Baptiste Lamy often escaped clerical politics by hiking into a valley north of town called Little Tesuque. He built a retreat and chapel that, years later, have become the Bishop's Lodge. All rooms are spacious and feature handcrafted furniture and local artwork. Activities include horseback riding, hiking, tennis, and swimming. See p. 79.

- **Encantado Resort,** 198 NM 592, Santa Fe (© **877/262-4666;** www.encantado resort.com): An architectural artwork, this Auberge Resort 15 minutes from Santa Fe provides world-class accommodations and views. A spa and fine-dining restaurant add to the all-inclusive nature of the experience. See p. 72.

- **Hotel Andaluz,** 125 Second St. NW, at Copper Avenue, Albuquerque (© **877/987-9090** or 505/242-9090; www.hotelandaluz.com): A $30-million makeover to this 1939 classic has brought a cozy Mediterranean ambience. For a real splurge, get a suite here to partake of city views, sumptuous bedding, granite counters, comfy robes, and other luxuries. See p. 244.

- **Inn of the Anasazi,** 113 Washington Ave., Santa Fe (© **800/688-8100** or 505/988-3030; www.innoftheanasazi.com): Just steps from the plaza, this elegant hotel offers a taste of Anasazi architecture. The interior utilizes stacked sandstone with touches of Navajo artwork to create a warm atmosphere. Add to that excellent amenities and stellar service. See p. 73.

- **Inn of the Five Graces,** 150 E. de Vargas St., Santa Fe (© **505/992-0957;** www.fivegraces.com): Just a few blocks from the plaza, this Relais & Chateaux inn spoils guests with floral-decked courtyards and elaborately decorated suites with *kilim* rugs and ornately carved beds.

- **La Posada de Santa Fe Resort and Spa,** 330 E. Palace Ave., Santa Fe (© **800/727-5276** or 505/986-0000; http://laposada.rockresorts.com): With the feel of a meandering adobe village but the service of a fine hotel, this has become one of New Mexico's premier resorts. Most rooms don't have views but do have outdoor patios, and most are tucked back into the quiet compound. See p. 73.

- **Rancho de San Juan Country Inn,** US 285 near Española (© **505/753-6818;** www.ranchodesanjuan.com): Just 38 miles from Santa Fe, in the enchanting country near Ojo Caliente, this award-winning inn offers complete luxury and the quiet of the country. The rooms in the inn, as well as the casitas set among the hills, are all decorated with impressive art and antiques, and have spectacular views. See p. 174.

- **El Monte Sagrado,** 317 Kit Carson Rd., Taos (© **800/828-8267** or 575/758-3502; www.elmontesagrado.com): With guest rooms and casitas set around a grassy "Sacred Circle," this eco-resort is the quintessence of luxury. Every detail, from the waterfalls and chemical-free pool and hot tubs to the authentic theme decor in the rooms, has been created with conscious care. See p. 189.

- **Hyatt Regency Tamaya Resort and Spa,** 1300 Tuyuna Trail, Santa Ana Pueblo (© **800/554-9288** or 505/867-1234; www.tamaya.hyatt.com): Situated on Santa Ana Pueblo land, this grand resort has all a human might need to get away from the world. Three swimming pools; a 16,000-square-foot, full-service spa and fitness center; the 18-hole Twin Warriors Championship Golf Course designed by Gary Panks; and views of the Sandia Mountains make for plenty to do. Meanwhile, spacious rooms offer quiet for those who'd rather do nothing. It's only 25 minutes from Albuquerque and 45 minutes from Santa Fe. See p. 249.

THE best MODERATELY PRICED HOTELS

- **Santa Fe Motel and Inn,** 510 Cerrillos Rd., Santa Fe (© **800/930-5002** or 505/982-1039; www.santafemotel.com): Rooms at this inn, walking distance from the plaza, combine the ambience of the Southwest—bold colors and some hand-made furniture—with a standard motel price tag. See p. 77.
- **El Rey Inn,** 1862 Cerrillos Rd., Santa Fe (© **800/521-1349** or 505/982-1931; www.elreyinnsantafe.com): If old-style court motels awaken the road warrior in you, this is your place. Built in the 1930s and added on to over the years, the King provides a variety of room types, all nicely appointed. See p. 82.
- Though it's actually an inn, one of the best moderately priced accommodations in Taos—with more luxurious options as well—is the **Old Taos Guesthouse,** 1028 Witt Rd., Taos (© **800/758-5448** or 575/758-5448; www.oldtaos.com). Surrounded by acres of country, it provides a lovely rural stay. See p. 196.
- Providing comfortable rooms with a Native American theme, the **Nativo Lodge,** 6000 Pan American Fwy. NE, Albuquerque (© **888/628-4861** or 505/798-4300; www.nativolodge.com), offers a bit of New Mexico culture at a reasonable price. See p. 246.
- **Hotel Albuquerque at Old Town,** 800 Rio Grande Blvd. NW, Albuquerque (© **800/237-2133** [reservations only] or 505/843-6300; www.hotelabq.com): Under the same ownership as the Nativo but with a prime location steps from Old Town, this hotel has artfully decorated rooms and excellent service.

THE best DINING EXPERIENCES

- **The Compound,** 653 Canyon Rd., Santa Fe (© **505/982-4353;** www.compound restaurant.com): This reincarnation of one of Santa Fe's classic restaurants serves daring contemporary American food in a soulful setting. Such delicacies as the grilled beef tenderloin with Italian potatoes and foie gras hollandaise will please sophisticated palates—and probably simpler ones, too. See p. 92.
- **Santacafé,** 231 Washington Ave., Santa Fe (© **505/984-1788;** www.santacafe. com): The food here borrows from an international menu of preparations and offerings. The minimalist decor accentuates the graceful architecture of the 18th-century Padre Gallegos House. One of my favorite dishes is the grilled rack of lamb with potato-leek gratin. See p. 96.
- **Geronimo,** 724 Canyon Rd., Santa Fe (© **505/982-1500;** www.geronimo restaurant.com): Set in the 1756 Borrego House on Canyon Road, this restaurant offers brilliant flavors in a serene adobe atmosphere. The elk tenderloin here is Santa Fe's most prized entree. See p. 94.
- **The Shed,** 113½ E. Palace Ave., Santa Fe (© **505/982-9030;** www.sfshed. com): The Shed, a Santa Fe luncheon institution since 1953, occupies several rooms in part of a rambling hacienda that was built in 1692. The sauces here have been refined over the years, creating amazing flavors in basic dishes like

enchiladas, burritos, and stuffed *sopaipillas*. The mocha cake is renowned. See p. 104. Sister restaurant **La Choza** is just as good, with a similar menu. See p. 103.

o **Stakeout Grill & Bar,** 101 Stakeout Dr., Taos (*C* **575/758-2042;** www.stake-outrestaurant.com): This elegant restaurant offers delicious New American cuisine and a broad view across sage forest and the Rio Grande Gorge. The filet mignon with béarnaise sauce is excellent. See p. 204.

o **Jennifer James 101,** 4615-A Menaul Blvd. NE., Albuquerque (*C* **505/884-3860;** www.jenniferjames101.com). In a contemporary setting, one of Albuquerque's best chefs serves imaginative fare using local and seasonal ingredients. The seared duck with a scallion pancake and plum sauce is delicious. See p. 258.

o **Bien Shur,** 30 Rainbow Rd. NE, at Sandia Resort & Casino, Albuquerque (*C* **800/526-9366;** www.sandiaresort.com): With views overlooking Albuquerque's city lights and the mountains, Bien Shur offers inventive food with a hint of Native America. The rack of lamb with a garlic mint au jus is excellent. See p. 258.

THE best THINGS TO DO FOR FREE

o **The Galleries Along Canyon Road:** Originally a Pueblo Indian route over the mountains and later an artists' community, Santa Fe's Canyon Road is now gallery central—the arts capital of the Southwest. The narrow one-way street is lined with more than 100 galleries, in addition to restaurants and private residences. Artwork ranges from the beautiful to the bizarre. You can step into artists' simple studio galleries as well as refined galleries showing world-renowned artists' works, such as paintings by Georgia O'Keeffe and sculptures by Frederic Remington. Be sure to stop for lunch at one of the street-side cafes. See "Walking Tour 2: Barrio de Analco & Canyon Road," in chapter 8.

o **Pueblo Dances:** These native dances, related to the changing cycles of the earth, offer a unique chance to see how an indigenous culture worships and rejoices. Throughout the year, the pueblos' people participate in ceremonies ranging from harvest and deer dances to those commemorating the feast days of their particular saints—all in the mystical light of the northern New Mexico sun. See chapter 11 for more information on visiting pueblos.

o **Rio Grande Gorge:** A hike into this dramatic gorge is unforgettable. You'll first see it as you come over a rise heading toward Taos, a colossal slice in the earth formed 130 million years ago. Drive about 35 miles north of Taos, near the village of Cerro, to the Wild Rivers Recreation Area. From the lip of the canyon, you descend through millions of years of geologic history on land inhabited by Indians since 16,000 B.C. When you reach the river, you can dip your toes in the fabled *rio*. If you're not a hiker, you can get a sense of the canyon by walking across the Rio Grande Gorge Bridge. See chapter 15.

o **Old Town:** Albuquerque's commercial center until about 1880, Old Town still gives a remarkable sense of what life was once like in a Southwestern village. You can meander down crooked streets and narrow alleys and rest in the cottonwood-shaded plaza. Though many of the shops are now very touristy, you can still happen upon some interesting shopping and dining finds here. Native Americans sell jewelry, pottery, and weavings under a portal on the plaza. See p. 265.

THE best OUTDOOR ACTIVITIES

o **Taos Ski Valley:** World renowned for its challenging runs and the ridge where skiers hike for up to 2 hours to ski fresh powder, Taos has long been a pilgrimage site for extreme skiers. Over the years, the ski area has opened up new bowls to accommodate intermediate and beginning skiers, and most recently snowboarders have become welcome, too! See p. 218.

o **Sandia Peak Tramway:** The world's longest tramway ferries passengers 2¾ miles, from Albuquerque's city limits to the summit of the 10,378-foot Sandia Peak. On the way, you'll likely see rare Rocky Mountain bighorn sheep and birds of prey. Go in the evening to watch the sun set, and then enjoy the glimmering city lights on your way down. See p. 266.

o **Bandelier National Monument:** These ruins provide a spectacular peek into the lives of the ancestral Puebloan culture, which reached its peak in this area around 1100 A.D. Less than 15 miles south of Los Alamos, the ruins spread across a peaceful canyon. You'll probably see deer and rabbits as you make your way through the canyon to the most dramatic site, a kiva and dwelling in a cave 140 feet above the canyon floor. See p. 162.

o **White-Water Rafting on the Rio Grande:** In spring and early summer, the region's most notorious white-water trip, the Taos Box, takes rafters on an 18-mile jaunt through the Rio Grande Gorge. Less extreme types can enjoy a trip down Pilar and still get plenty wet. See p. 225.

o **Llama Trekking:** Also in the Taos area, two outfitters take hikers on day or multi-day trips. You get to enjoy the scenery while the stout and docile creatures do the work. The trips come with gourmet food. See p. 224.

o **Hot-Air Ballooning:** One of the biggest treats about being in Albuquerque is waking each day and looking at the sky. Unless it's very windy or extremely cold, you'll likely see some colorful globes floating serenely on the horizon. You might even be startled with the sound of flames blasting as one flies over your head. The experience of riding in one is indescribable. You're literally floating, being carried along by nothing but the wind. Try it! See p. 272.

o **Bosque del Apache National Wildlife Refuge,** Socorro (© **505/835-1828**): About 80 miles south of Albuquerque, this is one of the nation's finest refuges. In winter, visitors come to see volumes of birds. In early December, the refuge may harbor as many as 45,000 snow geese, 57,000 ducks of many different species, and 18,000 sandhill cranes. Seeing them "fly out" to the fields in the morning or "fly in" to the lakes in the evening is a life-altering experience. See p. 273.

THE best OFFBEAT EXPERIENCES

o **Watching Zozobra Burn,** Santa Fe (© **505/284-1598**): Part of Las Fiestas de Santa Fe held in early September, this ritual draws crowds to the core of the city to cheer as "Old Man Gloom," a giant marionette, moans and struggles as he burns. The Fiestas also include Masses, parades, dances, food, and arts. See p. 34.

o **Theater Grottesco,** 551 W. Cordova Rd., no. 8400, Santa Fe (© **505/474-8400;** www.theatergrottesco.org): This theater troupe likes to shock, confuse, confound, and tickle its audience's funny bones. Their original works—presented for about a month each fall, and sometimes other seasons as well—combine adept movement with sound, story, and, well . . . complete brilliance. See p. 153.

o **Black Hole,** 4015 Arkansas Ave., Los Alamos (© **505/662-5053**): Oddball history buffs will love wandering among this shrine to the nuclear age. Packed to the ceiling with the remains of the nuclear age, from Geiger counters to a giant Waring blender, it's peace activist Edward Grothus's statement about the proliferation of war and the materials that make it happen. See p. 164.

o **D. H. Lawrence Ranch,** NM 522, San Cristobal (© **575/776-2245**): North of Taos, this memorial offers a look into the oddly touching devotion for this controversial author, who lived and wrote in the area in the early 1920s. The guest book reveals a wellspring of stories of pilgrimages to the site. See p. 216.

o **American International Rattlesnake Museum,** 202 San Felipe St. NW (© **505/242-6569;** www.rattlesnakes.com): This Albuquerque museum offers a glimpse of reptilian life. You'll see living specimens of common, uncommon, and very rare rattlesnakes of North, Central, and South America, in naturally landscaped habitats. More than 30 species are included, along with oddities such as albino and patternless rattlesnakes. See p. 269.

NORTHERN NEW MEXICO IN DEPTH

When I was a child in New Mexico, we'd sing a song while driving the dusty roads en route to such ruins as Chaco Canyon or Puye Cliff Dwellings. Sung to the tune of "Oh Christmas Tree," it went like this:

New Mexico, New Mexico
Don't know why we love you so.
It never rains
It never snows
The winds and sand
They always blow.
And how we live
God only knows
New Mexico, we love you so.

Although this song exaggerates the conditions here, the truth remains that, in many ways, New Mexico has an inhospitable environment. So why are so many people drawn here, and why do so many of us stay?

Ironically, the very extremes that this song presents are the reason. From the moment you set foot in this 121,666-square-mile state, you're met with wildly varied terrain, temperature, and temperament. On a single day, you might experience temperatures from 25° to 75°F (–4° to 24°C). From the vast heat and dryness of White Sands in the summer to the 13,161-foot subzero, snow-encrusted Wheeler Peak in the winter, New Mexico's beauty is carved by extremes.

Culturally, this is also the case. Pueblo, Navajo, and Apache tribes occupy much of the state's lands, many of them still speaking their native languages and observing the traditions of their people. Some even live without running water and electricity. Meanwhile, the Hispanic culture remains deeply linked to its Spanish roots, practicing a devout Catholicism, and speaking a centuries-old Spanish dialect; some still live by subsistence farming in tiny mountain villages.

New Mexico has its very own sense of time and its own social mores. The pace is slow, the objectives of life less defined. People rarely arrive on time for appointments, and businesses don't always hold to their posted hours. In most cases, people wear whatever they want here. You'll see men dressed for formal occasions in a buttoned collar with a bolo tie and women in cowboy boots and skirts.

All this leads to a certain lost-and-not-caring-to-be-found spell the place casts on visitors. We find ourselves standing amid the dust or sparkling light, within the extreme heat or cold, not sure whether to speak Spanish or English. That's when we let go completely of society's common goals, its pace, and social mores. We slip into a kayak and let the river take us, or hike a peak and look at the world from a new perspective. Or we climb into a car and drive past ancient ruins being excavated at that instant, past ghost mining towns, and under hot-air balloons, by chile fields, and around hand-smoothed *santuarios*, all on the road to nowhere, New Mexico's best destination. At some point in your travels, you'll likely find yourself on this road, and you'll realize that there's no destination so fine.

And after that surrender, you may find yourself looking about with a new clarity. Having experienced the slower pace, you may question your own life's speediness. Having tasted New Mexico's relaxed style, you may look askance at those nylon stockings and heels or that suit and tie. And the next time you climb in the car in your own state or country, you might just head down a road you've never been on and hope that it goes nowhere.

NORTHERN NEW MEXICO TODAY

On rock faces throughout northern New Mexico, you'll find circular symbols carved in sandstone—the wavy mark of Avanu, the river serpent, or the ubiquitous Koko-pelli playing his magic flute. These petroglyphs are constant reminders of the enig-matic history of the ancestral Puebloans (Anasazi), the Indians who inhabited this area from A.D. 1100 until the arrival of the Spanish conquistadors, around 1550.

DATELINE

3000 B.C. First evidence of stable farming settlements in region.	**1680** Pueblo tribes revolt against Spanish.
A.D. 700 Earliest evidence of ancestral Puebloan presence.	**1692** Spanish recapture Santa Fe.
	1706 Albuquerque established.
1540 Francisco Vásquez de Coronado marches to Cíbola in search of a Native American "city of gold."	**1739** First French traders enter Santa Fe.
	1779 Tabivo Naritgant, leader of rebellious Comanche tribes, falls to Spanish forces.
1542 Coronado returns to New Spain, declaring his mission a failure.	
1610 Immigration to New Mexico increases; Don Pedro de Peralta establishes Santa Fe as capital.	**1786** Comanches and Utes sign treaty with Spanish.
	1821 Mexico gains independence from Spain.

The Spanish conquistadors, in their inimitable fashion, imposed a new, foreign order on the resident Native Americans and their land. As an inevitable component of conquest, they changed most Native American names—today, you'll find a number of Native Americans with Hispanic names—and renamed the villages "pueblos." The Spaniards' most far-reaching legacy, however, was the forceful conversion of Indian populations to Catholicism, a religion that many Indians still practice today. In each of the pueblos you'll see a large, often beautiful, Catholic church, usually made with sculpted adobe; during the holiday seasons, Pueblo people perform ritual dances outside their local Catholic churches. The churches, set against the ancient adobe dwellings, are symbolic of the melding of two cultures.

This mix of cultures is apparent in today's northern New Mexican cuisine. When the Spaniards came to the New World, they brought cows and sheep. They quickly learned to appreciate the indigenous foods here, most notably corn, beans, squash, and chiles, and also more rare foods such as the thin-layered blue *piki* bread, or *chauquehue*, a thick corn pudding similar to polenta.

Growing Pains

Northern New Mexico is experiencing a reconquest of sorts, as the Anglo population soars and outside money and values again make their way in. The process continues to transform New Mexico's three distinct cultures and their unique ways of life, albeit in a less violent manner than during the Spanish conquest.

Certainly, the Anglos—many of them from large cities—add a cosmopolitan flavor to life here. The variety of restaurants has greatly improved, as have entertainment options. For their small size, towns such as Taos and Santa Fe offer a broad variety of restaurants and cultural events. Santa Fe has developed a strong dance and drama scene, with treats such as flamenco and opera that you'd expect to find in New York or Los Angeles. And Albuquerque has an exciting nightlife scene downtown; you can walk from club to club and hear a wealth of jazz, rock, country, and alternative music.

1828 Kit Carson, the legendary frontiersman, arrives in Taos.

1846 Mexican War breaks out; Gen. Stephen Kearny takes possession of New Mexico for United States.

1847 Revolt in Taos against U.S. control; newly appointed governor Charles Bent killed.

1848 Under provisions of Treaty of Guadalupe Hidalgo, Mexico officially cedes New Mexico to United States.

1861 Victorious Confederate general proclaims all of New Mexico south of the 34th parallel the Confederate territory of Arizona.

1862 Confederates routed from New Mexico.

1864 Navajos relocated to Bosque Redondo Reservation.

1868 Navajos return to their native homeland.

1878–81 Lincoln County War erupts; epitomizes the lawlessness and violence of the Wild West.

continues

Yet many newcomers, attracted by the adobe houses and exotic feel of the place, often bring only a loose appreciation for the area. Some tend to romanticize the lifestyle of the other cultures and trivialize their beliefs. Native American symbology, for example, is employed in ever-popular Southwestern decorative motifs; New Age groups appropriate valued rituals, such as sweats (in which believers sit encamped in a very hot, enclosed space to cleanse their spirits). The effects of cultural and economic change are even apparent throughout the countryside, where land is being developed at an alarming rate.

Transformation of the local way of life and landscape is also apparent in the stores continually springing up in the area. For some of us, these are a welcome relief from Western clothing stores and provincial dress shops. The downside is that city plazas, which once contained pharmacies and grocery stores frequented by residents, are now crowded with T-shirt shops and galleries appealing to tourists. Many locals in these cities now rarely visit their plazas except during special events such as fiestas.

Environmental threats are another regional reality. Nuclear-waste issues form part of an ongoing conflict affecting the entire Southwest, and a section of southern New Mexico has been designated a nuclear-waste site. Because much of the waste must pass through Santa Fe, the U.S. government, along with the New Mexico state government, constructed a bypass that directs some transit traffic around the west side of the city.

Still, new ways of thinking have also brought positive changes to the life here, and many locals have directly benefited from New Mexico's influx of wealthy newcomers and popularity as a tourist destination. Businesses and industries large and small have come to the area. In Albuquerque, Intel Corporation now employs more than 3,000 workers, and in Santa Fe, the nationally renowned *Outside* magazine publishes monthly. Local artists and artisans also benefit from growth. Many craftspeople—furniture makers, tin workers, and weavers—have expanded their businesses. The influx of people has broadened the sensibility of a fairly provincial

---

1879   Atchison, Topeka, and Santa Fe Railroad routes main line through Las Vegas, Albuquerque, El Paso, and Deming, where connection is made with California's South Pacific Line.

1881   Legendary outlaw Billy the Kid killed by Pat Garrett.

1886   Apache chief Geronimo captured; signals end of New Mexico's Indian wars.

1898   Painters Ernest Blumenschein and Bert Phillips settle in Taos.

1912   New Mexico becomes the 47th state.

1914   Blumenschein and Phillips form Taos Society of Artists; Taos becomes a major center of influence in midcentury American art and letters.

1916   Construction of Elephant Butte Dam brings irrigation to southern New Mexican farms.

1924   Native Americans granted full U.S. citizenship.

1943   Los Alamos National Laboratory built; "Manhattan Project" scientists spend 2 years in complete seclusion developing nuclear weapons.

state. The area has become a refuge for many gays and lesbians, as well as for political exiles, such as Tibetans. With them has developed a level of creativity and tolerance you would generally find only in very large cities.

Cultural Questions

Faced with new challenges to their ways of life, both Native Americans and Hispanics are marshaling forces to protect their cultural identities. A prime concern is language. Through the years, many Pueblo people have begun to speak more and more English, with their children getting little exposure to their native tongue. In a number of the pueblos, elders are working with school children in language classes. Some of the pueblos have even developed written dictionaries, the first time their languages have been presented in this form.

Many pueblos have introduced programs to conserve the environment, preserve ancient seed strains, and protect religious rites. Because their religion is tied closely to nature, a loss of natural resources would threaten the entire culture. Certain rituals have been closed off to outsiders, the most notable being some of the rituals of Shalako at Zuni, a popular and elaborate series of year-end ceremonies.

Hispanics, through art and observance of cultural traditions, are also embracing their roots. In northern New Mexico, murals depicting important historic events, such as the Treaty of Guadalupe Hidalgo of 1848, adorn many walls. The **Spanish Market** in Santa Fe has expanded into a grand celebration of traditional arts—from tin working to *santo* (icon) carving. Public schools in the area have bilingual education programs, allowing students to embrace their Spanish-speaking roots.

Hispanics are also making their voices heard, insisting on more conscientious development of their neighborhoods and rising to positions of power in government. Congressman Bill Richardson, Hispanic despite his Anglo surname, was appointed U.S. ambassador to the United Nations and then left that post to become energy secretary in President Clinton's cabinet. Currently, he is governor of New Mexico.

1945 First atomic bomb exploded at Trinity Site.

1947 Reports of a flying saucer crash near Roswell make national headlines, despite U.S. Air Force's denials that it has occurred.

1972 Pioneer balloonist Sid Cutter establishes Albuquerque International Balloon Fiesta.

1981 The Very Large Array, the world's most powerful radio telescope, begins observations of distant galaxies from the desert west of Socorro.

1982 U.S. space shuttle Columbia lands at Holloman Air Force Base, near White Sands National Monument.

1984 New Mexico's last remaining section of famed Route 66, near San Jon, is abandoned.

1990 New Mexico's last uranium mine, near Grants, closes.

1994 Under pressure from Congress, U.S. Air Force reopens investigation of the 1947 flying saucer crash reports, concluding that the debris found was likely from tests of a secret Cold War spy balloon; UFO believers allege a cover-up.

continues

Gambling Wins & Losses

Gambling, a fact of life and source of much-needed revenue for Native American populations across the country, has been a center of controversy in northern New Mexico for a number of years. In 1994, Governor Gary Johnson signed a pact with tribes in New Mexico, ratified by the U.S. Department of the Interior, to allow full-scale gambling. **Tesuque Pueblo** was one of the first to begin a massive expansion, and many other pueblos followed suit.

Many New Mexicans are concerned about the tone gambling sets in the state. The casinos are for the most part large, neon-bedecked buildings that stand out sorely on some of New Mexico's most picturesque land. Though most residents appreciate the boost that gambling can ultimately bring to the Native American economies, many critics wonder where gambling profits actually go—and if the casinos can possibly be a good thing for the pueblos and tribes. Some detractors suspect that profits go directly into the pockets of outside backers.

Santa Fe

Santa Fe is where the splendor of diverse cultures really shines, and it does so in a setting that's unsurpassed. There's a magic in Santa Fe that's difficult to explain, but you'll sense it when you glimpse an old adobe building set against blue mountains and giant billowing thunderheads, or when you hear a ranchero song come from a low-rider's radio and you smell chicken and chile grilling at a roadside vending booth. Although it's quickening, the pace of life here is still a few steps slower than that in the rest of the country. We use the word *mañana* to describe the pace—which doesn't mean "tomorrow" exactly, it just means "not today." There's also a level of creativity here that you'll find in few other places in the world. Artists who have fled big-city jobs are here to follow their passions, as are locals who grew up making crafts and continue to do so. Conversations often center on how to structure one's day so as to take advantage of the incredible outdoors while still making enough money to survive.

1998 The Waste Isolation Pilot Project, the nation's first deep-geologic repository for permanent disposal of radioactive waste, receives go-ahead to begin storage operations.	**2006** Spaceport America, the world's first purpose-built commercial spaceport, initiated in the desert 45 miles north of Las Cruces, with plans to one day launch commercial flights into outer space.
2002 80th anniversary of the Inter-Tribal Indian Ceremonial is held at Gallup.	**2010** Santa Fe celebrates 400-year anniversary.

Meanwhile, Santa Fe's precipitous growth and enduring popularity with tourists have been a source of conflict and squabbling. Outsiders have bought up land in the hills around the city, building housing developments and sprawling single-family homes. The hills that local populations claimed for centuries as their own are being overrun, while property taxes for all have skyrocketed. Local outcry has prompted the city to implement zoning restrictions on where and how development can proceed. Some of the restrictions include banning building on ridge tops and on steep slopes and limiting the size of homes built.

Only in recent years have Santa Fe's politicians become conscientious about the city's growth. Mayor Debbie Jaramillo was one of the first local politicians to take a strong stand against growth. A fiery native of Santa Fe, she came into office in the 1990s as a representative of *la gente* (the people) and set about discouraging tourism and rapid development. Subsequent mayors have taken a middle-of-the-road approach to the issue, which has resulted in a calmer community and an increase in tourism and development.

Taos

A funky town in the middle of a beautiful, sage-covered valley, Taos is full of narrow streets dotted with galleries and artisan shops. You might find an artist's studio tucked into a century-old church or a furniture maker working at the back of his own small shop.

More than any other major northern New Mexico community, Taos has successfully opposed much of the heavy development slated for the area. In the 1980s, locals stalled indefinitely plans to expand their airport; in the 1990s, they blocked plans for a $40-million golf course and housing development; and in 2003, they prevented a Super Wal-Mart from opening. It's hard to say where Taos gets its rebellious strength; the roots may lie in the hippie community that settled here in the '60s, or possibly the Pueblo community around which the city formed. After all, Taos Pueblo was at the center of the 17th-century Pueblo revolt.

Still, changes are upon Taoseños. The blinking light that for years residents used as a reference point has given way to a real traffic light. You'll also see the main route through town becoming more and more like Cerrillos Road in Santa Fe, as fast-food restaurants and service businesses set up shop. Though the town is working on alternate routes to channel through-traffic around downtown, there's no feasible way of widening the main drag because the street—which started out as a wagon trail—is bordered closely by historic buildings.

Albuquerque

The largest city in New Mexico, Albuquerque has borne the brunt of the state's most massive growth. Currently, the city sprawls more than 20 miles, from the lava-crested mesas on the west side of the Rio Grande to the steep alluvial slopes of the Sandia Mountains on the east, and north and south through the Rio Grande Valley. New subdivisions sprout up constantly.

Despite the growth, this town is most prized by New Mexicans for its genuineness. You'll find none of the self-conscious artsy atmosphere of Santa Fe here. Instead, there's a traditional New Mexico feel that's evident when you spend some time in the heart of the city. It centers on downtown, a place of shiny skyscrapers built around the original Route 66, which still maintains some of its 1950s charm.

The most emblematic growth problem concerns the **Petroglyph National Monument** on the west side. The area is characterized by five extinct volcanoes. Adjacent lava flows became a hunting and gathering place for prehistoric Native Americans, who left a chronicle of their beliefs etched in the dark basalt boulders. Over 25,000 petroglyphs have been found in the preserve. Now, a highway is being constructed through the center of the monument. Opponents fought it for more than a decade, with Native American groups likening the highway to building a road through a church.

Northern New Mexico's extreme popularity as a tourist destination has leveled out in the 21st century. Though many artists and other businesspeople lament the loss of the crowds we had back in the '80s, most people are glad that the wave has subsided. It's good news for travelers, too; they no longer have to compete so heavily for restaurant seats or space when hiking through ruins. Though parts of northern New Mexico have lost some of the unique charm that attracted so many to the area, the overall feeling is still one of mystery and a cultural depth unmatched in the world.

HOW NEW MEXICO WAS WON—& LOST

The Pueblo tribes of the upper Rio Grande Valley are descendants of the Anasazi, better known today as the ancestral Puebloans, who from the mid-9th to the 13th centuries lived in the Four Corners Region—where the states of New Mexico, Arizona, Colorado, and Utah now meet. The ancestral Puebloans built spectacular structures; you get an idea of their scale and intricacy at the ruins at **Chaco Canyon** and **Mesa Verde.** It isn't known exactly why they abandoned their homes (some archaeologists believe it was due to drought; others claim social unrest), but most theories suggest that they moved from these sites to such areas as Frijoles Canyon **(Bandelier National Monument)** and **Puye,** where they built villages resembling the ones they had left. Then several hundred years later, for reasons not yet understood, they moved down from the canyons onto the flat plain next to the Rio Grande. By the time the Spaniards arrived in the 1500s, the Pueblo culture was well established throughout what would become northern and western New Mexico.

Architectural style was a unifying mark of the otherwise diverse ancestral Puebloan and today's Pueblo cultures. Both built condominium-style communities of stone and mud adobe bricks, three and four stories high. Grouped around central plazas, the villages incorporate circular spiritual chambers called kivas. As farmers, the ancestral Puebloan and Pueblo peoples used the waters of the Rio Grande and its tributaries to irrigate fields of corn, beans, and squash. They were also the creators of elaborate works of pottery.

The Spanish Occupation

The Spanish ventured into the upper Rio Grande after conquering Mexico's Aztecs from 1519 to 1521. In 1540, Francisco Vásquez de Coronado led an expedition in search of the fabled Seven Cities of Cíbola, coincidentally introducing horses and sheep to the region. Neither Coronado nor a succession of fortune-seeking conquistadors could locate the legendary cities of gold, so the Spanish concentrated their efforts on exploiting the Native Americans.

Spots of Regional Historic Interest

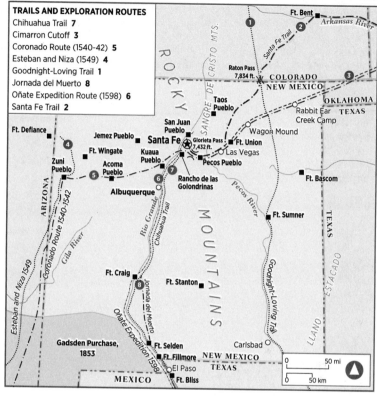

TRAILS AND EXPLORATION ROUTES

Chihuahua Trail **7**
Cimarron Cutoff **3**
Coronado Route (1540-42) **5**
Esteban and Niza (1549) **4**
Goodnight-Loving Trail **1**
Jornada del Muerto **8**
Oñate Expedition Route (1598) **6**
Santa Fe Trail **2**

Franciscan priests attempted to turn the Pueblo people into model peasants. Their churches became the focal points of every pueblo, with Catholic schools an essential adjunct. By 1625, there were approximately 50 churches in the Rio Grande Valley. (Two of the Pueblo missions, at Isleta and Acoma, are still in use today.) The Pueblos, however, weren't enthused about doing "God's work" for the Spanish—building new adobe missions, tilling fields, and weaving garments for export to Mexico—so Spanish soldiers came north to back the padres in extracting labor. In effect, the Pueblo people were forced into slavery.

Santa Fe was founded in 1610 as the seat of Spanish government in the upper Rio Grande. Governor Don Pedro de Peralta named the settlement La Villa Real de la Santa Fe de San Francisco de Asis (The Royal City of the Holy Faith of St. Francis of Assisi). The **Palace of the Governors** has been used continuously as a public building ever since—by the Spanish, Pueblos (1680–92), Mexicans, and Americans. Today it stands as the flagship of the state museum system.

Decades of oppression by the Spanish colonials led to Pueblo unrest. Uprisings in the 1630s at Taos and Jemez left village priests dead and triggered even more repression. In 1680, a unified Pueblo rebellion, orchestrated from Taos, succeeded in driving the Spaniards from the upper Rio Grande. The leaders of the revolt defiled or destroyed the churches, just as the Spanish had destroyed the religious symbols of the native people. Revolutionaries took the Palace of the Governors, where they burned archives and prayer books, and converted the chapel into a kiva. They also burned much of the property in Santa Fe that had been built by the Europeans and laid siege to Spanish settlements up and down the Rio Grande Valley. Forced to retreat to Mexico, the colonists were not able to retake Santa Fe until 12 years later. Bloody battles raged for the next several years, but by the beginning of the 18th century, Nuevo Mexico was firmly in Spanish hands.

It remained so until Mexico gained its independence from Spain in 1821. The most notable event in the intervening years was the mid-1700s departure of the Franciscans, exasperated by their failure to wipe out all vestiges of traditional Pueblo religion. Throughout the Spanish occupation, eight generations of Pueblos had clung tenaciously to their way of life. However, by the 1750s, the number of Pueblo villages had shrunk by half.

The Arrival of the Anglos

The first Anglos to spend time in the upper Rio Grande Valley were mountain men: itinerant hunters, trappers, and traders. Trailblazers of the U.S. westward expansion, they began settling in New Mexico in the first decade of the 19th century. Many married into Pueblo or Hispanic families. Perhaps the best known was **Kit Carson,** a sometime federal agent, sometime scout, whose legend is inextricably interwoven with that of early Taos. Though he seldom stayed in one place for long, he considered the Taos area his home. He married Josepha Jaramillo, the daughter of a leading Taos citizen. Later he became a prime force in the final subjugation of the Plains Indians. The Taos home where he lived off and on for 40 years, until his death in 1868, is now a museum.

Wagon trains and eastern merchants followed Carson and the other early settlers. Santa Fe, Taos, and Albuquerque, already major trading and commercial centers at the end of the **Chihuahua Trail** (the Camino Real from Veracruz, Mexico, 1,000 miles south), became the western terminals of the new **Santa Fe Trail** (from Independence, Missouri, 800 miles east).

Even though independent Mexico granted the Pueblo people full citizenship and abandoned restrictive trade laws instituted by their former Spanish rulers, the subsequent 25 years of direct rule from Mexico City were not peaceful in the upper Rio Grande. Instead, they were marked by ongoing rebellion against severe taxation, especially in Taos. Neither did things quiet down when the United States assumed control of the territory during the U.S.–Mexican War. Shortly after General Stephen Kearney occupied Santa Fe (in a bloodless takeover) on orders of President James Polk in 1846, a revolt in Taos, in 1847, led to the slaying of Charles Bent, the new governor of New Mexico. In 1848, the Treaty of Guadalupe Hidalgo officially transferred title of New Mexico, along with Texas, Arizona, and California, to the United States.

Impressions

"In New Mexico he always awoke a young man; not until he rose and began to shave did he realize that he was growing older."
—Archbishop Latour in Willa Cather's *Death Comes for the Archbishop*, 1927

Reflections

"I am become death, the shatterer of worlds."

—J. Robert Oppenheimer, quoting from ancient Hindu texts, shortly after the successful detonation of the first atomic bomb

Aside from Kit Carson, perhaps the two most notable personalities of 19th-century New Mexico were priests. **Father José Martínez** (1793–1867) was one of the first native-born priests to serve his people. Ordained in Durango, Mexico, he jolted the Catholic church after assuming control of the Taos parish: Martínez abolished the obligatory church tithe because it was a hardship on poor parishioners, published the first newspaper in the territory (in 1835), and fought large land acquisitions by Anglos after the United States annexed the territory.

On all these issues Martínez was at loggerheads with **Bishop Jean-Baptiste Lamy** (1814–88), a Frenchman appointed in 1851 to supervise the affairs of the first independent New Mexican diocese. Lamy, on whose life Willa Cather based her novel *Death Comes for the Archbishop,* served the diocese for 37 years. Lamy didn't take kindly to Martínez's independent streak and, after repeated conflicts, excommunicated the maverick priest in 1857. But Martínez was steadfast in his preaching. He established an independent church and continued as northern New Mexico's spiritual leader until his death.

Nevertheless, Lamy made many positive contributions to New Mexico, especially in the fields of education and architecture. Santa Fe's Romanesque **Cathedral of St. Francis** and the nearby Gothic-style **Loretto Chapel,** for instance, were constructed under his aegis. But he was adamant about adhering to strict Catholic religious tenets. Martínez, on the other hand, embraced the folk tradition, including the craft of *santero* (religious icon) carving and a tolerance of the Penitentes, a flagellant sect that flourished after the departure of the Franciscans in the mid–18th century.

With the advent of the **Atchison, Topeka & Santa Fe Railway** in 1879, New Mexico began to boom. Albuquerque in particular blossomed in the wake of a series of major gold strikes in the Madrid Valley, close to ancient Native American turquoise mines. By the time the gold lodes began to shrink in the 1890s, cattle and sheep ranching had become well entrenched. The territory's growth culminated in statehood in 1912.

Territorial governor Lew Wallace, who served from 1878 to 1881, was instrumental in promoting interest in the arts, which today flourish in northern New Mexico. While occupying the Palace of the Governors, Wallace penned the great biblical novel *Ben-Hur.* In the 1890s, Ernest Blumenschein, Bert Phillips, and Joseph Sharp launched the Taos art colony; it boomed in the decade following World War I when Mabel Dodge Luhan, D. H. Lawrence, Georgia O'Keeffe, Willa Cather, and many others visited or established residence in the area.

During World War II, the federal government purchased an isolated boys' camp west of Santa Fe and turned it into the **Los Alamos National Laboratory,** where the Manhattan Project and other top-secret atomic experiments were developed and perfected. The science and military legacies continue today; Albuquerque is among the nation's leaders in attracting defense contracts and high technology.

ART & ARCHITECTURE
Land of Art

It's all in the light—or at least that's what many artists claim drew them to northern New Mexico. In truth, the light is only part of the attraction: Nature in this part of the country, with its awe-inspiring thunderheads, endless expanse of blue skies, and rugged desert, is itself a canvas. To record the wonders of earth and sky, the Anasazi imprinted images—in the form of **petroglyphs** and **pictographs**—on the sides of caves and on stones, as well as on the sides of pots they shaped from clay dug in the hills.

Today's Native American tribes carry on that legacy, as do the other cultures that have settled here. Life in northern New Mexico is shaped by the arts. Everywhere you turn, you see pottery, paintings, jewelry, and weavings. You're liable to meet an artist whether you're having coffee in a Taos cafe or walking along Canyon Road in Santa Fe.

The area is full of little villages that maintain their own artistic specialties. Each Indian pueblo has a trademark design, such as Santa Clara's and San Ildefonso's black pottery and Zuni's needlepoint silver work. Bear in mind that the images used often have deep symbolic meaning. When purchasing art or an artifact, you may want to talk to its maker about what the symbols mean.

Hispanic villages are also distinguished by their artistic identities. Chimayo has become a center for Hispanic weaving, while the village of Cordova is known for its *santo* (icon) carving. *Santos, retablos* (paintings), and *bultos* (sculptures), as well as works in tin, are traditional devotional arts tied to the Roman Catholic faith. Often, these works are sold out of artists' homes in these villages, allowing you to glimpse the lives of the artists and the surroundings that inspire them.

Hispanic and Native American villagers take their goods to the cities, where, for centuries, people have bought and traded. Under the portals along the plazas of Santa Fe, Taos, and Albuquerque, you'll find a variety of works in silver, stone, and pottery for sale. In the cities, you'll find streets lined with galleries, some very slick, some more modest. At major markets, such as the Spanish Market and Indian Market in Santa Fe, some of the top artists from the area sell their works. Smaller shows at the pueblos also attract artists and artisans. The **Northern Pueblo Artists and Craftsman Show,** revolving each July to a different pueblo, continues to grow.

Drawn by the beauty of the local landscape and respect for indigenous art, artists from all over have flocked here, particularly during the 20th and 21st centuries. They have established locally important art societies; one of the most notable is the **Taos Society of Artists.** An oft-repeated tale explains the roots of this society. The artists **Bert Phillips** and **Ernest L. Blumenschein** were traveling through the area from Colorado on a mission to sketch the Southwest when their wagon broke down north of Taos. The scenery so impressed them that they abandoned their journey and stayed. Joseph Sharp joined them, and still later came Oscar Berninghaus, Walter Ufer, Herbert Dunton, and others. You can see a brilliant collection of some of their romantically lit portraits and landscapes at the **Taos Art Museum.** The 100th anniversary marking the artists' broken wheel was celebrated in 1998.

A major player in the development of Taos as an artists' community was the arts patron **Mabel Dodge Luhan.** A writer who financed the work of many an artist, in the 1920s Luhan held court for many notables, including Georgia O'Keeffe, Willa Cather, and D. H. Lawrence. This illustrious history goes a long way to explaining how it is that Taos—a town of about 5,000 inhabitants—has more than 100 arts-and-crafts galleries and many resident painters.

Santa Fe has its own art society, begun in the 1920s by a nucleus of five painters who became known as **Los Cinco Pintores.** Jozef Bakos, Fremont Ellis, Walter Mruk, Willard Nash, and Will Shuster lived in the area of dusty Canyon Road (now the arts center of Santa Fe, with countless artists, approximately 100 galleries, and many museums). Despite its small size, Santa Fe, remarkably, is considered one of the top three art markets in the United States.

Perhaps the most celebrated artist associated with northern New Mexico is **Georgia O'Keeffe** (1887–1986), a painter who worked and lived most of her later years in the region. O'Keeffe's first sojourn to New Mexico in 1929 inspired her sensuous paintings of the area's desert landscape and bleached animal skulls. The house where she lived in Abiquiu (42 miles northwest of Santa Fe on US 84) is now open for limited public tours (see "Along the High Road to Taos," in chapter 11 for details). The **Georgia O'Keeffe Museum,** the only museum in the United States dedicated entirely to an internationally renowned woman artist, opened in Santa Fe in 1997.

> ### Impressions
>
> [Sun-bleached bones] were most wonderful against the blue—that blue that will always be there as it is now after all man's destruction is finished.
> —Georgia O'Keeffe, on the desert skies of New Mexico

Santa Fe is also home to the **Institute of American Indian Arts,** where many of today's leading Native American artists have studied, including the Apache sculptor Allan Houser (whose works you can see near the State Capitol building and in other public areas in Santa Fe). Possibly the best-known Native American painter is R. C. Gorman, an Arizona Navajo who made his home in Taos for more than 2 decades. Now deceased, Gorman is internationally acclaimed for his bright, somewhat surrealistic depictions of Navajo women. Also in the spotlight is Dan Namingha, a Hopi artist who weaves native symbology into contemporary concerns.

If you look closely, you'll find notable works from a number of local artists. There's Tammy Garcia, a young Taos potter who year after year continues to sweep the awards at Indian Market with her intricately shaped and carved pots. Cippy Crazyhorse, a Cochiti, has acquired a steady following of patrons for his silver jewelry. All around the area you'll see the frescoes of Frederico Vigil, a noted muralist and Santa Fe native.

For the visitor interested in art, however, some caution should be exercised; there's a lot of schlock out there, targeting the tourist trade. Yet if you persist, you're likely to find much inspiring work as well. The museums and many of the galleries are excellent repositories of local art. Their offerings range from small-town folk art to works by major artists who show internationally.

A Rich Architectural Melting Pot

Northern New Mexico's distinctive architecture reflects the diversity of cultures that have left their imprint on the region. The first people in the area were the ancestral Puebloans or Anasazi, who built stone and mud homes at the bottom of canyons and inside caves. **Pueblo-style adobe architecture** evolved and became the basis for traditional New Mexican homes: sun-dried clay bricks mixed with grass for strength, mud-mortared, and covered with additional protective layers of mud. Roofs are supported by a network of vigas—long beams whose ends protrude through the outer facades—and *latillas,* smaller stripped branches layered between the vigas. Other adapted Pueblo architectural elements include plastered adobe-brick kiva fireplaces, *bancos* (adobe benches that protrude from walls), and *nichos* (small indentations within a wall in which religious icons are placed). These adobe homes are characterized by flat roofs and soft, rounded contours.

Spaniards wedded many elements to Pueblo style, such as portals (porches held up with posts, often running the length of a home) and enclosed patios, as well as the simple, dramatic sculptural shapes of Spanish mission arches and bell towers. They also brought elements from the Moorish architecture found in southern Spain: heavy wooden doors and elaborate *corbels*—carved wooden supports for the vertical posts.

With the opening of the Santa Fe Trail in 1821 and later the 1860s gold boom, both of which brought more Anglo settlers, came the next wave of building. New arrivals contributed architectural elements such as neo-Grecian and Victorian influences popular in the middle part of the United States at the time. Distinguishing features of what came to be known as **Territorial-style** architecture can be seen today; they include brick facades and cornices as well as porches, often placed on the second story. You'll also note millwork on doors and wood trim around windows and doorways, double-hung windows, and Victorian bric-a-brac.

Santa Fe Plaza is an excellent example of the convergence of these early architectural styles. On the west side is a Territorial-style balcony, while the Palace of the Governors is marked by Pueblo-style vigas and oversize Spanish/Moorish doors.

Nowhere else in the United States are you likely to see such extremes of architectural style as in northern New Mexico. In Santa Fe, you'll see the Romanesque architecture of the **St. Francis Cathedral** and the Gothic-style **Loretto Chapel,** brought by Archbishop Lamy from France, as well as the railroad station built in the **Spanish Mission style**—popular in the early part of the 20th century.

Since 1957, strict city building codes have required that all new structures within the circumference of the Paseo de Peralta conform to one of two revival styles: Pueblo or Territorial. The regulation also limits the height of the buildings and restricts the types of signs permitted, and it requires buildings to be topped by flat roofs.

Albuquerque also has a broad array of styles, most evident in a visit to **Old Town.** There, you'll find the large Italianate brick house known as the **Herman Blueher home,** built in 1898; throughout Old Town you'll find little *placitas,* homes, and haciendas built around courtyards, a strategy developed not only for defense purposes but also as a way to accommodate several generations of the same family in different wings of a single dwelling. **The Church of San Felipe de Neri** at the center of Old Town is situated between two folk Gothic towers. This building was begun in a cruciform plan in 1793; subsequent architectural changes resulted in an interesting mixture of styles.

The most notable architecture in Taos is the **Taos Pueblo,** the site of two structures emulated in homes and business buildings throughout the Southwest. Built to resemble Taos Mountain, which stands behind it, the two structures are pyramidal in form, with the different levels reached by ladders. Also quite prevalent is architecture echoing colonial hacienda style. What's nice about Taos is that you can see historic homes inside and out. You can wander through artist **Ernest Blumenschein's home.** Built in 1797 and restored by Blumenschein in 1919, it represents another New Mexico architectural phenomenon: homes that were added onto year after year. Doorways are typically low, and floors rise and fall at the whim of the earth beneath them. The **Martinez Hacienda** is an example of a hacienda stronghold. Built without windows facing outward, it originally had 20 small rooms, many with doors opening out to the courtyard. One of the few refurbished examples of colonial New Mexico architecture and life, the hacienda is on the National Historic Registry.

As you head into villages in the north, you'll see steep-pitched roofs on most homes. This is because the common flat-roof style doesn't shed snow; the water builds up and causes roof problems. In just about any town in northern New Mexico, you may detect the strong smell of tar, a sure sign that another resident is laying out thousands to fix his enchanting but frustratingly flat roof.

Today, very few new homes are built of adobe. Instead, most are constructed with wood frames and plasterboard, and then stuccoed over. Several local architects are currently employing innovative architecture to create a Pueblo-style feel. They incorporate straw bails, pumice-crete, rammed earth, old tires, even aluminum cans in the construction of homes. Most of these elements are used in the same way bricks are used, stacked and layered, and then covered over with plaster and made to look like adobe. Often it's difficult to distinguish homes built with these materials from those built with wood-frame construction. West of Taos, a number of "earthships" have been built. Many of these homes are constructed with alternative materials, most bermed into the sides of hills, utilizing the earth as insulation and the sun as an energy source.

A visitor could spend an entire trip to New Mexico focusing on the architecture. As well as relishing the wealth of architectural styles, you'll find more subtle elements everywhere. You may encounter an ox-blood floor, for example. An old Spanish tradition, ox blood is spread in layers and left to dry, hardening into a glossy finish that's known to last centuries. You're also likely to see coyote fences—narrow cedar posts lined up side by side—a system early settlers devised to ensure safety of their animals. Winding around homes and buildings you'll see *acequias,* ancient irrigation canals still maintained by locals for watering crops and trees. Throughout the area you'll notice that old walls are whimsically bowed, and windows and floors are often crooked, constant reminders of the effects time has had on even these stalwart structures.

ANTHROPOLOGY 101: BELIEFS & RITUALS

Religion has always been a central, defining element in the life of the Pueblo people. Within the cosmos, which they view as a single whole, all living creatures are mutually dependent. Thus, every relationship a human being may have, whether with a person, an animal, or a plant, has spiritual significance. A hunter prays before killing a deer, asking the creature to sacrifice itself to the tribe. A slain deer is treated as a guest of honor, and the hunter performs a ritual in which he sends the animal's soul back to its community, so that it may be reborn. Even the harvesting of plants requires prayer, thanks, and ritual.

The Pueblo people believe that their ancestors originally lived under the ground, which, as the place from which plants spring, is the source of all life. According to their beliefs, the original Pueblos, encouraged by burrowing animals, entered the world of humans—the so-called "fourth" world—through a hole, a *sipapu.* The ways in which this came about and the deities that the Pueblo people revere vary from tribe

danse MACABRE

The **Dance of the Matachines,** a ritualistic dance performed at northern New Mexico pueblos and in many Hispanic communities, reveals the cultural miscegenation, identities, and conflicts that characterize northern New Mexico. It's a dark and vivid ritual in which a little girl, Malinche, is wedded to the church. The dance, depicting the taming of the native spirit, is difficult even for historians to decipher.

Brought to the New World by the Spaniards, the dance has its roots in the painful period during which the Moors were driven out of Spain. However, some symbols seem obvious: At one point, men bearing whips tame "El Toro," a small boy dressed as a bull who has been charging about rebelliously. The whip-men symbolically castrate him and then stroll through the crowd, pretending to display the

dismembered body parts, as if to warn villagers of the consequences of disobedience. At another point, a hunched woman-figure births a small troll-like doll, perhaps representative of the union between Indian and Hispanic cultures.

The Dance of the Matachines ends when two *abuelo* (grandparent) figures dance across the dirt, holding up the just-born baby, while the Matachines, adorned with bishop-like headdresses, follow them away in a recessional march. The Matachines' dance, often performed in the early mornings, is so dark and mystical that every time I see it, my passion for this area deepens. The image of that baby always stays with me, and in a way represents New Mexico itself: a place born of disparate beliefs that have melded with the sand, sage, and sun, and produced incredible richness.

to tribe. Most, however, believe this world is enclosed by four sacred mountains, where four sacred colors—coral, black, turquoise, and yellow or white—predominate.

There is no single great spirit ruling over this world; instead, it is watched over by a number of spiritual elements. Most common are Mother Earth and Father Sun. In this desert land, the sun is an element of both life and death. The tribes watch the skies closely, tracking solstices and planetary movements, to determine the optimal time for crop planting.

Ritualistic dances are occasions of great symbolic importance. Usually held in conjunction with the feast days of Catholic saints (including Christmas Eve), Pueblo ceremonies demonstrate the parallel absorption of Christian elements without the surrendering of traditional beliefs. To this day, communities enact medicine dances, fertility rites, and prayers for rain and for good harvests. The spring and summer corn, or *tablita*, dances are among the most impressive. Ceremonies begin with an early-morning Mass and procession to the plaza; the image of the saint is honored at the forefront. The rest of the day is devoted to song, dance, and feasting, with performers masked and clad as deer, buffalo, eagles, or other creatures.

Visitors are usually welcome to attend Pueblo dances, but they should respect the tribe's requests not to be photographed or recorded. It was exactly this lack of respect that led the Zunis to ban outsiders from attending many of their famous Shalako ceremonies.

Catholicism, imposed by the Spaniards, has infused northern New Mexico with an elaborate set of beliefs. This is a Catholicism heavy with iconography, expressed in carved *santos* (statues) and beautiful *retablos* (paintings) that adorn the altars of many cathedrals. Catholic churches are the focal points of most northern New Mexico villages. If you take the high road to Taos, be sure to note the church in **Las Trampas,** as well as the one in **Ranchos de Taos;** both have 3- to 4-foot-thick walls sculpted from adobe and inside have old-world charm, with beautiful *retablos* decorating the walls and vigas supporting the ceiling.

Hispanics in northern New Mexico, in particular, maintain strong family and Catholic ties, and they continue to honor traditions associated with both. Communities plan elaborate celebrations such as the *quinceañera* for young girls reaching womanhood, and weddings with big feasts and dances in which well-wishers pin money to the bride's elaborately laced gown.

If you happen to be in the area during a holiday, you may even get to see a religious procession or pilgrimage. Most notable is the **pilgrimage to the Santuario de Chimayo,** an hour's drive north of the state capital. Constructed in 1816, the sanctuary has long been a pilgrimage site for Catholics who attribute miraculous healing powers to the earth found in the chapel's anteroom. Several days before Easter, fervent believers begin walking the highway headed north or south to Chimayo, some carrying large crosses, others carrying nothing but small bottles of water, most praying for a miracle.

In recent years, New Mexico has become known (and in some circles, ridiculed) for **New Age pilgrims and celebrations.** The roots of the local movement are hard to trace. It may have something to do with northern New Mexico's centuries-old reputation as a place where rebel thinkers come to enjoy the freedom to believe what they want. Pueblo spirituality and deeply felt connection to the land are also factors that have drawn New Agers. At any rate, the liberated atmosphere here has given rise to a thriving New Age network, one that now includes alternative churches, healing centers, and healing schools. You'll find all sorts of alternative medicine and fringe practices here, from aromatherapy to rolfing (a form of massage that realigns the muscles and bones in the body) and chelation therapy (in which an IV drips ethylene diamine tetra-acetic acid into the blood to remove heavy metals). If those sound too invasive, you can always try psychic surgery.

New Age practices and beliefs have given rise to a great deal of local humor targeting their supposed psychobabble. One pointed joke asks: "How many New Agers does it take to change a light bulb?" Answer: "None. They just form a support group and learn to live in the dark." For many, however, there's much good to be found in the movement. The Dalai Lama visited Santa Fe because the city is seen as a healing center and has become a refuge for Tibetans. Notable speakers such as Ram Dass and Thomas Moore have also come to the area. Many practitioners find the alternatives—healing resources and spiritual paths—they are looking for in the receptive northern New Mexico desert and mountains.

BOOKS, FILMS & MUSIC
Books

Many well-known writers made their homes in New Mexico in the 20th century. In the 1920s, the most celebrated were **D. H. Lawrence** and **Willa Cather,** both short-term Taos residents. Lawrence, the romantic and controversial English novelist, spent time here between 1922 and 1925; he reflected on his sojourn in *Mornings in Mexico* and *Etruscan Places.* Lawrence's Taos period is described in *Lorenzo in*

Taos, which his patron, Mabel Dodge Luhan, wrote. Cather, a Pulitzer-prize winner famous for her depictions of the pioneer spirit, penned _Death Comes for the Archbishop,_ among other works. This fictionalized account of the 19th-century Santa Fe bishop, Jean-Baptiste Lamy, grew out of her stay in the region. Frank Waters gives a strong sense of Native American tradition in the region in his classics _People of the Valley_ and _The Man Who Killed the Deer._

Many contemporary authors also live in and write about New Mexico. John Nichols, of Taos, whose _Milagro Beanfield War_ was made into a Robert Redford movie in 1987, writes insightfully about the problems of poor Hispanic farming communities. Albuquerque's Tony Hillerman has for decades woven mysteries around Navajo tribal police in books such as _Listening Woman_ and _A Thief of Time._ In more recent years, Sarah Lovett has joined Hillerman's ranks with a series of gripping mysteries, most notably _Dangerous Attachments._ The Hispanic novelist Rudolfo Anaya's _Bless Me, Ultima,_ and Pueblo writer Leslie Marmon Silko's _Ceremony_ capture the lifestyles of their respective peoples. A coming-of-age story, Richard Bradford's _Red Sky at Morning_ juxtaposes the various cultures of New Mexico. Edward Abbey wrote of the desert environment and politics; his _Fire on the Mountain,_ set in New Mexico, was one of his most powerful works.

Excellent works about Native Americans of New Mexico include _The Pueblo Indians of North America_ (Holt, Rinehart & Winston, 1970) by Edward P. Dozier and _Living the Sky: The Cosmos of the American Indian_ (University of Oklahoma Press, 1987) by Ray A. Williamson. Also look for _American Indian Literature 1979–1994_ (Ballantine, 1996), an anthology edited by Paula Gunn Allen.

For general histories of the state, try Myra Ellen Jenkins and Albert H. Schroeder's _A Brief History of New Mexico_ (University of New Mexico Press, 1974) and Marc Simmons's _New Mexico: An Interpretive History_ (University of New Mexico Press, 1988). In addition, Claire Morrill's _A Taos Mosaic: Portrait of a New Mexico Village_ (University of New Mexico Press, 1973) does an excellent job of portraying the history of that small New Mexican town. I have also enjoyed Tony Hillerman's (ed.) _The Spell of New Mexico_ (University of New Mexico Press, 1976) and John Nichols and William Davis's _If Mountains Die: A New Mexico Memoir_ (Alfred A. Knopf, 1979). _Talking Ground_ (University of New Mexico Press, 1996), by Santa Fe author Douglas Preston, tells of a contemporary horseback trip through Navajoland, exploring the native mythology. One of my favorite texts is _Enchantment and Exploitation_ (University of New Mexico Press, 1985), by William deBuys. A very extensive book that attempts to capture the multiplicity of the region is _Legends of the American Southwest_ (Alfred A. Knopf, 1997), by Alex Shoumatoff.

Enduring Visions: 1,000 Years of Southwestern Indian Art, by the Aspen Center for the Visual Arts (Publishing Center for Cultural Resources, 1969), and Roland F. Dickey's _New Mexico Village Arts_ (University of New Mexico Press, 1990) are both excellent resources for those interested in Native American art. If you become intrigued with Spanish art during your visit to New Mexico, you'll find E. Boyd's _Popular Arts of Spanish New Mexico_ (Museum of New Mexico Press, 1974) to be quite informative.

If you like to combine walking with literary history, pick up Barbara Harrelson's _Walks in Literary Santa Fe: A Guide to Landmarks, Legends, and Lore_ (Gibbs-Smith, 2008).

2

Books, Films & Music

NORHTERN NEW MEXICO IN DEPTH

King of the Road

If you like road trip stories to small New Mexico towns, check out my book *King of the Road* (New Mexico Magazine Press, 2007). It's a compilation of articles from my monthly column in *New Mexico Magazine,* in which locals tell the stories of their hometowns. It's illustrated with my photos, too. You can order the book online at www.nm magazine.com and www.amazon.com.

Films

If you like to start traveling before you climb on the plane or into the car, you can do so easily by watching any number of movies filmed in the state. Over the years, so many have been filmed that I won't list them all. Instead, I'll give the ones that provide a glimpse into the true nature of New Mexico. *Silverado* (1985), a light-hearted western, and the heartfelt miniseries *Lonesome Dove* (1989), based on a Larry McMurtry novel, start my list. Billy Bob Thorton's film adaptation (2000) of the novel *All the Pretty Horses,* Ron Howard's film version of *The Missing* (2003), and Billy Crystal in *City Slickers,* are also some of my favorite westerns.

Favorite classics include *Butch Cassidy and the Sundance Kid* (1969), filmed in Taos and Chama; *The Cowboys* (1972), with John Wayne; Clint Eastwood's *Every Which Way But Loose* (1978); and Dennis Hopper in the 1960s classic *Easy Rider* (1969).

More contemporary themes are explored in *Contact* (1997), which features the National Radio Astronomy Very Large Array in western New Mexico, as did *Independence Day* (1996). Also exploring alien themes, *The Man Who Fell to Earth* (1976), with David Bowie, was filmed in southern New Mexico.

In recent years, thanks to state tax credits given to film companies, many films have been shot in New Mexico. Among these recent additions is the 2009 double-Oscar winner *Crazy Heart.*

Music

Such musical legends as Bo Diddley, Buddy Holly, Roy Orbison, and the Fireballs basked in New Mexico's light for parts of their careers. More recent musicians whose music really reflects the state include Mansanares, two brothers who grew up in Abiquiu, known for their Spanish guitar and soulful vocals. Look for their album *Nuevo Latino.* Master flute player Robert Mirabal's music is informed by the ceremonial music he grew up with at Taos Pueblo. Check out his 2006 Grammy Award–winning album *Sacred Ground.* Using New Mexico as his creative retreat since the 1980s, Michael Martin Murphey often plays live here, where fans always cheer for his most notable song, "Wildfire." *The Best of Michael Martin Murphey* gives a good taste of his music. Country music superstar Randy Travis calls Santa Fe home. His newest release, *Around the Bend,* is a treasure, as are his classics. My favorite musician who resides in Santa Fe is Ottmar Liebert and his band the Luna Negra. All of their flamenco-inspired music is rich with New Mexico tones. Check out their CD *Leaning into the Night.*

YOU SAY chili, **WE SAY** Chile

You'll never see "chili" on a menu in New Mexico. New Mexicans are adamant that *chile,* the Spanish spelling of the word, is the only way to spell it—no matter what your dictionary may say.

Virtually anything you order in a restaurant is likely to be topped with a chile sauce. If you're not accustomed to spicy foods, certain varieties will make your eyes water, your sinuses drain, and your palate feel as if it's on fire. **Warning:** No amount of water or beer will alleviate the sting. (Drink milk. A *sopaipilla* drizzled with honey is also helpful.)

But don't let these words of caution scare you away from genuine New Mexico chiles. The pleasure of eating them far outweighs the pain. Start slowly, with salsas and chile sauces first, perhaps *rellenos* (stuffed peppers) next. Before long, you'll be buying chile *ristras* (chiles strung on rope).

EATING & DRINKING IN NORTHERN NEW MEXICO

You know you're in a food-conscious place when the local newspaper uses chiles (and onions) to rate movies, as does Santa Fe's *New Mexican.* A large part of that city's cachet as a chic destination derives from its famous cuisine, while Taos and Albuquerque are developing notable reputations themselves. The competition among restaurants is fierce, which means that visitors have plenty of options from which to choose. Aside from establishments serving New Mexican cuisine that the region is famed for, you can also find French, Italian, Asian, Indian, and interesting hybrids of those. Luckily, not all the top restaurants are high end; several hidden gems satisfy your taste buds without emptying your wallet.

Reservations are always recommended at the higher-end restaurants and are essential during peak seasons. Only a few restaurants serve late, so be sure to plan dinner before 8pm. Most restaurants are casual, so almost any attire is fine, though for the more expensive ones, dressing up is a good idea.

At the beginning of each city's dining section, I give more details about the dining scene there.

Food here isn't the same as Mexican cuisine or even those American variations of Tex-Mex and Cal-Mex. New Mexican cooking is a product of Southwestern history: Native Americans taught the Spanish conquerors about corn—how to roast it and how to make corn pudding, stewed corn, cornbread, cornmeal, and *posole* (hominy)—and they also taught the Spanish how to use chile peppers, a crop indigenous to the New World, having been first harvested in the Andean highlands as early as 4000 B.C. The Spaniards brought the practice of eating beef to the area.

Newcomers have introduced other elements to the food here. From Mexico came the interest in seafood. Regional New American cuisine combines elements from various parts of Mexico, such as sauces from the Yucatán Peninsula, and fried bananas served with bean dishes, typical of Central American locales. You'll also find Asian elements mixed in.

The basic ingredients of New Mexico cooking are three indispensable, locally grown foods: **chile, beans,** and **corn.** Of these, perhaps the most crucial is the **chile,** whether brilliant red or green and with various levels of spicy bite. Chile forms the base for the red and green sauces that top most New Mexico dishes such as enchiladas and burritos. One is not necessarily hotter than the other; spiciness depends on the type, and where and during what kind of season (dry or wet) the chiles were grown.

Spotted or painted **pinto beans** with a nutty taste are simmered with garlic, onion, cumin, and red chile powder and served as a side dish. When mashed and refried in oil, they become *frijoles refritos.* **Corn** supplies the vital dough, called *masa,* for tortillas and tamales. New Mexican corn comes in six colors, of which yellow, white, and blue are the most common.

Even if you're familiar with Mexican cooking, the dishes you know and love are likely to be prepared differently here. The following is a rundown of some regional dishes, a number of which aren't widely known outside the Southwest.

BISCOCHITO   A cookie made with anise.

CARNE ADOVADA   Tender pork marinated in red chile sauce, herbs, and spices, and then baked.

CHILE RELLENOS   Peppers stuffed with cheese, deep-fried, and then covered with green chile sauce.

CHORIZO BURRITO   Mexican sausage, scrambled eggs, potatoes, and scallions wrapped in a flour tortilla with red or green chile sauce and melted Jack cheese. Also called a "breakfast burrito."

EMPANADA   A fried pie with nuts and currants.

ENCHILADAS   Tortillas either rolled or layered with chicken, beef, or cheese, topped with chile sauce.

GREEN CHILE STEW   Locally grown chiles cooked in a stew with chunks of meat, beans, and potatoes.

HUEVOS RANCHEROS   Fried eggs on corn tortillas, topped with cheese and red or green chile, served with pinto beans.

PAN DULCE   A sweet Native American bread.

POSOLE   A corn soup or stew (called hominy in other parts of the south), sometimes prepared with pork and chile.

SOPAIPILLA   A lightly fried puff pastry served with honey as a dessert or stuffed with meat and vegetables as a main dish. *Sopaipillas* with honey have a cooling effect on your palate after you've eaten a spicy dish.

TACOS   Spiced chicken or beef served either in soft tortillas or crispy shells.

TAMALES   A dish made from cornmeal mush, wrapped in husks and steamed.

PLANNING YOUR TRIP TO NORTHERN NEW MEXICO

3

A trip to northern New Mexico may affect your attitude. You may return home and find that your response to the world is completely different from the way it used to be. (That is, if you return at all.) The Land of Enchantment has few customary points of reference. Rather than sharp-cornered buildings, you find adobe ones made of mud bricks. Rather than hearing a single language on the street, you hear many, from Navajo and the Pueblo Tiwa and Tewa to Spanish and English. The pace here is slow and the objectives are less obvious than in most places.

And the northern part of the state has its own unique terrain and climate as well. Travelers often think that because this is the desert, it should have saguaro cactus and always be warm. Think again. Much of the area lies upwards of 5,000 feet in elevation, which means that four full seasons act upon the land. So, when you're planning, be sure to take a look at the "When to Travel" sections so you can be prepared.

That said, preparation to come here is simple. Even though many people mistake New Mexico for our lovely neighbor to the south, really, traveling here is much like anywhere in the U.S. You can drink the water and eat all the food you care to eat, except you'll want to take care, as some of the chiles can be very hot. The sun at these elevations can also be scorching, so come readied with a hat and plenty of sunscreen. In fact, the elements here may present the greatest challenge, so be sure to review the section on health below.

Another point to be aware of is the distance between cities. Your best bet is to travel by car here, as many of the "must see" attractions are located off the main thoroughfares, traversed by the few public transportation options available. Besides, there are few enjoyments so great as driving in the sparkling light through crooked farming villages, past ancient ruins, around plazas, and over mountain passes.

As with any trip, a little preparation is essential before you start your journey to northern New Mexico. This chapter provides a variety of planning tools, including information on when to go and how to get there. For additional help in planning your trip and for more on-the-ground resources in northern New Mexico, please turn to chapter 17, "Fast Facts."

WHEN TO GO

Forget any preconceptions you may have about the New Mexico "desert." The high desert climate of this part of the world is generally dry, but not always warm. Santa Fe and Taos, at 7,000 feet above sea level, have **midsummer** highs in the 90s (30s Celsius) and lows in the 50s (teens Celsius). This is the busiest time of year in New Mexico, when most cultural activities are in full swing and prices and temperatures rise. You'll want to make hotel reservations in advance.

Spring and fall are some of New Mexico's most pleasant seasons, with highs in the 60s (teens Celsius), and lows in the 30s (as low as −1°C). Spring can be windy, but the skiing can be excellent, with sunny days and the season's accumulated deep snow. Fall is a particularly big draw because the aspens turn golden in the mountains. In both spring and fall, tourist traffic is sparse and room rates are lower.

Average Temperatures (High/Low) & Annual Rainfall (In.)

		JAN	APR	JULY	OCT	RAINFALL
Albuquerque	Temp (°F)	46/21	70/38	92/64	74/45	8.5
	Temp (°C)	8/−6	21/3	33/18	22/7	
Santa Fe	Temp (°F)	47/18	64/33	85/56	67/38	11.4
	Temp (°C)	8/−8	18/1	29/13	19/3	
Taos	Temp (°F)	40/10	64/29	87/50	75/32	12.0
	Temp (°C)	4/−12	18/−2	31/10	24/0	

Winter can be delightful in northern New Mexico, when typical daytime temperatures are in the low 40s (single digits Celsius), and overnight lows are in the teens (−7°C and below). The snowy days here are some of the prettiest you'll ever see, and during a good snow year (as much as 300 in. at Taos Ski Valley), skiers can really enjoy the region. However, during holidays, the slopes can get crowded. During all the seasons, temperatures in Albuquerque, at 5,300 feet, often run about 10° warmer than elsewhere in the northern region.

Northern New Mexico Calendar of Events

A good resource for events is **www.newmexico.org/calendar**. Here are some of my favorites. For an exhaustive list of events beyond those listed here, check **http://events. frommers.com**, where you'll find a searchable, up-to-the-minute roster of what's happening in cities all over the world.

JANUARY

New Year's Day. Transfer of canes to new officials and various dances at most pueblos. Turtle Dance at Taos Pueblo (no photography allowed). Call (✆) **575/758-1028,** or go to

www.taospueblo.com for more information. January 1.

Winter Wine Festival. A variety of wine offerings and food tastings prepared by local chefs take place in the Taos Ski Valley.

Call ✆ **505/438-8060** for details, or go to www.taoswinterwinefest.com. Mid-January.

FEBRUARY

Candelaria Day Celebration, Picuris Pueblo. Traditional dances. Call ✆ **575/587-2519** for more information. February 2.

Mt. Taylor Winter Quadrathlon. Hundreds of athletes come from all over the West to bicycle, run, cross-country ski, and snowshoe up and down this mountain. For information, call ✆ **800/748-2142.** Early February.

Just Desserts Eat, Ski or Snowshoe. Cross-country skiers and snow-shoers travel from point to point on the Enchanted Forest course near Red River, tasting decadent desserts supplied by area restaurants. Call ✆ **575/754-2374,** or go to www.enchanted forestxc.com. Late February.

MARCH

National Fiery Foods/Barbecue Show. Here's your chance to taste the hottest of the hot and plenty of milder flavors, too. Some 13,000 general public attendees show up to taste sauces, salsas, candies, and more at the Sandia Resort & Casino. For information, call ✆ **505/873-8680,** or go to www.fiery-foods.com. Early March.

Rio Grande Arts and Crafts Festival. A juried show featuring 200 artists and craftspeople from around the country takes place at Expo New Mexico in Albuquerque. Call ✆ **505/292-7457** for more information, or visit www.riograndefestivals.com. Second week of March. Also check out their October Balloon Fiesta show and November holiday show.

Chimayo Pilgrimage. On Good Friday, thousands of pilgrims trek on foot to the Santuario de Chimayo, a small church north of Santa Fe that's believed to aid in miracles. For information, call ✆ **505/351-9961,** or check out the church's website at www.elsantuariodechimayo.org.

APRIL

Easter Weekend Celebration. Celebrations include Masses, parades, corn dances, and other dances, such as the bow and arrow dance at Nambe. Call ✆ **505/843-7270** for information.

American Indian Week, Indian Pueblo Cultural Center, Albuquerque. A celebration of Native American traditions and culture. Call ✆ **505/843-7270,** or go to www.indian pueblo.org. Late April.

Gathering of Nations Powwow, University Football Stadium, Albuquerque. Dance competitions, arts-and-crafts exhibitions, and Miss Indian World contest. Call ✆ **505/836-2810,** or visit www.gathering ofnations.com. Late April.

MAY

Taos Spring Arts Festival. Contemporary visual, performing, and literary arts are highlighted during 2 weeks of gallery openings, studio tours, performances by visiting theatrical and dance troupes, live musical events, traditional ethnic entertainment, literary readings, and more.

Events are held at venues throughout Taos and Taos County. For dates and ticket info, contact the Taos County Chamber of Commerce, 108 Kit Carson Rd., Taos, NM 87571 (✆ **575/751-8800;** www.taos chamber.com). All month.

JUNE

San Antonio Feast Day. Corn dances at many of the pueblos. For information, call ✆ **505/843-7270,** or go to www.indian pueblo.org. June 13.

Rodeo de Santa Fe. This 4-day event features a Western parade, free concert, and five rodeo performances with more than 600 contestants from all over the world, who compete for sizable purses in such events as Brahma bull and bronco riding, roping, steer wrestling, barrel racing, and clown antics.

The rodeo grounds are at 3237 Rodeo Rd., at Richards Avenue, 5½ miles south of the plaza. Performances are in the evening Wednesday to Saturday, and on Saturday afternoon. For tickets and information, call ✆ **505/471-4300,** or visit www.rodeode santafe.org. It takes place sometime around the fourth weekend in June.

Rodeo de Taos, County Fairgrounds, Taos. A fun event featuring local and regional participants. For information, call ✆ **575/758-5700,** or, in mid-to late June, call

☎ **575/758-3974.** Third or fourth weekend in June.

Taos Solar Music Festival, Kit Carson Municipal Park, Taos. Sit out on the grass under the sun, and listen to major players at this event celebrating the summer solstice. A tribute to solar energy, the event has a stage powered by a solar generator and educational displays within the Solar Village. For information, call ☎ **575/758-9191,** or visit www.solarmusicfest.com. Late June.

New Mexico Arts and Crafts Fair. A tradition for 43 years, this juried show offers work from more than 200 New Mexico artisans, accompanied by nonstop entertainment for the whole family. This can be a good place to find Hispanic arts and crafts.

The fair is held at Expo New Mexico in Albuquerque. Admission cost varies. For information, call ☎ **505/884-9043,** or check online at www.nmartsandcraftsfair.org. Last full weekend in June.

JULY

Fourth of July celebrations (including fireworks displays) are held all over New Mexico. Call the chambers of commerce in specific towns and cities for information. July 4th.

Pancake Breakfast on the Plaza. Rub elbows with Santa Fe residents at this locals' event on the plaza that raises funds for charities and draws some 10,000 hungry folks. For information, call ☎ **505/982-2002,** or check out www.uwsfc.org. July 4th.

Taos Pueblo Powwow. Intertribal competition in traditional and contemporary dances. Call ☎ **575/758-1028** for more information, or visit www.taospueblo powwow.com. Second weekend in July.

Taste of Santa Fe. Sample some 50 of Santa Fe's best chefs' food, including appetizers, entrees, and desserts at the Santa Fe Railyard. For information, call ☎ **505/982-6366,** ext. 107, or look online at www.taste ofsantafe.com. Mid-July.

Eight Northern Pueblos Artist and Craftsman Show. More than 600 Native American artists exhibit their work at the eight northern pueblos. Traditional dances and food

booths; location varies. Contact ☎ **505/747-1593,** or go to www.enipc.org for location and exact dates. Third weekend in July.

Fiestas de Santiago y Santa Ana. The celebration begins with a Friday-night Mass at one of the three Taos-area parishes, where the fiesta queen is crowned. During the weekend, there are candlelight processions, special Masses, music, dancing, parades, crafts, and food booths.

Taos Plaza hosts many events and most are free. For information, contact ☎ **800/732-8267** or www.fiestasdetaos.com. Third weekend in July.

Spanish Market. More than 500 traditional and contemporary Hispanic artists from New Mexico and southern Colorado exhibit and sell their work in this lively community event. Artists are featured in special demonstrations, while an entertaining mix of traditional Hispanic music, dance, foods, and pageantry creates the ambience of a village celebration. Artwork for sale includes *santos* (painted and carved saints), textiles, tinwork, furniture, straw appliqué, and metalwork.

The markets are found at the Santa Fe plaza. For information, contact the Spanish Colonial Arts Society (☎ **505/982-2226;** www.spanishmarket.org). Last full weekend in July.

AUGUST

San Lorenzo Feast Day, Picuris Pueblo. Traditional dances and foot races. Contact ☎ **575/587-2519,** or go to www.indian pueblo.org for details. August 10.

Pueblo Independence Day, Jemez State Monument. Participants from many of the Pueblos convene to celebrate the Pueblo Revolt of 1680. Food, art booths, dances, and live music fill the sunny plaza. Contact ☎ **575/829-3530,** or go to www.nmmonuments.org. Mid-August.

The Indian Market. This is the largest all–Native American market in the country. About 1,000 artisans display their baskets and blankets, jewelry, pottery, woodcarvings, rugs, sand paintings, and sculptures at rows of booths around Santa Fe Plaza.

Costumed tribal dancing and crafts demonstrations are scheduled in the afternoon.

The market is free, but hotels are booked months in advance. For information, contact the **Southwestern Association for Indian Arts** at 𝄐 **505/983-5220,** or check www.swaia.org. Third weekend in August.

Music from Angel Fire. World-class musicians gather in Angel Fire to perform classical and chamber music. For information and schedules, contact 𝄐 **888/377-3300** or www.musicfromangelfire.org. Mid-August to the first week in September.

SEPTEMBER

New Mexico Wine Festival. New Mexico wines are showcased at this annual event in Bernalillo, near Albuquerque, which features wine tastings, an art show, and live entertainment. For a schedule of events, call 𝄐 **505/867-3311** or go to www.newmexico winefestival.com. Labor Day weekend.

Las Fiestas de Santa Fe. An exuberant combination of spirit, history, and general merrymaking, Las Fiestas is the oldest community celebration in the United States. The first fiesta was celebrated in 1712, 20 years after the peaceful resettlement of New Mexico by Spanish conquistadors in 1692. The celebration includes Masses, a parade for children and their pets, a historical/hysterical parade, mariachi concerts, dances, food, and arts, as well as local entertainment on the plaza. Zozobra, "Old Man Gloom," a 40-foot-tall effigy made of wood, canvas, and paper, is burned at dusk on Thursday to revitalize the community. For information, contact 𝄐 **505/204-1598,** or go to www.santa fefiesta.org. Weekend following Labor Day.

Enchanted Circle Century Bike Tour. About 600 cyclists turn out to ride 100 miles of scenic mountain roads, starting and ending in Red River. All levels of riders are welcome, though not everyone completes this test of endurance. Call 𝄐 **575/754-2366,** or go to www.redrivernewmex.com. Weekend following Labor Day.

New Mexico State Fair and Rodeo. This is one of America's top state fairs; it features pari-mutuel horse racing, a nationally acclaimed rodeo, entertainment by top country artists, Native American and Spanish villages, the requisite midway, livestock shows, and arts and crafts.

The fair and rodeo, which last 17 days, are held at Expo New Mexico in Albuquerque. Advance tickets can be ordered by calling 𝄐 **505/265-3976** or by visiting www. exponm.com. Early September.

Taos Trade Fair, La Hacienda de los Martinez, Lower Ranchitos Road, Taos. This 1-day affair reenacts Spanish colonial life of the mid-1820s and features Hispanic and Native American music, weaving and crafts demonstrations, traditional foods, dancing, and visits by mountain men. Call 𝄐 **575/758-0505.** Last full weekend in September.

San Geronimo Vespers Sundown Dance and Trade Fair, Taos Pueblo. This event features a Mass and procession; traditional corn, buffalo, and Comanche dances; an arts-and-crafts fair; foot races; and pole climbs by clowns. Call 𝄐 **575/758-1028** for details, or go to www.taospueblo.com. Last weekend in September.

Santa Fe Wine & Chile Fiesta. This lively celebration boasts 5 days of wine and food events, including seminars, guest chef demonstrations and luncheons, tours, a grand tasting and reserve tasting, an auction, and a golf tournament. It takes place at many venues in downtown Santa Fe, with the big event on the last Saturday. Tickets go on sale in early July and sell out quickly. For information, call 𝄐 **505/438-8060,** or visit www.santafewineandchile.org. Last Wednesday through Sunday in September.

Taos Fall Arts Festival. Highlights include arts-and-crafts exhibitions and competitions, studio tours, gallery openings, lectures, concerts, dances, and stage plays. Simultaneous events include the **Trade Fair, Wool Festival,** and **San Geronimo Day** at Taos Pueblo.

The festival is held throughout Taos and Taos County. Events, schedules, and tickets (where required) can be obtained from the **Taos County Chamber of Commerce,** 108 Kit Carson Rd., Taos, NM 87571 (✆ **800/732-8267** or 575/751-8800; www.taosfallarts.com). Mid-September (or the third weekend) to the first week in October.

OCTOBER

Albuquerque International Balloon Fiesta. The world's largest balloon rally, this 9-day festival brings together more than 600 colorful balloons and includes races and contests. There are mass ascensions at sunrise, "balloon glows" in the evening, and balloon rides for those desiring a little lift. Various special events are staged all week.

Balloons lift off at Balloon Fiesta Park (at I-25 and Alameda NE) on Albuquerque's northern city limits. For information, call ✆ **505/821-1000,** or visit www.balloonfiesta.com. First full week in October.

NOVEMBER

Weems Artfest. Approximately 260 artisans, who work in a variety of media, come from throughout the world to attend this 3-day fair, held at the State Fairgrounds in Albuquerque. It's one of the top-100 arts-and-crafts fairs in the country. For details, call ✆ **505/293-6133,** or go to www.weemsgallery.com. Early November.

Festival of the Cranes. People come from all over the world to attend this bird-watching event, just an hour and a half south of Albuquerque at Bosque del Apache National Wildlife Refuge, near Socorro. Call ✆ **575/835-1828,** or go to www.friendsofthebosque.org. Weekend before Thanksgiving.

Yuletide in Taos. This holiday event emphasizes northern New Mexican traditions, cultures, and arts, with carols, festive classical music, Hispanic and Native American songs and dances, historic walking tours, art exhibitions, dance performances, candlelight dinners, and more.

Events are staged by the **Taos County Chamber of Commerce,** 108 Kit Carson Rd., Taos, NM 87571 (✆ **800/732-8267;** www.taoschamber.com). From Thanksgiving through New Year's Day.

DECEMBER

Santa Fe Film Festival, at venues throughout the city. Presents engaging world cinema, including local New Mexican films and international films in a variety of genres. Postscreening parties often feature film stars. Call ✆ **505/988-7414,** or go to www.santafefilmfestival.com. Early December.

Winter Spanish Market, Santa Fe Community Convention Center, Santa Fe. Approximately 150 artists show their wares at this little sister to July's major event. See the Spanish Market in July (above) for more information. Call ✆ **505/982-2226,** or go to www.spanishmarket.org. First full weekend in December.

Christmas in Madrid Open House. Even if you never get out of your car, it's worth going to see the spectacular lights display in this village between Albuquerque and Santa Fe on the Turquoise Trail. You'll also find entertainment, refreshments in shops, and Santa Claus. For additional information, call ✆ **505/471-1054.** First two weekends in December.

Canyon Road Farolito Walk, Santa Fe. Locals and visitors bundle up and stroll Canyon Road, where streets and rooftops are lined with *farolitos* (candle lamps). Musicians play and carolers sing around luminarias. Though it's not responsible for the event, the **Santa Fe Convention and Visitors Bureau** (✆ **505/955-6200**) can help direct you there; or ask your hotel concierge. Christmas Eve at dusk.

Dance of the Matachines and Other Dances. Many pueblos celebrate the Christmas holiday with dances. The Dance of the Matachines takes place at Picuris and San Juan pueblos on Christmas Day. Call ✆ **505/843-7270,** or go to www.indianpueblo.org. Christmas Eve through Christmas Day.

Torchlight Procession, Taos Ski Valley. Brave skiers carve down a steep run named Snakedance in the dark while carrying golden fire. For information call ✆ **866/968-7386,** or visit www.skitaos.org. December 31.

ENTRY REQUIREMENTS

Passports

Virtually every air traveler entering the U.S. is required to show a passport. All persons, including U.S. citizens, traveling by air between the United States and Canada, Mexico, Central and South America, the Caribbean, and Bermuda are required to present a valid passport. **Note:** U.S. and Canadian citizens entering the U. S. at land and sea ports of entry from within the Western Hemisphere must now also present a passport or other documents compliant with the Western Hemisphere Travel Initiative (WHTI; see www.gctyouhome.gov for details). Children 15 and under may continue entering with only a U.S. birth certificate, or other proof of U.S. citizenship.

It is advised to always have at least one or two consecutive blank pages in your passport to allow space for visas and stamps that need to appear together. It is also important to note when your passport expires. Many countries require your passport to have at least 6 months left before its expiration in order to allow you into the destination.

Visas

For information on obtaining a visa, please visit "Fast Facts," on p. 293.

The U.S. State Department has a **Visa Waiver Program (VWP)** allowing citizens of the following countries to enter the United States without a visa for stays of up to 90 days: Andorra, Australia, Austria, Belgium, Brunei, Czech Republic, Denmark, Estonia, Finland, France, Germany, Greece, Hungary, Iceland, Ireland, Italy, Japan, Latvia, Liechtenstein, Lithuania, Luxembourg, Malta, Monaco, the Netherlands, New Zealand, Norway, Portugal, San Marino, Singapore, Slovakia, Slovenia, South Korea, Spain, Sweden, Switzerland, and the United Kingdom. (**Note:** This list was accurate at press time; for the most up-to-date list of countries in the VWP, consult http://travel.state.gov/visa.) Even though a visa isn't necessary, in an effort to help U.S. officials check travelers against terror watch lists before they arrive at U.S. borders, visitors from VWP countries must register online through the Electronic System for Travel Authorization (ESTA) before boarding a plane or a boat to the U.S. Travelers must complete an electronic application providing basic personal and travel eligibility information. The Department of Homeland Security recommends filling out the form at least 3 days before traveling. Authorizations will be valid for up to 2 years or until the traveler's passport expires, whichever comes first. Currently, there is no fee for the online application. **Note:** Any passport issued on or after October 26, 2006, by a VWP country must be an **e-Passport** for VWP travelers to be eligible to enter the U.S. without a visa. Citizens of these nations also need to present a round-trip air or cruise ticket upon arrival. E-Passports contain computer chips capable of storing biometric information, such as the required digital photograph of the holder. If your passport doesn't have this feature, you can still travel without a visa if the valid passport was issued before October 26, 2005, and includes a machine-readable zone; or if the valid passport was issued between October 26, 2005, and October 25, 2006, and includes a digital photograph. For more information, go to **http://travel.state.gov/visa**. Canadian citizens may enter the United States without visas, but will need to show passports and proof of residence.

Citizens of all other countries must have (1) a valid passport that expires at least 6 months later than the scheduled end of their visit to the U.S., and (2) a tourist visa.

Customs

WHAT YOU CAN BRING INTO THE U.S.

Every visitor 21 years of age or older may bring in, free of duty, the following: (1) 1 U.S. quart of alcohol; (2) 200 cigarettes, 50 cigars (but not from Cuba), or 3 pounds of smoking tobacco; and (3) $100 worth of gifts. These exemptions are offered to travelers who spend at least 72 hours in the United States and who have not claimed them within the preceding 6 months. It is forbidden to bring into the country almost any meat products (including canned, fresh, and dried meat products such as bouillon, soup mixes, and so on). Generally, condiments including vinegars, oils, pickled goods, spices, coffee, tea, and some cheeses and baked goods are permitted. Avoid rice products, as rice can often harbor insects. Bringing fruits and vegetables is prohibited, as they may harbor pests or disease. International visitors may carry in or out up to $10,000 in U.S. or foreign currency with no formalities; larger sums must be declared to U.S. Customs on entering or leaving, which includes filing form CM 4790. For details regarding U.S. Customs and Border Protection, consult your nearest U.S. embassy or consulate, or **U.S. Customs** (www.customs.gov).

WHAT YOU CAN TAKE HOME

For information on what you're allowed to bring home, contact one of the following agencies:

U.S. Citizens: **U.S. Customs & Border** Protection **(CBP),** 1300 Pennsylvania Ave. NW, Washington, DC 20229 (ⓒ **877/287-8667;** www.cbp.gov).

Canadian Citizens: Canada Border Services Agency, Ottawa, Ontario, K1A 0L8 (ⓒ **800/461-9999** in Canada, or 204/983-3500; www.cbsa-asfc.gc.ca).

U.K. Citizens: HM Customs & Excise, Crownhill Court, Tailyour Road, Plymouth, PL6 5BZ (ⓒ **0845/010-9000;** from outside the U.K., 020/8929-0152; www.hmce.gov.uk).

Australian Citizens: Australian Customs Service, Customs House, 5 Constitution Ave., Canberra City, ACT 2601 (ⓒ **1300/363-263;** from outside Australia, 612/6275-6666; www.customs.gov.au).

New Zealand Citizens: New Zealand Customs, the Customhouse, 17–21 Whitmore St., Box 2218, Wellington, 6140 (ⓒ **04/473-6099** or 0800/428-786; www.customs.govt.nz).

Medical Requirements

Unless you're arriving from an area known to be suffering from an epidemic (particularly cholera or yellow fever), inoculations or vaccinations are not required for entry into the United States.

GETTING THERE & AROUND

Getting to Northern New Mexico

BY PLANE

The gateway to Santa Fe, Taos, Albuquerque, and other northern New Mexico communities is the **Albuquerque International Sunport** (ABQ; ⓒ **505/244-7700** for the administrative offices; www.cabq.gov/airport). To find out which airlines travel to northern New Mexico, please see "Airline Websites," in the "Fast Facts" chapter. Though a little more costly, visitors can now fly into the **Santa Fe Municipal Airport** (SAF; ℭ **505/955-2900;** www.santafenm.gov). In conjunction with American Airlines, flights are offered by **American Eagle** (ℭ **800/433-7300;** www.aa.com).

Getting Into Town from the Airport

Most hotels have courtesy vans to meet their guests and take them to their respective destinations. In addition, **Sunport Shuttle** (ℭ **505/883-4966;** www.sunport shuttle.com) in Albuquerque runs vans to and from city hotels. In Santa Fe, Roadrunner Shuttle (ℭ **505/424-3367**) meets flights and takes visitors anywhere in Santa Fe. See "By Bus" and "By Train" below to find out how to get from the Albuquerque Sunport to Santa Fe.

BY CAR

Driving is the best way to see northern New Mexico, so you'll want to either drive here or rent a car. All major rental-car companies are represented here.

Albuquerque is at the crossroads of two major interstate highways. I-40 runs from Wilmington, North Carolina (1,870 miles east), to Barstow, California (580 miles west). I-25 extends from Buffalo, Wyoming (850 miles north), to El Paso, Texas (265 miles south). I-25 skims past Santa Fe's southern city limits. To reach Taos, you have to leave I-25 at Santa Fe and travel north 74 miles via U.S. 84/285 and N.M. 68; or exit I-25 9 miles south of Raton, near the Colorado border, and proceed 100 miles west on US 64.

Parking is quite available and reasonably priced throughout the region both at meters and in city parking garages.

International visitors should note that insurance and taxes are almost never included in quoted rental-car rates in the U.S. Be sure to ask your rental agency about additional fees for these. They can add a significant cost to your car rental.

BY TRAIN

Northern New Mexico recently gained rail transport with **New Mexico Rail Runner** Express (ℭ **866/795-7245;** www.nmrailrunner.com). Trains run daily from various points in Albuquerque to various ones in Santa Fe, with connecting buses to the Albuquerque International Sunport and to Taos.

Amtrak (ℭ **800/**872-**7245** or 505/842-9650; www.amtrak.com) passes through northern New Mexico twice daily. The *Southwest Chief,* which runs between Chicago and Los Angeles, stops once eastbound and once westbound in Gallup, Albuquerque, Lamy (for Santa Fe), Las Vegas, and Raton. The Albuquerque train station is in the center of downtown, with easy access to hotels. A spur runs on a limited schedule from Lamy approximately 20 miles to downtown Santa Fe, within walking distance to the plaza. A photo ID is required to ride Amtrak trains.

BY BUS

Because Santa Fe is only about 58 miles northeast of Albuquerque via I-40, most visitors to Santa Fe take the bus directly from the Albuquerque airport, at a cost of about $20 to $25 one-way. **Sandia Shuttle Express** buses (ℭ **888/775-5696** or 505/474-5696; www.sandiashuttle.com) make the 70-minute run between the airport and Santa Fe hotels 10 times daily each way (from Albuquerque to Santa Fe, 6:30am–6pm; from Santa Fe to Albuquerque, 8:45am–8:20pm). Reservations are required, ideally 48 hours in advance. Two other bus services shuttle between Albuquerque and Taos (via Santa Fe) for $25 to $35 one-way: **Faust's** Transportation

(© **888/830-3410** or 505/758-3410) and **Twin Heart Express & Transportation** (© **800/654-9456** or 575/751-1201).

The **public bus depot** in Albuquerque is located at 100 1st St. SW. Contact **Greyhound** © **800/231-2222**; www.greyhound.com) for information and schedules. Greyhound buses no longer run to Santa Fe and Taos.

Getting Around

BY PLANE

Northern New Mexico doesn't have carriers flying between its cities, which is just as well. The best parts of the region happen between the major destinations.

Some large airlines offer transatlantic or transpacific passengers special discount tickets under the name **Visit USA,** which allows mostly one-way travel from one U.S. destination to another at very low prices. Unavailable in the U.S., these discount tickets must be purchased abroad in conjunction with your international fare. This system is the easiest, fastest, and cheapest way to see the country.

BY CAR

The most convenient, and scenic, way to get around northern New Mexico is by private car. Auto and RV rentals are widely available for those who arrive without their own transportation, either at the Albuquerque airport or at locations around each city.

Drivers who need wheelchair-accessible transportation should call **Wheelchair Getaways of New** Mexico, 1015 Tramway Lane NE, Albuquerque (© **800/408-2626** or 505/247-2626; www.wheelchairgetaways.com); the company rents vans by the day, week, or month.

If you're visiting from abroad and plan to rent a car in the United States, keep in mind that foreign driver's licenses are usually recognized in the U.S., but you may want to consider obtaining an international driver's license.

BY TRAIN

New Mexico **Rail Runner Express** (© **866/795-7245;** www.nmrailrunner.com) runs daily from various points in Albuquerque to various ones in Santa Fe, with connecting buses to the Albuquerque International Sunport and to Taos.

Amtrak (© **800/872-7245** or 505/842-9650; www.amtrak.com) runs from Albuquerque to Lamy, with a small spur railroad running to Santa Fe.

International visitors can buy a **USA Rail Pass,** good for 15, 30, or 45 days of unlimited travel on **Amtrak** The pass is available online or through many overseas travel agents. See Amtrak's website for the cost of travel within the western, eastern, or northwestern United States. Reservations are generally required and should be made as early as possible. Regional rail passes are also available.

BY BUS

Greyhound (© **800/231-2222;** www.greyhound.com) is the sole nationwide bus line. Although Greyhound maintains a station in Albuquerque (see above), it no longer runs between northern New Mexico cities; however, I do list shuttle buses that do those routes in the "Getting There" section, above. International visitors can obtain information about the Greyhound **North American Discovery Pass.** The pass, which offers unlimited travel and stopovers in the U.S. and Canada, can be obtained from foreign travel agents or through www.discoverypass.com.

MONEY & COSTS

THE VALUE OF U.S. DOLLARS VS. OTHER POPULAR CURRENCIES

US$	Can$	UK£	Euro (€)	Aus$	NZ$
$1	C$1.03	£.70	€.80	A$1.14	NZ$1.43

Frommer's lists exact prices in the local currency. The currency conversions quoted above were correct at press time. However, rates fluctuate, so before departing consult a currency exchange website such as www.xe.com to check up-to-the-minute rates.

If you come from a major city such as New York or London, you may find northern New Mexico overall fairly inexpensive. In Taos and Albuquerque, you can still get good accommodations and meals without wincing. Santa Fe, however, may hurt a bit, especially if you hit the hottest spots in town, which cater to sophisticated tastes.

The easiest and best way to get cash away from home is from an ATM (automated teller machine), sometimes referred to as a "cash machine," or "cashpoint." They are available all over northern New Mexico. The **Cirrus** (✆ 800/424-7787; www. mastercard.com) and **PLUS** (www.visa.com) networks span the globe; look at the back of your bank card to see which network you're on, then call or check online for ATM locations at your destination. Be sure you know your personal identification number (PIN) and daily withdrawal limit before you depart. *Note:* Remember that many banks impose a fee every time you use a card at another bank's ATM, and that fee can be higher for international transactions (up to $5 or more) than for domestic ones (where they're rarely more than $2). In addition, the bank from which you withdraw cash may charge its own fee. For international withdrawal fees, ask your bank

Beware of hidden credit-card fees while traveling. Check with your credit or debit card issuer to see what fees, if any, will be charged for overseas transactions. Recent reform legislation in the U.S., for example, has curbed some exploitative lending practices. But many banks have responded by increasing fees in other areas, including fees for customers who use credit and debit cards while out of the country—even if those charges were made in U.S. dollars. Fees can amount to 3% or more of the purchase price. Check with your bank before departing to avoid any surprise charges on your statement.

WHAT THINGS COST IN SANTA FE

Double room in high season at La Posada de Santa Fe Resort and Spa	$361.00
Double room in high season at Santa Fe Sage Inn	$140.00
Dinner for two at Geronimo, without drinks, tax, or tip	$115.00
Dinner for two at La Choza, without drinks, tax, or tip	$25.00
Imported Mexican beer at the Dragon Room	$4.00
Hour massage at Ten Thousand Waves Japanese Health Spa	$99.00
Adult admission to the Museum of International Folk Art	$9.00

STAYING HEALTHY

One thing that sets New Mexico apart from most other states is its elevation. Santa Fe and Taos are about 7,000 feet above sea level; Albuquerque is more than 5,000 feet above sea level. The reduced oxygen and humidity can yield some unique problems, as noted below. The desert environment can also present some challenges.

Regional Health Concerns

HIGH DESERT CHALLENGES   One of the most common ailments in northern New Mexico is acute mountain sickness. In its early stages, you might experience headaches, shortness of breath, loss of appetite and/or nausea, tingling in the fingers or toes, lethargy, and insomnia. The condition can usually be treated by taking aspirin as well as getting plenty of rest, avoiding large meals, and drinking lots of nonalcoholic fluids (especially water). If the condition persists or worsens, you must return to a lower altitude. Other dangers of higher elevations include hypothermia and sun exposure, and these should be taken seriously. To avoid dehydration, drink water as often as possible.

Limit your exposure to the sun, especially during the first few days of your trip and, thereafter, between 11am and 2pm. Liberally apply sunscreen with a high protection factor. Remember that children need more protection than adults do. It's important to monitor your children's health while in New Mexico. They are just as susceptible to mountain sickness, hypothermia, sunburn, and dehydration as you are.

DIETARY RED FLAGS   Though some places in northern New Mexico can have the feel of towns in our neighboring Mexico, the food and water here are safe. As well, a broad range of food is available, so that even vegetarians can usually find something to eat; small cafes often offer beans and rice. One of the few dietary concerns is the spicy chile, so be sure to ask how hot it is before ordering.

BUGS, BITES & OTHER WILDLIFE CONCERNS   If you're an outdoorsperson, be on the lookout for snakes—particularly rattlers. Avoid them. Don't even get close enough to take a picture (unless you have a very good zoom lens). As well, watch for black widows, which have a bulbous body and an hourglass image on their belly; a bite from this spider can make you very sick. The same goes for scorpions, which are crablike spiders with a curled stinging tail. If you get bitten by a snake or spider, or stung by a scorpion, seek professional medical help immediately.

Visitors to the state should also be careful of contracting the plague and hantavirus, a few cases of each reported annually in the state. Both diseases can be fatal, and both are transmitted through exposure to infected rodent droppings. Though it's unlikely that you'll be exposed to such things while traveling, be careful anytime you note the presence of mice or other rodents.

WEATHER CONCERNS   You'll also want to be wary of arroyos, or creek beds in the desert where flash floods can occur without warning. If water is flowing across a road, *do not* try to drive through it because chances are the water is deeper and flowing faster than you think. Just wait it out. Arroyo floods don't last long.

If You Get Sick

The most reliable hospitals in the area are **Christus St. Vincent Regional Medical Center,** 455 St. Michaels Dr. in Santa Fe (✆ **505/983-5250;** www.stvn.org), and **Presbyterian Hospital,** 1100 Central Ave. SE in Albuquerque (© **505/841-1819,** or 505/841-1111 for emergency service; www.phs.org). Additional **emergency numbers** are listed in "Fast Facts," p. 293.

CRIME & SAFETY

Tourist areas as a rule are safe, but, despite recent reports of decreases in violent crime in Santa Fe, it would be wise to check with the tourist offices in Santa Fe, Taos, and Albuquerque if you are in doubt about which neighborhoods are safe. (See the "Orientation" sections in chapters 5, 12, and 16 for the names and addresses of the specific tourist bureaus.)

Remember that hotels are open to the public, and in a large hotel, security may not be able to screen everyone who enters. Always lock your room door; don't assume that once inside your hotel you are automatically safe and no longer need to be aware of your surroundings.

Be aware that New Mexico has a higher-than-average reported incidence of rape. Women should not walk alone in isolated places, particularly at night.

SPECIALIZED TRAVEL RESOURCES

In addition to the destination-specific resources listed below, please visit Frommers. **com** for other specialized travel resources.

GLBT Travelers

New Mexico is a pretty gay-friendly place in general, especially in Santa Fe, with its cosmopolitan attitude. Only in the smaller villages will locals look askance.

Common Bond (© **505/891-3647;** www.commonbond.org) provides information and outreach services for Albuquerque's gay and lesbian community, as well as referrals for other New Mexico cities. A recorded message on this phone line gives lists of bars and clubs, businesses, and publications, as well as health and crisis information and a calendar of events. Volunteers are on hand (generally in the evenings) to answer questions. Another good resource is **www.gaynm.org**, a website that provides news, resources, and lists of events.

For more gay and lesbian travel resources, visit www.frommers.com.

Travelers with Disabilities

Throughout New Mexico, measures have been taken to provide access for travelers with disabilities. Several bed-and-breakfasts have made one or more of their rooms completely wheelchair accessible. The **Center for Development & Disability Info in NM** (© **800/552-8195** or 505/272-8549) accesses a database with lists of services ranging from restaurants and hotels to wheelchair rentals. The *Access New Mexico* guide lists accessible hotels, attractions, and restaurants throughout the state. For more information, contact the **Governor's Commission on Disabilities,** 491 Old Santa Fe Trail, Lamy Building Room 117, Santa Fe, NM 87503 (© **505/827-6465;** www.gcd.state.nm.us).

The chambers of commerce in Santa Fe, Taos, and Albuquerque will answer questions regarding accessibility in their areas. It is advisable to call hotels, restaurants, and attractions in advance to be sure that they are fully accessible.

Family Travel

If you have enough trouble getting your kids out of the house in the morning, dragging them thousands of miles away may seem like an insurmountable challenge. But family travel can be immensely rewarding, giving you new ways of seeing the world through smaller pairs of eyes.

Be aware that family travel in northern New Mexico may be a little different from what you're accustomed to. You'll find few huge Disney-like attractions here. Instead, the draws are culture and the outdoors. Rather than spending time in theme parks, you may go white-water rafting down the Rio Grande, skiing at one of the many family-friendly areas, climbing a wooden ladder up to a cliff dwelling, or trekking through the wilderness with a llama.

If your brood is not very adventurous, don't worry. Some of the hotels and resorts listed in this book have inviting pools to laze around or on-site activities planned especially for kids. Whatever your choice, northern New Mexico will definitely offer your children a new perspective on the United States by exposing them to ancient ruins, Southwestern cuisine, and Hispanic and Native American cultures that they may not experience elsewhere.

The Santa Fe quarterly *Tumbleweeds* (© **505/984-3171;** www.sftumbleweeds.com) offers useful articles on family-oriented subjects in the Santa Fe area, a quarterly day-by-day calendar of family events, and a seasonal directory of children's classes, camps, and programs. It's available free in locations all over Santa Fe, or by mail for $15.

To locate accommodations, restaurants, and attractions that are particularly kid-friendly, look for the "Kids" icon throughout this guide.

Senior Travel

Recommended publications offering travel resources and discounts for seniors include the Albuquerque-based monthly tabloid *Prime Time* (© **505/880-0470;** www.primetimemonthly.com), which publishes a variety of articles aimed at those 50 years and older.

RESPONSIBLE TOURISM

New Mexico is the first state in the U.S. to launch an eco-tourism initiative. It has three foci: Cultural Heritage, Nature and Conservancy, and Outdoor Adventure. What this means to travelers is yet to be seen, but it is important that the state is looking to help expand this part of its travel offering.

Most of New Mexico's 19 Native American communities still preserve their traditional ways. In order for them to continue to do so, we all must respect their requests. When visiting these cultures, be sure to honor their posted boundaries and their rules. In Chapter 11, I list some important tips in the box, "Pueblo Etiquette."

The main environmental challenge in northern New Mexico's high desert is **water.** For many years, the region has been experiencing a drought to the degree that

GENERAL RESOURCES FOR responsible TRAVEL

In addition to the resources for northern New Mexico listed above, the following websites provide valuable wide-ranging information on sustainable travel.

o **Responsible Travel** (www.responsibletravel.com) is a great source of sustainable travel ideas; the site is run by a spokesperson for ethical tourism in the travel industry. **Sustainable Travel International** (www.sustainabletravelinternational.org) promotes ethical tourism practices, and manages an extensive directory of sustainable properties and tour operators around the world.

o **Carbonfund** (www.carbonfund.org), **TerraPass** (www.terrapass.org), and **Cool Climate** (http://coolclimate.berkeley.edu) provide info on "carbon offsetting," or offsetting the greenhouse gas emitted during flights.

o **Greenhotels** (www.greenhotels.com) recommends green-rated member hotels around the world that fulfill the company's stringent environmental requirements. **Environmentally Friendly Hotels** (www.environmentallyfriendlyhotels.com) offers more green accommodation ratings.

o **Volunteer International** (www.volunteerinternational.org) has a list of questions to help you determine the intentions and the nature of a volunteer program. For general info on volunteer travel, visit **www.volunteerabroad.org** and **www.idealist.org**.

---

citizens in Albuquerque and Santa Fe monitor their landscape irrigation. This has led businesses to become more accountable for their water use as well. Some recycle their water, using it to irrigate landscaping. Others plant xeric (natural) gardens. Many have extended their green practices to include recycling paper, glass, and other materials, and, when possible, eliminating paper filing systems in favor of electronic ones. Northern New Mexico has also become conscious of its **CO_2 footprint** in relation to food. More and more residents and restaurants now buy produce from local farmers, rather than large suppliers who ship long distances. Such practices support small, often organic, agriculture, which helps protect the region's clean water from pesticides and rural land from development. Yet, there is still massive waste of water and other resources here. Golf courses, including those on Native American-owned lands, have become more and more common, with only a few that are desert oriented.

Public transportation in the area is relatively scarce, though the recent introduction of the New Mexico Rail Runner Express train has helped reduce some of the automobile travel between Albuquerque and Santa Fe and outlying communities. Visitors to the region will likely still want to have a car handy because many of the sights and activities are in outlying areas. But you can help in other ways. Look for hotels that are taking steps toward the green measures mentioned above and eat in restaurants that use local, seasonal ingredients when possible. Play golf at the few desert courses, even if they may be more challenging than standard ones.

A few eco-tourism lodgings in the region have initiated green measures. These include in Santa Fe **Bishop's Lodge Ranch Resort & Spa** (𝒞 505/983-6377; www.bishopslodge.com) and **La Posada Resort & Spa** (𝒞 800/727-5276; www.rockresorts.com); in Taos, **El Monte Sagrado** (𝒞 800/828-8267; www.elmontesagrado.com)

and the **Old Taos Guesthouse** (© 800/758-5448; www.oldtaos.com); and in Albuquerque, the new Andaluz (© 505/242-9090; www.hotelandaluz.com).

In the "Where to Dine" sections in this book, I mention a number of restaurants that use local, seasonal ingredients, which will help you support the region's green efforts.

If you're a duffer and want to play on an eco-friendly course, check out **Marty Sanchez Links de Santa Fe** (© 505/955-4400; www.linksdesantafe.com), **Paa-Ko Ridge** (© 866/361-7443; www.resortlifestylecommunities.com/paakoridge) east of Albuquerque, and the **Twin** Warriors **Golf Club** at the Hyatt Regency Tamaya Resort & Spa (© 505/867-1234; www.tamaya.hyatt.com).

For more all-inclusive travel in Santa Fe, **Santa Fe Mountain Adventures** (© 800/965-4010 or 505/988-4000; www.santafemountainadventures.com) leads programs that combine outdoor adventures with arts and cultural experiences, and spa treatments. This eco-conscious business is a collaborative effort in conjunction with Outside magazine.

SPECIAL-INTEREST & ESCORTED TRIPS

Academic & Cultural Trips

Those who like a scholarly bent to their vacations can hook up with **Southwest Seminars** (© 505/466-2775; www.southwestseminars.org) and their "Travels with a Scholar" program. This organization arranges tours throughout the Southwest, led by museum directors, historians, geologists, archaeologists, anthropologists, and authors. Southwest Seminars is able to arrange visits to sites that are not open to the general public, such as archaeological sites, petroglyph panels, volcanic calderas, contemporary Indian pueblos, and native artists' homes and studios. ***Note:*** Each Monday at 6pm, talks are given by regional scholars that are well worth checking out.

Photography & Art Trips

Some of the world's most outstanding photographers convene in Santa Fe at various times during the year for the **Santa Fe Workshops,** at a delightful campus in the hills on the east side of town (© 505/983-1400; www.santafeworkshops.com). Most courses are full time, lasting a week. Food and lodging packages are available.

If you'd like to pursue an artistic adventure, check out the weeklong classes in such media as painting, Native American pottery making, and weaving offered by **Taos Art School** (© 505/758-0350; www.taosartschool.org). This organization is especially known for its weaving and horseback-riding creative "odyssey." Open since 1989, the school is a virtual campus in which classes go where they need to be. For instance, a painting class on Georgia O'Keeffe is held in Abiquiu and a Pueblo pottery class at Taos Pueblo. The fees vary from class to class and include lodging and meals.

Great Expeditions (© 800/663-3364; www.greatexpeditions.com) offers an "Opera in Santa Fe" trip, which focuses on more than the opera, but also partakes of this world-class entertainment.

Adventure & Wellness Trips

If you're looking for an active adventure and some relaxation too there are a few options. One excellent operator is **Santa Fe Mountain Adventures**

(© **800/965-4010** or 505/988-4000; www.santafemountainadventures.com), which combines outdoor adventures, such as hiking and river running, with cultural activities, such as visits to pueblos or museums, with more relaxing ones, such as spa treatments and meditation practices. A collaborative effort in conjunction with *Outside* magazine, the business is eco-conscious. See p. 133 for more details.

Bicycle Adventures (© **800/443-6060** or 425/250-5540; www.bicycle adventures.com) offers tours to northern New Mexico. Riders get to experience some of the region's loveliest routes, such as the High Road to Taos and the Enchanted Circle. Participants visit major sights such as Santa Fe's Canyon Road and Taos Pueblo and can even opt for a river trip. In business for over 2 decades, this company knows how to put together a good tour.

Food & Wine Trips

Jane **Butel Cooking School,** 2655 Pan American NE, Ste. F (© **800/473-8226** or 505/243-2622; www.janebutelcooking.com), offers weeklong and weekend packages with a hotel stay and full-participation classes. The weekend classes are held in noted chef and television personality Jane Butel's home kitchen in Corrales, a village along the Rio Grande on the edge of Albuquerque. The weeklong classes are in Santa Fe.

Volunteer & Working Trips

Sierra Club Outings (© **415/977-5522;** www.sierraclub.org/outings/national/service.asp) organizes working vacations all over the world, with some work to be done in New Mexico. **Global Citizens Network** offers volunteer vacations to worldwide destinations as well, including, at times, New Mexico. To check their schedule, contact (© **800/644-9292;** www.globalcitizens.org).

Escorted General-Interest Tours

Escorted tours are structured group tours, with a group leader. The price usually includes everything from airfare to hotels, meals, tours, admission costs, and local transportation.

Not many escorted tours are offered in New Mexico. Most visitors have such disparate interests it's difficult to create packages to please everyone. Still, a few tour companies can help you arrange a variety of day trips during your visit and can also secure lodging. **Tauck World Discovery,** 10 Norden Place, Norwalk, CT 06855 (© **800/788-7885;** www.tauck.com), offers weeklong cultural trips to northern New Mexico. **Destination Southwest, Inc.,** 20 First Plaza Galeria, Ste. 212, Albuquerque, NM 87102 (© **800/999-3109** or 505/766-9068; www.destinationsouthwest.com), offers an escorted tour to the Albuquerque International Balloon Fiesta. **Rojotours & Services,** P.O. Box 15744, Santa Fe, NM 87506-5744 (© **505/474-8333;** www.rojotours.com), can help with a variety of day trips during your visit.

For more information on escorted tours, including questions to ask before booking your trip, visit **www.frommers.com.**

STAYING CONNECTED

Mobile phones

Because this region is a GSM network, your cellphone will likely work in the major cities. Be aware, though, that in rural areas, reception will be spotty.

Internet & E-Mail

Wi-Fi and traditional Internet access are widely available in the cities in the region. Most hotels now offer free Wi-Fi, and all cities in the region have cafes with wireless access. In order to find one near you, log onto **www.jiwire.com**; its Hotspot Finder holds the world's largest directory of public wireless hot spots. To find wireless cafes, check out **www.cybercafe.com**.

Newspapers & Magazines

National newspapers include the *New York Times, USA Today,* and the *Wall Street Journal.* National news weeklies include *Newsweek, Time,* and *U.S. News & World Report.* In large cities, most newsstands offer a small selection of the most popular foreign periodicals and newspapers, such as *The Economist* and *Le Monde.* For information on local publications, see the "Fast Facts" sections in chapters 5, 12, and 16.

Telephones

Many convenience groceries and packaging services sell **prepaid calling cards** in denominations up to $50. Many public pay phones at airports now accept American Express, MasterCard, and Visa. **Local calls** made from most pay phones cost either 25¢ or 35¢. Most long-distance and international calls can be dialed directly from any phone. **To make calls within the United States and to Canada,** dial 1 followed by the area code and the seven-digit number. **For other international calls,** dial 011 followed by the country code, city code, and the number you are calling.

Calls to area codes **800, 888, 877,** and **866** are toll-free. However, calls to area codes **700** and **900** (chat lines, bulletin boards, "dating" services, and so on) can be expensive—charges of 95¢ to $3 or more per minute. Some numbers have minimum charges that can run $15 or more.

For **reversed-charge or collect calls,** and for person-to-person calls, dial the number 0 then the area code and number; an operator will come on the line, and you should specify whether you are calling collect, person-to-person, or both. If your operator-assisted call is international, ask for the overseas operator.

For **directory assistance** ("Information"), dial 411 for local numbers and national numbers in the U.S. and Canada. For dedicated long-distance information, dial 1, then the appropriate area code, plus 555-1212.

TIPS ON ACCOMMODATIONS

No two travelers are alike; fortunately, New Mexico has a broad-enough range of accommodations to satisfy even the most eccentric adventurer. If you long to be pampered, you'll find a few swanky resorts within the region, with a variety of luxury options such as pool and exercise facilities, golf, tennis, horseback riding, and spa treatments. Of course, none of it comes cheap.

If you're looking to really savor the flavor of New Mexico, you may want to opt for one of its historic hotels. This may include a hacienda-style inn—an adobe one- or two-story structure often built around a courtyard. You'll also find some Victorian inns that have a frontier flavor. Within this variety of architecture, the amenities vary, from places with antique but workable plumbing and no television, to those with hot tubs and Wi-Fi in rooms.

In recent years, bed-and-breakfast inns (B&Bs) have proliferated in New Mexico. Though you can find traditional Victorian-style B&Bs here (and some lovely ones at that), complete with lacy bedding and elaborately carved accents, you can also choose from old hacienda-style homes or tiered adobe structures. All are comfortable and a few luxurious, with prices in the moderate to expensive range.

We all have those nights when only predictability will do. That's when a chain hotel comes in handy. You'll find all the major ones in northern New Mexico, though not quite everywhere. The small villages still shun such cookie-cutter establishments, but most everywhere else you can find them along the highways or in the town centers.

For tips on surfing for hotel deals online, visit www.frommers.com.

SUGGESTED NORTHERN NEW MEXICO ITINERARIES

You may already have an idea of how you want to spend your time in New Mexico—power shopping, perhaps, or time-traveling through ancient culture. But if you're not sure what to do, here are four suggested itineraries, outlined in 1-week and 2-week segments. For each one, I assume that you're starting in Albuquerque, either by driving in your own car or flying into the Albuquerque International Sunport, the air transportation hub of the state, and then renting a car.

4

Northern New Mexico has a mix of museums and indoor activities, but the real attractions here are the living culture and spectacular scenery en route. With this in mind, I've combined scenic drives with city stays in these tours. In order to get a true sense of this place, take your time—linger at a country cafe or wander a plaza for an hour. You might be surprised at how easily you get enveloped in the experience of being a New Mexican.

NORTHERN NEW MEXICO IN A WEEK

A week in northern New Mexico isn't quite long enough to do justice to the area's rich and varied landscape, but if that's all the time you have, you can definitely hit the highlights. You can gaze at the ancient petroglyphs etched on stone at Petroglyph National Monument, shop one of the world's top art markets on Canyon Road in Santa Fe, marvel at the play of light on the Rio Grande Gorge in Taos—and maybe even take a white-water rafting trip through it. See map on p. 51.

Days 1 & 2: Albuquerque

If you have some energy left after traveling, head to **Old Town** (p. 265), where you can wander through the **plaza** and peruse some shops. Be sure to duck into some of the back alleyways and little nooks—you'll uncover some of the city's most inventive shops in these areas. Next, head over to the **Albuquerque Museum of Art and History** (p. 262) to get a good sense of the story of this land. Finish the day with one of New Mexico's premier treats—an enchilada—at **Mary & Tito's** (p. 257).

On Day 2, start out at the **Indian Pueblo Cultural Center** (p. 264), where you'll get a sense of the cultures you'll encounter up north, and then head to the **Albuquerque Biological Park** (p. 269), both in the vicinity of **Old Town Plaza.** From here, go west of town to visit the **Petroglyph National Monument** (p. 267). (If it's summer, you may want to go during the cooler early morning.) In the late afternoon, find your way to Central Avenue, just south of Old Town, and drive east on **Route 66.** This takes you right through downtown, to the Nob Hill district and the Sandia Mountains foothills, respectively. Finish your day with a ride up the **Sandia Peak Tramway** (p. 266). After you reach the top, you may want to hike along the crest, though this isn't safe for young kids. Ideally, you should ride up during daylight and back down at night for a view of the city lights. You may even want to dine at **High Finance Restaurant and Tavern** on the top.

Day 3: The Turquoise Trail ★★ & Santa Fe

Strike out for the ghost towns and other sights along the **Turquoise Trail** (p. 290) to Santa Fe, stopping to peruse some of the galleries in **Madrid** (p. 290). This will put you in Santa Fe in time to do some sightseeing. Head straight to the **plaza** (p. 113), the **New Mexico History Museum and the Palace of the Governors** (p. 112), and the **St. Francis Cathedral** (p. 113). If you shop from the Native Americans selling under the portal, be sure to ask about the art you buy; the symbols on it may have interesting significance. Next, make your way over to the **Georgia O'Keeffe Museum** (p. 110). Finish your day with an enchilada at **The Shed** (p. 104). In the evening, depending on the season, you may want to check out Santa Fe's excellent arts scene; try the **Santa Fe Opera** (p. 151) or the **Santa Fe Chamber Music Festival** (p. 152).

Day 4: Santa Fe Arts

In the morning, head up to Museum Hill, where you can take your pick from four very unique museums: the **Museum of International Folk Art** (p. 117), the **Museum of Indian Arts & Culture** (p. 116), the **Wheelwright Museum of the American Indian** (p. 119), and the **Museum of Spanish Colonial Art** (p. 117). You can have lunch at the **Museum Hill Café** (p. 116). On your way back to the plaza, take a stroll and do some shopping on **Canyon Road** (p. 139). At sunset during the warmer months, you can enjoy a cocktail at the bell tower of the historic **La Fonda** hotel (p. 74). Eat dinner at **Santacafé** (p. 96)—or if you lingered over your shopping, stop in at **Geronimo** (p. 94) or the **Compound** (p. 92) on Canyon Road.

Day 5: Bandelier National Monument ★★★ & North to Taos

Head out of town to **Bandelier National Monument** (p. 162). Linger among the ruins and be sure to climb the ladders to see the kiva set high above the canyon floor.

Northern New Mexico in a Week

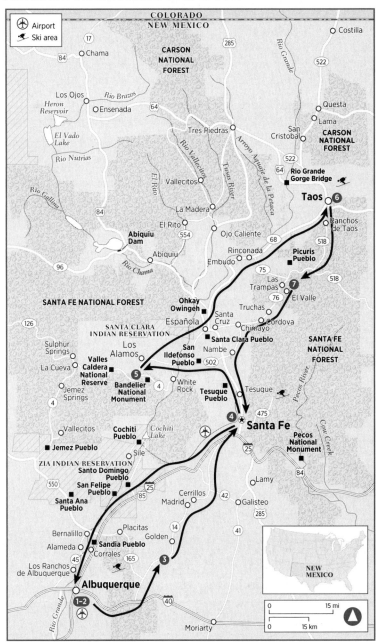

Then continue north to Taos. On your way into the city, stop at the **San Francisco de Asis church** (p. 212). And if you like music, head out to the **Sagebrush Inn** (p. 232) for some country-and-western dancing.

Day 6: Taos ★★★
Spend your morning exploring **Taos Pueblo** (p. 218), the **Millicent Rogers Museum** (p. 211), and the **Rio Grande Gorge Bridge** (p. 217). You can then ditch your car for the afternoon and step out on foot. Do some shopping around **Taos Plaza.** At cocktail hour, head to the **Adobe Bar** (p. 232) at the Historic Taos Inn or the **Anaconda Bar** (p. 232) at the new El Monte Sagrado.

Day 7: The High Road ★★
On your last day, enjoy a leisurely morning and then head south on the **High Road to Taos** (see chapter 11). Be sure to spend some time at the **Santuario de Chimayo** (p. 167), where you can rub healing dust between your fingers. You may want to spend the night at a bed-and-breakfast in **Chimayo** (p. 167) along the way. Depending on your flight time the next morning, stay the night in Santa Fe or Albuquerque.

NORTHERN NEW MEXICO IN 2 WEEKS

If you have 2 weeks to spend exploring the region, consider yourself fortunate. In addition to hitting the highlights, you'll be able to spend time getting to know such places as Chama and Chaco National Cultural Park. See map on p. 53.

Days 1 to 4: Albuquerque & Santa Fe
For days 1 to 4, follow the previous itinerary, "Northern New Mexico in a Week."

Day 5: Santa Fe
In the morning, take the **Plaza Area** walking tour (p. 125), spending time at the **Museum of Fine Arts** and the **Loretto Chapel** (p. 119). If you're visiting during the warm seasons, have lunch in the Sena Plaza at **La Casa Sena** (p. 94). In the afternoon, take the **Barrio de Analco** walking tour (p. 129) up Canyon Road, allowing you more time for shopping that lovely street. Be sure to stop in at **El Zaguan** (p. 130) to see an old New Mexico hacienda.

Day 6: High Road to Taos ★★
On Day 6, travel the **High Road to Taos** (see chapter 11), stopping to rub healing dust between your fingers at the **Santuario de Chimayo** (p. 167). On the way into Taos, stop at the **San Francisco de Asis church** (p. 212). While there, take note of the thickness of the structure's walls. If you like music, head out to the **Sagebrush Inn** (p. 232) for some country-and-western music or to the **Anaconda Bar** (p. 232) to hear some jazz or other live music.

Day 7: Taos ★★★
Spend your morning at **Taos Pueblo** (p. 214), where you may want to sample some fry bread. Next head to the **Millicent Rogers Museum** (p. 211) and the **Rio Grande Gorge Bridge** (p. 217). During the afternoon, do some shopping around

Northern New Mexico in 2 Weeks

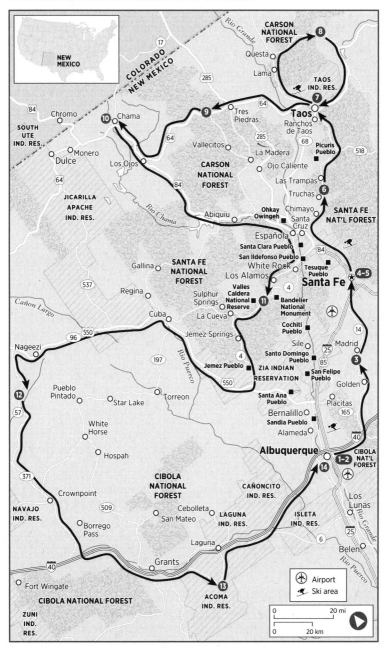

the **Taos Plaza,** and then visit the **Taos Art Museum** (p. 212). Don't just look at the art there. The Fechin Home where the museum is housed is a work of art itself. At cocktail hour, head to the **Adobe Bar** (p. 232) at the Historic Taos Inn or the **Anaconda Bar** (p. 232) at El Monte Sagrado to hear live music.

Day 8: The Enchanted Circle ★★
Take the 90-mile loop north of Taos through old Hispanic villages and mining towns to see some of the region's most picturesque landscapes. If you're a literary type, be sure to stop at the **D.H. Lawrence Ranch** (p. 216), and if you're a hiker, stretch your legs at the **Wild Rivers Recreation Area** (p. 234).

Day 9: West to Chama
If you're traveling in the spring, summer, or fall, take a scenic drive west to Chama. En route, stop in at **Tierra Wools** (p. 180) to see the weaving. Then wander around Chama to learn about the area's train history. In the afternoon, prepare for tomorrow's train ride on the **Cumbres & Toltec Scenic Railroad** (p. 177). Be sure to make your train reservations well in advance. As well as offering a great ride, the Cumbres & Toltec is a living train museum, so take some time to wander the grounds. Often volunteers will tell fun stories about the train and its history. Spend the night in Chama. If it's wintertime, the train won't be running, so you'll want to stay in Taos and head to **Taos Ski Valley** (p. 218) for a day of skiing. Or, if you're not a train buff and it's spring, take a white-water raft trip down the **Taos Box** (p. 225) or **Pilar** (p. 225).

Day 10: Cumbres & Toltec Scenic Railroad ★★
Spend the day riding the **Cumbres & Toltec Scenic Railroad** (p. 177). Your best bet is to ride the train to the halfway point and turn around and come back. Spend the night in Chama. If you don't ride the train and have stayed in Taos, take a **llama trek** (p. 224), with a gourmet lunch.

Day 11: Head South to Bandelier National Monument ★★★
This will be a day of pure scenery. You'll drive through **Abiquiu** and see the crimson-and-white hills that Georgia O'Keeffe painted, and then head into the Jemez Mountains. Stop at **Bandelier National Monument** (p. 162). Here you'll hike among ancient ruins. Follow the Frijoles Trail as far up as you'd like, making sure you stop to climb the ladders to the kiva perched high on the canyon wall. From Bandelier, you'll make your way west past the **Valles Caldera National Preserve** (p. 166), pausing to look out across this amazing collapsed volcano. From here, head south on the **Jemez Mountain Trail** (p. 287). Spend the night in Jemez Springs.

Day 12: Chaco Culture National Historic Park ★★★
Though it's a long, dusty drive to **Chaco Culture National Historic Park** (p. 175), its combination of a stunning setting and expansive ruins makes it worthwhile. In fact, Chaco is the Holy Grail for Southwest history buffs. Be sure to hike up the **Pueblo Alto Trail** (p. 177) to get a full view of the grand kivas and amazing network of dwellings. If you have camping equipment, spend the night at Chaco. If not, you can spend the night at one of the chain hotels in Grants.

Day 13: Acoma Pueblo ★★★

Head to **Acoma Pueblo** (p. 284). Tour the village with the requisite bus and walking tour, but then be sure to hike down on your own in order to get a good sense of this mesa-top village, where people still live as their ancestors did hundreds of years ago. Spend the night in Albuquerque.

Day 14: Albuquerque

On your last day in Albuquerque, take a **balloon ride** (p. 272) in the early morning. (And if you want to do this, be sure to make your reservations in advance.) Then head to the new **Balloon Museum** (p. 264) to learn more about the sport. Finish the afternoon cooling off at your hotel pool, or if you're energetic, visit the **National Hispanic Cultural Center** (p. 265). Have dinner at **Seasons Rotisserie & Grill** (p. 252).

NORTHERN NEW MEXICO IN A WEEK FOR KIDS

Although New Mexico lacks the major theme park variety of attractions, it makes up for it by offering experiences that have a deeper impact. This trip takes families to the region's most notable sights—including Petroglyph National Monument and Bandelier National Monument—but it's not too jampacked; it also fits in some time for poolside lounging. When planning this trip, keep in mind that the climate in this region is fairly mild, but summers in Albuquerque can be scorching and winters in Santa Fe and Taos can be cold. See map on p. 56.

Days 1 & 2: Albuquerque

If you have some energy after traveling, head to **Old Town** (p. 265), where you can wander the **plaza,** peruse some shops, and, if you have time, head over to the **Explora** science center (p. 270) or the **New Mexico Museum of Natural History and Science** (p. 270). Finish the day with one of New Mexico's premier treats—an enchilada—at **Mary & Tito's** (p. 257).

On Day 2, start out at the **Indian Pueblo Cultural Center** (p. 264), and then head to the **Albuquerque Biological Park** (p. 269). Be sure to visit the Biological Park's butterfly exhibit. Alternatively, you may want to visit the **Rio Grande Zoo** (p. 271). Don't miss the polar bears there. Both are in the vicinity of **Old Town Plaza.** Then head out to **Petroglyph National Monument** (p. 267), west of town. (If it's summer, you may want to go first thing in the morning while the air is cool.) In the late afternoon, find your way to Central Avenue, just south of Old Town, and drive east on **Route 66** (p. 261). This takes you right through downtown to the Nob Hill district and the Sandia Mountains foothills, respectively. Finish your day with a ride up the **Sandia Peak Tramway** (p. 266). After you reach the top, you may want to hike along the crest, though this isn't safe for young kids. Ideally, you should ride up during daylight and ride down at night for a view of the city lights. You may even want to dine at **High Finance Restaurant and Tavern** at the top.

Day 3: The Turquoise Trail ★★ & Santa Fe

In the morning, strike out for the ghost towns and other sights along the **Turquoise Trail** to Santa Fe. Stop in at the **Tinkertown Museum** in Sandia Crest and then

Northern New Mexico in a Week for Kids

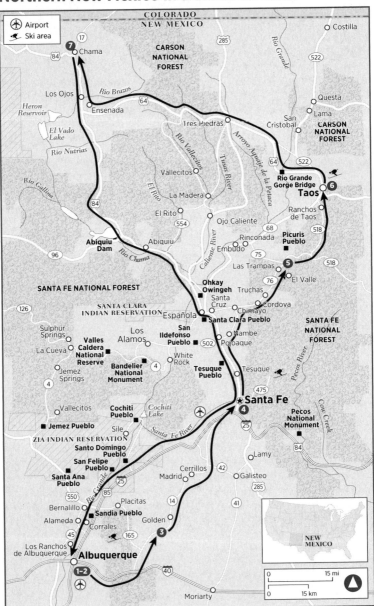

roam **Madrid** to peruse the **Old Coal Mine Museum** (p. 290). You'll arrive in Santa Fe in time to do some sightseeing. Head straight to the **plaza,** the **New Mexico History Museum and the Palace of the Governors** (p. 112), and the **St. Francis Cathedral** (p. 113). Next, make your way over to the **Santa Fe Children's Museum** (p. 124), where the kids can do some rock climbing or other fun activities. Finish your day with an enchilada at **the Shed** (p. 104). In the evening, depending on the season, you may want to get a sitter and take in some of Santa Fe's excellent arts, such as the **Santa Fe Opera** (p. 151) or the **Santa Fe Chamber Music Festival** (p. 152). Alternatively, if you'd like to take the kids along, head to **La Casa Sena** (p. 94) to hear some show tunes.

Day 4: Santa Fe Arts

Head up to **Museum Hill,** and visit the **Museum of International Folk Art** (p. 117) so your kids can see the excellent toy collection. Also noteworthy are the **Museum of Indian Arts & Culture** (p. 116) and the **Wheelwright Museum of the American Indian** (p. 119), which often have kids-oriented activities such as craft making and storytelling. Check their schedules in advance. Head back downtown via **Canyon Road** to peruse the arts scene. In the afternoon, go to the living history site **El Rancho de las Golondrinas** (p. 121).

Day 5: The High Road to Taos ★★

Travel the High Road to Taos, following the directions in chapter 11. Stop for lunch at **Leona's** (p. 167) and visit the **Santuario de Chimayo** (p. 167). On the way into Taos, stop at the **San Francisco de Asis church** (p. 212). If you like music, get a sitter and head to the **Sagebrush Inn** (p. 232) for some country-and-western tunes or to the **Anaconda Bar** (p. 232) to hear some jazz or other live performance.

Day 6: Taos ★★★

Spend the morning at **Taos Pueblo** (p. 214) and the **Rio Grande Gorge Bridge** (p. 217). On the west side of the Gorge, the **West Rim Trail** (p. 224) offers a fun hike with stunning views over the canyon, though you'll want to watch the kids carefully. During the afternoon, do some shopping around the **Taos Plaza,** and then visit the **Kit Carson Home and Museum** (p. 217). For a fun dinner, head to **Taos Pizza Out Back** (p. 207).

Day 7: Enjoying the Outdoors

Head west and spend the day riding the **Cumbres & Toltec Scenic Railroad** (p. 117). Be sure to check departure times for the train and make reservations in advance. Alternatively, depending on the season, you might want to go skiing at **Taos Ski Valley** (p. 218) or white-water rafting at **Pilar** (p. 225) on the Rio Grande. Spend the night either in Chama or Taos and then drive south to Albuquerque to catch your plane.

AN ACTIVE TOUR OF NORTHERN NEW MEXICO

Anyone who skis, hikes, mountain bikes, or rafts knows that the Southwest is unsurpassed in its offerings for outdoors enthusiasts. New Mexico is no exception, and the highest concentration of sports lies in the north. You can ski world-class terrain at Taos Ski Valley, bike the edge of the Rio Grande Gorge, and hike the mountains among ancient Anasazi ruins at Bandelier National Monument. Be aware that the region is known for its mercurial weather conditions—always be prepared for extremes. Also, northern New Mexico is over 6,000 feet in elevation, so it may take you time to catch your breath. Be patient on the long upward hills. The sports you do will, of course, depend a lot on the season. For the full benefit of this trip, take it in late March or early April. With a little advance preparation, you might be able to ski and river raft on the same trip! See map on p. 59.

Days 1 & 2: Albuquerque

When you arrive in Albuquerque, you may want to get acclimated to the city by strolling through **Old Town** (p. 256) and visiting the **Albuquerque Biological Park** (p. 269) to get a sense of the nature in the area. A visit to the **Indian Pueblo Cultural Center** (p. 264) will get you acquainted with the culture you'll encounter as you head north. On Day 2, for a truly unique experience, you may want to schedule a **balloon ride** (p. 272) first thing in the morning. Just be sure to make advance reservations for this exhilarating activity. If you're a bike rider or hiker, head to **Petroglyph National Monument** (p. 267) to see thousands of symbols etched on stone. In the evening, ride the **Sandia Peak Tramway** (p. 266) and go hiking along the crest. If you'd like, you can have dinner at the **High Finance Restaurant and Tavern** and view the city lights as you come down.

Day 3: The Turquoise Trail ★★ to Santa Fe

Head for the ghost towns and other sights along the **Turquoise Trail** (p. 290) to Santa Fe. If you like to ride horses, schedule a ride in Cerrillos with **Broken Saddle Riding Company** (p. 291). This will put you in Santa Fe in time to do some late-afternoon sightseeing. Head straight to the **plaza** (p. 113), the **New Mexico History Museum and the Palace of the Governors** (p. 112), and **St. Francis Cathedral** (p. 113). When you've had enough touring for one day, and you've worked up an appetite, treat yourself to an enchilada at **the Shed** (p. 104).

Day 4: Santa Fe

Use your own bike or rent a cruiser in town to ride around the plaza and up **Canyon Road** (p. 139). Stop at the top of Canyon at the **Randall Davey Audubon Center** (p. 121) to do some bird-watching. Alternatively, you may want to head to the mountains to do some hiking on the **Borrego Trail** (p. 136) or, if it's winter, some skiing at **Ski Santa Fe** (p. 137). Finish your day at one of the fun restaurants or cafes on **Canyon Road** (p. 139). In the evening, depending on the season, you may want to take in some of Santa Fe's excellent arts, such as the **Santa Fe Opera** (p. 151) or the **Santa Fe Chamber Music Festival** (p. 152).

Day 5: Bandelier National Monument ★★★

Head out from Santa Fe to **Bandelier National Monument** (p. 162) and hike among ancient ruins. Follow the Frijoles Trail as far up as you'd like, making sure you stop to climb the ladders to the kiva perched high on the canyon wall. Trail runners like to jog the Frijoles Trail, with its easy descent back to the start. Follow the Rio Grande River north, and you'll come to Taos. Spend the evening strolling around the **plaza** (p. 185) to get a feel of the city.

An Active Tour of Northern New Mexico

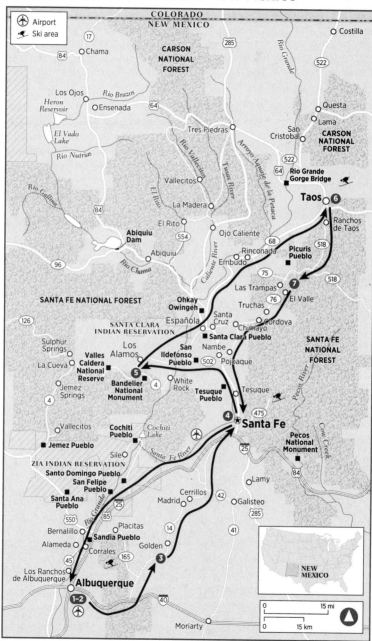

Day 6: Taos

Sports lovers have many options in this town. If you like to ride horses, take a ride on Taos Pueblo land. Alternatively, you may want to take a **llama trek** (p. 224) into the Rio Grande Gorge, or hike up to the top of **Wheeler Peak** (p. 221), New Mexico's highest, a full-day trek. If it's ski season, you'll definitely want to spend the day at **Taos Ski Valley** (p. 218). If you're visiting in the spring and the rivers are running, take the full-day heart-throbbing romp through the **Taos Box** (p. 225) or a half-day trip at **Pilar** (p. 225).

Day 7: The High Road ★★

On your last day, take a leisurely drive south toward Santa Fe. You'll want to take the **High Road** (p. 166), through the art villages of **Cordova** (p. 168) and **Chimayo** (p. 167). Stop at the **Santuario de Chimayo** (p. 167) and have lunch on the patio at **Rancho de Chimayo** (p. 168). Depending on your plane reservations, you can spend the night in Santa Fe or Albuquerque.

GETTING TO KNOW SANTA FE

After visiting Santa Fe, Will Rogers reportedly once said, "Whoever designed this town did so while riding on a jackass backwards and drunk." You, too, may find yourself perplexed when maneuvering through the meandering lanes and one-way streets in this, the oldest capital city in the United States.

But Santa Fe's crooked streets, combined with its Pueblo-style architecture and setting at the base of elegantly sloping mountains, provides a sense of exotic sophistication. Just remember to pack your walking shoes, because exploring the city by foot is the best way to get a feel for its idiosyncrasies. And if you do get lost, ask one of the 72,000 inhabitants living here—7,000 feet above sea level—for directions.

Native Americans enlighten the area with viewpoints and lifestyles deeply tied to nature and completely contrary to the American norm. Many of the Hispanics in this area still live within extended families and practice a devout Catholicism; they bring a slower pace to the city and an appreciation for deep-rooted ties. Meanwhile, a strong cosmopolitan element contributes cutting-edge cuisine, world-class opera, first-run art films, and some of the finest artwork in the world.

Like most cities of Hispanic origin, Santa Fe contains a **plaza** in its center. Here, you'll find tall shade trees and lots of grass. The area is full of restaurants, shops, art galleries, and museums, many within centuries-old buildings, and is dominated by the beautiful **St. Francis Cathedral,** a French Romanesque structure.

On the plaza, you'll see Native Americans selling jewelry under the portal of the **Palace of the Governors,** teenagers in souped-up low-riders cruising along, and people young and old hanging out in the ice-cream parlor. Such diversity, coupled with the variety of architecture—which ranges from Pueblo style to Romanesque to Gothic—prompted the tourism department here to call this city "The City Different."

Not far away is **Canyon Road,** a narrow, mostly one-way street packed with galleries and shops. Once it was the home of many artists, and today you'll still find some who work within gallery studios. A number of fine restaurants are in this district as well.

Farther to the east slopes the rugged **Sangre de Cristo** mountain range. Locals spend a lot of time in these mountains—picnicking, hiking, and skiing. When you look up at the mountains, you see the peak of **Santa Fe Baldy** (with an elevation of over 12,600 ft.). Back in town, to the south of the plaza, is the **Santa Fe River,** a tiny tributary of the Rio Grande that runs most of the year.

North is the **Española Valley,** and beyond that, the village of Taos, about 66 miles away. South of the city are ancient Native American **turquoise mines** in the Cerrillos Hills, and to the southwest is metropolitan Albuquerque, some 58 miles away. To the west, across the Caja del Rio Plateau, is the **Rio Grande,** and beyond that, the 11,000-foot **Jemez Mountains** and **Valles Caldera**—an ancient and massive volcanic caldera that offers a variety of outdoor activities. Pueblos dot the entire Rio Grande Valley, within an hour's drive in any direction.

ORIENTATION

Arriving

BY PLANE   Many people choose to fly into the Albuquerque International Sunport. However, if you want to save time and don't mind paying a bit more, you may be able to fly into the **Santa Fe Municipal Airport** (SAF; ✆ 505/955-2900; www.santafenm.gov), just outside the southwestern city limits on Airport Road. In conjunction with American Airlines, commuter flights are offered by **American Eagle** (✆ 800/433-7300; www.aa.com).

If you do fly into Albuquerque, you can rent a car or take one of the bus services. See "Getting There & Around," in chapter 3, for details.

From the Santa Fe Municipal Airport, **Roadrunner Shuttle** (✆ 505/424-3367) meets every commercial flight and takes visitors anywhere in Santa Fe. From the Albuquerque Sunport to Santa Fe, **Sandia Shuttle Express** (✆ 888/775-5696 or 505/474-5696; www.sandiashuttle.com) runs shuttles daily from 8:45am to 10:45pm. **New Mexico Rail Runner Express** (see below) also runs to Santa Fe, with a shuttle bus taking travelers from the airport to the train.

BY TRAIN & BUS   Daily train service from Albuquerque to Santa Fe is now provided by **New Mexico Rail Runner Express** (✆ 866/795-7245; www. nmrailrunner.com). For more information about train and bus service to Santa Fe, see "Getting There & Getting Around," in chapter 3.

BY CAR   I-25 skims past Santa Fe's southern city limits, connecting it along one continuous highway from Billings, Montana, to El Paso, Texas. I-40, the state's major east–west thoroughfare, which bisects Albuquerque, affords coast-to-coast access to Santa Fe. (From the west, motorists leave I-40 in Albuquerque and take I-25 north; from the east, travelers exit I-40 at Clines Corners and continue 52 miles to Santa Fe on US 285. For those coming from the northwest, the most direct route is via Durango, Colorado, on US 160, entering Santa Fe on US 84.

For information on car rentals in Albuquerque, see "Getting Around," in chapter 3; for agencies in Santa Fe, see "Getting Around," below.

Visitor Information

The **Santa Fe Convention and Visitors Bureau** is located downtown at 201 W. Marcy St. (P.O. Box 909), Santa Fe, NM 87504-0909 (© **800/777-2489** or 505/955-6200). You can also log on to the bureau's website, at www.santafe.org.

City Layout

MAIN ARTERIES & STREETS The limits of downtown Santa Fe are demarcated on three sides by the horseshoe-shaped Paseo de Peralta and on the west by St. Francis Drive, otherwise known as US 84/285. Alameda Street follows the north side of the Santa Fe River through downtown, with the State Capitol and other government buildings on the south side of the river, and most buildings of historic and tourist interest on the north, east of Guadalupe Street.

The plaza is Santa Fe's universally accepted point of orientation. Its four diagonal walkways meet at a central fountain, around which a strange and wonderful assortment of people of all ages, nationalities, and lifestyles can be found at nearly any hour of the day or night.

If you stand in the center of the plaza looking north, you'll be gazing directly at the Palace of the Governors. In front of you is Palace Avenue; behind you, San Francisco Street. To your left is Lincoln Avenue, and to your right is Washington Avenue, which divides the downtown avenues into east and west. St. Francis Cathedral is the massive Romanesque structure a block east, down San Francisco Street. Alameda Street is 2 full blocks behind you.

Near the intersection of Alameda Street and Paseo de Peralta, you'll find Canyon Road running east toward the mountains. Much of this street is one-way. The best way to see it is to walk up or down, taking time to explore shops and galleries and even have lunch or dinner.

Running to the southwest from the downtown area, beginning opposite the state office buildings on Galisteo Avenue, is Cerrillos Road. Once the main north–south highway connecting New Mexico's state capital with its largest city, Albuquerque, it is now a 6-mile-long motel and fast-food strip. St. Francis Drive, which crosses Cerrillos Road 3 blocks south of Guadalupe Street, is a far less tawdry byway, linking Santa Fe with I-25, 4 miles southwest of downtown. The Old Pecos Trail, on the east side of the city, also joins downtown and the freeway. St. Michael's Drive connects the three arteries.

FINDING AN ADDRESS The city's layout makes it difficult to know exactly where to look for a particular address. It's best to call ahead for directions.

MAPS Free city and state maps can be obtained at tourist information offices. An excellent state highway map is published by the **New Mexico Department of Tourism,** 491 Old Santa Fe Trail, Lamy Building, Santa Fe, NM 87501 (© **800/733-6396** or 505/827-7400, www.newmexico.org; to receive a tourism guide call © **800/777-2489**). There's also a Santa Fe visitor center in the same building. More specific county and city maps are available from the **State Highway and Transportation Department,** 1120 Cerrillos Rd., Santa Fe, NM 87504 (© **505/827-5100**). Members of the **American Automobile Association (AAA),** 1644 St. Michael's Dr. (© **505/471-6620;** www.aaa.com), can obtain free maps from the AAA office. Other good regional maps can be purchased at area bookstores (for a list of these, see chapter 9).

5

GETTING TO KNOW SANTA FE

Orientation

Santa Fe Orientation

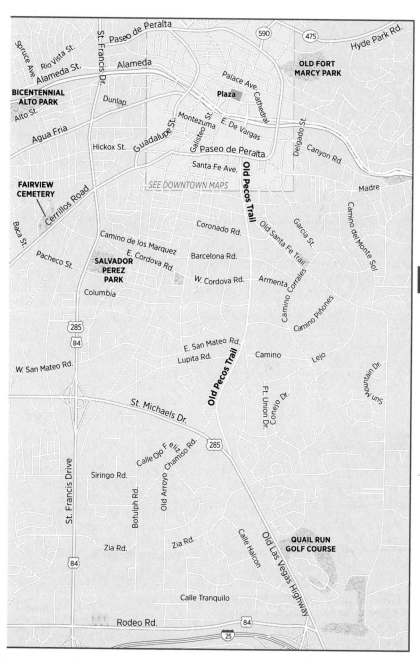

GETTING AROUND

The best way to see downtown Santa Fe is on foot. Free **walking-tour maps** are available at the **Santa Fe Convention and Visitors Bureau,** 201 W. Marcy St. (✆ **800/777-2489** or 505/955-6200), and several guided walking tours, as well as two self-guided tours, are included in chapter 8.

By Bus

In 1993, Santa Fe opened **Santa Fe Trails** (✆ **505/955-2001;** www.santafenm. gov), its first public bus system. There are seven routes, and visitors can pick up a map from the Convention and Visitors Bureau. Most buses operate Monday to Friday 6:30am to 9:30pm and Saturday 8am to 8pm. There is limited service on Sunday and holidays. Call for a current schedule and fare information. Be aware that the buses don't always run on time.

By Car

Cars can be rented from any of the following firms in Santa Fe: **Avis,** Santa Fe Airport (✆ **505/471-5892**); **Budget,** 1946 Cerrillos Rd. (✆ **505/984-1596**); **Enterprise,** 4462 Cerrillos Rd. and 1611 St. Michael's; ✆ **505/473-3600**); and **Hertz,** Santa Fe Airport (✆ **505/471-7189**).

If Santa Fe is merely your base for an extended driving exploration of New Mexico, be sure to give the vehicle you rent a thorough road check before starting out. There are a lot of wide-open desert and wilderness spaces here, so if you break down, you could be stranded for hours before someone passes by, and cellphones don't tend to work in these remote areas.

Make sure your driver's license and auto club membership (if you have one) are valid before you leave home. Check with your auto-insurance company to make sure you're covered when out of state and/or when driving a rental car.

Note: In 2002, the Santa Fe City Council imposed a law prohibiting use of cellphones while driving within the city limits, with strict fines imposed. If you need to make a call, be sure to pull off the road or use a hands-free device.

Street parking is difficult to find during summer months. There's a metered parking lot near the federal courthouse, 2 blocks north of the plaza; a city lot behind Santa Fe Village, a block south of the plaza; another city lot at Water and Sandoval streets, and one underneath the Santa Fe Community Convention Center. If you stop by the Santa Fe Convention and Visitors Bureau (see above), you can pick up a wallet-size guide to Santa Fe parking areas. The map shows both street and lot parking.

Driving Warning

New Mexico has one of the highest per-capita rates of traffic deaths in the nation (mostly due to drunk driving). Although the number has been dropping in recent years, it's still a good idea to drive carefully!

Unless otherwise posted, the speed limit on freeways is 75 mph; on most other two-lane open roads it's 60 to 65 mph. The minimum age for drivers is 16. Seat belts are required for drivers and all passengers ages 5 and over; children 4 and under must use approved child seats.

Because Native American reservations enjoy a measure of self-rule, they can legally enforce certain designated laws. For instance, on the Navajo reservation, it is forbidden to transport alcoholic beverages, leave established roadways, or go without a seat belt. Motorcyclists must wear helmets. If you are caught breaking reservation laws, you are subject to reservation punishment—often stiff fines and, in some instances, detainment.

The **State Highway and Transportation Department** has a toll-free hot line (📞 800/ 432-4269) that provides up-to-the-hour information on road closures and conditions.

By Taxi

Cabs are difficult to flag from the street, but you can call for one. Expect to pay a standard fee of $3 for the service and an average of about $3 per mile. **Capital City Cab** (📞 505/438-0000) is the main company in Santa Fe. On Friday and Saturday nights from 5:30pm to 2:30am, service is $5 for two people ($10 for three or more) anywhere within the city limits. This reduced cost service is provided between a bar, club, or restaurant and a person's home, not from bar to bar.

By Bicycle

Riding a bicycle is a good way to get around town, though you'll have to ride cautiously because there are few designated bike paths. Check with **Mellow Velo,** 638 Old Santa Fe Trail (📞 505/982-8986; www.mellowvelo.com); **Bike-N-Sport,** 524 Cordova Rd. (📞 505/820-0809; www.nmbikensport.com); or **Santa Fe Mountain Sports,** 1221 Flag Man Way (📞 505/988-3337; www.santafemountain sports.com), for rentals.

[FastFACTS] SANTA FE

Airport See "Orientation," p. 62.

Area Code In 2007, New Mexico added a new area code. The northwestern section, including Santa Fe and Albuquerque, retained the **505** code, while the rest of the state changed to 575.

ATM Networks As in most U.S. destinations, ATMs are ubiquitous in the cities of northern New Mexico. However, in the small mountain towns, they're scarce. ATMs are linked to a network that most likely includes your bank at home. **Cirrus** (📞 800/424-7787; www.mastercard.com) and

PLUS (📞 800/843-7587; www.visa.com) are the two most popular networks in the United States and in this region.

Babysitters Most hotels can arrange for sitters on request. Alternatively, call the professional, licensed sitter **Linda Iverson** (📞 505/982-9327).

Business Hours Offices and **stores** are generally open Monday to Friday, 9am to 5pm, with many stores also open Friday night, Saturday, and Sunday in the summer season. Most **banks** are open Monday to Thursday, 9am to 5pm, and

Friday, 9am to 6pm. Some may also be open Saturday morning. Most branches have ATMs available 24 hours. Call establishments for specific hours.

Car Rentals See "Getting Around," in chapter 3, and "Getting Around," above.

Climate See "When to Go," in chapter 3.

Currency Exchange You can exchange foreign currency at **Wells Fargo** for $5 at 241 Washington St. (📞 505/984-0500).

Dentists Dr. Gilman Stenzhorn (📞 505/982-4317 or 505/983-4491) offers emergency service.

He's located at 1496 St. Francis Dr., in the St. Francis Professional Center.

Doctors ABQ Health Partners, 465 St. Michaels Dr., Ste. 101 (© **505/995-2400**), is open Monday to Friday 8am to 5pm. For physician and surgeon referral and information services, call the **American Board of Medical Specialties** (© **866/275-2267**).

Emergencies For police, fire, or ambulance emergencies, dial © **911.**

Etiquette & Customs Certain rules of etiquette should be observed when visiting the pueblos. See chapter 11 for details.

Hospitals Christus St. Vincent Regional Medical Center, 455 St. Michaels Dr. (© **505/983-3361,** or 505/995-3934 for emergency services; www.stvin. org), is a 248-bed regional health center. Patient services include urgent and emergency-room care and ambulatory surgery. Health services are also available at the **Women's Health Services Family Care and Counseling Center** (© **505/988-8869;** www. whssf.org). **Ultimed,** 707 Paseo de Peralta (© **505/989-8707;** www. ultimed.com), an urgent-care facility near the plaza, offers comprehensive health care.

Hot Lines The following hot lines are available in Santa Fe: **battered families** (© **505/473-5200;** www. esperanzashelter.org),

poison control (© **800/432-6866**), **psychiatric emergencies** (© **888/920-6333** or 505/820-6333), and **sexual assault** (© **505/986-9111**).

Internet Access Head to the **Santa Fe Public Library** at 145 Washington Ave. (© **505/955-6780**), or **FedEx,** 301 N. Guadalupe (© **505/982-6311**).

Libraries The Santa Fe Public Library is half a block from the plaza, at 145 Washington Ave. (© **505/955-6780**). The Oliver La Farge Branch library is at 1730 Llano St., just off St. Michael's Drive, and the Southside Library is at 6599 Jaguar Dr., at the intersection with Country Club Road. **The New Mexico State Library** is at 1209 Camino Carlos Rey (© **505/476-9700**).

Liquor Laws The legal drinking age is 21 throughout New Mexico. Bars may remain open until 2am Monday to Saturday and until midnight on Sunday. Wine, beer, and spirits are sold at licensed supermarkets and liquor stores, but there are no package sales on election days until after 7pm, and on Sundays before noon. It is illegal to transport liquor through most Native American reservations.

Lost Property Contact the **city police** at © **505/955-5030.**

Newspapers & Magazines The **New Mexican**— Santa Fe's daily paper—is the oldest newspaper in the

West. Its main office is at 202 E. Marcy St. (© **505/983-3303;** www.santafenew mexican.com). The weekly **Santa Fe Reporter,** 132 E. Marcy St. (© **505/988-5541;** www.sfreporter.com), published on Wednesdays and available free at stands all over town, is often more controversial, and its entertainment listings are excellent. Regional magazines published locally are **New Mexico** magazine (monthly, statewide interest; www.nm magazine.com) and the **Santa Fean** magazine (six times a year, Southwestern lifestyles; www.santafean.com).

Pharmacies Del Norte Pharmacy, at 1691 Galisteo St. (© **505/988-9797**), is open Monday to Friday 8am to 6pm, and Saturday 8am to noon. Delivery service is available.

Police In case of emergency, dial © **911.** For all other inquiries, call the **Santa Fe Police Department,** 2515 Camino Entrada (© **505/428-3710**). The **Santa Fe County Sheriff,** with jurisdiction outside the city limits, is at 35 Camino Justicia (© **505/986-2400**).

Post Offices The **main post office** is at 120 S. Federal Place (© **505/988-2239**), 2 blocks north and 1 block west of the plaza. It's open Monday to Friday 7:30am to 5:30pm and Saturday 9am to 4pm. The **Coronado Station branch** is at 2071 S. Pacheco St. (© **800/275-8777**), and is open Monday to Friday

8am to 6pm, and Saturday 9am to 4pm. Some of the major hotels have stamp machines and mailboxes with twice-daily pickup.

Radio Local radio stations are **KLBU** (102.9), which plays contemporary jazz, and **KBAC** (98.1), which plays alternative rock and folk music.

Safety Although the tourist district appears very safe, Santa Fe is not on the whole a safe city; theft and the number of reported rapes have risen. The good news is that Santa Fe's overall crime statistics do appear to be falling. Still, when walking the city streets, guard your purse carefully because there are many bag-grab thefts, particularly during the summer tourist months. Also, be as aware of your surroundings as you would in any other major city.

Taxes A tax of about 8% is added to all purchases, with an additional 7% added to lodging bills.

Taxis See "Getting Around," above.

Television There are five Albuquerque network affiliates: **KOB-TV** (Channel 4, NBC), **KOAT-TV** (Channel 7, ABC), **KQRE-TV** (Channel 13, CBS), **KASA-TV** (Channel 2, FOX), and **KNME-TV** (Channel 5, PBS).

Time Zone New Mexico is on **Mountain Standard**

Time, 1 hour ahead of the West Coast and 2 hours behind the East Coast. When it's 10am in Santa Fe, it's noon in New York, 11am in Chicago, and 9am in San Francisco. Daylight saving time is in effect from early March to early November.

Useful Telephone Numbers Information on road conditions in the Santa Fe area can be obtained by calling the **State Highway and Transportation Department** (✆ **800/432-4269**). For **time and temperature,** call ✆ **505/473-2211.**

Weather For **weather forecasts,** call ✆ **505/988-5151.**

WHERE TO STAY IN SANTA FE

The City Different offers a broad range of accommodations. From downtown hotels to Cerrillos Road motels, ranch-style resorts to quaint bed-and-breakfasts, the standard is almost universally high.

You should be aware of the seasonal nature of the tourist industry in Santa Fe. Accommodations are often booked through the summer months, the Christmas holiday, and Easter, and most places raise their prices accordingly. Rates increase even more during Indian Market, the third weekend of August. During these periods, it's essential to make reservations well in advance.

No matter the season, discounts are often available to seniors, affiliated groups, corporate employees, and others. If you have any questions about your eligibility for these lower rates, be sure to ask.

A combined city-state tax of about 15% is added to every hotel bill in Santa Fe. And unless otherwise indicated, all recommended accommodations come with a private bathroom.

RESERVATIONS SERVICES   Year-round reservation assistance is available from **Santafehotels.com** (© **800/745-9910**), the **Accommodation Hot Line** (© **800/338-6877**), **All Santa Fe Reservations** (© **877/737-7366**), and **Santa Fe Stay,** which specializes in casitas (© **800/995-2272**). **Emergency Lodging Assistance** is available free daily after 4pm (© **505/986-0038**). All of the above are private companies and may have biases toward certain properties. Do your own research before calling.

DOWNTOWN

Everything within the horseshoe-shaped Paseo de Peralta and east a few blocks along either side of the Santa Fe River is considered downtown Santa Fe. All these accommodations are within walking distance of the plaza.

Very Expensive

Eldorado Hotel & Spa ★★   Since its opening in 1986, the Eldorado has been a model hotel for the city. In a large structure, the architects

Downtown Santa Fe Accommodations

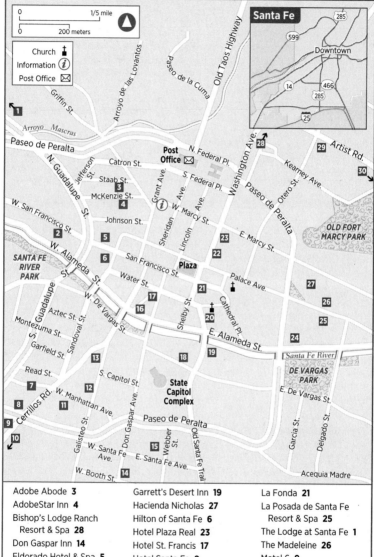

Adobe Abode **3**

AdobeStar Inn **4**

Bishop's Lodge Ranch Resort & Spa **28**

Don Gaspar Inn **14**

Eldorado Hotel & Spa **5**

El Farolito **12**

El Paradero **11**

Encantado Resort **28**

Fort Marcy Hotel Suites **29**

Four Kachinas Inn **15**

Garrett's Desert Inn **19**

Hacienda Nicholas **27**

Hilton of Santa Fe **6**

Hotel Plaza Real **23**

Hotel St. Francis **17**

Hotel Santa Fe **8**

Inn & Spa at Loretto **20**

Inn of the Anasazi **22**

Inn of the Five Graces **18**

Inn of the Governors **16**

Inn on the Alameda **24**

La Fonda **21**

La Posada de Santa Fe Resort & Spa **25**

The Lodge at Santa Fe **1**

The Madeleine **26**

Motel 6 **9**

Old Santa Fe Inn **13**

Santa Fe Motel and Inn **7**

Santa Fe Sage Inn **10**

Ten Thousand Waves **30**

Water Street Inn **2**

managed to meld pueblo revival style with an interesting cathedral feel, inside and out. The lobby has a high ceiling that continues into the court area and the cafe, all adorned with well over a million dollars' worth of Southwestern art. The spacious, quiet rooms received a makeover in 2006, maintaining an artistic motif, with a warm feel created by custom-made furniture in all and kiva fireplaces in many. You'll find families, businesspeople, and conference-goers staying here. Most of the rooms have views of downtown Santa Fe, many from balconies. The Nidah Spa offers a full range of treatments, including turquoise gemstone therapy. The Eldorado also manages the nearby Zona Rosa condominiums, which are two-, three-, and four-bedroom suites with full kitchens. The hotel's innovative and elegant restaurant, the Old House (p. 95), serves creative American cuisine.

309 W. San Francisco St., Santa Fe, NM 87501. **(** **800/955-4455** or 505/988-4455. Fax 505/995-4544. www.eldoradohotel.com. 219 units. $139–$389 double. Seasonal package rates available. AE, DC, DISC, MC, V. Valet parking $18 per night. Pets welcome for a $50 fee. **Amenities:** 2 restaurants; lounge; concierge; executive-level rooms; medium-size health club; Jacuzzi; heated rooftop pool; room service; his-and-hers saunas and steam baths; spa. In room: A/C, TV, CD player, hair dryer, MP3 docking station, Wi-Fi.

Encantado Resort ★★★ This Auberge Resort, set in pink foothills of the Sangre de Cristo Mountains about 15 minutes from Santa Fe, offers 65 elegant casitas, an artfully kiva-shaped spa, and gourmet dining. The resort melds contemporary architecture with traditional Pueblo style, using textured art and earth tones to add warmth to the design. Broad windows blur the boundary between indoor and out, with views from nearly every vantage point. In the casitas, polished concrete floors, kiva fireplaces, vaulted ceilings, and patios with stunning vistas west toward the Jemez Mountains add to the "mystical" quality the resort touts. In addition, the spa features a full range of treatments, including Ayurvedic techniques and regionally inspired massages. Steam rooms, soaking pools, and a fitness facility add to the experience. Also on-site is **LewAllen Encantado,** a satellite gallery for one of Santa Fe's most reputable contemporary art spaces. The resort's restaurant, Terra, opened to national rave reviews.

198 NM 592, Santa Fe, NM 87506. **(** **877/262-4666.** Fax 505/946-5888. www.encantadoresort. com. 65 casitas. $305–$695 casita double; $650–$1,100 suite. AE, DISC, MC, V. **Amenities:** Restaurant; lounge; concierge; exercise room; Jacuzzi; outdoor pool; room service; sauna; spa. In room: A/C, TV/ DVD, hair dryer, minibar, MP3 docking station, Wi-Fi.

Hilton of Santa Fe ★ With its landmark bell tower, the Hilton encompasses a full city block (1 block from the plaza) and incorporates most of the historic landholdings of the 350-year-old Ortiz family estate. It's built around a lovely courtyard pool and patio area, and it's a fine blend of ancient and modern styles. A renovation in 2007 has brought new fine linens and carpeting to most of the rooms, though the furniture could still use some updating. The rooms range in size from medium to large, with comfortable beds and functional medium-size bathrooms with marble countertops. My favorite rooms have small balconies opening onto the courtyard. The Hilton also has the Casa Ortiz de Santa Fe, luxury casitas with kitchens situated in a 1625 coach house adjacent to the hotel.

100 Sandoval St. (P.O. Box 25104), Santa Fe, NM 87501-2131. **(** **800/336-3676,** 800/445-8667, or 505/988-2811. Fax 505/986-6439. www.santafe.hilton.com. 158 units. $119–$229 double; $350–$400 suite; $400–$600 casita, depending on time of year. Additional person $20. AE, DC, DISC, MC, V. Parking $15 per night. **Amenities:** 2 restaurants; lounge; concierge; exercise room; Jacuzzi; outdoor pool; room service. In room: A/C, TV, fridge (in suites), hair dryer, MP3 player, Wi-Fi.

Inn of the Anasazi ★★★   The designers of this fine luxury hotel have crafted a feeling of grandness in a very limited space. The rooms have bold splashes of color, and flagstone floors create a warm and welcoming ambience that evokes the feeling of an Anasazi cliff dwelling. Oversize cacti complete the look. A half-block off the plaza, this hotel was built in 1991 to cater to travelers who know their hotels. On the ground floor are a living room and library with oversize furniture and replicas of Anasazi pottery and Navajo rugs. The rooms range from medium-size to spacious, with pearl-finished walls, comfortable four-poster beds, and novelties such as iron candle sconces, gas-lit kiva fireplaces (in some), and humidifiers. All the rooms are quiet and comfortable, though none have dramatic views. The Anasazi Restaurant (p. 90) serves creative Southwestern cuisine.

113 Washington Ave., Santa Fe, NM 87501. ✆ **800/688-8100** or 505/988-3030. Fax 505/988-3277. www.innoftheanasazi.com. 57 units. Jan–Feb $217–$269 double; Mar–Apr $217–$362 double; May–Dec $325–$525 double. AE, DC, DISC, MC, V. Valet parking $15 per day. **Amenities:** Restaurant; concierge; library/boardroom; room service. *In room:* A/C, TV/DVD, hair dryer, minibar, Wi-Fi.

Inn of the Five Graces ★★★ 🏨   In the historic Barrio de Analco, just a few blocks from the plaza, this Relais & Châteaux inn holds true to its stated theme: "Here the Orient and the Old West meet, surprisingly at home in each other's arms." With floral-decked courtyards, elaborately decorated suites with *kilim* rugs, embroidered bedspreads, and ornately carved beds, this is a chic place. All rooms are suites, with sitting areas and fireplaces. Most have large bathrooms with elaborate broken-tile mosaics and soaking or jetted tubs. It's of the same caliber as Inn of the Anasazi, but with more flair. In recent years, the inn acquired the atmospheric **Pink Adobe** restaurant (p. 95) next door; every other evening the inn holds a wine-and-cheese reception in the Pink's lounge. All rooms have robes, stocked fridges, patios, and CD players; some have kitchenettes. This is a nontipping property, and all amenities are included with the room rate.

150 E. de Vargas St., Santa Fe, NM 87501. ✆ **505/992-0957.** www.fivegraces.com. 24 units. $360–$900 double, depending on the season and type of room. Price includes full breakfast with specialty items and afternoon treats. AE, MC, V. Free parking. Pets welcome for $75 per night. **Amenities:** Restaurant; lounge; concierge. *In room:* A/C, TV, CD player, fridge, hair dryer, kitchen (in some), MP3 docking station, Wi-Fi.

Inn & Spa at Loretto ★★   This much-photographed hotel, just 2 blocks from the plaza, was built in 1975 to resemble Taos Pueblo. Light and shadow dance upon the five-level structure as the sun crosses the sky. With a multi-million-dollar renovation in 2008, this has become a comfortable and elegant place to stay. The medium-size rooms employ a Navajo motif, with comfortable beds and fine linens, while the medium-size bathrooms have fine tiling and robes. Be aware that the Loretto likes convention traffic, so sometimes service lags for travelers. Overall, it is fairly quiet and has nice views—especially on the northeast side, where you'll see both the historic St. Francis Cathedral and the Loretto Chapel (with its "miraculous" spiral staircase; p. 119). The Spa Terre offers a range of treatments, from facials to massages, in intimate, Southwest-meets-Asia rooms. Their restaurant, Luminaria, and lobby lounge are excellent places to relax and sate your hungers.

211 Old Santa Fe Trail (P.O. Box 1417), Santa Fe, NM 87501. ✆ **800/727-5531** or 505/988-5531. Fax 505/984-7968. www.innatloretto.com. 134 units. Jan–Mar $189–$279 double; Apr–June $219–$349 double; July–Oct $329–$499 double; Nov–Dec $209–$299 double. Additional person $30. Children 17 and under stay free in parent's room. Resort fee of $12 per night. AE, DC, DISC, MC, V. Valet parking $18 per night. AE, DC, DISC, MC, V. **Amenities:** Restaurant; lounge; concierge; exercise room; outdoor pool (heated year-round); room service; spa. *In room:* A/C, TV, hair dryer, stocked minibar, MP3 docking station (some rooms), Wi-Fi.

La Fonda ★★   This historic hotel right on the plaza offers a glimpse into Santa Fe's past. It was once the inn at the end of the Santa Fe Trail, hosting trappers and traders, as well as notables such as President Rutherford B. Hayes and General Ulysses S. Grant. The original inn was razed in 1920 and replaced by the current La Fonda, built in pueblo revival style. Inside, the lobby is richly textured and slightly dark, with people bustling about, sitting in the cafe, and buying jewelry from Native Americans.

No two rooms are the same, but all have fine bedding and graceful touches such as hand-painted furnishings and some have fireplaces and private balconies. The elegant Terrace suites have handcrafted furniture, balconies, and city views. La Fiesta Lounge draws many locals, and the newly renovated La Plazuela offers excellent Southwestern cuisine in a skylit garden patio. The Bell Tower Bar, the highest point downtown, is a great place for a cocktail and a view of the city.

100 E. San Francisco St. (P.O. Box 1209), Santa Fe, NM 87501. ✆ **800/523-5002** or 505/982-5511. Fax 505/988-2952. www.lafondasantafe.com. 168 units. $229–$319 double; $249–$359 deluxe double; $309–$469 suite. Additional person $15. Children 12 and under stay free in parent's room. AE, DC, DISC, MC, V. Parking $12 per day in a covered garage. **Amenities:** Restaurant; 2 lounges; babysitting; concierge; exercise room; Jacuzzi; outdoor pool (heated in summer); room service; sauna; spa. *In room:* A/C, TV, hair dryer, Wi-Fi.

La Posada de Santa Fe Resort and Spa ★★   Three blocks from the plaza, this century-old New Mexico adobe hotel was once an art colony, and the original part was a Victorian mansion built in 1882. It is said that the first owner's widow, who died in 1896, continues to haunt the place. If you like tasteful Victorian interiors more than Santa Fe style, these rooms are a good bet.

The rest of the hotel offers pueblo-style architecture. Here, you get to experience squeaky maple floors, vigas and *latillas*, and kiva fireplaces. Be aware that unless you've secured a deluxe room or suite, the rooms tend to be fairly small. Fortunately, the hotel benefited from major remodels in recent years, including a $6-million one in 2008, so all the bathrooms are modern with artful granite throughout. Most notable are the Zen-Southwestern-style spa rooms, as well as a few "gallery suites," appointed with original artwork. Most rooms don't have views but have outdoor patios, and most are tucked back into the quiet compound. The top-notch restaurant, Fuego (p. 93), serves artfully prepared New Mexican and New American cuisine. The Rockresorts Spa offers a full range of treatments. This hotel has taken many actions toward being "green."

330 E. Palace Ave., Santa Fe, NM 87501. ✆ **800/727-5276** or 505/986-0000. Fax 505/982-6850. http://laposada.rockresorts.com. 157 units. $169–$361 double; $239–$401 deluxe double; $419–$1,131 suite. Various vacation packages available. AE, DC, DISC, MC, V. $30 resort fee per day includes parking. **Amenities:** Restaurant; lounge; babysitting; concierge; exercise room; Jacuzzi; outdoor pool (heated year-round); room service; spa w/full treatments. *In room:* A/C, TV, hair dryer, minibar, Wi-Fi.

Expensive

Don Gaspar Inn ★★ 📖   In a historic neighborhood only a 10-minute walk from the plaza, the Don Gaspar occupies three homes, connected by brilliant gardens and brick walkways. Rooms vary in size, though all are plenty spacious, most with patios, some with kitchenettes, and there's even a full house for rent. Travelers looking for an adventure beyond a hotel stay, but without the close interaction of a B&B, enjoy this place. Though the rooms don't have views, all are quiet. The Courtyard Casita, with a kitchenette and a sleeper couch in its own room, is nice for a small family.

The Territorial Suite, with carpet throughout and Italian marble in the bathroom, is perfect for a romantic getaway. All rooms have bathrobes and fireplaces. The friendly staff serves a full breakfast such as green-chile stew with fresh baked items on the patio under a peach tree (the fruit from which they make cobbler) in the warm months and in the atrium in winter.

623 Don Gaspar Ave., Santa Fe, NM 87505. © **888/986-8664** or 505/986-8664. Fax 505/986-0696. www.dongaspar.com. 10 units. $165–$185 double; $165–$225 suite; $205–$255 casita; $345–$385 house. Rates include full breakfast. AE, DISC, MC, V. Free parking. *In room:* A/C, TV/DVD, hair dryer, Wi-Fi.

Hotel Plaza Real ★ ✔ This Territorial–style hotel provides comfortable, creatively appointed rooms near the plaza. The lobby is rustically elegant, built around a fireplace with balconies perched above. Clean and attractively decorated rooms have Southwestern-style furniture, many with French doors opening onto balconies or terraces that surround a quiet courtyard decorated with *ristras* (strung chiles). Beds are comfortably soft and bathrooms are small but with outer sink vanities. The junior suites have an especially nice layout, with a sitting area near a fireplace and good light from the north and south.

125 Washington Ave., Santa Fe, NM 87501. © **877/901-7666** or 505/988-4900. Fax 505/983-9322. www. hhandr.com. 56 units. $109–$149 double; $149–$289 suite, depending on time of year and type of room. Additional person $20. Children 11 and under stay free in parent's room. AE, DC, DISC, MC, V. Parking $14 per day. Pets welcome for $50 per stay. **Amenities:** Lounge; concierge. *In room:* A/C, TV, fridge (in some), Wi-Fi.

Hotel St. Francis ★★ Two blocks from the plaza, this 1880 building was renovated in 2009 with an artful Spanish monastery atmosphere. The lobby is crowned by a stone fireplace and has marble arches and travertine tile floors. Devotional art decorates all public spaces and rooms. The standard rooms here are small, but sparsely enough decorated so they feel more cozy than cramped. If possible, opt for a deluxe room and you'll have more space. Each room in the hotel has a unique footprint, some with hardwood floors, some with carpets. All have a carved *trastero* housing the television, a sink in the room, and fairly small but nicely tiled bathroom. Request a room facing east, and you'll wake each day to a view of the mountains. Enjoy high tea in the lobby Thursday to Saturday from 3 to 5pm. Their restaurant, called Table, serves quality New Mexican/American food.

210 Don Gaspar Ave., Santa Fe, NM 87501. © **800/529-5700** or 505/983-5700. Fax 505/989-7690. www.hotelstfrancis.com. 81 units. $109–$349 all rooms, depending on the season. Children 11 and under stay free in parent's room. AE, DC, DISC, MC, V. Parking $9 per day. **Amenities:** Restaurant; lounge; babysitting; concierge; exercise room; room service; access to nearby spa. *In room:* A/C, TV, fridge (in deluxe rooms), MP3 docking station, Wi-Fi.

Hotel Santa Fe ★★ 📖 A 10-minute walk south of the plaza, this is the only Native American–owned hotel in Santa Fe. Picuris Pueblo is the majority stockholder, and part of the pleasure of staying here is the culture the Picuris bring to your visit. This is not to say that you'll experience the rusticity of a pueblo—this is a sophisticated hotel decorated in Southwestern style. The rooms are medium size, with clean lines and comfortable beds, the decor accented with pine Taos-style furniture. Rooms on the north side get less street noise and have better views of the mountains, but they don't have the sun shining onto their balconies. In the summer, Picuris dancers come to perform and bread bakers uncover the *horno* (oven) and prepare loaves for sale.

The **Hacienda at Hotel Santa Fe ★★** is a unique addition and features 35 luxurious rooms and suites, all with cozy fireplaces, 10-foot ceilings, handcrafted Southwestern furnishings, and plush duvets to snuggle under on chilly nights. The Amaya restaurant serves a standard breakfast, but for lunch and dinner you can dine on what they call "native" cuisine from all over the Americas.

1501 Paseo de Peralta, Santa Fe, NM 87501. ℭ **800/825-9876** or 505/982-1200. Fax 505/984-2211. www.hotelsantafe.com. 163 units. $129–$199 double; $239–$459 suite, depending on the season. Hacienda rooms and suites $199–$459. Additional person $20. Children 17 and under stay free in parent's room. AE, DC, DISC, MC, V. Free parking. Pets welcome with $20 fee. **Amenities:** Restaurant; babysitting; concierge; executive-level rooms; exercise room; Jacuzzi; outdoor pool; room service. *In room:* A/C, TV, minibar (in suites), Wi-Fi.

Inn of the Governors ★   Rooms in this inn tucked 2 blocks from the plaza have the feel of a Southwestern home but come with the service and amenities of a fine hotel. The building (situated where the governor's mansion once was) is Territorial style, with a brick-trimmed roofline and distinctive portals. The medium-size rooms have a plush feel, with white down comforters, set against the bold reds and blacks of Native American weavings hanging on the walls. They have Mexican tile in the bathrooms, robes, and comfortable beds; many have fireplaces. Rooms on the north side look toward downtown and the mountains, and many have balconies. Unlike any other downtown hotel, this one serves a complimentary full breakfast buffet in the morning and hot tea, sherry, and cookies in the afternoon. The Del Charro Saloon serves food until midnight, a rarity in Santa Fe. Wireless Internet access is available in the lobby.

101 W. Alameda St., Santa Fe, NM 87501. ℭ **800/234-4534** or 505/982-4333. Fax 505/989-9149. www.innofthegovernors.com. 100 units. $109–$289 double; $169–$429 suite. Additional person $15. Children 16 and under stay free in parent's room. AE, DC, DISC, MC, V. Free parking. **Amenities:** Restaurant; bar; concierge; outdoor pool (heated year-round); limited room service. *In room:* A/C, TV, fridge, hair dryer, minibars (in suites), Wi-Fi.

Inn on the Alameda ★★   Just across the street from the bosque-shaded Santa Fe River sits the Inn on the Alameda, a cozy stop for those who like the services of a hotel with the intimacy of an inn. It's a little like a village, with a number of pueblo-style adobe buildings and casitas. The owner has used red brick in the dining area and Mexican *equipae* (wicker) furniture in the lobby, as well as thick vigas and shiny *latillas* in a sitting area set around a grand fireplace. Some rooms have kiva fireplaces, and all have comfortable beds, good linens, robes, and well-planned bathrooms with tile. The trees surrounding the inn—cottonwoods and aspens—add a bit of a rural feel to the property. If you're an art shopper, this is an ideal spot because it's a quick walk to Canyon Road. A full-service bar is open nightly. Breakfast is delicious, with bakery and organic items, as well as dairy-free and gluten-free options.

303 E. Alameda, Santa Fe, NM 87501. ℭ **800/289-2122** or 505/984-2121. Fax 505/986-8325. www.innonthealameda.com. 71 units. $125–$230 queen; $180–$305 king; $240–$390 suites. Additional adult $25. Reduced off-season rates are available. Rates include breakfast and afternoon wine-and-cheese reception. AE, DC, DISC, MC, V. Free parking. Small pets under 30 lbs. welcome with $30 fee. **Amenities:** Lounge; babysitting; concierge; exercise room; 2 open-air Jacuzzis; pet amenities and a pet-walking map. *In room:* A/C, TV, CD player, fridge (in some), hair dryer, Wi-Fi.

Ten Thousand Waves ★ 📷   This inn provides minimalist Japanese-adobe accommodations nestled within *piñon* trees below Ten Thousand Waves Japanese health spa (p. 138), a unique place renowned for its hot tubs and spa treatments. Inn guests receive complimentary use of communal baths. About a 10-minute drive from the plaza, the place is en route to Ski Santa Fe. Guests need to be fit because the paths connecting the rooms with the spa have enough steps to make you gasp. Rooms are aesthetically bare, medium size with clean lines and paper lamps and kimonos hanging about. All have wood-burning fireplaces, robes, CD players, and balconies; three have full kitchens; and most have TV/DVDs. Fresh fruit, rice milk, granola, coffee, and tea are provided in each room. The High Moon is the most elaborate room, with a full kitchen, two balconies, and lots of space. More spartan and small is the Zen room, decorated in minimalist decor, and with no TV.

3451 Hyde Park Rd., Santa Fe, NM 87501. ⓒ **505/982-9304** or 505/992-5025. Fax 505/989-5077. www.tenthousandwaves.com. 12 units. $125–$306 double. Additional person $40. Rates include use of communal baths. AE, DISC, MC, V. Free parking. One or more pets welcome, with advance notice, for $20 per night. **Amenities:** Spa w/full treatments. *In room:* TV (in some), CD player, DVD player (in some), fridge, hair dryer, Wi-Fi.

Moderate

Garrett's Desert Inn 🌙 The closest budget hotel to the plaza (just 3 blocks), Garrett's offers decent and comfortable accommodations. It's a clean, two-story, concrete-block building around a broad parking lot. Renovation on the hotel is ongoing but don't expect the consistency of a chain hotel here. Instead you'll find some '50s elements, such as Art Deco tile in the bathrooms and plenty of space in the rooms. If you're traveling in winter, ask for a south-facing room and you might be able to sunbathe under the portal. Minisuites have refrigerators and microwaves. The outdoor pool here is one of the nicest in town.

311 Old Santa Fe Trail, Santa Fe, NM 87501. ⓒ **800/888-2145** or 505/982-1851. Fax 505/989-1647. www.garrettsdesertinn.com. 83 units. $89–$169, depending on season and type of room. AE, DISC, MC, V. **Amenities:** Restaurant; exercise room; heated outdoor pool (open in summer). *In room:* A/C, TV, hair dryer, Wi-Fi.

Old Santa Fe Inn ★ 🏨 Want to stay downtown and savor Santa Fe–style ambience without wearing out your plastic? This is your hotel. A multi-million-dollar renovation to this 1930s court motel has created a comfortable, quiet inn just a few blocks from the plaza. Rooms verge on small but are decorated with such lovely handcrafted colonial-style furniture that you probably won't mind. All have small Mexican-tiled bathrooms, and some have gas fireplaces and DVD players. You have a choice of king, queen, or twin bedrooms as well as suites. Breakfast is served in an atmospheric dining room next to a comfortable library. This inn jacks prices *way* up during special event times such as the Indian Market.

320 Galisteo St., Santa Fe, NM 87501. ⓒ **800/745-9910** or 505/995-0800. Fax 505/995-0400. www.oldsantafeinn.com. 43 units. $90–$129 double, $179–$500 suite depending on season. Rates include full hot breakfast. AE, DC, DISC, MC, V. *In room:* A/C, TV, DVD players (in some), Wi-Fi.

Santa Fe Motel and Inn ★ If you like walking to the plaza and restaurants but don't want to pay big bucks, this little compound is a good choice. Rooms here are larger than at the Old Santa Fe Inn and have more personality than those at Garrett's Desert Inn. Ask for one of the casitas in back—you'll pay more but get a little turn-of-the-20th-century charm, plus more quiet and privacy. Some have vigas; others have skylights, fireplaces, and patios. The main part of the motel, built in 1955, is two-story Territorial style, with upstairs rooms that open onto a portal with a bit of a view. All guest rooms are decorated with a Southwest motif and some have antique furnishings. All have medium-size bathrooms and comfortable beds. A full breakfast, including

Sage Bakehouse bread, is served each morning in the Southwest-style dining room or on a quaint patio.

510 Cerrillos Rd., Santa Fe, NM 87501. ℂ **800/930-5002** or 505/982-1039. Fax 505/986-1275. www.santafemotel.com. 23 units. $79–$139 double, $99–$159 deluxe double depending on season. Additional person $10. Rates include full breakfast. AE, DC, MC, V. Free parking. *In room:* A/C, TV, hair dryer, kitchenette (in some), Wi-Fi.

Inexpensive

Santa Fe Sage Inn If you're looking for a convenient, almost-downtown location at a reasonable price, this is one of your best bets. This two-story stucco adobe motel with portals is spread through five buildings and is about a 10-minute walk from the plaza. The hotel also provides shuttle service to local businesses. Built in 1985, it was remodeled in 2005. The smallish rooms have Southwestern furnishings, with comfortable beds and small bathrooms. There's a park in the back and an outdoor pool set in a secluded fenced area, a good place for kids. To avoid street noise, ask for a room at the back of the property.

725 Cerrillos Rd., Santa Fe, NM 87501. ℂ **866/433-0335** or 505/982-5952. Fax 505/984-8879. www.santafesageinn.com. 156 units. $50–$140 double. Rates include continental breakfast. Additional person $10. Pets welcome ($25). AE, DC, DISC, MC, V. Free parking. **Amenities:** Exercise room; heated outdoor pool. *In room:* A/C, TV, hair dryer, Wi-Fi.

Motel 6 You can count on this motel for comfort and convenience. It's near Hotel Santa Fe (6 blocks to the plaza) on busy Cerrillos Road. Rooms have furnishings with clean lines, some with a rustic, pine, Santa Fe–style. All rooms are nicely lit, and, despite the busy location, relatively quiet. They offer a little more space than those at Santa Fe Sage, but Sage offers some rooms farther back from the road; choose according to your needs.

646 Cerrillos Rd., Santa Fe, NM 87501. ℂ **800/578-7878** or 505/982-3551. Fax 505/983-8624. www.motel6.com. 48 units. May–Oct $79–$90 double; Nov–Apr $42–$75 double. AE, DC, DISC, MC, V. Free parking. **Amenities:** Outdoor pool (in summer). *In room:* A/C, TV, fridge, Wi-Fi.

---

family-friendly HOTELS

Bishop's Lodge Ranch Resort & Spa (p. 79) Riding lessons, tennis courts with instruction, a pool with a lifeguard, a stocked trout pond just for kids, a summer daytime program, horseback trail trips, and more make this a veritable day camp for all ages.

El Rey Inn (p. 82) A picnic area and playground in a courtyard set back away from the street make this a nice place for families to commune in summer.

Fort Marcy Hotel Suites (p. 79) An indoor pool and condo amenities, such as kitchens and patios, make these a good option for families that don't like to eat out every meal.

The Lodge at Santa Fe (p. 79) Built above the city, with a bit of a country-club feel, this place offers a nice outdoor pool and condo units that serve family needs well.

Residence Inn (p. 80) Spacious suites house families comfortably. An outdoor pool, fully equipped kitchens, and patio grills add to the appeal.

Santa Fe Sage Inn (above) With its fenced-in pool and reasonable prices, this is a good spot for families.

THE NORTH SIDE

Within easy reach of the plaza, the north side encompasses the area that lies north of the loop of Paseo de Peralta.

Very Expensive

Bishop's Lodge Ranch Resort & Spa ★★★ ☺ 📷 This resort holds special significance for me because my parents met in the lodge and were later married in the chapel. More than a century ago, when Bishop Jean-Baptiste Lamy was the spiritual leader of northern New Mexico's Roman Catholic population, he often escaped clerical politics by hiking into this valley called Little Tesuque. He built a retreat and a humble chapel (now on the National Register of Historic Places) with high-vaulted ceilings and a hand-built altar. Today, Lamy's 450-acre getaway has become Bishop's Lodge.

In recent years, a $17-million renovation spruced up the place and added a spa. The guest rooms, spread through many buildings, feature handcrafted furniture and regional artwork, and many have balconies or patios. The newer Ridge Rooms are spacious, with high ceilings, vigas, gas fireplaces, patios or balconies, and most with views. The newest addition are villas: spectacular two- and three-bedroom town houses, filled with amenities, including full kitchens, fireplaces, patios, and views, a great option for families or couples who travel together. The Bishop's Lodge is an active resort three seasons of the year, with activities such as horseback riding, nature walks, and cookouts; in the winter, it takes on the character of a romantic country retreat. A children's program keeps kids busy for much of the day.

Bishop's Lodge Rd. (P.O. Box 2367), Santa Fe, NM 87504. © **505/983-6377.** Fax 505/989-8939. www. bishopslodge.com. 111 units. Summer $299–$489 double; fall and spring $259–$399 double; mid-winter $189–$309 double; villas $599–$1,800. Resort fee $15 per person per day. Additional person $15. Children 3 and under stay free in parents' room. Ask about packages that include meals. AE, DC, DISC, MC, V. Free parking. **Amenities:** Restaurant; lounge; babysitting; children's center; concierge; Jacuzzi; outdoor pool; room service; spa; tennis courts. *In room:* A/C, TV, fridge, hair dryer, Wi-Fi.

Expensive

Fort Marcy Hotel Suites ☺ About a 6-minute walk from the plaza, these con-dominiums climb up a hill north of town and are a decent choice for those who like the amenities a condo offers. They are privately owned, so decor and upkeep vary. Most have fireplaces and full kitchens (with dishwashers), with microwave ovens, ranges, and refrigerators. The units have plenty of space, and the grounds are well kept, with some nature trails winding about. Some of the units, however, are show-ing their age (built in 1975).

320 Artist Rd., Santa Fe, NM 87501. © **888/570-2775** or 505/988-2800. Fax 505/992-1804. www. fortmarcy.com. 100 units. $79–$229 1-bedroom (up to 3 adults); $109–$349 2-bedroom (up to 5 adults); $149–$469 3-bedroom (up to 7 adults). Children 18 and under stay free in parent's room. Rates include continental breakfast. AE, DC, DISC, MC, V. Free on- and off-street parking. **Amenities:** Indoor pool; spa. *In room:* A/C, TV/DVD, CD player, hair dryer, kitchen (in some), MP3 docking station (in some), Wi-Fi.

The Lodge at Santa Fe ★ ☺ Set on a hill as you head north toward the Santa Fe Opera, this three-story hotel is a convenient and relaxing place to stay. The theme is Native American, with Anasazi-style stacked sandstone throughout the lobby and dining room, a theme that carries into the guest rooms. They are medium size, decorated in earth tones with bold prints, some with views of the mountains, others overlooking the pool. Premium rooms are more spacious, some with large living rooms and private balconies. Each parlor suite has a Murphy bed and kiva fireplace in the living room, a big dining area, a wet bar and refrigerator, and a jetted bathtub. The suites nearby come with fully equipped kitchens, fireplaces, and private decks. The lodge offers free shuttle service to downtown.

750 N. St. Francis Dr., Santa Fe, NM 87501. © **800/563-4373** or 505/992-5800. Fax 505/992-5856. www.lodgeatsantafe.com. 128 units. $89–$179 double; $129–$199 suite; $200–$300 condo. AE, DC, DISC, MC, V. Free parking. **Amenities:** Restaurant; bar; babysitting; exercise room; Jacuzzi; heated outdoor pool. *In room:* A/C, TV, fridge, hair dryer, kitchen (in suites), Wi-Fi.

THE SOUTH SIDE

Santa Fe's major strip, Cerrillos Road, is US 85, the main route to and from Albuquerque and the I-25 freeway. It's about 5¼ miles from the plaza to the Santa Fe mall, which marks the southern boundary of the city. Most motels are on this strip, although several of them are to the east, closer to St. Francis Drive (US 84) or the Las Vegas Highway.

Expensive

Residence Inn by Marriott ★ ☺   Designed to look like a neighborhood, this inn provides the efficient stay you'd expect from a Marriott. It's a 10-minute drive from the plaza, through a few quiet neighborhoods. The lobby and breakfast area are warmly decorated in tile, with a fireplace and Southwestern accents. There are three sizes of suites, each roomy, each with a fully equipped kitchen. All rooms have fireplaces and are decorated with Southwestern furnishings. Many have balconies. Outside, plenty of amenities keep family members happy, including barbecue grills on the patio. Most who stay here are leisure travelers, but you'll also encounter some government workers and business travelers. Guests gather for complimentary hors d'oeuvres Monday through Wednesday from 5 to 6:30pm.

1698 Galisteo St., Santa Fe, NM 87505. © **800/331-3131** or 505/988-7300. Fax 505/988-3243. www.marriot.com. 120 units. $139–$249 studio suite and double suite; $179–$289 penthouse suite. Rates vary according to season. Rates include hot breakfast buffet and Mon–Wed evening hors d'oeuvres. AE, DC, DISC, MC, V. Free parking. **Amenities:** Exercise room; 3 Jacuzzis; jogging trail; outdoor pool; sports court. *In room:* A/C, TV, kitchen, Wi-Fi.

Sunrise Springs Resort and Spa ★★ 📷   About 20 minutes south of Santa Fe, set along a series of ponds, this resort offers graceful accommodations on a 70-acre compound. Its first incarnation was as a meeting center and parts of it retain that feel. But other parts provide some of Santa Fe's most reasonably priced luxury rooms. The resort has a spa, biodynamic gardens, a Japanese tea house, and an arts and yoga center. All rooms have comfortable beds with good linens and very functional bathrooms stocked with locally crafted bath products. The Pond View rooms are perfect for solo travelers; small but well appointed, they overlook the shady waters. The casitas have vaulted ceilings and plenty of space, as well as gas fireplaces, private patios, and kitchenettes. Some have a "meditation studio" that can be used as an extra room, a great option for families. The Garden rooms are pleasant—medium size, with patios or balconies—but the furniture could use updating. Service is accommodating.

Accommodations & Dining on Cerrillos Road

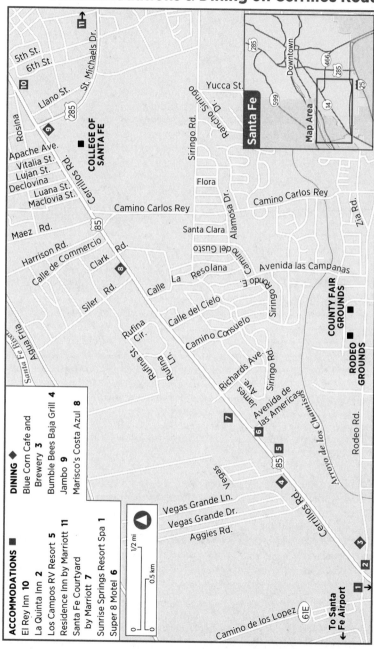

ACCOMMODATIONS ■

El Rey Inn **10**
La Quinta Inn **2**
Los Campos RV Resort **5**
Residence Inn by Marriott **11**
Santa Fe Courtyard
 by Marriott **7**
Sunrise Springs Resort Spa **1**
Super 8 Motel **6**

DINING ◆

Blue Corn Cafe and
 Brewery **3**
Bumble Bees Baja Grill **4**
Jambo **9**
Marisco's Costa Azul **8**

242 Los Pinos Rd., Santa Fe, NM 87507. ℂ **800/955-0028** or 505/471-3600. Fax 505/471-7365. www.sunrisesprings.com. 58 units. $90–$200 double; $185–$290 casita. Additional person $20. AE, MC, V. Free parking. **Amenities:** Lounge; art center; concierge; exercise room; 2 Jacuzzis; outdoor pool (summer only); 2 saunas; spa. *In room:* A/C, hair dryer, Wi-Fi.

Moderate

El Rey Inn ★ 🔪🏠 ☺ Staying at "the King" makes you feel like you're traveling the old Route 66 through the Southwest. Opened in the 1930s, it received additions in the 1950s, and remodeling is ongoing. No two rooms are alike. The oldest section, nearest the lobby, feels a bit cramped, though the rooms have Art Deco tile in the bathrooms and vigas on the ceilings. Some have little patios. Be sure to request a room as far back as possible from Cerrillos Road. The two stories of suites around the Spanish colonial courtyard make you feel like you're at a Spanish inn, with carved furniture and cozy couches. Some rooms have kitchenettes. To the north sit 10 deluxe units around the courtyard. These rooms offer more upscale amenities and gas log fireplaces, as well as distinctive furnishings and artwork. There's also a sitting room with a library and games tables, as well as a picnic area, a playground, and an exercise room.

1862 Cerrillos Rd. (P.O. Box 4759), Santa Fe, NM 87502. ℂ **800/521-1349** or 505/982-1931. Fax 505/989-9249. www.elreyinnsantafe.com. 86 units. $99–$165 double; $125–$225 suite. Rates include continental breakfast. AE, DC, DISC, MC, V. Free parking. **Amenities:** Exercise room; 2 Jacuzzis; outdoor pool (summer only); sauna. *In room:* A/C, TV, fridge, hair dryer, kitchenette (in some), Wi-Fi.

Inexpensive

La Quinta Inn 🐾 Though it's a good 15-minute drive from the plaza, this is a good choice among the economical Cerrillos Road chain hotels. Built in 1986, it has had ongoing remodeling to keep the rooms comfortable and tasteful. The rooms within the three-story building have an unexpectedly elegant feel, with lots of deep colors and Art Deco tile in the bathrooms. There's plenty of space in these rooms, and they're lit for mood as well as for reading. The heated outdoor kidney-shaped pool has a nice lounging area. The hotel is just across a parking lot from the Santa Fe Place mall, which shoppers and moviegoers will appreciate. The Flying Tortilla coffee shop is adjacent.

4298 Cerrillos Rd., Santa Fe, NM 87507. ℂ **800/753-3757** or 505/471-1142. Fax 505/438-7219. www.lq.com. 130 units. June to mid-Oct $92–$119 double; late Oct–May $79–$89 double. Children 18 and under stay free in parent's room. Rates include continental breakfast. AE, DC, DISC, MC, V. Free parking. Maximum 2 pets stay free. **Amenities:** Executive-level rooms; outdoor heated pool (May–Oct). *In room:* A/C, TV, fridge, hair dryer, microwave (in some), Wi-Fi.

Santa Fe Courtyard by Marriott This is a good choice if you don't mind mixing business with pleasure. Because it caters to a lot of conference traffic, there's a definite business feel to this hotel. Built in 1986, the rooms are set around grassy yards, lending a relaxed feel. The decor is tasteful Southwestern, with rooms opening onto cave-like balconies or walkways. Though it's situated on busy Cerrillos Road, the rooms are placed so that they are quiet. The newly remodeled cafe serves breakfast and dinner.

3347 Cerrillos Rd., Santa Fe, NM 87505. ℂ **800/777-3347** or 505/473-2800. Fax 505/473-4905. www.santafecourtyard.com. 209 units. $89–$129 double; $129–$199 suite. AE, DC, DISC, MC, V. Free parking. **Amenities:** Restaurant; executive-level rooms; exercise room; Jacuzzi; indoor pool; room service; free airport transfers. *In room:* A/C, TV, fridge, hair dryer, Wi-Fi.

Super 8 Motel 🐾 It's nothing flashy, but this pink-stucco, boxy motel, which has received the Pride of Super 8 award, attracts regulars who know precisely what to expect. You'll get a clean room with a comfortable bed and a few other amenities at a great price.

3358 Cerrillos Rd., Santa Fe, NM 87507. ✆ **800/800-8000** or 505/471-8811. Fax 505/471-3239. www. super8.com. 96 units. $47–$80 double, depending on the season. Rates include continental breakfast. AE, DC, DISC, MC, V. Free parking. **Amenities:** Exercise room. *In room:* A/C, TV, fridge (some rooms), hair dryer, Wi-Fi.

BED & BREAKFASTS

If you prefer a homey, intimate setting to the sometimes-impersonal ambience of a large hotel, one of Santa Fe's bed-and-breakfast inns may be right for you. All those listed here are in or close to the downtown area and offer comfortable accommodations at expensive to moderate prices.

Adobe Abode ★ A short walk from the plaza, in the same quiet residential neighborhood as the Georgia O'Keeffe Museum, Adobe Abode is one of Santa Fe's most imaginative B&Bs. The living room is cozy, decorated with folk art. The creativity shines in each of the guest rooms as well, some in the main house, which was built in 1907. Others, in back, are newer. The Galisteo Suite is decorated with Spanish colonial furniture and artwork, while the Bronco Room is filled with cowboy paraphernalia: hats, Pendleton blankets, pioneer chests, and an entire shelf lined with children's cowboy boots. Two rooms have fireplaces, and several have private patios. Complimentary sherry, fruit, and cookies are served daily in the living room. Every morning, a full breakfast of fresh fruit and a hot dish such as green-chile corn soufflé is served in the country-style kitchen.

202 Chapelle St., Santa Fe, NM 87501. ✆ **505/983-3133.** Fax 505/983-3132. www.adobeabode.com. 6 units. $155–$225 double. Rates include full gourmet breakfast and afternoon snacks. DISC, MC, V. Limited free parking. *In room:* A/C, TV, hair dryer, Wi-Fi.

AdobeStar Inn ★ This inn, formerly the Spencer House B&B, is near the O'Keeffe Museum, and offers a cozy, homelike feel with a bit of Southwest elegance. Each of the small- to medium-size rooms has a different Southwestern theme. The O'Keeffe room has bold primary colors along with O'Keeffe prints on the walls, while the Chimayo room—my favorite—is set in a quiet spot in back of the house and has wood floors, a kiva fireplace and warm earth tones. Also in back, an 800-square-foot casita has been split into two separate rooms, each with a full bathroom and whirlpool tub, one with a full kitchen, fireplace, and private patio. It's a great space but could use an update. All bathrooms are modern and very clean. In summer, a full breakfast—delights such as a *chile relleno* casserole or blueberry bread pudding—is served on the outdoor patio. In winter, guests dine in an atrium. Some rooms have coffeemakers, TVs, and telephones.

222 McKenzie St., Santa Fe, NM 87501. ✆ **800/647-0530** or 505/988-3024. Fax 505/983-3132. www. adobestarinn.com. 7 units. $135–$215 double. Rates include full breakfast. DISC, MC, V. **Amenities:** Concierge. *In room:* A/C, hair dryer, Wi-Fi.

El Farolito ★★ Within walking distance of the plaza, themes here include the Native American Room, decorated with rugs and pottery; the South-of-the-Border Room, with Mexican folk art; and the elegant Santa Fe–style Opera Room, with hand-carved, lavishly upholstered furniture. A two-room suite has been added in the main building, with a queen-size iron bed and Southwestern decor. The walls of most of the rooms were rubbed with beeswax during plastering to give them a golden finish. All rooms have kiva fireplaces and private patios. Part of the inn was built before 1912, and the rest is new, but the old-world elegance carries through. For breakfast, the focus is on healthy food with a little decadence thrown in. You'll enjoy fresh fruit and home-baked breads and pastries. Under the same stellar ownership (but a little less expensive) is the nearby **Four Kachinas Inn ★** (*©* **888/634-8782;** www.fourkachinas.com), where Southwestern-style rooms sit around a sunny courtyard.

514 Galisteo St., Santa Fe, NM 87501. *©* **888/634-8782** or 505/988-1631. Fax 505/988-4589. www. farolito.com. 8 units. $150–$280 casita. Rates include hot entree breakfast buffet. AE, DISC, MC, V. Free parking. **Amenities:** Babysitting by appointment. *In room:* A/C, TV, fridge, hair dryer, Wi-Fi.

El Paradero ★ A 10-minute walk from the plaza, El Paradero ("the Stopping Place") provides reliable, unpretentious accommodations and good service. It began in 1810 as a Spanish adobe farmhouse. The newly decorated living and breakfast rooms have a festive Mexican feel, with brightly colored walls and folk art set about. Nine ground-level rooms surround a central courtyard and offer a fairly basic stay, with hardwood or brick floors and Southwestern furniture. Three more luxurious upstairs rooms feature tile floors and bathrooms as well as private balconies. Some rooms have fireplaces. Two suites, occupying a brick 1912 coachman's house, are elegantly decorated with period antiques and provide living rooms with fireplaces, kitchen nooks, TVs, and phones. A full gourmet breakfast and afternoon tea are served daily. A complimentary computer is available for use in the library.

220 W. Manhattan Ave., Santa Fe, NM 87501. *©* **505/988-1177.** Fax 505/988-3577. www.elparadero. com. 15 units. May–Oct $115–$185 double; Nov–Dec and Mar–Apr $100–$155 double; Jan–Feb $90–$140 double. Rates include full breakfast and afternoon tea. AE, DISC, MC, V. Free parking. Pets welcome in some rooms $20 per night. **Amenities:** Concierge. *In room:* A/C, TV (in some), hair dryer, Wi-Fi.

Hacienda Nicholas ★★ A few blocks from the plaza, this inn has a delightful Southwest hacienda feel. Rooms surround a sunny patio; my favorite is the bright Cottonwood, with a serene feel created by the sunshine-colored walls, wood floors, and a kiva fireplace. The luxurious Sunflower has French doors, plenty of space, and also a fireplace. The rooms off the sitting room are more modest but have a warm "Southwest meets Provence" feel. All beds are comfortable and bathrooms range from small (with showers only) to larger (with tub/showers). A full breakfast—including such delicacies as homemade granola and red- and green-chile breakfast burritos—and afternoon wine and cheese are served in the lovely Great Room or on the patio, both with fireplaces. Under the same ownership, **Alexander's Inn** (*©* **888/321-5123** or 505/986-1431; www.alexanders-inn.com) has long been one of the city's finest B&Bs. The inn itself has closed, but the same managers rent four charming casitas in the older district of Santa Fe.

320 E. Marcy St., Santa Fe, NM 87501. *©* **888/284-3170** or 505/992-0888. Fax 505/982-8572. www. haciendanicholas.com. 7 units. $100–$240 double. Additional person $25. Rates include breakfast and afternoon wine and cheese. AE, DISC, MC, V. Free parking. Pets welcome with $20 fee. **Amenities:** Concierge. *In room:* A/C, TV, hair dryer, Wi-Fi.

The Madeleine ★★ Lace and stained glass surround you at this 1886 Queen Anne–style inn just 5 blocks east of the plaza. One of my favorite rooms is the Morning Glory, with a king-size bed, a corner fireplace, and lots of sun. An adjacent cottage built in 1987 received an award for compatible architecture from the Santa Fe Historical Association. The two rooms in the cottage are larger than the other rooms, with king-size beds and bay windows, some of the nicest rooms in the city. In winter, a full breakfast is served at the adjacent Hacienda Nicholas (see above), which is under the same excellent management. In the Victorian-cum-Asian lobby and out on a flagstone patio surrounded by flowers and fruit trees, guests enjoy chai from the Absolute Nirvana Spa & Gardens, which offers imaginative treatments and facials; see p. 138.

106 E. Faithway St., Santa Fe, NM 87501. © **888/877-7622** or 505/982-3465. Fax 505/982-8572. www. madeleineinn.com. 7 units. $100–$240 double. Additional person $25. Rates include full breakfast and afternoon wine and cheese. AE, DISC, MC, V. Free parking. **Amenities:** Concierge; spa w/steam showers and soaking tubs. *In room:* A/C, TV/DVD, hair dryer, Wi-Fi.

Water Street Inn ★★   An award-winning adobe restoration 4 blocks from the plaza, this friendly inn features elegant Southwestern-style rooms, with antique furnishings, and several with kiva fireplaces. Rooms are medium size to large, some with four-poster beds, all comfortable with fine linens and well-planned Mexican-tiled bathrooms. Four suites have elegant contemporary Southwestern furnishings and outdoor private patios with fountains. Most rooms have balconies or patios. The hot breakfast here is always gourmet.

427 W. Water St., Santa Fe, NM 87501. © **800/646-6752** or 505/984-1193. Fax 505/984-6235. www. waterstreetinn.com. 11 units. $195–$275 double. Rates include hot gourmet breakfast. AE, DISC, MC, V. Free parking. Children 12 and under and pets (free) welcome with prior approval. **Amenities:** Jacuzzi; concierge; room service. *In room:* A/C, TV/DVD/VCR, hair dryer, Wi-Fi.

RV PARKS & CAMPGROUNDS
RV Parks

At least four private camping areas, mainly for recreational vehicles, are located within a few minutes' drive of downtown Santa Fe. Typical rates are $30 for full RV hookups, $20 for tents. Be sure to book ahead at busy times.

Los Campos RV Resort   The resort has 95 spaces with full hookups, picnic tables, and covered pavilion for use with reservation at no charge. It's just 5 miles south of the plaza, so it's plenty convenient, but keep in mind that it is surrounded by the city. The campground honors a variety of discounts. Wireless Internet access is available in half the park.

3574 Cerrillos Rd., Santa Fe, NM 87507. © **800/852-8160.** Fax 505/471-9220. $36–$45 daily; $220–$258 weekly; $500 monthly in winter, $550 monthly in summer. AE, DISC, MC, V. Pets welcome (free). **Amenities:** Free cable TV; grills; coin-op laundry; outdoor pool; restrooms; showers; vending machines.

Rancheros de Santa Fe Campground ★   Tents, motor homes, and trailers requiring full hookups are welcome here. The park's 127 sites are situated on 22 acres of *piñon* and juniper forest. Cabins are also available. It's about 6 miles southeast of Santa Fe and is open March 15 to October 31. Wireless Internet access is available throughout the park and high-speed Internet access is available in the lobby. Free nightly movies are shown May through September.

736 Old Las Vegas Hwy. (exit 290 off I-25), Santa Fe, NM 87505. © **800/426-9259** or 505/466-3482. www.rancheros.com. Tent site $20–$22; RV hookup $24–$38. AE, DISC, MC, V. **Amenities:** Cable TV hookup; grills; grocery store; coin-op laundry; nature trails; picnic tables; playground; outdoor pool; propane; recreation room; restrooms; showers.

Santa Fe KOA   This campground, about 11 miles northeast of Santa Fe, sits among the foothills of the Sangre de Cristo Mountains, an excellent place to enjoy northern New Mexico's pine-filled high desert. It offers full hookups, pull-through sites, and tent sites. Ten cabins are available. Wireless Internet access is available throughout the park.

934 Old Las Vegas Hwy. (exit 290 or 294 off I-25), Santa Fe, NM 87505. © **800/KOA-1514** (562-1514) or 505/466-1419 for reservations. www.santafekoa.com. Tent site $14; cabins $55; RV hookup $29–$40. AE, MC, V. **Amenities:** Cable TV hookup; dumping station; gift shop; coin-op laundry; picnic tables; playground; propane; recreation room; restrooms; showers.

Campgrounds

There are three forested sites along NM 475 on the way to Ski Santa Fe. All are open from May to October. Overnight rates start at about $12.

Hyde Memorial State Park ★   About 8 miles from the city, this pine-surrounded park offers a quiet retreat. Seven RV pads with electrical pedestals and an RV dumping station are available. There are nature and hiking trails and a playground.

740 Hyde Park Rd., Santa Fe, NM 87501. © **505/983-7175.** www.nmparks.com. **Amenities:** Picnic tables; group shelters (for social events in inclement weather); vault toilets; water.

Santa Fe National Forest ★★   You'll reach **Black Canyon campground,** with 44 sites, before you arrive at Hyde State Park. It's one of the only campgrounds in the state for which you can make a reservation (© **877/444-6777;** www.recreation.gov). The sites sit within thick forest, with hiking trails nearby. **Big Tesuque,** a first-come, first-served campground with 10 newly rehabilitated sites, is about 12 miles from town. The sites here are closer to the road and sit at the edge of aspen forests. Both Black Canyon and Big Tesuque campgrounds, along the Santa Fe Scenic Byway, NM 475, are equipped with vault toilets.

1474 Rodeo Rd., Santa Fe, NM 87505. © **505/438-5300** or 505/753-7331 (Espanola District). www.fs.fed.us/r3/sfe. **Amenities:** Vault toilets; drinking and all-purpose water.

WHERE TO DINE IN SANTA FE

Santa Fe abounds in dining options, with hundreds of restaurants in all categories. Competition among them is steep, and spots are continually opening and closing. Locals watch closely to see which ones will survive. Some chefs create dishes that incorporate traditional Southwestern foods with ingredients not indigenous to the region; their restaurants are referred to in the listings as New American. There is also standard regional New Mexican cuisine, and beyond that, diners can opt for excellent steak and seafood, as well as Continental, European, Asian, and, of course, Mexican menus. On the south end of town, Santa Fe has the requisite chain establishments such as **Outback Steakhouse,** 2574 Camino Entrada (✆ **505/424-6800**), **Olive Garden,** 3781 Cerrillos Rd. (✆ **505/438-7109**), and **Red Lobster,** 4450 Rodeo Rd. (✆ **505/473-1610**).

Especially during peak tourist seasons, dinner reservations may be essential. Reservations are always recommended at better restaurants.

RESTAURANTS BY CUISINE

AMERICAN
Cowgirl Hall of Fame ★ (Downtown, $$, p. 98)
Harry's Roadhouse ★★ (Southeast, $, p. 104)
Plaza Cafe ★ (Downtown, $, p. 103)
Second Street Brewery ★ (South Side, $, p. 108)
Tesuque Village Market ★ (North Side, $$, p. 106)
Zia Diner ★ (Downtown, $, p. 105)

AFRICAN
Jambo ★★ (Downtown, $$, p. 99)

ASIAN
Body ★★ (Downtown, $, p. 102)

Chow's ★ (South Side, $$, p. 108)
Mu Du Noodles ★★ (South Side, $$, p. 108)
Shohko Cafe ★★ (Downtown, $$, p. 100)

BARBECUE/CAJUN

Cowgirl Hall of Fame ★ (Downtown, $$, p. 98)

BISTRO

315 Restaurant & Wine Bar ★★ (Downtown, $$$, p. 97)
Vinaigrette ★★ (Downtown, $$, p. 101)

CARIBBEAN

Jambo ★★ (Downtown, $$, p. 99)

CONTINENTAL

The Compound ★★★ (Downtown, $$$, p. 92)
Geronimo ★★★ (Downtown, $$$, p. 94)
Old House ★★★ (Downtown, $$$, p. 95)
The Pink Adobe ★ (Downtown, $$$, p. 95)

DELI/CAFE

Plaza Cafe ★ (Downtown, $, p. 103)
Sage Bakehouse ★ (Downtown, $, p. 103)

FRENCH

Clafoutis French Bakery & Restaurant ★★ (Downtown, $, p. 102)
Ristra ★★ (Downtown, $$$, p. 96)
315 Restaurant & Wine Bar ★★ (Downtown, $$$, p. 97)

GREEK

Plaza Cafe ★ (Downtown, $, p. 103)

HEALTH FOOD

Body ★★ (Downtown, $, p. 102)

INDIAN

India Palace ★★ (Downtown, $$, p. 99)

ITALIAN

Andiamo! ★★ (Downtown, $$, p. 98)
Café Café ★★ (Downtown, $$, p. 98)
Il Piatto Cucina Italiano ★★ (Downtown, $$, p. 99)

Osteria d'Assisi ★★ (Downtown, $$, p. 100)
Pranzo Italian Grill ★★ (Downtown, $$, p. 100)
Trattoria Nostrani ★★ (Downtown, $$$, p. 97)
Upper Crust Pizza ★ (Downtown, $, p. 105)

MEDITERRANEAN

Amavi ★★ (Downtown, $$$, p. 90)
La Boca ★★ (Downtown, $$, p. 99)

MEXICAN

Bumble Bee's Baja Grill ★ (Downtown, $, p. 102)
Cafe Pasqual's ★★ (Downtown, $$$, p. 90)
Gabriel's ★★ (North Side, $$, p. 106)
Marisco's La Playa ★ (South Side, $, p. 108)
San Marcos Café ★ (South Side, $, p. 104)

MICROBREWERY

Blue Corn Cafe ★ (Downtown, $, p. 101)
Second Street Brewery ★ (South Side, $, p. 108)

NEW AMERICAN

¡A La Mesa! Bistro & Wine Bar ★★ (Downtown, $$$, p. 89)
Anasazi Restaurant ★★ (Downtown, $$$, p. 90)
Aqua Santa ★★★ (Downtown, $$$, p. 90)
Atomic Grill (Downtown, $, p. 101)
Cafe Pasqual's ★★ (Downtown, $$$, p. 90)
The Compound ★★★ (Downtown, $$$, p. 92)
Coyote Café, ★★ (Downtown, $$$, p. 92)
Fuego ★★ (Downtown, $$$, p. 93)
Galisteo Bistro & Wine Bar ★★★ (Downtown, $$$, p. 93)
Geronimo ★★★ (Downtown, $$$, p. 94)
Las Fuentes Restaurant & Bar ★★ (North Side, $$, p. 106)

KEY TO ABBREVIATIONS:
$$$$** = Very Expensive **$$$** = Expensive **$$** = Moderate **$ = Inexpensive

La Casa Sena ★★ (Downtown, $$$, p. 94)

O'Keeffe Café ★★ (Downtown, $$$, p. 94)

Old House ★★★ (Downtown, $$$, p. 95)

The Pink Adobe ★ (Downtown, $$$, p. 95)

Real Food Nation ★★ (South Side, $$, p. 104)

Restaurant Martín ★★★ (Downtown, $$$, p. 96)

Ristra ★★ (Downtown, $$$, p. 96)

Santacafé ★★★ (Downtown, $$$, p. 96)

Terra ★★ (North Side, $$$, p. 106)

NEW MEXICAN

Blue Corn Cafe ★ (Downtown, $, p. 101)

Fuego ★★ (Downtown, $$$, p. 93)

Guadalupe Cafe ★★ (Downtown, $, p. 102)

La Casa Sena ★★ (Downtown, $$$, p. 94)

La Choza ★★ (Downtown, $, p. 103)

Ore House on the Plaza ★ (Downtown, $$$, p. 95)

Plaza Cafe ★ (Downtown, $, p. 103)

The Shed ★★ (Downtown, $, p. 104)

Tesuque Village Market ★ (North Side, $$, p. 106)

Tía Sophia's ★ (Downtown, $, p. 104)

Tomasita's Cafe ★ (Downtown, $, p. 105)

PIZZA

Andiamo! ★★ (Downtown, $$, p. 98)

Café Café ★★ (Downtown, $$, p. 98)

Upper Crust Pizza ★ (Downtown, $, p. 105)

SPANISH

El Farol ★★ (Downtown, $$$, p. 92)

El Meson ★★ (Downtown, $$$, p. 93)

La Boca ★★ (Downtown, $$, p. 99)

STEAK/SEAFOOD

Marisco's La Playa ★ (South Side, $, p. 108)

Ore House on the Plaza ★ (Downtown, $$$, p. 95)

Rio Chama Steakhouse ★★ (Downtown, $$$, p. 96)

Steaksmith at El Gancho ★★ (South Side, $$, p. 104)

Vanessie of Santa Fe ★★ (Downtown, $$$, p. 97)

DOWNTOWN

This area includes the circle defined by the Paseo de Peralta and St. Francis Drive, as well as Canyon Road.

Expensive

¡A La Mesa! Bistro & Wine Bar ★★ NEW AMERICAN   Since its opening in late 2008, this cozy restaurant has drawn crowds. Serving what it calls "classy comfort food from all over the world," it lives up to its goal. The atmosphere melds the curves of a century-old adobe with modern touches such as a beaded shimmer screen covering one wall. The service is refined. Your meal might start with a frisee salad with mushroom confit, bacon, and basil vinaigrette. For a main course, the steak frites with green peppercorn and cognac sauce and, of course, french fries, offers brilliant flavor, as does the honey-lacquered duck with sour cherry sauce and mascarpone polenta. A diverse and reasonable international wine list accompanies the menu. For dessert, try the *pithivier*, a puff pastry with almond marzipan cream on a bed crème anglaise.

428 Agua Fria St. ℂ **505/988-2836.** June–Aug Wed–Sun 11:30am–2pm (with a brunch menu on Sun) and daily 5:30–9:30pm; Sept–May Mon–Sat 5:30–9:30pm. The schedule may change, so call to confirm. AE, DISC, MC, V. Reservations recommended. Main courses $18–$25; brunch $8–$20.

Amavi ★★ 🖼 MEDITERRANEAN   The experience of eating in this downtown restaurant holds true to its name, Amavi, which means "love of life." Golden walls, viga ceilings, and contemporary lighting enfold the diner in a rich ambience, while the friendly and knowledgeable service guides you through the evening. Using local and seasonal ingredients, the restaurant creates new and interesting flavors with a base in the foods from Italy, France, and Spain. A must-taste offering is the ricotta gnocchi with cauliflower, walnuts, purple kale, and mushrooms in a brown-butter sauce. Recently a friend and I split that entree and a duck with risotto in a pomegranate sauce. The wine list is created to pair well with the old-world flavors, while accenting the innovative ones as well. For dessert try the peach turnover with vanilla ice cream. **Note:** The chef driving this restaurant recently departed, so fans are waiting to see if the quality will hold.

221 Shelby St. ⓒ **505/988-2355.** www.amavirestaurant.com. Reservations recommended. Main courses $22–$35. AE, DISC, MC, V. Daily 5:30–9pm (later Fri–Sat).

Anasazi Restaurant ★★ NEW AMERICAN   This ranks as one of Santa Fe's more interesting dining experiences. It's part of the Inn of the Anasazi (p. 73), but it's a fine restaurant in its own right. Named for the ancient people who once inhabited the area, the restaurant features diamond-finished walls and stacked flagstone. The waitstaff is friendly but not overbearing, and tables are spaced nicely, making it a good place for a romantic dinner. All the food is inventive, utilizing regional and seasonal ingredients. A day here might start with a breakfast burrito with asadero cheese. At lunch the chicken fajitas with guacamole are tasty, and at dinner the Alaskan halibut with fingerling potatoes is excellent. There are daily specials, as well as a nice list of wines by the glass and special wines of the day. The Anasazi's patio dining is a great way to sample flavors from a variety of "small plates."

At the Inn of the Anasazi, 113 Washington Ave. ⓒ **505/988-3236.** www.innoftheanasazi.com. Reservations recommended. Main courses $7–$16 breakfast, $10–$18 lunch, $25–$36 dinner. AE, DISC, MC, V. Daily 7–10:30am, 11:30am–2:30pm, and 5:30–10pm.

Aqua Santa ★★★ 🍴 NEW AMERICAN   This is one of my favorite Santa Fe restaurants. Tucked into a little nook along the Santa Fe River, it could easily go unnoticed, but it already has a strong following of locals who enjoy the serene environment and fresh artisanal food. The atmosphere is like a quaint country hacienda with a touch of elegance created by hardwood floors, a kiva fireplace, cream-colored walls, and fine art. Service is excellent, though cooking times run a little long. The chef employs organic meats and seasonal vegetables. At lunch, I've enjoyed the local lamb braised with rapini greens and pistachios. At dinner, a great start is the escarole salad with feta and grapefruit, and one of many exquisite entrees is the sautéed sea scallops in duck fat with shiitake mushrooms and lemon. For dessert, try the buttermilk panna cotta or espresso mascarpone parfait. A carefully chosen beer and wine list compliments the menu. In warmer months, you might want to request a table on the patio where you can sit under a cherry tree.

451 W. Alameda St. ⓒ **505/982-6297.** Reservations recommended. Main courses $10–$15 lunch, $11–$29 dinner. AE, MC, V. Wed–Fri noon–2pm; Tues–Sat 5:30–9pm.

Cafe Pasqual's ★★ NEW AMERICAN/MEXICAN   Pasqual's owner uses mostly organic ingredients in her dishes, and the walls are lined with murals depicting villagers playing guitars and drinking. It's a festive place, though it's also excellent for a romantic dinner. My favorite dish for breakfast or lunch is the *huevos motuleños* (two eggs over

Downtown Santa Fe Dining

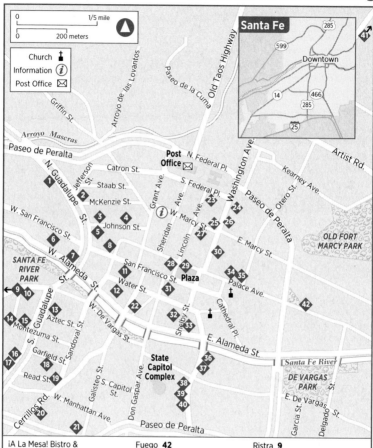

¡A La Mesa! Bistro & Wine Bar **10**
Amavi **33**
Anasazi Restaurant **30**
Andiamo! **18**
Aqua Santa **7**
Atomic Grill **31**
Blue Corn Cafe **11**
Bumble Bee's Baja Grill **2**
Café Café **19**
Cafe Pasqual's **31**
Clafoutis French Bakery & Restaurant **1**
Cowgirl Hall of Fame **13**
Coyote Cafe **12**
El Meson **26**

Fuego **42**
Galisteo Bistro & Wine Bar **22**
Guadalupe Café **40**
Il Piatto Cucina Italiano **25**
India Palace **32**
La Boca **27**
La Casa Sena **35**
O'Keeffe Café **4**
Old House **8**
Ore House on the Plaza **28**
Osteria d' Assisi **23**
The Pink Adobe **38**
Plaza Cafe **29**
Pranzo Italian Grill **14**
Restaurant Martín **21**
Rio Chama Steakhouse **39**

Ristra **9**
Sage Bakehouse **20**
Santacafé **24**
Second Street Brewery **17**
The Shed **34**
Shohko Café **3**
Tía Sophia's **11**
Trattoria Nostrani **5**
Tesuque Village Market **41**
Tomasita's Cafe **16**
315 Restaurant & Wine Bar **36**
Upper Crust Pizza **37**
Vanessie of Santa Fe **6**
Zia Diner **15**

easy on blue-corn tortillas and black beans topped with sautéed bananas, feta cheese, salsa, and green chile). Soups and salads are also served for lunch, and there's a delectable grilled-salmon burrito with herbed goat cheese and cucumber salsa. The frequently changing dinner menu offers grilled meats and seafood, plus vegetarian specials. Start with the Mexican prawn cocktail with lime, tomato, and avocado, and move on to the chicken mole enchiladas with cilantro rice and orange-jicama salad. There's a communal table for those who would like to meet new people over a meal. Pasqual's offers imported beers and wine by the bottle or glass. Try to go at an odd hour—late morning or afternoon—or make a reservation for dinner; otherwise, you'll have to wait.

121 Don Gaspar Ave. © **505/983-9340,** www.pasquals.com. Reservations recommended for dinner. Main courses $8–$15 breakfast, $9–$17 lunch, $19–$39 dinner. AE, MC, V. Daily 8am–3pm and 5:30–9.30pm.

The Compound ★★★ NEW AMERICAN/CONTINENTAL This reincarnation of one of Santa Fe's classic restaurants serves some of the most flavorful and daring food in the Southwest. Inside, it's an elegant old adobe with white walls often offset by bold splashes of flowers. Outside, during warm months, a broad patio shelters diners from the city bustle. With friendly, efficient service, this is an excellent place for a romantic dinner or a relaxing lunch. Chef and owner Mark Kiffin (a James Beard award winner and the former chef at Coyote Café) lets his creativity soar. For lunch, monkfish chorizo with watercress is outrageously tasty. At dinner, you might start off with tuna tartare topped with Osetra caviar. For an entree, a signature dish is the grilled beef tenderloin with Italian potatoes and foie gras hollandaise, the beef so tender you won't quite believe it. Finish with a warm bittersweet liquid chocolate cake. A carefully selected beer and wine list accompanies the menu.

653 Canyon Rd. © **505/982-4353.** www.compoundrestaurant.com. Reservations recommended. Main courses $12–$20 lunch, $25–$40 dinner. AE, DC, DISC, MC, V. Mon–Sat noon–2pm; daily 6–9pm. Bar opens nightly at 5pm.

Coyote Café ★★ NEW AMERICAN World-renowned chef and cookbook author Mark Miller put this place on the map decades ago. Now under new ownership, it has gained new popularity as a place for innovative food in a festive environment. The atmosphere blends warm colors, sculpted adobe, and creative lighting to make for a memorable meal. The waitstaff is efficient and friendly. The menu changes seasonally. Past favorites have included sautéed Italian porcinis or prawns over corn cakes with chipotle butter and guacamole. For a main course, look for delights such as pan-seared white miso halibut with roasted lobster jus, wasabi mashed potatoes, and braised baby bok choy; or the Cowboy Cut, a rib-eye with "borracho" beans, red-chile onion rings, and roasted fingerling potatoes. You can order drinks from the full bar or wine by the glass.

Coyote Café has an adjunct establishment. In summer, the place to be seen is the **Rooftop Cantina,** where light Mexican fare and cocktails are served on a festively painted terrace. Try the guacamole and chips, tacos, and burgers.

132 Water St. © **505/983-1615.** www.coyotecafe.com. Reservations recommended. Main courses $19–$36 (Coyote Café), $6–$16 (Rooftop Cantina). AE, DC, DISC, MC, V. Dining room daily 5:30–10pm; Rooftop Cantina daily 11:30am–9:30pm.

El Farol ★★ SPANISH This is the place to head for local ambience and flavors of Spain, Santa Fe, and Mexico. El Farol (the Lantern), set in an 1835 adobe building, is the Canyon Road artists' quarter's original neighborhood bar. The restaurant has cozy low ceilings and hand-smoothed adobe walls. Thirty-five varieties of tapas are offered, including such delicacies as *gambas al ajillo* (shrimp with chile, garlic, Madeira, and lime) and *puerco asado* (pork tenderloin with figs). You can make a meal out of two or three tapas shared with your friends, or order a full dinner such as the paella or the mixed grill, with lamb, chorizo, and shrimp over potatoes. There is live entertainment 7 nights a week—including jazz/swing, folk, and Latin guitar music—starting at 9:30pm. In summer, two outdoor patios are open to diners. Check the web to find out about their flamenco dinner shows. The restaurant offers some of the finest wines and sherries in the world.

808 Canyon Rd. © **505/983-9912.** www.elfarolsf.com. Reservations recommended. Tapas $5–$10; main courses $8.75–$18 lunch, $26–$33 dinner. AE, DC, DISC, MC, V. Daily 11:30am–3pm and 5:30–10pm. Bar until 2am Mon–Sat; until midnight Sun.

El Meson ★★ SPANISH   In an elegantly rustic setting reminiscent of an old Spanish hacienda, this restaurant serves up enticing tapas and dynamic entertainment. The service is efficient and knowledgeable. My favorite tapas are the steamed mussels in herbs and the blue-crab cakes with a garlic-caper aioli. But most of all I can't pass up the paella here, made the way the Spaniards do in Valencia, with prawns, calamari, shrimp, mussels, chicken, and chorizo all cooked slowly with saffron rice. For dessert, try the crema Catalana, one of the creamiest concoctions imaginable. **Chispa!** (p. 154), the neighboring tapas bar, offers live entertainment— jazz combos, guitar duos—Tuesday through Saturday nights. Most notable are the Tango Tuesdays, in which the city's tango adepts turn out to burn up the floor.

213 Washington Ave. © **505/983-6756.** www.elmeson-santafe.com. Reservations recommended. AE, MC, V. Tapas $6–$12; main courses $20–$28. Tues–Sat 5–10pm (bar until 11pm).

Fuego ★★ NEW AMERICAN/NEW MEXICAN   Set in a contemporary Spanish atmosphere, with elegant chandeliers, Venetian glass walls, and cozy *bancos*, Fuego offers what they call "innovative foods infused with classic traditions." Their broad dining patio is one of Santa Fe's best lunch locales. Service is good. Lunch should definitely start with house-made tortilla chips and Fuego's signature salsa and guacamole. Follow with chicken or steak fajitas or a taco salad. At dinner, a bistro menu offers light fare such as shrimp tacos, while the main menu highlights such dishes as rack of lamb with corn custard and Brussels sprouts or a Spanish bouillabaisse. For dessert, try selections from a world-class artisanal farmhouse cheese cart or variety of sweets. The Rancher's Brunch is one of the town's finest. An excellent wine list accompanies the menu.

330 E. Palace Ave. (at La Posada de Santa Fe Resort and Spa). © **800/727-5276** or 505/954-9670. www.laposada.rockresorts.com. Reservations recommended. Main courses $8–$14 lunch, $12–$34 dinner; $45 brunch. AE, DC, DISC, MC, V. Daily 11:30am–2pm, 4:30–10pm; Sun brunch 11:30am–2:30pm.

Galisteo Bistro & Wine Bar ★★★ 📖 NEW AMERICAN   In a cozy setting that sparkles with conviviality, chefs Robert and Marge Chickering serve innovative cuisine that spans the globe. The bistro features an exhibition kitchen that puts on an active show during the busy dining hours here. Chef Robert greets diners at the door and follows up throughout the meal. Each night features a short list of specials, as well as a carefully planned menu with seasonal offerings. You might start with a buffalo bratwurst with mushrooms and sauerkraut. A popular entree is the chicken saltimbocca—pan-roasted chicken layered with sage, prosciutto, and fontina in a

Madeira sauce with vegetables and orzo. As a recent special I had a delectable duck Marsala—served over gnocchi and finished with mushrooms, tomatoes, and cream. For dessert, definitely choose the Mud Puddle—layers of coffee ice cream, chocolate mousse and whipped cream, large enough to share. The wine list here features local and international selections that compliment the menu.

227 Galisteo St. © **505/982-3700.** www.galisteobistro.com. Reservations highly recommended. Tapas $9–$12; main courses $23–$29. AE, DISC, MC, V. Wed–Sun 5–9pm.

Geronimo ★★★ NEW AMERICAN/CONTINENTAL   This elegant restaurant offers one of Santa's Fe's most delectable and atmospheric dining experiences. Occupying an adobe structure known as the Borrego House—which was built by Geronimo Lopez in 1756—it retains the feel of an old Santa Fe home. The food is simply fantastic, always utilizing seasonal produce. If you enjoy dining outside, reserve a spot under the portal and watch the action on Canyon Road. You might order the pan-roasted caramel quail with brie and Reggiano polenta, or *Kurobuta* pork tenderloin with a soy peach glaze and scallion risotto. If you want to try one of Santa Fe's most renowned entrees, order the peppery elk tenderloin with applewood-smoked bacon served with mashed Yukon gold potatoes. For dessert try the white-chocolate mascarpone cheesecake. The menu changes seasonally, and there's a thoughtful wine list, with a primary focus on boutique American vineyards.

724 Canyon Rd. © **505/982-1500.** www.geronimorestaurant.com. Reservations recommended. Main courses $28–$43 dinner. AE, MC, V. Daily 5:45–9:30pm.

La Casa Sena ★★ NEW AMERICAN/NEW MEXICAN   This is one of Santa Fe's favorite restaurants, though the food here isn't as precise and flavorful as at Santacafé or Geronimo. It sits in a Territorial-style adobe house built in 1867 by Civil War hero Major José Sena. The house, which surrounds a garden courtyard, is today a veritable art gallery, with museum-quality landscapes on the walls and Taos-style hand-crafted furniture. During the warm months, this restaurant has the best patio in town. One of my favorite lunches is the fish tacos with Cuban-*mojo napa* slaw. In the evening, diners might start with a salad of garden greens and New Mexico feta cheese, then move onto a red-chile-crusted pork loin with roasted sweet potatoes.

In the adjacent **La Cantina,** waitstaff sing Broadway show tunes as they carry platters. The Cantina offers the likes of enchiladas with black beans and Mexican rice. Both restaurants have exquisite desserts; try the black-and-white bittersweet chocolate terrine with raspberry sauce. The award-winning wine list features more than 850 selections.

125 E. Palace Ave. © **505/988-9232.** www.lacasasena.com. Reservations recommended. La Casa Sena main courses $8–$19 lunch, $21–$39 dinner; 5-course chef's tasting menu $63, varies with wine price. La Cantina main courses $13–$28. AE, DC, DISC, MC, V. Mon–Sat 11:30am–3pm; Sun brunch 11am–3pm; daily 5:30–10pm.

O'Keeffe Café ★★ NEW AMERICAN   Following Georgia O'Keeffe's appreciation for sparse interiors, this restaurant has refined minimalist decor, with much more elaborate food. Large black-and-white photographs of O'Keeffe stirring stew and serving tea adorn the walls. This is a good place to stop in between museums or, in the warm months, to sit on the open patio and watch the summer scene. The food is excellent, but for a nice dinner (in winter), the atmosphere lags behind that of places in a similar price range, such as Santacafé and Geronimo. The menu is eclectic, with a good balance of chicken, lamb, fish, and vegetarian dishes, some in salad and sandwich form (at lunch), along with more elaborate entree offerings. Most recently for lunch I had the pink-horseradish-crusted Atlantic salmon. Dinner might start with a crispy shrimp-and-watercress salad and move onto fennel-crusted halibut with Parisienne potatoes. Finish with a coconut crème brûlée. There's also a children's menu. The restaurant has a notable wine list and offers periodic wine-tasting menus.

217 Johnson St. ℂ **505/946-1065.** www.okeeffecafe.com. Main courses $11–$27 lunch, $9–$35 dinner. AE, MC, V. Daily 11am–3pm; Mon–Sat 5:30–8:30 or 9pm (wine bar 3–5:30pm).

Old House ★★★ NEW AMERICAN/CONTINENTAL   Located within the Eldorado Hotel (p. 70), this restaurant consistently rates as one of Santa Fe's best in local publications' polls. In a Southwestern atmosphere, rich with colorful Native American art (though without the historic ambience of Geronimo or the Santacafé), the Old House serves quality meats, poultry, and seafood in refined sauces. The menu changes seasonally, using local and organic ingredients, when possible. Your meal might start with barbecued quail and move on to sea bass with asparagus and green chile, or lamb chops with Parmesan polenta chimichurri and broccolini. Each entree is paired with a wine selection from the *Wine Spectator* award-winning list. For dessert, the vanilla crème brûlée with sugar toile is delectable.

309 W. San Francisco St. (in the Eldorado Hotel). ℂ **505/995-4530.** www.eldoradohotel.com. Reservations recommended. Main courses $29–$43 dinner. AE, DC, DISC, MC, V. Daily 5:30–10pm. Lounge 11:30am–closing.

Ore House on the Plaza ★ STEAK/SEAFOOD/NEW MEXICAN   The Ore House's second-story balcony, at the southwest corner of the plaza, is an ideal spot from which to watch the passing scene while you enjoy cocktails and hors d'oeuvres. In fact, it is the place to be between 4 and 6pm every afternoon and the main reason to come here. Though the food is fine and the Southwestern ambience cozy, with plants and lanterns hanging amid pale walls and booths, other restaurants eclipse this place in terms of flavors. The menu offers fresh seafood and steaks, as well as some Nueva Latina dishes that incorporate some interesting sauces. The bar, offering live music nightly Thursday to Sunday, serves more than 65 different custom margaritas. An appetizer menu is served daily from 2:30 to 10pm, and the bar stays open until midnight or later.

50 Lincoln Ave. ℂ **505/983-8687.** www.orehouseontheplaza.com. Reservations recommended. Main courses $9–$16 lunch, $16–$37 dinner. AE, MC, V. Daily 11:30am–10pm (bar until midnight or later).

The Pink Adobe ★ CONTINENTAL/NEW AMERICAN   This restaurant, a few blocks off the plaza, has remained popular since it opened in 1944. (I remember eating my first lamb curry here, and my mother ate her first blue-corn enchilada, back in the '50s.) The restaurant occupies an adobe home believed to be at least 350 years old. Adobe colored walls, ceiling vigas, and kiva fireplaces yield a Santa Fe feel. For lunch, a favorite is the gypsy stew (chicken, green chile, tomatoes, onions, and mozzarella in a sherry broth). At dinner, steak Dunigan, a New York strip with sautéed mushrooms and green chile, is their signature dish, though the cut of meat isn't as good as you'll find next door at the Rio Chama (see below). Lighter eaters will like the half-order portions available for some entrees. You can't leave without trying the hot French apple pie.

Under the same ownership, the charming bar (a real local scene) has its own menu, offering traditional New Mexican food.

406 Old Santa Fe Trail. ℂ **505/983-7712.** www.thepinkadobe.com. Reservations recommended. Main courses $8–$20 lunch, $20–$38 dinner. AE, DC, DISC, MC, V. Mon–Fri 11:30am–2pm; daily 5:30pm–closing. Bar Mon–Fri 11:30am–midnight; Sat–Sun 5pm–midnight.

Restaurant Martín ★★★ NEW AMERICAN   Santa Fe's stand-out newcomer offers casual elegance in the historic 1944 Ortiz home, with hardwood floors and bold paintings, as well as sprawling patios perfect for a summer lunch. Opened in 2009, the restaurant is the creation of Chef Martín Rios. A native of Guadalajara, Mexico, he grew up in Santa Fe, where he started his career as a dishwasher. After formal training, he became executive chef at some of the city's finest restaurants. Finally at his own eatery, he serves innovative flavors often utilizing chile peppers and local, seasonal ingredients. At lunch the delicious grilled-vegetable panini has eggplant, camembert, and golden tomatoes. The restaurant's signature appetizer is as an ahi tuna tartare with avocado and jalapeño parfait and toasted nori pancakes. For a dinner entree, the Maine Diver sea scallops with potato-shallot puree and chorizo offers a tasty mix of flavors. For dessert try the bittersweet chocolate truffle cake. The well-conceived wine and beer list is accessible to many wallets.

526 Galisteo St. ⓒ **505/820-0919.** www.restaurantmartinsantafe.com. Reservations recommended. Main courses $9-$14 lunch, $19-$30 dinner. AE, DISC, MC, V. Tues-Sun 11:30am-2pm and 5:30-9pm.

Rio Chama Steakhouse ★★ STEAK/SEAFOOD   Serving up tasty steaks in a refined ranch atmosphere, this is one of Santa Fe's most popular restaurants, with a bright patio during warm months. I suggest sticking to the meat dishes here, though the fish and pasta dishes can be quite good, too. At lunch or dinner you might start with the Capitol Salad, with lots of fresh greens, *piñon* nuts, and blue cheese crumbles. My favorite for lunch is the green-chile cheeseburger made with New Mexico grass-fed beef. Lunch also brings more formal dishes such as a grilled Atlantic salmon with grilled vegetables and mango salsa. At dinner, the prime rib is a big hit, as is the filet mignon, both served with a potato and vegetable. For dessert, try the chocolate pot. The bar here romps during happy hour, when the booths fill up, martinis nearly overflow, and reasonably priced menu items sate postwork appetites.

414 Old Santa Fe Trail. ⓒ **505/955-0765.** www.riochamasteakhouse.com. Reservations recommended Fri-Sat night. Main courses $8.50-$17 lunch, $18-$39 dinner. AE, DC, DISC, MC, V. Daily 11am-3pm and 5-10pm. Patio bar 5pm-closing.

Ristra ★★ FRENCH/NEW AMERICAN   Anything you order here will likely be unique, with flavors that you'll remember. Hearing the specials alone is like poetry: a blend of American favorites prepared with French and Southwestern accents. It's a quiet, comfortable restaurant, within a century-old Victorian house decorated with contemporary art. Best of all is the patio during warm months, when you can watch the sun set. At lunch you might try the lobster ciabatta sandwich with a spinach salad. Dinner might start with butternut squash soup. For a main course, try the crispy king salmon with fennel and roasted potatoes. For dessert, try the chocolate soufflé. A long wine list covers the best wine regions of California and France; beer is also served. During warm months, request a table on the lovely patio. Locals like to sit at the candlelit bar and sample wines by the glass and selections from the appetizer menu.

548 Agua Fria St. ⓒ **505/982-8608.** www.ristrarestaurant.com. Reservations recommended. Main courses $22-$38. AE, MC, V. Tues-Sat 11:30-2:30; daily 5:30-9:30pm.

Santacafé ★★★ 📷 NEW AMERICAN   This is where I go to celebrate special occasions. The food combines the best of many cuisines, from Asian to Southwestern, served in an elegant setting with minimalist decor. The white walls are decorated only with deer antlers, and each room contains a fireplace. In warm months you can sit under elm trees in the charming courtyard. Beware that on busy nights, the rooms are noisy. Their Sunday brunch menu offers such delights as a mascarpone-stuffed French toast and poached eggs with corned beef. For a lunch or dinner starter, try the shiitake and cactus spring rolls with Southwestern *ponzu*. One of my favorite lunches is the baby spinach niçoise salad with tuna seared to perfection. At dinner I've enjoyed the grilled rack of lamb with rosemary risotto. There's an extensive whole- and half-bottle wine list, with wine by the glass as well. Desserts, as elegant as the rest of the food, are made in-house; try the warm chocolate upside-down cake with vanilla ice cream.

231 Washington Ave. (©) **505/984-1788.** www.santacafe.com. Reservations recommended. Main courses $6.50–$11 lunch, $19–$33 dinner. AE, DISC, MC, V. Daily 11:30am–2pm and 5:30–9pm.

315 Restaurant & Wine Bar ★★ BISTRO/FRENCH   This classy French bistro enjoyed instant success when it opened in 1995 because the food is simply excellent. The cozy atmosphere provides a perfect setting for a romantic meal, and during warm months the patio is a popular place to people-watch, with little white lights setting the whole place aglow. Service is excellent. The menu changes seasonally and more recently offers a number of Italian dishes. The daily prix-fixe menu offers some great deals. You might start with the grilled prawn skewer with tomato chutney and move on to the roasted halibut served with baby carrots and asparagus. Save room for dessert, such as the flourless chocolate cake with pistachio ice cream and Grand Marnier sauce. The wine list includes over 250 offerings from France to California to Australia, with many by-the-glass selections served at table or at the new wine bar.

315 Old Santa Fe Trail. (©) **505/986-9190.** www.315santafe.com. Reservations recommended. Main courses $9–$17 lunch, $18–$33 dinner. AE, DISC, MC, V. Sun–Thurs 5:30–9pm; Fri–Sat 5:30–9:30pm; summer only Fri 11:30–2pm.

Trattoria Nostrani ★★ NORTHERN ITALIAN   This award-winning Italian treasure, on a side street a few blocks from the plaza, offers creative flavors in a cozy romantic-chic setting accented by the wood floors and smooth walls of a historic building. It was the only restaurant in the state to receive the International Wine and Food Society Award of Excellence and the Wine Enthusiast Ultimate Award of Distinction. *Mountain Living Magazine* named it one of the top 10 restaurants in the western United States. Classically trained chefs Nelli Maltezos and Eric Stapelman spend time in Italy to keep expanding their talents. They serve such delicacies as roasted quail with scallops, and a green-peppercorn-crusted pork tenderloin with brandy. A range of pastas, including duck ravioli with plums and red wine, are all house made. Over 500 wine selections are available to accompany your meal.

304 Johnson St. (©) **505/983-3800.** www.trattorianostrani.com. Reservations recommended. Main courses $16–$35. MC, V. Tues–Sat 5:30–10pm.

Vanessie of Santa Fe ★★ STEAK/SEAFOOD   Vanessie is as much a piano bar as it is a restaurant. Doug Montgomery holds forth at the keyboard, caressing the ivories with a repertoire that ranges from Bach to Barry Manilow. The food, served at wooden tables surrounded by bright paintings by notable local artists or on a covered patio, varies little: rotisserie chicken, fresh fish, New York sirloin, filet mignon, Australian rock lobster, grilled shrimp, and rack of lamb. Portions are large; however, most are served a la carte, which bumps this restaurant up into the expensive category. For sides, you can order fresh vegetables, sautéed mushrooms, a baked potato, or an onion loaf (my mom raves about this). The "specialty dinners" come with potato, polenta, or rice and vegetable sides, and are more reasonably priced. I especially like the rotisserie chicken. For dessert, the slice of cheesecake served is large enough for three diners. There's a short wine list.

434 W. San Francisco St. (parking entrance on Water St.). ✆ **505/982-9966.** www.vanessiesantafe.com. Reservations recommended. Dinner $15–$34. AE, DC, DISC, MC, V. Daily 5:30–9:30pm (earlier in off season).

Moderate

Andiamo! ★★ CONTEMPORARY ITALIAN/PIZZA A local favorite, this neighborhood trattoria features an excellent daily-changing menu with antipasto, pasta, pizza, and delectable desserts. It's set in an atmospheric old home with golden walls and hardwood floors. The place buzzes with activity most nights and can be a bit noisy. Service is friendly and knowledgeable. In the summer, you can dine on a patio. For a starter, I've enjoyed the crispy polenta with Gorgonzola sauce. Their lamb sausage pizza is an excellent entree, as is the spaghetti putanesca. Nightly fish specials are always good. For dessert, I'd recommend the panna cotta. Beer and an award-winning wine list accompany the menu.

322 Garfield St. ✆ **505/995-9595.** www.andiamoonline.com. Reservations recommended. Main courses $10–$20. AE, DISC, MC, V. Daily 5:15–9:30pm.

Café Café ★★ 🍴 REGIONAL ITALIAN/PIZZA In a cozy, casual atmosphere created by hardwood floors, pine tables, and a *banco* along one wall, this new restaurant serves some of Santa Fe's most flavorful Italian food. The menu changes seasonally, taking advantage of what's fresh. Service is friendly and knowledgeable. The only downside is the place gets busy and can be noisy. Pizza is one big draw here, with a thin crispy crust and lots of cheese. I like the chicken pesto, with artichoke hearts and red onion. Diners can select from a number of burgers and salads, such as the grilled fish of the day atop greens with roasted potatoes, green beans, tomato, and balsamic vinaigrette. For entrees, the baked cannelloni is delicious. A lemon mascarpone brownie I had recently still visits me in sweet dreams. A carefully selected beer and wine list accompanies the menu.

500 Sandoval St. ✆ **505/466-1391.** www.cafecafesantafe.com. Reservations recommended at dinner. AE, DISC, MC, V. Main courses lunch $7–$12, dinner $7.50–$22. Mon–Sat 11am–9pm; Sun 11am–3pm and 5:30–8:30pm.

Cowgirl Hall of Fame ★ REGIONAL AMERICAN/BARBECUE/CAJUN This raucous bar/restaurant serves decent food in a festive atmosphere. The main room is a bar—a hip hangout spot, and a good place to eat as well. The back room is quieter, with wood floors and tables and plenty of cowgirl memorabilia. Best of all is

 family-friendly RESTAURANTS

Blue Corn Cafe (p. 101) A relaxed atmosphere and their own menu pleases kids, while excellent brewpub beer pleases parents.

Bumble Bee's Baja Grill (p. 102) A casual atmosphere allows parents to relax while their kids chow down on quesadillas and burritos.

Upper Crust Pizza (p. 105) Many people feel it has the best pizza in town, and they'll deliver to tired tots and their families at downtown hotels.

sitting out on a brick patio lit with strings of white lights during the warm season. The service is at times brusque, and the food varies. In winter, my favorite is a big bowl of gumbo or crawfish étoufée, and the rest of the time, I order Jamaican jerk chicken or pork tenderloin when it's a special. Careful, both can be hot. The daily blue-plate special is a real buy, especially on Tuesday nights, when it's *chile rellenos.* There's even a special "kid's corral" that has horseshoes, a rocking horse, a horse-shaped rubber tire swing, hay bales, and a beanbag toss. Happy hour is daily from 3 to 6pm. There is also live music almost every night, a pool hall, and a deli.

319 S. Guadalupe St. ✆ **505/982-2565.** www.cowgirlsantafe.com. Reservations recommended. Main courses $7–$13 lunch, $8–$23 dinner. AE, DISC, MC, V. Mon–Fri 11am–midnight; Sat 10am–midnight; Sun 10am–11pm. Bar Mon–Sat until 2am; Sun until midnight.

Il Piatto Cucina Italiano ★★ 🗲 NORTHERN ITALIAN   This simple Italian cafe brings innovative flavors to thinner wallets. It's simple and elegant, with contemporary art on the walls—nice for a romantic evening. Service is efficient, though on a busy night, overworked. The menu changes seasonally, complemented by a few perennial standards. For a starter, try the grilled calamari with shaved fennel and aioli. Among entrees, my favorite is the pancetta-wrapped trout with grilled polenta and wild mushrooms. The Gorgonzola-walnut ravioli is a favorite of many, though not quite enough food to fill me up, so I order an appetizer. A full wine and beer menu is available.

95 W. Marcy St. ✆ **505/984-1091.** www.ilpiattosantafe.com. Reservations recommended. Main courses $15–$22. AE, DISC, MC, V. Mon–Fri 11:30am–2pm; daily 5:30–9pm. Closed July 4.

India Palace ★★ INDIAN   Once every few weeks, I get a craving for the lamb vindaloo served at this restaurant in the center of downtown. A festive ambience, with pink walls painted with mosque rooflines, makes this a nice place for a relaxed meal. The service is efficient, and most of the waiters are from India, as is the chef. The tandoori chicken, fish, lamb, and shrimp are rich and flavorful, and the *baingan bhartha* (eggplant) makes a nice accompaniment. A lunch buffet provides an excellent selection of both vegetarian and nonvegetarian dishes at a reasonable price. Beer and wine are available, or you might want some chai tea.

227 Don Gaspar Ave. (inside the Water St. parking compound). ✆ **505/986-5859.** www.indiapalace. com. Reservations recommended. Main courses $11–$26; luncheon buffet $9.50. AE, DC, DISC, MC, V. Daily 11:30am–2:30pm and 5–10pm. Closed Super Bowl Sun.

Jambo ★★ 🗲 EAST AFRICAN/CARRIBBEAN   A newcomer in 2009, this cafe serves tasty comfort food in a casual atmosphere. Glass-topped tables and African decorations disguise its mall location well. Chef Ahmed Obo cooks a variety of dishes from Lamu, an island off the coast of Kenya. You might start with a phyllo pastry stuffed with spinach, olives, feta, peppers, and chickpeas over greens. For an entree try the coconut chicken (or tofu) curry with basmati rice, or the spice-rubbed lamb sandwich with onions, tomatoes, and cucumber-yogurt sauce on pita bread. Watch for daily specials as well. A variety of beers and wines accompany the menu. Finish with rum rice pudding.

2010 Cerrillos Rd. (at St. Michaels Dr.). ✆ **505/473-1269.** www.jambocafe.net. Main courses $7–$14. MC, V. Mon–Sat 11am–9pm.

La Boca ★★ 🏛 SPANISH/MEDITERRANEAN   Amid cream-colored walls and sparse decor, with simple white-clothed tables set close together, Chef James Campbell Caruso brings the sensations of southern Spain to your palate. Utilizing traditional Spanish foods with mixtures of Arabic and Moroccan flavors, the menu always has welcome surprises. Such artistry has garnered the restaurant acclaim in *Travel + Leisure, Esquire,* and the *New York Times.* Only tapas are served at dinner, emphasizing a social way of dining, since dishes circulate—along with conversation—around the table. You may sample Velarde peaches wrapped in *jamón serrano* or a grilled hanger steak draped with smoked sea-salt-caramel sauce. Full entrees such as paella are available as well. Accenting the experience are selections from a handpicked wine list focusing on Spanish, Italian, and South American vineyards—all served by a knowledgeable and conscientious waitstaff. The meal culminates with a dessert such as *helado de Turrón,* an almond-nougat *semifreddo*—like an ice-cream cake.

72 W. Marcy St. (℃) **505/982-3433,** www.labocasf.com. Reservations recommended. Main courses $8–$24 lunch; dinner tapas $6–$14; 3-, 4-, and 5-course tasting menus $45–$65. AE, DISC, MC, V. Mon-Sat 11:30am–10pm; Sun 5–10pm.

Osteria d'Assisi ★★ NORTHERN ITALIAN A couple blocks from the plaza, this restaurant offers authentic Italian food in a fun atmosphere. The place has a cozy country Italian decor with wooden furniture, white tablecloths, and Italian from the kitchen punctuating the air. In summer, the patio offers a country villa feel. For antipasto, I've enjoyed the Caprese (fresh mozzarella with tomatoes and basil, garnished with baby greens in a vinaigrette dressing). For pasta, I recommend the lasagna, and for fish, try the delightful Italian seafood stew. All meals are served with homemade Italian bread, and there are a number of special desserts, as well as a full bar.

58 S. Federal Place. (℃) **505/986-5858.** www.osteriadassisi.net. Main courses $9–$13 lunch, $12–$25 dinner. AE, MC, V. Mon-Sat 11am–3pm and 5–10pm; Sun 5–10pm.

Pranzo Italian Grill ★★ REGIONAL ITALIAN Housed in a renovated warehouse and freshly decorated in warm Tuscan colors, this Santa Fe staple has a contemporary atmosphere of modern abstract art and very fresh food prepared on an open grill. Homemade pastas, soups, salads, and creative thin-crust pizzas are among the less expensive menu items. *Linguine alla capasante* (linguine with bay scallops, artichoke hearts, and diced tomatoes in a white-wine butter sauce) and *pizza con funghi* (pizza with marinara, mushrooms, sun-dried tomatoes, artichokes, mozzarella, and truffle oil) are consistent favorites. Steak, chicken, veal, and fresh seafood grills dominate the dinner menu. The bar offers the Southwest's largest collection of grappas, as well as a wide selection of wines and champagnes by the bottle or glass. The upstairs rooftop terrace is lovely for seasonal moon-watching over a glass of wine.

540 Montezuma St. (Sanbusco Center). (℃) **505/984-2645.** www.pranzosantafe.com. Reservations recommended. Main courses $8–$18 lunch, $9–$30 dinner. AE, DC, DISC, MC, V. Mon-Sat 11:30am–3pm and 5pm–midnight; Sun noon–10pm.

Shohko Cafe ★★ ASIAN Santa Fe's favorite sushi restaurant serves fresh fish in a 150-year-old adobe building that was once a bordello. The atmosphere is sparse and comfortable, a blending of New Mexican decor (such as ceiling vigas and Mexican tile floors) with traditional Japanese decorative touches (rice-paper screens, for instance). Up to 30 fresh varieties of raw seafood, including sushi and sashimi, are served at plain pine tables in various rooms or at the sushi bar. Request the sushi bar, where the atmosphere is coziest, and you can watch the chefs at work. My mother likes the tempura combination with veggies, shrimp, and scallops. On an odd night, I'll order the salmon teriyaki, but most nights I have sushi, particularly the *anago* and spicy tuna roll—though if you're daring, you might try the Santa Fe Roll (with green chile, shrimp tempura, and *masago*). My new favorite is a caterpillar, with eel and lots of avocado, shaped like its crawling namesake. Wine, imported beers, and hot sake are available.

321 Johnson St. (© **505/982-9708.** Reservations recommended. Main courses $5–$19 lunch, $8.50–$25 dinner. AE, DISC, MC, V. Mon–Fri 11:30am–2pm; Mon–Thurs 5:30–9pm; Fri–Sat 5:30–9:30pm.

Vinaigrette ★★ BISTRO   This new restaurant serves inventive salads, soups, and sandwiches on one of the city's best patios. It's a delightful place to sit and sip herbal iced tea under shade trees, but allow plenty of time because the patio fills quickly. Inside, vermillion-colored chairs and butcher-block tables create a contemporary ambience that appeals to some more than others and tends to be noisy. Still, the food utilizes seasonal ingredients, much of them sourced from the chef's own farm in Nambé, north of Santa Fe. The salad selections include classics such as a Greek and Cobb, but also signature ones such as an Asian beef—marinated steak over arugula, roasted cherry tomatoes, and rice noodles with a Thai peanut vinaigrette. Daily soup and sandwich specials also accompany the regular menu, as does an inventive wine and beer list.

709 Don Cubero Alley. (© **505/820-9205.** Reservations accepted for dinner only. Main courses $8–$16. AE, DISC, MC, V. Mon–Sat 11am–9pm.

Inexpensive

Atomic Grill NEW AMERICAN   A block south of the plaza, this cafe offers decent patio dining at reasonable prices. (Of course, there's indoor dining as well.) The whole place has a hip and comfortable feel, and the food is prepared imaginatively. This isn't my choice for downtown restaurants, but it's great if you're dining at an odd hour, particularly late at night. For breakfast try the raspberry French toast made with home-baked challah bread, served with maple syrup. For lunch, or dinner, the fish tacos are nice, and the burgers are juicy and come with many toppings. They also have wood-fired pizzas; try the grilled chicken pesto one. For dessert, the carrot cake is big enough to share and is quite tasty. Wine by the glass and 100 different beers are available.

103 E. Water St. (© **505/820-2866.** Most items under $10. AE, DC, DISC, MC, V. Mon–Thurs 11am–3am; Fri 10am–3am; Sat 9am–3am; Sun 9am–1am.

Blue Corn Cafe ★ ☺ NEW MEXICAN/MICROBREWERY   Within a breezy decor—wooden tables and abstract art—you'll find a raucous and buoyant atmosphere. The overworked waitstaff may be slow, but they're friendly. I recommend sampling dishes from the combination menu, which includes such favorites as enchiladas and tamales. You can get two to five items served with your choice of rice, beans, or one of the best *posoles* (hominy and chile) that I've tasted. Kids have their own menu and crayons to keep them occupied. Nightly specials include the tasty shrimp fajitas, served with guacamole and the usual toppings. Because this is also a brewery, you might want to sample the High Altitude Pale Ale or Sleeping Dog Stout. My beverage choice is the prickly-pear iced tea (black tea with enough cactus juice to give it a zing). The Spanish flan is tasty and large enough to share. **The Blue Corn Cafe & Brewery,** 4056 Cerrillos Rd., Suite G (© **505/438-1800**), on the south side at the corner of Cerrillos and Rodeo roads, has similar fare and atmosphere.

133 W. Water St. (© **505/984-1800.** Reservations accepted for parties of 6 or more. www.bluecorncafe.com. Main courses $10–$12. AE, DC, DISC, MC, V. Daily 11am–10pm.

Body ★★ ASIAN/HEALTH FOOD   My best friend and I eat lunch here every week in order to partake of the calming atmosphere. The cafe atmosphere is quiet, with wood floors and dark wood tables. The service, though good-natured, seems to be perpetually in training. The main draws for us are the mostly organic offerings that always leave us feeling healthy. Breakfast, served all day, includes an excellent granola and a number of egg dishes such as an omelet with goat cheese, basil pesto, tomatoes, and spinach, served with potatoes and toast. Lunch and dinner (same menu) offer such simply delicious food as grilled vegetables with tofu (or chicken or salmon, if you'd prefer), and a very light lemon grass, coconut, and ginger curry, with lots of vegetables. Salads, sandwiches, and a selection of raw entrees, as well as smoothies, chai tea, and such desserts as a yummy mixed berry pie round out the menu. Organic beers and wines are offered as well.

333 Cordova Rd. ✆ **505/986-0362.** www.bodyofsantafe.com. Main courses $6–$11. AE, DISC, MC, V. Daily 7am–9pm.

Bumble Bee's Baja Grill ★ 👜 ☺ MEXICAN   This new "beestro" offers a refreshing twist on fast food: It's actually healthy! The secret? Tacos are made Mexican style, with a tortilla folded around quality meat, fish, and poultry grilled with veggies. You pick from an array of salsas. Waist watchers can sample from a selection of salads, including one with grilled chicken and avocado. Rotisserie chicken and various burritos round out the main menu, while kids have their own options, such as the quesadillas. Diners order at a counter, and a waiter brings the food. The decor is a bit Formica-esque for my tastes, though the primary colors are fun. During warm months, I try to nab a patio table. Evenings often offer live jazz music, when folks sit back and sip beer and wine. There's also a drive-through window. There's another **Bumble Bee's Baja Grill** at 3777 Cerrillos Rd (✆ **505/988-3278**), with similar decor and offerings, on the south side of town.

301 Jefferson St. (from W. San Francisco St., take Guadalupe 2 blocks north). ✆ **505/820-2862.** www.bumblebeesbajagrill.com. Main courses $7–$12. AE, MC, V. Daily 11am–9pm.

Clafoutis French Bakery & Restaurant ★★ COUNTRY FRENCH   Set in a cozy building on the north end of town, this restaurant serves delectable meals in a country kitchen environment. There's always a wait during mealtime, though it's usually not long. The ambience is simple, with wooden utensils and jars of herbs adorning the walls and wooden chairs and a padded *banco* for seating. At lunch, the place can get noisy, with excited diners remarking on the food. All of it is prepared fresh with seasonal ingredients. Breakfast might include an egg croissant with bacon or ham and cheese, or a variety of crepes (served all day). For lunch, you can select from a number of quiches, served with a mixed green salad. My favorite lunch, though, is the chicken-mango salad, with lots of fresh vegetables and tasty but simple vinaigrette. The sandwiches made on homemade organic bread are also popular. Order dessert from the pastry counter (strawberry tart!) and even take home some croissants. A selection of good coffees and teas accompanies the menu.

402 Guadalupe St. ✆ **505/988-1809.** Reservations suggested for 5 or more. All menu items under $11. AE, DISC, MC, V. Mon–Sat 7am–4pm.

Guadalupe Cafe ★★ NEW MEXICAN   A real locals' choice for New Mexican food, this casually elegant cafe occupies a white stucco building that's warm and friendly and has a nice-size patio for dining in warmer months. Service is conscientious. For breakfast, try the spinach-mushroom burritos or huevos rancheros, and for lunch, the chalupas or stuffed *sopaipillas.* Any other time, I'd start with fresh roasted *ancho* chiles (filled with a combination of Montrachet and Monterey Jack cheeses and *piñon* nuts, and topped with your choice of chile) and move on to the sour-cream chicken enchilada or any of the other New Mexican dishes. Order both red and green chile ("Christmas"), so you can sample some of the best sauces in town. Beware, though: The chile here can be hot, and the chef won't put it on the side. Diners can order from a choice of delicious salads, such as a Caesar with chicken. Daily specials are available, and don't miss the famous chocolate-amaretto adobe pie for dessert. Beer and wine are served.

422 Old Santa Fe Trail. ✆ **505/982-9762.** Main courses $5.50-$10 breakfast, $6-$12 lunch, $8-$17 dinner. DISC, MC, V. Tues-Fri 7am-2pm; Sat-Sun 8am-2pm; Tues-Sat 5-9pm.

La Choza ★★ NEW MEXICAN This sister restaurant of the Shed (see below) offers some of the best New Mexican food in town at a convenient location near the intersection of Cerrillos Road and St. Francis Drive. When other restaurants are packed, you'll only wait a little while here. It's a warm, casual eatery with vividly painted walls; it's especially popular on cold days, when diners gather around the wood-burning stove and fireplace. The patio is delightful in summer. Service is friendly and efficient. The menu offers enchiladas, tacos, and burritos, as well as green-chile stew, chile con carne, and *carne adovada.* The portions are medium size, so if you're hungry, start with guacamole or nachos. For dessert, you can't leave without trying the mocha cake (chocolate cake with a mocha pudding filling, served with whipped cream). Vegetarians and children have their own menus. Beer and wine are available. La Choza now boasts a full bar.

905 Alarid St. ✆ **505/982-0909.** Main courses $9-$12. AE, DISC, MC, V. Summer Mon-Sat 11am-2:30pm and 5-9pm; winter Mon-Thurs 11am-2:30pm and 5-8pm, Fri-Sat 11am-2:30pm and 5-9pm.

Plaza Cafe ★ AMERICAN/DELI/NEW MEXICAN/GREEK Santa Fe's best example of diner-style eating, this cafe has excellent food in a bright and friendly atmosphere right on the plaza. A restaurant since the turn of the 20th century, the decor has changed only enough to stay comfortable and clean, with red upholstered banquettes, Art Deco tile, and a soda fountain–style service counter. Service is always quick and conscientious, and only during the heavy tourist seasons will you have to wait long for a table. Breakfasts are excellent and large, and the hamburgers and sandwiches at lunch and dinner are good. I also like the soups and New Mexican dishes, such as the bowl of green-chile stew, or, if you're more adventurous, the pumpkin *posole.* Check out the Greek dishes, such as vegetable moussaka or beef and lamb gyros. Wash it down with an Italian soda, in flavors from vanilla to Amaretto. Alternatively, you can have a shake, a piece of coconut cream pie, or Plaza Cafe's signature dessert, *cajeta* (apple and pecan pie with Mexican caramel). Beer and wine are available.

54 Lincoln Ave. (on the plaza). ✆ **505/982-1664.** www.thefamousplazacafe.com. No reservations. Main courses $8-$17. AE, DISC, MC, V. Daily 7am-9pm.

Sage Bakehouse ★ GOURMET CAFE Restaurants all over Santa Fe use elegantly sharp sourdough bread from this bakery on Cerrillos Road across from the Hotel Santa Fe. And whenever I'm going visiting, I'll stop and pick up a peasant loaf or some rich olive bread. If you're a bread lover, you might want to stop in for breakfast or lunch. The atmosphere is quiet and hip, with lots of marble and metal, a rounded counter, and a few small tables, as well as sidewalk seating during the warm months. Breakfasts include good espressos and mochas, and a bread basket that allows you to sample some of the splendid treats. There are also large blueberry muffins. Lunches are simple, with only a few sandwiches from which to choose, but you can bet they're good. Try the Black Forest ham and Gruyère on rye, or the roasted red bell pepper and goat cheese on olive. People all over town are talking about the chocolate-chip cookies—rumor has it there's more chocolate than cookie in them.

535-C Cerrillos Rd. ✆ **505/820-7243.** All menu items under $10. MC, V. Mon–Fri 7am–5pm; Sat 7am–2pm.

The Shed ★★ NEW MEXICAN This longtime locals' favorite is so popular that during lunch lines often form outside. Half a block east of the plaza and a luncheon institution since 1953, it occupies several rooms and the patio of a rambling hacienda that was built in 1692. Festive folk art adorns the doorways and walls. The food is delicious, some of the best in the state, and a compliment to traditional Hispanic and Pueblo cooking. The red-chile cheese enchilada is renowned in Santa Fe. Tacos and burritos are good, too. The green-chile stew is a local favorite. The Shed has added vegetarian and low-fat Mexican foods to the menu, as well as a variety of soups and salads and grilled chicken and steak. Don't leave without trying the mocha cake, possibly the best dessert you'll ever eat. In addition to wine and a number of beers, there's full bar service. The cantina-style bar is a fun place to schmooze, and the brick patio is well shaded.

113½ E. Palace Ave. ✆ **505/982-9030.** www.sfshed.com. Reservations accepted at dinner. Main courses $6.75–$11 lunch, $8–$19 dinner. AE, DC, DISC, MC, V. Mon–Sat 11am–2:30pm and 5:30–9pm. Bar opens at 4pm.

Tía Sophia's ★ 🍴 NEW MEXICAN If you want to see how real Santa Fe locals look and eat, go to this friendly downtown restaurant, now in its third decade, serving

---

DINING ON THE outskirts

If you're on the south or east side of Santa Fe, you might want to try some of the excellent restaurants on the city's outskirts. Toward the east is the famed **Harry's Roadhouse** ★★, Old Las Vegas Highway (✆ **505/989-4629**), always packed with locals, but worth a wait to sample from their menu of inventive diner-style food. Try the burgers or the salmon with a mustard glaze. It's open daily 7am to 9:30pm. Nearby, if you'd like a steak, stop in at **Steaksmith at El Gancho** ★★, Old Las Vegas Highway and El Gancho Way (✆ **505/988-3333;** www.santafesteaksmith.com). It's most popular for shrimp and steak dishes, both served with a good 'ole baked potato, if you'd like. It's open daily 4 to 9:30pm. Also in that vicinity, try **Real**

Food Nation ★★, 624 Old Las Vegas Hwy. (✆ **505/466-3886;** www.realfood nation.biz). With greenhouses, orchards, and gardens on-site, nearly every item is locally grown. Their veggie burger is homemade and hearty, and the cookies are big enough to share. South of town, on the Turquoise Trail, check out **San Marcos Café** ★, 3877 NM 14, near Lone Butte (✆ **505/471-9298**). Set in an old adobe house with wood plank floors, the restaurant serves excellent cinnamon rolls and New Mexican food. Try the eggs San Marcos—tortillas stuffed with scrambled eggs and topped with guacamole, pinto beans, Jack cheese, and red chile. It's open daily 8am to 2pm (the cafe stops serving at 1:50pm.)

some of the best *sopaipillas* in town. You'll sit at big wooden booths and sip diner coffee. Daily breakfast specials include eggs with blue-corn enchiladas (Tues) and burritos with chorizo, potatoes, chile and cheese (Sat). My favorites are the breakfast burrito and huevos rancheros. Beware of what you order because, as the menu states, Tía Sophia's is "not responsible for too hot chile." Because this is a popular place, be prepared to wait for a table.

210 W. San Francisco St. ✆ **505/983-9880.** Main courses $3–$10 breakfast, $5–$11 lunch. MC, V. Mon-Sat 7am–2pm.

Tomasita's Cafe ★ NEW MEXICAN When I was in high school, I used to eat at Tomasita's, a little dive on a back street. I always ordered a burrito, and I think people used to bring liquor in bags. It's now in a modern building near the train station, and its food has become renowned. The atmosphere is simple—hanging plants and wood accents—with lots of families sitting at booths or tables and a festive spillover from the bar, where many come to drink margaritas. Service is quick, even a little rushed, which is my biggest gripe about Tomasita's. Sure, the food is still tasty, but unless you go at some totally odd hour, you'll wait for a table, and once you're seated, you may eat and be out again in less than an hour. The burritos are still excellent, though you may want to try the *chile rellenos*, a house specialty. Vegetarian dishes, burgers, steaks, and daily specials are also offered. There's full bar service.

500 S. Guadalupe St. ✆ **505/983-5721.** Main courses $6–$15 lunch, $6.25–$16 dinner. AE, DISC, MC, V. Mon-Sat 11am–10pm.

Upper Crust Pizza ★ ☺ PIZZA/ITALIAN Upper Crust serves some of Santa Fe's best pizzas, in an adobe house near the old San Miguel Mission. The atmosphere is plain, with wooden tables; in summer, the outdoor patio overlooking Old Santa Fe Trail is more inviting. Options include the Grecian gourmet pizza (feta and olives) and the whole-wheat vegetarian pizza (topped with sesame seeds). You can either eat here or request free delivery (it takes about 30 min.) to your downtown hotel. Beer and wine are available, as are salads, calzones, sandwiches, and stromboli.

329 Old Santa Fe Trail. ✆ **505/982-0000.** www.uppercrustpizza.com. Pizzas $13–$20. DISC, MC, V. Summer daily 11am–11pm; winter daily 11am–10pm.

Zia Diner ★ AMERICAN Santa Fe's alternative weekly, *The Reporter*, awarded this local favorite the prize for the "Best Comfort Food" in town. The setting is comfortable, too. In a renovated 1880 coal warehouse, it's an Art Deco diner with a turquoise-and-mauve color scheme. It boasts a stainless-steel soda fountain and a shaded patio. Extended hours make it a convenient stopover after a movie or late outing; however, during key meals on weekends, it can get crowded and the wait can be long. The varied menu features homemade soups, salads, fish and chips, scrumptious *piñon* meatloaf, and, of course, enchiladas. Specials range from turkey potpie to Yankee pot roast to three-cheese calzone. I like the corn, green-chile, and Asiago pie, as well as the soup specials. There are fine wines, a full bar, great desserts (for example, tapioca pudding, apple pie, and strawberry-rhubarb pie), and an espresso bar. You can get malts, floats, and shakes anytime.

326 S. Guadalupe St. ✆ **505/988-7008.** www.ziadiner.com. Reservations accepted only for parties of 6 or more. Main courses $6–$10 breakfast and lunch, $5–$14 dinner. AE, DISC, MC, V. Daily 7am–10pm.

DINING ON THE outskirts—north

If you'd like to take a little drive en route to dinner, or are cruising into Santa Fe from the north, you'll find a number of excellent dining options. You can have a little history with your crab cakes or filet mignon at **Las Fuentes Restaurant & Bar ★★** at Bishop's Lodge Ranch Resort & Spa, 1297 Bishop's Lodge Rd. (*©* **505/819-4035;** www.bishopslodge. com). When you finish feasting, ask for a key at the front desk and then take a short walk up some steps to the 1853 chapel, which once served as Bishop Jean-Baptiste Lamy's retreat. Las Fuentes is open daily for breakfast, lunch, and dinner.

Among the pink hills north of Santa Fe at Encantado Resort, **Terra ★★**, 198 NM 592 (*©* **877/262-4666;** www.encantado resort.com) serves New American cuisine with one of the city's finest sunset views. You might try lobster spaghettini. Terra is open daily for breakfast, lunch, and dinner. Feast on the region's best guacamole, mixed tableside at **Gabriel's ★★** on US 84/285 (*©* **505/455-7000;** www. restauranteur.com/gabriels), 15 minutes north of Santa Fe. The steak tacos are excellent. The restaurant is open Sunday to Thursday 11:30am to 9pm and Friday and Saturday 11:30am to 10pm.

THE NORTH SIDE
Moderate

Tesuque Village Market ★ AMERICAN/NEW MEXICAN Located under a canopy of cottonwoods at the center of this quaint village, the restaurant doesn't have the greatest food but makes for a nice adventure 10 minutes north of town. During warmer months, you can sit on the porch; in other seasons, the interior is comfortable, with plain wooden tables next to a deli counter and upscale market. For me, this is a breakfast place, where blue-corn pancakes rule. Friends of mine like the breakfast burritos and huevos rancheros. Lunch and dinner are also popular, and there's always a crowd (though, if you have to wait for a table, the wait is usually brief). For lunch, I recommend the burgers, and for dinner, one of the hearty specials, such as lasagna. For dessert, there's a variety of house-made pastries and cakes at the deli counter, as well as fancy granola bars and oversize cookies in the market. A kids' menu is available.

At the junction of Bishop's Lodge Rd. and NM 591, in Tesuque Village. *©* **505/988-8848.** www. tesuquevillagemarket.com. Reservations recommended for holidays. Main courses $4–$15 breakfast, $7–$14 lunch and dinner. MC, V. Daily 7am–9pm.

THE SOUTH SIDE

Santa Fe's motel strip and other streets south of Paseo de Peralta have their share of good, reasonably priced restaurants. Take note that the highly recommended **Bumble Bee's Baja Grill** and the **Blue Corn Cafe** have south-side location (see earlier in the chapter for both). Also, Marisco's La Playa (see below) has a second location on Cerrillos Road, called **Marisco's Costa Azul.**

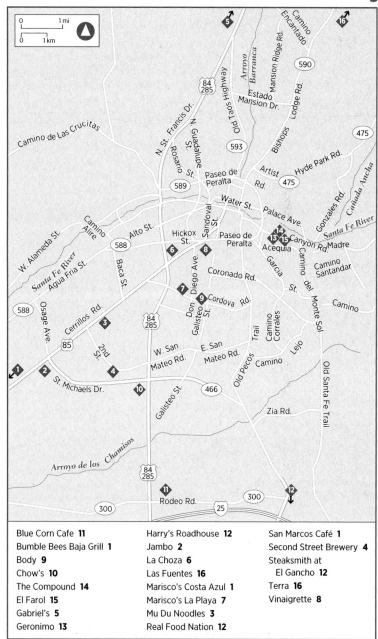

Blue Corn Cafe **11**	Harry's Roadhouse **12**	San Marcos Café **1**
Bumble Bees Baja Grill **1**	Jambo **2**	Second Street Brewery **4**
Body **9**	La Choza **6**	Steaksmith at
Chow's **10**	Las Fuentes **16**	El Gancho **12**
The Compound **14**	Marisco's Costa Azul **1**	Terra **16**
El Farol **15**	Marisco's La Playa **7**	Vinaigrette **8**
Gabriel's **5**	Mu Du Noodles **3**	
Geronimo **13**	Real Food Nation **12**	

Moderate

Chow's ★ ASIAN   This refined but casual restaurant, near the intersection of St. Francis and St. Michael's, is Chinese with a touch of health-conscious Santa Fe. The tasteful decor has lots of wood and earth tones, while the food is unconventional and cooked without MSG. You can get standard pot stickers and fried rice here, but you may want to investigate imaginatively named dishes such as Firecracker Dumplings (carrots, onions, ground turkey, and chile in a Chinese pesto-spinach sauce), Nuts and Birds (chicken, water chestnuts, and zucchini in a Szechuan sauce), or my favorite, Pearl River Splash (whole steamed boneless trout in a ginger onion sauce). For dessert, try the chocolate-dipped fortune cookies. Wine by the bottle or glass as well as beer is available.

720 St. Michaels Dr. ✆ **505/471-7120.** www.mychows.com. Main courses $8–$17. MC, V. Mon–Sat 11:15am–2pm and 4:45–9pm.

Mu Du Noodles ★★ ASIAN   If you're ready for a light, healthy meal with lots of flavor, head to this small restaurant about an 8-minute drive from downtown. The two main rooms, with coral- and butter-colored walls, plain pine tables and chairs, and Asian prints on the walls provide a cozy ambience. The woodsy-feeling patio is definitely worth requesting during the warmer months. Chef Mu uses organic produce and meats and wild seafood whenever she can. My favorite appetizer is the lamb *martabak,* Indonesian dumplings served with a cilantro-mint dipping sauce. For an entree I often order the Malaysian *laksa,* thick rice noodles in a blend of coconut milk, hazelnuts, onions, and red curry, stir-fried with chicken or tofu and julienned vegetables and sprouts. If you're eating with others, you may each want to order a different dish and share. Definitely check out the daily specials, which usually include a fish dish. An interesting selection of beers, wines, and boutique sakes is available, tailored to the menu.

1494 Cerrillos Rd. ✆ **505/983-1411.** www.mudunoodles.com. Reservations for parties of 3 or larger only. Main courses $9–$18. AE, DC, DISC, MC, V. Tues–Sat 5:30–9pm (sometimes 10pm in summer).

Inexpensive

Marisco's La Playa ★ MEXICAN/SEAFOOD   Set in a shopping mall, this little cafe has brightly painted chairs and a mural with a beach scene, all setting the tone for the rollicking flavors served here. It was opened by two cousins who wanted to bring good Mexican *playa* (beach) food to the dry lands, and judging from the crowds here (you may have to wait 15–20 min., but it's worth it), they've succeeded. It features such dishes as shrimp or fish tacos and *pescado a la plancha* (trout seasoned with butter, garlic, and paprika). It has lots of other shrimp dishes, all served with fries, rice, avocado, tomatoes, and lettuce. Chicken and steak fajitas are also popular. Wash it all down with a domestic or imported beer. There is a now a second location, called **Marisco's Costa Azul,** at 2875 Cerrillos Rd. (✆ **505/473-4594**).

537 Cordova Rd. ✆ **505/982-2790.** Main courses $10–$15. AE, DISC, MC, V. Daily 11am–9pm.

Second Street Brewery ★ MICROBREWERY/AMERICAN   In both its 2nd Street location and its Santa Fe Railyard one, this brewery creates a lively pub scene and fairly warm atmosphere. The decor includes contemporary art and wooden tables. It's a party type of place, especially during the warm months, when diners and beer drinkers sit out on the patio. The beers are quite tasty, and you can get a 4-ounce sampler size for $1.25 and try a few different brews. The food isn't extremely memorable, but in winter, it can warm a hearty appetite with such home-style dishes as chicken potpie (as a special) and shepherd's pie. The fish and chips is a big seller, as are the burgers topped with green chile and cheese. The menu also offers lighter fare, such as quiches, soups, and salads. There's a kids' menu, and wines are available. Look for their "Hoppy" Hour, when beer prices are reduced. There are also darts all the time and live entertainment several nights a week.

1814 2nd St. (at the railroad tracks). © **505/982-3030.** Downtown Railyard location: 1607 Paseo del Peralta. © **505/989-3278.** www.secondstreetbrewery.com. Main courses $5-$13. AE, DISC, MC, V. Mon–Thurs 11am–10pm; Fri–Sat 11am–11pm (bar until later); Sun noon–9pm.

WHAT TO SEE & DO IN SANTA FE

One of the oldest cities in the United States, Santa Fe has long been a center for the creative and performing arts, so it's not surprising that most of the city's major sights are related to local history and the arts. The city's Museum of New Mexico, art galleries and studios, historic churches, and cultural sights associated with local Native American and Hispanic communities all merit a visit. It would be easy to spend a full week sightseeing in the city, without ever heading out to any nearby attractions.

THE TOP ATTRACTIONS

Georgia O'Keeffe Museum ★★　The Georgia O'Keeffe Museum, inaugurated in July 1997, contains the largest collection of O'Keeffes in the world: currently 1,149 paintings, drawings, and sculptures, and 1,851 works by other artists of note. It's the largest museum in the United States dedicated solely to an internationally known woman artist. You can see such remarkable O'Keeffes as *Jimson Weed*, painted in 1932, and *Evening Star No. VI*, from 1917. The museum presents special exhibitions that are either devoted entirely to O'Keeffe's work or combine examples of her art with works by her American modernist contemporaries. My favorite in recent years brought together works of O'Keeffe and photographer Ansel Adams. The rich and varied collection adorns the walls of a cathedral-like, 13,000-square-foot space—a former Baptist church with adobe walls. O'Keeffe's images are tied inextricably to local desert landscapes. She first visited New Mexico in 1929 and returned for extended periods from the '20s through the '40s. In 1949, she moved here permanently. An excellent film at the museum depicts her life.

217 Johnson St. ✆ **505/946-1000.** www.okeeffemuseum.org. Admission $9, free for students and children 18 and under, free for all first Fri of each month 5–8pm. Daily 10am–5pm (Fri until 8pm). Closed Tues Nov–May.

Downtown Santa Fe Attractions

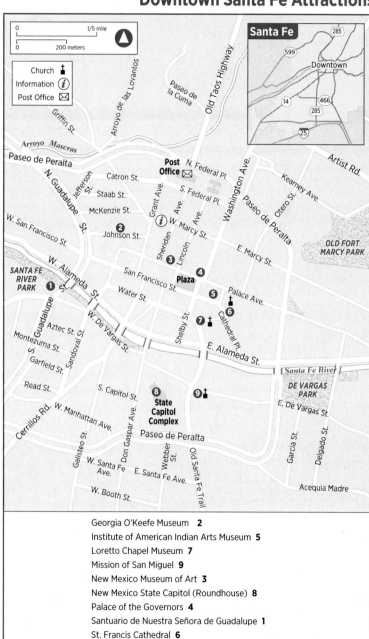

Georgia O'Keefe Museum **2**
Institute of American Indian Arts Museum **5**
Loretto Chapel Museum **7**
Mission of San Miguel **9**
New Mexico Museum of Art **3**
New Mexico State Capitol (Roundhouse) **8**
Palace of the Governors **4**
Santuario de Nuestra Señora de Guadalupe **1**
St. Francis Cathedral **6**

museum BINGEING

If you're a museum buff, pick up a **Museum of New Mexico's 4-day pass.** It's good at all branches of the Museum of New Mexico: the Palace of the Governors, the Museum of Art, the Museum of International Folk Art, and the Museum of Indian Arts & Culture, with the Museum of Spanish Colonial Art thrown in for good measure. The cost is $20 for adults. Also ask about the new **Culture Pass,** which provides full one-time admission to each of the state's 14 museums during a 12-month period for $25.

New Mexico History Museum and the Palace of the Governors ★★   Open in 2009, the New Mexico History Museum presents the state's unique role in world history. Set in 96,000 square feet of exhibit space, the museum offers visitors an interactive experience utilizing voice recordings, music and electronic media to explore the region occupied by Pueblo, Navajo, and Apache people, followed by the arrival of the Spanish in the 1500s, and, finally, the present day.

You'll enter through the Palace of the Governors. Built in 1610 as the original capital of New Mexico, the palace has been in continuous public use longer than any other structure in the United States. Its defining moment was when the Pueblo people took it over during the Pueblo Revolt of 1680. Begin out front, where Native Americans sell jewelry, pottery, and some weavings under the protection of the portal. This is a good place to buy, and it's a fun place to shop, especially if you take the time to visit with the artisans about their work. When you buy a piece, you may learn its history, a treasure as valuable as the piece itself. Plan to spend 2 or more hours exploring the museum and shopping here.

Two shops are of particular interest. One is the bookstore/gift shop, which has an excellent selection of art, history, and anthropology books. The other is the print shop and bindery, where limited-edition works are produced on hand-operated presses. Free docent tours are offered daily, as are downtown walking tours April through October. Call for the schedule.

North plaza. (℗ **505/476-5100.** www.palaceofthegovernors.org. Admission $8 adults, free for children 16 and under, free for all Fri 5–8pm. 4-day passes (good at all branches of the Museum of New Mexico and the Museum of Spanish Colonial Art) $20 for adults. Tues–Sun in winter and daily in summer 10am–5pm (Fri until 8pm).

New Mexico Museum of Art ★   Opposite the Palace of the Governors, this was one of the first Pueblo revival–style buildings constructed in Santa Fe (in 1917). The museum's permanent collection of more than 20,000 works emphasizes regional art and includes landscapes and portraits by all the Taos masters, *los Cincos Pintores* (a 1920s organization of Santa Fe artists), and contemporary artists. The museum also has a collection of photographic works by such masters as Ansel Adams and Eliot Porter. Modern artists are featured in temporary exhibits throughout the year. Two sculpture gardens present a range of three-dimensional art, from the traditional to the abstract.

Graceful **St. Francis Auditorium,** patterned after the interiors of traditional Hispanic mission churches, adjoins the art museum (see "The Performing Arts," in chapter 10). A museum shop sells gifts, art books, prints, and postcards of the collection.

107 W. Palace (at Lincoln Ave.). *℃* **505/476-5072.** www.nmartmuseum.org. Admission $9 adults, free for seniors Wed, free for children 16 and under, free for all Fri 5–8pm. 4-day passes (good at all branches of the Museum of New Mexico and the Museum of Spanish Colonial Art) $20 for adults. Tues–Sun 10am–5pm (Fri until 8pm). Closed New Year's Day, Easter, Thanksgiving, Christmas.

St. Francis Cathedral ★   Santa Fe's grandest religious structure is an architectural anomaly in Santa Fe because its design is French. Just a block east of the plaza, it was built between 1869 and 1886 by Archbishop Jean-Baptiste Lamy in the style of the great cathedrals of Europe. French architects designed the Romanesque building—named after Santa Fe's patron saint—and Italian masons assisted with its construction. The small adobe Our Lady of the Rosary chapel on the northeast side of the cathedral has a Spanish look. Built in 1807, it's the only portion that remains from Our Lady of the Assumption Church, founded along with Santa Fe in 1610. The new cathedral was built over and around the old church.

A wooden icon set in a niche in the wall of the north chapel, Our Lady of Peace, is the oldest representation of the Madonna in the United States. Rescued from the old church during the 1680 Pueblo Rebellion, it was brought back by Don Diego de Vargas on his (mostly peaceful) reconquest 12 years later—thus, the name. Today, Our Lady of Peace plays an important part in the annual Feast of Corpus Christi in June and July.

The cathedral's front doors feature 16 carved panels of historic note and a plaque memorializing the 38 Franciscan friars who were martyred during New Mexico's early years. There's also a large bronze statue of Archbishop Lamy himself; his grave is under the main altar of the cathedral.

Cathedral Place at San Francisco St. *℃* **505/982-5619.** Donations appreciated. Daily 8am–5pm. Mass Mon–Sat 7am and 5:15pm; Sun 8, 10am, noon, and 5:15pm. Free parking in city lot next to the cathedral.

Santa Fe Plaza ★★ 📷   This square has been the heart and soul of Santa Fe, as well as its literal center, since the city was established in 1610. Originally designed as a meeting place, it has been the site of innumerable festivals and other historical, cultural, and social events. Long ago the plaza was a dusty hive of activity as the staging ground and terminus of the Santa Fe Trail. Today, those who congregate around the central monument enjoy the best people-watching in New Mexico. Live music and dancing are often staged on the gazebo/bandstand in summer. At Christmastime the plaza is decked out with lights. Santa Feans understandably feel nostalgic for the days when the plaza, now the hub of the tourist trade, still belonged to locals rather than outside commercial interests.

At the corner of San Francisco St. and Lincoln Ave. Daily 24 hr.

MORE ATTRACTIONS
Museums

Indian Arts Research Center ★   Having grown up in New Mexico, surrounded by Native American arts, I had a hodgepodge knowledge of whose work looked like what. The center put my knowledge into a more coherent framework. The School for Advanced Research, of which the Indian Arts Research Center is a division, was established in 1907 as a center for advanced studies in anthropology and related fields. It sponsors scholarship, academic research, and educational programs, all in the name of keeping traditional arts alive.

Greater Santa Fe Attractions

ATTRACTIONS ●

College of Santa Fe **22**
Cristo Rey **14**
El Rancho de las Golondrinas **24**
Governor's Mansion **3**
Indian Arts Research Center **15**
Museum of Indian Arts & Culture **18**
Museum of International Folk Art **19**
Museum of Spanish Colonial Art **17**
Old Fort Marcy Park **11**
Planetarium at Santa Fe Community College **25**
Randall Davey Audubon Center **13**
Rockin' Rollers Event Arena **6**
Rodeo de Santa Fe **23**
Santa Fe Children's Museum **16**
Santa Fe Climbing Center **9**
Santa Fe Indian School **21**
Santa Fe Opera **1**
Santa Fe Public Library **4**
Santa Fe River Park **12**
Santa Fe Southern Railway **7**
Santuario de Nuestra Señora de Guadalupe **5**
SITE Santa Fe **8**
Skateboard Park **10**
Wheelwright Museum of the American Indian **20**

ACCOMMODATIONS ■

Bishop's Lodge Ranch Resort & Spa **2**

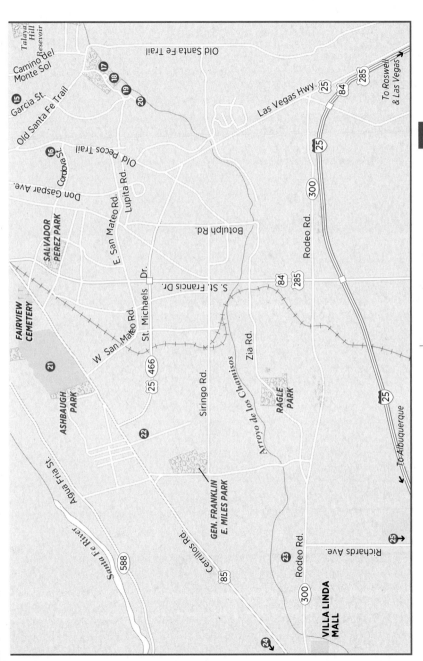

The school has collected more than 12,000 objects, in the process compiling one of the world's finest collections of Southwest Indian pottery, jewelry, weavings, paintings, baskets, and other arts that span from the prehistoric era (around 300–500 A.D.) to the present. You'll be led through temperature- and humidity-controlled rooms filled with work separated by tribe. Admission, however, is by tour only; see below for details.

School of American Research, 660 Garcia St. (off Canyon Rd.). ℂ **505/954-7205.** www.sarweb.org. Free admission for Native Americans and SAR members; $15 for all others. Public tours given most Fri at 2pm (call for reservations). Private tours available for an additional fee. Group tours can also be arranged. Limited parking.

Institute of American Indian Arts Museum ★ A visit to this museum (with over 7,000 works, often called the "national collection of contemporary Native American art") offers a profound look into the lives of a people negotiating two worlds: traditional and contemporary. Here, you'll see cutting-edge art that pushes the limits of many media, from creative writing to textile manufacturing to painting. Much of the work originates from artists from the Institute of American Indian Arts (IAIA), the nation's only congressionally chartered institute of higher education devoted solely to the study and practice of the artistic and cultural traditions of all American Indian and Alaskan native peoples.

Exhibits change periodically, while a more permanent collection of Allan Houser's monumental sculpture is on display in the museum's Art Park. The museum store offers a broad collection of contemporary jewelry, pottery, and other crafts, as well as books and music.

108 Cathedral Place. ℂ **505/983-1777.** www.iaia.edu. Admission $5 adults, $2.50 seniors and students, free for children 16 and under. Mon–Sat 10am–5pm; Sun noon–5pm.

Museum of Indian Arts & Culture ★★ An interactive permanent exhibit here has made this one of the most exciting Native American museum experiences in the Southwest. "Here, Now and Always" takes visitors through thousands of years of Native American history. More than 70,000 pieces of basketry, pottery, clothing, carpets, and jewelry—much of it quite old—are on continual rotating display. You begin by entering through a tunnel that symbolizes the *sipapu,* the ancestral Puebloan entrance into the upper worlds; you're greeted by the sounds of trickling water, drums, and Native American music. Videos show Native Americans telling creation stories. Visitors can reflect on the lives of modern-day Native Americans by seeing a traditional Pueblo kitchen juxtaposed with a modern kitchen. You can step into a Navajo hogan (log and mud hut) and stroll through a trading post. The rest of the museum houses an expansive pottery collection as well as changing exhibits. There's always a contemporary show.

Cultural Chow

If you get hungry while visiting the Museum of Indian Arts & Culture, the Museum of International Folk Art, the Wheelwright Museum of the American Indian, and the Museum of Spanish Colonial Art (all located together, southeast of the plaza), you can now feast on more than your fingernails. The **Museum Hill Café** ★, 710 Camino Lejo (ℂ **505/984-8900**), is open daily for breakfast and lunch from 9am to 5pm, and for a light dinner on Friday until 8pm.

Look for demonstrations of traditional skills by tribal artisans and regular programs in a 70-seat multimedia theater. Call for information on year-round lectures and classes on native traditions and arts, as well as performances of Native American music and dancing by tribal groups. The Roland Discovery Corner offers space for kids to build puzzles and stack fake sandstone into a house. The museum shop offers a broad range of jewelry, pottery, books, and music.

The laboratory, founded in 1931 by John D. Rockefeller, Jr., is itself a point of interest. Designed by the well-known Santa Fe architect John Gaw Meem, it's an exquisite example of pueblo revival architecture.

710 Camino Lejo. © **505/476-1250.** www.miaclab.org. Admission $9 adults, free for children 16 and under. 4-day passes (good at all branches of the Museum of New Mexico and the Museum of Spanish Colonial Art) $20 for adults. Tues–Sun 10am–5pm (also Mon in summer). Drive southeast on Old Santa Fe Trail (beware: Old Santa Fe Trail takes a left turn; if you find yourself on Old Pecos Trail, you missed the turn). Look for signs pointing right onto Camino Lejo.

Museum of International Folk Art ★★★ ☺ This branch of the Museum of New Mexico may not seem quite as typically Southwestern as other Santa Fe museums, but it's the largest of its kind in the world. With a collection of some 130,000 objects from more than 100 countries, it's my favorite city museum, well worth an hour or two of perusing. It was founded in 1953 by the Chicago collector Florence Dibell Bartlett, who said, "If peoples of different countries could have the opportunity to study each other's cultures, it would be one avenue for a closer understanding between men." That's the basis on which the museum operates today.

The special collections include Spanish colonial silver, traditional and contemporary New Mexican religious art, Mexican tribal costumes and majolica ceramics, Brazilian folk art, European glass, African sculptures, and East Indian textiles. Particularly delightful are numerous dioramas of people around the world at work and play in typical town, village, and home settings.

Children love to look at the hundreds of toys on display throughout the museum, many of which are from a collection donated in 1982 by Alexander Girard, a notable architect and interior designer, and his wife, Susan. The couple spent their lives traveling the world collecting dolls, animals, fabrics, masks, and dioramas. They had a home in Santa Fe, where they spent many years. Their donation included more than 100,000 pieces, 10,000 of which are exhibited at the museum.

The Hispanic Heritage Wing houses a fine collection of Spanish colonial and contemporary Hispanic folk art. Folk-art demonstrations, performances, and workshops are often presented here. The 80,000-square-foot museum also has a lecture room, a research library, and two gift shops, where a variety of folk art is available for purchase.

706 Camino Lejo. © **505/476-1200.** www.moifa.org. Admission $9 adults, free for children 16 and under. 4-day passes (good at all branches of the Museum of New Mexico and at the Museum of Spanish Colonial Art) $20 for adults. Daily 10am–5pm (closed Mon Labor Day–Memorial Day). The museum is about 2 miles southeast of the plaza. Drive southeast on Old Santa Fe Trail (beware: Old Santa Fe Trail takes a left turn; if you find yourself on Old Pecos Trail, you missed the turn). Look for signs pointing right onto Camino Lejo.

Museum of Spanish Colonial Art ★ Ironically, beauty sometimes follows in the wake of imperialism. A good example of this point is Spanish colonial art, which has flourished from Europe across the Americas and even in the Philippines. This newer museum, located in the same compound as the Museum of International Folk Art, the Museum of Indian Arts & Culture, and the Wheelwright Museum of the

American Indian, celebrates this art with a collection of 3,000 devotional and decorative works and utilitarian artifacts. Housed in a home built by noted architect John Gaw Meem, the museum displays *retablos* (religious paintings on wood), *bultos* (free-standing religious sculptures), furniture, metalwork, and textiles and, outside, an 18th-century wooden colonial house from Mexico.

750 Camino Lejo. © **505/982-2226.** www.spanishcolonial.org. Admission $9 adults, free for children 16 and under. 4-day passes (good at all branches of the Museum of New Mexico and this one) $20 for adults. Tues–Sun 10am–5pm. The museum is located about 2 miles southeast of the plaza. Drive southeast on Old Santa Fe Trail (beware: Old Santa Fe Trail takes a left turn; if you find yourself on Old Pecos Trail, you missed the turn). Look for signs pointing right onto Camino Lejo.

SITE Santa Fe ★   This not-for-profit, 18,000-square-foot contemporary art space without a permanent collection has made a place for itself in the City Different, as well as in the international art scene. It's no wonder, with shows by some of the world's most noted contemporary artists. As well as bringing cutting-edge visual art to Santa Fe, SITE sponsors an art and culture series of lectures, multidisciplinary programs, and artist dialogues.

1606 Paseo de Peralta. © **505/989-1199.** www.sitesantafe.org. $10 adults, $5 students and seniors, free for SITE Santa Fe members, free for all Fri and Sat 10am–noon during the Farmers' Market. Wed–Sat 10am–5pm (Fri until 7pm); Sun noon–5pm. Closed Thanksgiving, Christmas Eve, Christmas, New Year's Eve, New Year's Day. Call for information about docent tours and tours in Spanish.

 fetishes: **GIFTS OF POWER**

According to Zuni lore, in the early years of human existence, the Sun sent down his two children to assist humans, who were under siege from earthly predators. The Sun's sons shot lightning bolts from their shields and destroyed the predators. For generations, Zunis, traveling across their lands in western New Mexico, have found stones shaped like particular animals. The Zunis believe the stones to be the remains of those long-lost predators, still containing their souls or last breaths.

In many shops in Santa Fe, you too can pick up a carved animal figure called a *fetish*. According to belief, the owner of the fetish is able to absorb the power of that creature. Many fetishes were long ago used for protection and might in the hunt. Today, a person might carry a bear for health and strength, or an eagle for keen perspective. A mole might be placed in a home's foundation for protection from elements underground, a frog buried with crops for fertility and rain, a ram carried in the purse for prosperity. For love, some locals recommend pairs of fetishes—often foxes or coyotes carved from a single piece of stone.

Many fetishes, arranged with bundles on top and attached with sinew, serve as an offering to the animal spirit that resides within the stone. Fetishes are still carved by many of the pueblos. A good fetish is not necessarily one that is meticulously carved. Some fetishes are barely carved at all, as the original shape of the stone already contains the form of the animal. When you have a sense of the quality and elegance available, decide which animal (and power) suits you best. Native Americans caution, however, that the fetish cannot be expected to impart an attribute you don't already possess. Instead, it will help elicit the power that already resides within you. A good source for fetishes is **Keshi,** 227 Don Gaspar Ave. (© **505/989-8728;** www.keshi.com). Expect to pay $25 to $50 or more for a good one.

Wheelwright Museum of the American Indian ★ ☺ Next door to the folk art museum, this museum resembles a Navajo hogan, with its doorway facing east (toward the rising sun) and its ceiling formed in the interlocking "whirling log" style. It was founded in 1937 by Boston scholar Mary Cabot Wheelwright, in collaboration with a Navajo medicine man, Hastiin Klah, to preserve and document Navajo ritual beliefs and practices. Klah took the designs of sand paintings used in healing ceremonies and adapted them into the woven pictographs that are a major part of the museum's treasure. In 1976, the museum's focus was altered to include the living arts of all Native American cultures. The museum offers three or four exhibits per year. You may see a basketry exhibit, mixed-media Navajo toys, or contemporary Navajo rugs. An added treat here is the Case Trading Post, an arts-and-crafts shop built to resemble the typical turn-of-the-20th-century trading post found on the Navajo reservation. Docent tours of the exhibition are Monday through Friday at 2pm and Saturday at 1pm. Year-round each Saturday and Tuesday morning at 10:15am and Sunday at 2pm, the Trading Post presents a lively and informative introduction to Southwestern Indian art. The museum has excellent access for travelers with disabilities. Best of all here are the **storytelling sessions** ★★ given by Joe Hayes, scheduled in July and August on Saturday and Sunday evenings at 7pm. Check the Web schedule for more details.

704 Camino Lejo. ✆ **800/607-4636** or 505/982-4636. Fax 505/989-7386. www.wheelwright.org. Donations appreciated. Mon-Sat 10am-5pm; Sun 1-5pm. Closed New Year's Day, Thanksgiving, Christmas. Drive southeast on Old Santa Fe Trail (beware: Old Santa Fe Trail takes a left turn; if you find yourself on Old Pecos Trail, you missed the turn). Look for signs pointing right onto Camino Lejo.

Churches

Cristo Rey This Catholic church (Christ the King), a huge adobe structure, was built in 1940 to commemorate the 400th anniversary of Coronado's exploration of the Southwest. Parishioners did most of the construction work, even making adobe bricks from the earth where the church stands. The local architect John Gaw Meem designed the building, in missionary style, as a place to keep some magnificent stone *reredos* (altar screens) created by the Spanish during the colonial era and recovered and restored in the 20th century.

1120 Canyon Rd. ✆ **505/983-8528.** www.cristoreysantefe.parishesonline.com. Free admission. Mon-Fri 8am-5pm; Mass Sat 4:30pm and Sun 10am.

Loretto Chapel Museum ★★ Though no longer consecrated for worship, the Loretto Chapel is an important site in Santa Fe. Patterned after the famous Sainte-Chapelle in Paris, it was constructed in 1873—by the same French architects and Italian masons who were building Archbishop Lamy's cathedral—as a chapel for the Sisters of Loretto, who had established a school for young women in Santa Fe in 1852.

The chapel is especially notable for its remarkable spiral staircase: It makes two complete 360-degree turns, with no central or other visible support. The structure is steeped in legend. The building was nearly finished in 1878, when workers realized the stairs to the choir loft wouldn't fit. Hoping for a solution more attractive than a ladder, the sisters made a novena (9-day prayer) to St. Joseph—and were rewarded when a mysterious carpenter appeared astride a donkey and offered to build a staircase. Armed with only a saw, a hammer, and a T-square, the master constructed this work of genius by soaking slats of wood in tubs of water to curve them and holding them together with wooden pegs. Then he disappeared without bothering to collect his fee.

207 Old Santa Fe Trail (btw. Alameda and Water sts.). © **505/982-0092.** www.lorettochapel.com. Admission $2.50 adults, $2 children 7–12 and seniors 65 and over, free for children 6 and under. Mon–Sat 9am–5pm; Sun 10:30am–5pm.

Mission of San Miguel If you really want to get the feel of colonial Catholicism, visit this church. Better yet, attend Mass here. You won't be disappointed. Built in 1610, the church has massive adobe walls, high windows, an elegant altar screen (erected in 1798), and a 780-pound San José bell (now found inside), which was cast in Spain in 1356. It also houses buffalo-hide and deerskin Bible paintings used in 1630 by Franciscan missionaries to teach the Native Americans. Anthropologists have excavated near the altar, down to the original floor that some claim to be part of a 12th-century pueblo. A small store just off the sanctuary sells religious articles.

401 Old Santa Fe Trail (at E. de Vargas St.). © **505/983-3974.** Admission $1 adults, free for children 6 and under. Mon–Sat 9am–5pm; Sun 9am–4pm. Summer hours start earlier. Mass Sun 5pm.

Santuario de Nuestra Señora de Guadalupe ★ This church, built between 1776 and 1796 at the end of El Camino Real by Franciscan missionaries, is believed to be the oldest shrine in the United States honoring the Virgin of Guadalupe, the patron saint of Mexico. Better known as Santuario de Guadalupe, the shrine's adobe walls are almost 3 feet thick, and the deep-red plaster wall behind the altar was dyed with oxblood in traditional fashion when the church was restored early in the 20th century.

It is well worth a visit to see photographs of the transformation of the building over time; its styles have ranged from flat-topped pueblo to New England town meeting and today's northern New Mexico style. On one wall is a famous oil painting, *Our Lady of Guadalupe,* created in 1783 by the renowned Mexican artist José de Alzibar. Painted expressly for this church, it was brought from Mexico City by mule caravan. One of Santa Fe's newest landmarks, the graceful 12-foot, 4,000-pound statue of Our Lady of Guadalupe by Mexican sculptor Georgina "Gogy" Farias, was erected in 2008.

100 S. Guadalupe St. © **505/983-8868.** Donations appreciated. Mon–Fri 9am–4pm. Labor Day to Memorial Day Sun–Fri 9am–6pm. Mass Mon–Fri 6:30am, Sun noon.

Parks & Refuges

Arroyo de los Chamisos Trail This trail, which meanders through the southwestern part of town, is of special interest to those staying in hotels along Cerrillos Road. The 2.5-mile paved path follows a chamisa-lined arroyo (stream) and has mountain views. It's great for walking or bicycling; dogs must be leashed.

Begin at Santa Fe High School on Yucca St. or on Rodeo Road near Sam's Club. Contact the city of Santa Fe for more information (© **505/955-6977;** www.santafe.org).

Old Fort Marcy Park Marking the 1846 site of the first U.S. military reservation in the Southwest, this park overlooks the northeast corner of downtown. Only a few mounds remain from the fort, but the Cross of the Martyrs, at the top of a winding brick walkway from Paseo de Peralta near Otero Street, is a popular spot for bird's-eye photographs. The cross was erected in 1920 by the Knights of Columbus and the Historical Society of New Mexico to commemorate the Franciscans killed during the Pueblo Rebellion of 1680. It has since played a role in numerous religious processions. The park is open daily 24 hours, though it's dark and not safe at night.

617 Paseo de Peralta (or travel 3 blocks up Artist Rd. and turn right).

Randall Davey Audubon Center ★ Named for the late Santa Fe artist who willed his home to the National Audubon Society, this wildlife refuge occupies 135 acres at the mouth of Santa Fe Canyon. Just a few minutes' drive from the plaza, it's an excellent escape. More than 100 species of birds and 120 types of plants live here, and varied mammals have been spotted—including black bears, mule deer, mountain lions, bobcats, raccoons, and coyotes. Trails winding through more than 100 acres of the nature sanctuary are open to day hikers, but not to dogs. There's also a natural history bookstore on site.

1800 Upper Canyon Rd. © **505/983-4609.** http://nm.audubon.org. Trail admission $2 adults, $1 children. Daily 9am–5pm. House tours conducted Mon and Fri at 2pm, $5 per person. Free 1-hr. guided bird walk Sat at 8:30am. Gift shop daily 10am–4pm (call for winter hours).

Santa Fe River Park This is a lovely spot for an early morning jog, a midday walk beneath the trees, or perhaps a sack lunch at a picnic table. The green strip follows the midtown stream for about 4 miles as it meanders along Alameda from St. Francis Drive upstream beyond Camino Cabra, near its source. It's open daily 24 hours, but it's not safe at night.

Alameda St. © **505/955-6977.**

Other Attractions

El Rancho de las Golondrinas ★★ ☺ This 200-acre ranch, about 15 minutes south of the plaza via I-25, was once the last stopping place on the 1,000-mile El Camino Real from Mexico City to Santa Fe. Today, it's a living 18th- and 19th-century Spanish village, comprising a hacienda, a village store, a schoolhouse, and several chapels and kitchens. There's also a working molasses mill, wheelwright and blacksmith shops, shearing and weaving rooms, a threshing ground, a winery and vineyard, and four water mills, as well as dozens of farm animals. A walk around the entire property is 1¼ miles in length, with amazing scenery and plenty of room for the kids to romp.

The Spring Festival (the first full weekend of June) and the Harvest Festival (the first full weekend of Oct) are the year's highlights at Las Golondrinas (the Swallows). On these festival Sundays, the museum opens with a procession and Mass dedicated to San Ysidro, patron saint of farmers. Volunteers in authentic costumes demonstrate shearing, spinning, weaving, embroidery, woodcarving, grain milling, blacksmithing, tinsmithing, soap making, and other activities. There's an exciting atmosphere of Spanish folk dancing, music, theater, and food.

A tip: Plan your trip here around a meal, or even a spa treatment or swim, at Sunrise Springs Resort, just up the road (p. 80). You can cool down by the water.

334 Los Pinos Rd. © **505/471-2261.** www.golondrinas.org. Admission $6 adults, $4 seniors and teens, $2 children 5–12, free for children 4 and under. Festival weekends $8 adults, $5 seniors and teens, $3 children 5–12. June–Sept Wed–Sun 10am–4pm; Apr–May and Oct by advance arrangement. From Santa Fe, drive south on I-25, taking exit 276; this will lead to NM 599 going north; turn left on W. Frontage Rd.; drive ½ mile; turn right on Los Pinos Rd.; travel 3 miles to the museum.

New Mexico State Capitol (Roundhouse) This is the only round capitol building in the U.S. Built in 1966, it's designed in the shape of a Zia Pueblo emblem (or sun sign, which is also the state symbol). It symbolizes the Circle of Life: four winds, four seasons, four directions, and four sacred obligations. Surrounding the capitol is a lush 6½-acre garden boasting more than 100 varieties of plants, including roses, plums, almonds, nectarines, Russian olive trees, and sequoias. Inside you'll find standard functional offices, with New Mexican art hanging on the walls. Check out the Governor's Gallery and the Capitol Art Collection. Self-guided tours are available year-round Monday through Friday 7am to 6pm; Memorial Day to Labor Day guided tours are available Monday through Saturday at 10am and 2pm. All tours and self-guided brochures are free to the public.

Paseo de Peralta and Old Santa Fe Trail. ✆ **505/986-4589.** www.legis.state.nm.us. Free admission. Memorial Day to last Sat in Aug Mon–Sat 7am–7pm, tours Sat 10am and 2pm; rest of year Mon–Fri 7am–6pm, tours by appointment. Free parking.

Santa Fe Climbing Center   The walls of this two-story, cavernous gym are covered with foot- and handholds, making it a perfect place to frolic, especially in winter. Rental gear is available.

825 Early St. ✆ **505/986-8944.** www.climbsantafe.com. Daily pass $13 adults, children 12 and under $10. Mon, Wed, and Fri 3–10pm; Tues and Thurs 9am–9pm; Sat noon–8pm; Sun 10am–6pm.

Santa Fe Southern Railway ★   "Riding the old Santa Fe" always referred to riding the Atchison, Topeka & Santa Fe railroad. Ironically, the main route of the AT&SF bypassed Santa Fe, which probably forestalled some development for the capital city. A spur was run off the main line to Santa Fe in 1880, and today, an 18-mile ride along that spur offers views of some of New Mexico's most spectacular scenery.

The Santa Fe Depot is a well-preserved tribute to the Mission architecture that the railroad brought to the West in the early 1900s. Characterized by light-colored stuccoed walls, arched openings, and tiled roofs, this style was part of an architectural revolution in Santa Fe at a time when builders snubbed the traditional pueblo style.

Inside the restored coach, passengers are surrounded by aged mahogany and faded velvet seats. The train snakes through Santa Fe and into the Galisteo Basin, broad landscapes spotted with *piñon* and chamisa, with views of the Sandia and Ortiz mountains. Arriving in the small track town of Lamy, you get another glimpse of a Mission-style station, this one surrounded by spacious lawns where passengers picnic. Check out the sunset rides on weekends and specialty trains throughout the year.

410 S. Guadalupe St. ✆ **888/989-8600** or 505/989-8600. Fax 505/983-7620. www.thetraininsantafe. com. Tickets $32 adults, $18 children 3–13; evening High Ball Train $28–$35 adults, children not encouraged; evening Barbecue Train $58–$70 adults, $35–$55 children. Discounts available. Depending on the season, trains depart the Santa Fe Depot (call to check schedule) 9:30am–1pm Mon–Sat. Rides also available Fri–Sat evening and Sun afternoon.

Cooking, Art & Photography Classes

If you're looking for something to do that's a little off the beaten tourist path, you might consider taking a class.

You can master the flavors of Santa Fe with an entertaining 3-hour demonstration cooking class at the **Santa Fe School of Cooking and Market ★**, on the upper level of the Plaza Mercado, 116 W. San Francisco St. (✆ **800/982-4688** or 505/983-4511; www.santafeschoolofcooking.com). The class teaches about the flavors and history of traditional New Mexican and contemporary Southwestern cuisines. "Cooking Light" classes are available as well. Prices range from $40 to $150 and include a meal; call for a class schedule. The adjoining market offers a variety of regional foods and cookbooks, with gift baskets available.

retro DINING CAR

If you take the Santa Fe Southern to Lamy, or simply drive there, stop for lunch at the **Lamy Station Café** ★, 150 Old Lamy Trail (② **505/466-1904;** www. lamystationcafe.com). Set in a 1950s Atlantic Coastal dining car, it has curvy *bancos* at triangular shaped tables, with food that "pays homage to the Fred Har- vey menu at the height of the railroad years." Order up such sandwiches as open-faced roast beef with mashed pota- toes and gravy or grilled cheese with bacon and green chile. Pasta dishes and salads are available as well. It's open Wed- nesday to Friday 11am to 3pm, Saturday 9am to 3pm, and Sunday 10am to 3pm.

If Southwestern art has you hooked, you can take a drawing and painting class led by Santa Fe artist Jane Shoenfeld. Students sketch such outdoor subjects as the Santa Fe landscape and adobe architecture. In case of inclement weather, classes are held in the studio. Each class lasts for 3 hours, and art materials are included in the fee, which is $125. Private lessons can also be arranged. All levels of experience are wel- come. Children's classes can be arranged, and discounts are available for families. You can create your own personal art adventure with one of Shoenfeld's 1-day classes at Ghost Ranch in Abiquiu. Contact Jane at **Sketching Santa Fe** ★, P.O. Box 5912, Santa Fe, NM 87502 (② **505/986-1108;** www.skyfields.net).

Some of the world's most outstanding photographers convene in Santa Fe at various times during the year for the **Santa Fe Workshops** ★★, P.O. Box 9916, Santa Fe, NM 87504, at a delightful campus in the hills on the east side of town (② **505/983-1400;** www.santafeworkshops.com). Most courses are full time, lasting a week. Food and lodging packages are available.

Wine Tastings

If you enjoy sampling regional wines, consider visiting the wineries within easy driving distance of Santa Fe: **Santa Fe Vineyards,** with a retail outlet at 235 Don Gaspar Ave., in Santa Fe (② **505/982-3474;** www.nmwine.com), or the vineyard itself about 20 miles north of Santa Fe to the Nambe Road on 106 W. Shining Sun (② **505/455-2826**); and the **Black Mesa Winery,** 1502 Hwy. 68, in Velarde (② **800/852-6372**), north on US 84/285 to NM 68 (about 1-hr. drive). Be sure to call in advance to find out when the wineries are open for tastings and to get specific directions.

ESPECIALLY FOR KIDS

Don't miss taking the kids to the **Museum of International Folk Art** (p. 117), where they'll love the international dioramas and the toys. Also visit the tepee at the **Wheelwright Museum of the American Indian** (p. 119), where storyteller Joe Hayes spins traditional Spanish *cuentos*, Native American folk tales, and Wild West tall tales on weekend evenings. **The Bishop's Lodge Ranch Resort and Spa** (p. 79) has extensive children's programs during the summer. These include horse- back riding, swimming, arts-and-crafts programs, and special activities such as archery and tennis. Kids are sure to enjoy **El Rancho de las Golondrinas** (p. 121), a living 18th- and 19th-century Spanish village comprising a hacienda, a village store, a schoolhouse, and several chapels and kitchens.

The **Genoveva Chavez Community Center,** 3221 Rodeo Rd., is a full-service family recreation center on the south side of Santa Fe. The complex includes a 50m pool, a leisure pool, a therapy pool, an ice-skating rink, three gyms, a workout room, racquetball courts, and an indoor running track, as well as a spa and sauna. For hours and more information, call ℭ **505/955-4001** (www.chavezcenter.com).

Planetarium at Santa Fe Community College ★

The planetarium offers imaginative programs, combining star shows with storytelling and other interactive techniques. Among the planetarium's inventive programs: Rusty Rocket's Last Blast, in which kids launch a model rocket, and the Solar System Stakeout, in which kids build a solar system. There's also a 10-minute segment on the current night sky. Programs vary, from those designed for preschoolers to ones for high school kids.

6401 Richards Ave. (south of Rodeo Rd.). ℭ **505/428-1677** or 505/428-1777 for the information line. www.sfccnm.edu. Admission $5 adults, $3 seniors and children 12 and under. Live lecture 1st Wed of month 7–8pm; Celestial Highlights (live program mapping the night sky for that particular month) 1st Thurs of month 7–8pm; prerecorded shows 2nd and 4th Thurs of month.

Rockin' Rollers Event Arena

This roller rink offers public-skating sessions—what the owners call family nights—on Fridays, as well as lessons and rentals. There's also a concession area to buy snacks. In-line skates are allowed.

2915 Agua Fria St. ℭ **505/473-7755.** Admission $5 all ages. Fri 7–9pm.

Rodeo de Santa Fe ★★

The rodeo is usually held in late June. It's a colorful and fun Southwestern event for kids, teens, and adults. (See "Northern New Mexico Calendar of Events," in chapter 3, for details.)

3237 Rodeo Rd. ℭ **505/471-4300.** www.rodeodesantafe.org.

Santa Fe Children's Museum ★

This museum offers interactive exhibits and hands-on activities in the arts, humanities, and science. The most notable features include a 16-foot climbing wall that kids—outfitted with helmets and harnesses—can scale, and a 1-acre Southwestern horticulture garden, complete with animals, wetlands, and a greenhouse. This fascinating area serves as an outdoor classroom for ongoing environmental educational programs. Special performances and hands-on sessions with artists and scientists are regularly scheduled. *Family Life* magazine named this as one of the 10 hottest children's museums in the nation.

1050 Old Pecos Trail. ℭ **505/989-8359.** www.santafechildrensmuseum.org. Admission $8 for non-residents; $4 New Mexico residents; $4 children 12 and under. Wed-Sat 10am–5pm; Sun noon–5pm.

Santa Fe Public Library

Special programs, such as storytelling and magic shows, can be found here weekly throughout the summer. The library is in the center of town, 1 block from the plaza.

145 Washington Ave. ℭ 505/955-6780. www.santafelibrary.org. Mon-Thurs 10am–9pm; Fri-Sat 10am–6pm; Sun 1–5pm. Call for information on current events.

Skateboard Park

Split-level ramps for daredevils, park benches for onlookers, and climbing structures for youngsters are located at this park near downtown.

At the intersection of de Vargas and Sandoval sts. ℭ **505/955-2100.** Free admission. Daily 24 hr.

SANTA FE STROLLS

Santa Fe, with its intricate streets and resonant historical architecture, lends itself to walking. The city's downtown core extends only a few blocks in any direction from the plaza, and the ancient Barrio de Analco and the Canyon Road artists' colony are a mere stone's throw away.

WALKING TOUR 1: THE PLAZA AREA

START:	**The plaza.**
FINISH:	**Loretto Chapell**
TIME:	**1 to 5 hours, depending on the length of visits to the museums and churches.**
BEST TIMES:	**Any morning before the afternoon heat, but after the Native American traders have spread out their wares.**

1 The Plaza

This square (see "The Top Attractions," earlier in this chapter) offers a look at Santa Fe's everyday life as well as many types of architecture, ranging from the Pueblo-style Palace of the Governors to the Territorial-style row of shops and restaurants on its west side.

Facing the plaza on its north side is the:

2 Palace of the Governors

Today the flagship of the New Mexico State Museum system (see "The Top Attractions," earlier in this chapter), the Palace of the Governors has functioned continually as a public building since it was erected in 1610 as the capitol of Nuevo Mexico. Every day, Native American artisans spread out their crafts for sale beneath its portal.

3 Take a Break ☕

Even though you're only two stops into this walking tour, you might want to fortify your strength for the rest of the walk. I recommend the fajitas (grilled meat and chile in a tortilla) or tamales from the street vendor on the plaza.

At the corner of Lincoln and Palace avenues, you'll find the:

4 New Mexico Museum of Art

Located at 107 W. Palace Ave., this museum holds works by Georgia O'Keeffe and other famed 20th-century Taos and Santa Fe artists. The building is a fine example of Pueblo revival–style architecture, and it's home to the renowned St. Francis Auditorium (see "The Top Attractions," earlier in this chapter, and "The Performing Arts," in chapter 10).

Virtually across the street is the:

5 Delgado House

This Victorian mansion (at 124 W. Palace Ave.) is an excellent example of local adobe construction, modified by late-19th-century architectural detail. It was built in 1890 by Felipe B. Delgado, a merchant most known for his business of running mule and ox freight trains over the Santa Fe Trail to Independence and the Camino Real to Chihuahua. The home remained in the Delgado family until 1970. It now belongs to the Historic Santa Fe Foundation.

If you continue west on Palace Avenue, you'll come to a narrow lane—Burro Alley—jutting south toward San Francisco Street, with an interesting burro sculpture.

Head back to Palace Avenue, make your way north on Grant Avenue, and turn left on Johnson Street to the:

6 Georgia O'Keeffe Museum

Opened in 1997, this museum houses the largest collection of O'Keeffe works in the world (see "The Top Attractions," earlier in this chapter). The 13,000-square-foot space is the only museum in the United States dedicated solely to one internationally known woman's work. You might also want to stop next door at the **O'Keeffe Café** (discussed in more detail in chapter 7) for a creative lunch or dinner.

Head back to Grant Avenue, and continue north to Griffin Street, where you'll find the:

7 Oliver P. Hovey House

Constructed between 1857 and 1859 in Territorial style, this adobe, located at 136 Griffin St., is unique because it is actually painted brick. It's not surprising that a flamboyant man like Hovey would go to the trouble to dress up a home in such a fancy style (red brick was a rare commodity in this outpost town back then), but such stunts might be what made people call him the Great Lord Hovey, when he was no lord at all.

Just to the east and across Grant Ave. is the:

8 Bergere House

Built around 1870, this house, at 135 Grant Ave., hosted U.S. President Ulysses S. Grant and his wife Julia during their 1880 visit to Santa Fe.

Proceed north on Grant and turn right on Marcy. On the north side of the street is the Santa Fe Community Convention Center.

Three blocks farther east on Marcy, through an office and restaurant district, turn left on Washington Avenue. Walk a short distance to 227–237 Washington Ave., where you'll see the:

9 Padre de Gallegos House

This house was built in 1857 in the Territorial style. Padre de Gallegos was a priest who, in the eyes of newly arrived Archbishop Jean-Baptiste Lamy, kept too high a social profile and was therefore defrocked in 1852. Gallegos later represented the territory in Congress and eventually became the federal superintendent of Native American affairs.

Reverse course and turn south again on Washington Avenue, passing en route the public library.

Walking Tour 1: The Plaza Area

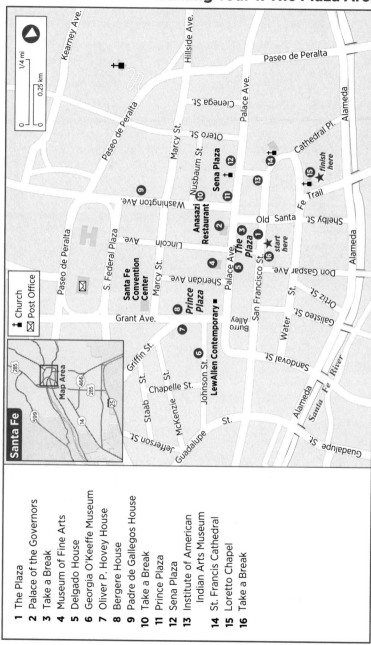

Santa Fe — Map Area

Church
⊠ **Post Office**

1 The Plaza
2 Palace of the Governors
3 Take a Break
4 Museum of Fine Arts
5 Delgado House
6 Georgia O'Keeffe Museum
7 Oliver P. Hovey House
8 Bergere House
9 Padre de Gallegos House
10 Take a Break
11 Prince Plaza
12 Sena Plaza
13 Institute of American Indian Arts Museum
14 St. Francis Cathedral
15 Loretto Chapel
16 Take a Break

8

WHAT TO SEE & DO IN SANTA FE | Walking Tour 1: The Plaza Area

127

10 Anasazi Restaurant & Bar ☕

This is a good time to stop for refreshments at Anasazi Restaurant & Bar at the Inn of the Anasazi, 113 Washington Ave. (© 505/988-3030). During the summer, you'll find a variety of drinks served on the veranda, and in the winter the atmospheric bar inside can be quite cozy.

Leaving the Anasazi, you'll notice the entrance to the Palace of the Governors Museum Shop, across the street, a good place to purchase quality regional memorabilia. As you approach the plaza, turn left (east) on Palace Avenue. A short distance farther on your left, at 113 E. Palace Ave., is:

11 Prince Plaza

A former governor's home, this Territorial-style structure, which now houses **the Shed** (a great lunch or dinner spot; p. 104), had huge wooden gates to keep out tribal attacks.

Next door is:

12 Sena Plaza

This city landmark offers a quiet respite from the busy streets, with its parklike patio. **La Casa Sena** restaurant (a great place to stop for lunch or dinner; p. 94) is the primary occupant of what was once the 31-room Sena family adobe hacienda, built in 1831. The Territorial legislature met in the upper rooms of the hacienda in the 1890s.

Turn right (south) on Cathedral Place to no. 108, which is the:

13 Institute of American Indian Arts Museum

Here you'll find the most comprehensive collection of contemporary Native American art in the world (see "More Attractions," earlier in this chapter).

Across the street, step through the doors of the:

14 St. Francis Cathedral

Built in Romanesque style between 1869 and 1886 by Archbishop Lamy, this is Santa Fe's grandest religious edifice. It has a famous 17th-century wooden Madonna known as *Our Lady of Peace* (see "The Top Attractions," earlier in this chapter).

After leaving the cathedral, walk around the backside of the illustrious La Fonda Hotel—south on Cathedral Place and west on Water Street—to the intersection of the Old Santa Fe Trail. Here, at the northwest corner of the Hotel Loretto, you'll find the:

15 Loretto Chapel

This chapel is more formally known as the Chapel of Our Lady of Light. Lamy was also behind the construction of this chapel, built for the Sisters of Loretto. It is remarkable for its spiral staircase, which has no central or other visible support (see "More Attractions," earlier in this chapter).

Follow Old Santa Fe Trail north back to the Plaza.

16 Five and Dime General Store ☕

By now you may be tired and hungry. I recommend heading to a small store called Five and Dime General Store, 58 E. San Francisco St. (© 505/992-1800), where F. W. Woolworth's, the now-defunct, legendary five-and-dime store, once stood. Like Woolworth's, the store serves a cherished local delicacy called Frito pie: a bag of Fritos smothered in chile con carne, served in a plastic bag with a spoon and a napkin.

BARRIO DE ANALCO & CANYON ROAD

START:	**Don Gaspar Avenue and East de Vargas Street.**
FINISH:	**Any of the quaint restaurants on Canyon Road.**
TIME:	**1 to 3 hours, depending on how long you spend in the art galleries.**
BEST TIMES:	**Anytime.**

The Barrio de Analco, now called East de Vargas Street, is one of the oldest continuously inhabited avenues in the United States. Spanish colonists, with their Mexican and Native American servants, built homes here in the early 1600s, when Santa Fe was founded; some of the structures survive to this day.

Most of the houses you'll see as you walk east on de Vargas are private residences, not open for viewing. Even so, they are well worth looking at because of the feeling they evoke of a Santa Fe now relegated to bygone days. Most have interpretive historical plaques on their outer walls.

The first house you'll see is:

1 Tudesqui House

Dating from the early 19th century, this house, at 135 E. de Vargas St., once owned by a merchant, is now recognizable for the wisteria growing over its adobe walls. The L-shaped Territorial-style residence is noted for its brick coping, 3-foot-thick adobe walls, and deeply inset windows.

Across the street is the:

2 Gregoria Crespin House

The records of this house, 132 E. de Vargas St., date back at least to 1747, when it was sold for 50 pesos. Originally of pueblo design, it later had Territorial embellishments added in the trim of bricks along its roofline.

Just down the road is the:

3 Santa Fe Playhouse

Home to the oldest existing thespian group in New Mexico, this original adobe theater, at 142 E. de Vargas St., still holds performances. (See "The Performing Arts," in chapter 10.)

On the next block, at 401 Old Santa Fe Trail, is the:

4 Mission of San Miguel

Built around 1612, this ranks as one of the oldest churches in the United States (see "More Attractions," earlier in this chapter). Today, it's maintained and operated by the Christian Brothers.

Across de Vargas Street from the Mission of San Miguel is the so-called:

5 Oldest House in the United States

Whether or not this is true is anybody's guess, but this is among the last of the poured-mud adobe houses and may have been built by Pueblo people. The new owners date the place between 1200 and 1646.

There are more homes at the east end of de Vargas, before its junction with Canyon Road. Among them is the:

6 Arthur Boyle House

This house, at 327 E. de Vargas St. on the left side of the street, was built in the mid–18th century as a hacienda.

Up the block and across the street is the:

7 José Alarid House

Built in the 1830s, this house, at 338 E. de Vargas St., is a one-story structure with a pitched metal roof in the grand style of a hacienda.

East de Vargas crosses Paseo de Peralta, entering an alleyway. Immediately on the right is the:

8 Adolph Bandelier House

This house, at 352 E. de Vargas St. (also listed as 1005 Paseo de Peralta), was the home of the famous archaeologist who unearthed the prehistoric ruins at Bandelier National Monument. It has undergone a fine restoration, and houses Sherwoods, a gallery specializing in Native American artifacts.

Extending for a mile or so before you, Canyon Road was once a trail used by the Pueblo tribes and traders. When the Pueblo tribes came to launch their 1680 insurrection against the Spanish colonists, they used this route. Today, it's lined with art galleries, shops, and restaurants. Its historic buildings include the:

9 Juan José Prada House

This house, at 519 Canyon Rd., dates from about 1760. A few doors before you get to it, you'll come to **Morning Star Gallery,** a great place to glimpse and buy museum-quality Native American arts and artifacts.

Farther up the road is:

10 El Zaguan

This building, located at 545 Canyon Rd., is a beautiful example of a Spanish hacienda. In warmer months, be sure to walk through the garden, subject of many Santa Fe paintings. El Zaguan is the headquarters of the **Historic Santa Fe Foundation** (© **505/983-2567;** www.historicsantafe.org). A publication of the foundation, *Old Santa Fe Today* ($10), gives detailed descriptions, with a map and photos, of approximately 80 sites within walking distance of the plaza. The office and garden are generally open Monday through Saturday 9am to 5pm.

11 Geronimo ☕

If you're ready for an elegant lunch or dinner, head to the 1756 Borrego House, which is now Geronimo, 724 Canyon Rd. (© 505/982-1500; p. 94), for lunch or dinner.

If you have the stamina to continue, turn right on Camino del Monte Sol, then right again on Camino del Poniente, and bear right onto Acequia Madre (Mother Ditch). This narrow lane winds through one of Santa Fe's oldest and most notable residential districts. It follows the mother ditch, used for centuries to irrigate gardens in the area. A 20- to 30-minute walk will bring you to **Downtown Subscription,** where you can have some excellent coffee and baked goods. From there, you can take Garcia Street north, back to the base of Canyon Road.

Walking Tour 2: Barrio de Analco & Canyon Road

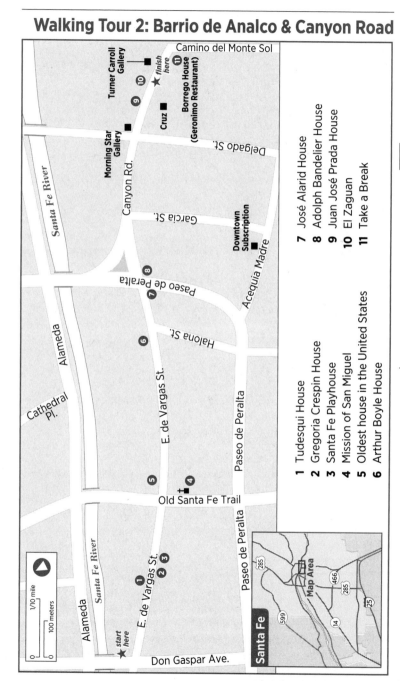

1 Tudesqui House
2 Gregoria Crespin House
3 Santa Fe Playhouse
4 Mission of San Miguel
5 Oldest house in the United States
6 Arthur Boyle House
7 José Alarid House
8 Adolph Bandelier House
9 Juan José Prada House
10 El Zaguan
11 Take a Break

ORGANIZED TOURS

Bus, Car & Tram Tours

Loretto Line ★   For an open-air tour of the city covering history and sights, contact this company that has been running tours for some 20 years. Tours last 1¼ hours and are offered daily from April to October. They depart at 10am, noon, and 2pm—and sometimes more frequently in high summer.

At the Hotel Loretto, 211 Old Santa Fe Trail. Tours depart from the Loretto Chapel. ✆ **505/983-3701.** www.toursofsantafe.com. Tours $14 adults, $10 children 12 and under.

Walking Tours

As with the independent strolls described above, the following are the best way to get an appreciable feel for Santa Fe's history and culture.

Storytellers and the Southwest: A Literary Walking Tour ★   Barbara Harrelson, a former Smithsonian museum docent and local writer, takes you on a 2-hour literary walking tour of downtown, exploring the history, legends, characters, and authors of the region through its landmarks and historic sites. It's a great way to absorb the unique character of Santa Fe. Tours take place by appointment. Harrelson's book, *Walks in Literary Santa Fe: A Guide to Landmarks, Legends, and Lore* ($13, Gibbs Smith) allows for self-guided tours and is available in local bookstores and online.

924 Old Taos Hwy. ✆ **505/989-4561.** barbarah@newmexico.com. Apr–Oct. Tours $20 per person, with a $40 minimum.

Walking Tour of Santa Fe ★   One of Santa Fe's best walking tours begins under the T-shirt tree at Tees & Skis, 107 Washington Ave., near the northeast corner of the plaza (daily at 9:30am and afternoons by reservation). It lasts about 2½ hours. From November through March, the tour runs by reservation only.

54½ E. San Francisco St. (tour meets at 107 Washington Ave.). ✆ **800/338-6877** or 505/983-6565. Tours $10 adults, free for children 12 and under.

Miscellaneous Tours

Pathways Customized Tours ★   Don Dietz offers several planned tours, including a downtown Santa Fe walking tour, a full city tour, a trip to the cliff dwellings and native pueblos, a "Taos adventure," and a trip to Georgia O'Keeffe country (with a focus on the landscape that inspired the art now viewable in the O'Keeffe Museum). He will try to accommodate any special requests you might have. These tours last anywhere from 2 to 9 hours, depending on the one you choose. Don has extensive knowledge of the area's culture, history, geology, and flora and fauna, and will help you make the most of your precious vacation time.

161-F Calle Ojo Feliz. ✆ **505/982-5382.** www.santafepathways.com. Tours for 2 or more people $60 (and up) per day. No credit cards.

Rain Parrish ★   A Navajo anthropologist, artist, and curator, Rain Parrish offers custom guide services focusing on cultural anthropology, Native American arts, and the history of the Native Americans of the Southwest. Some of these are true adventures to insider locations. Ms. Parrish includes visits to local Pueblo villages.

If you're one of those people who wants it all, hook up with **Santa Fe Mountain Adventures ★★** (© 800/965-4010 or 505/988-4000; www.santafemountain adventures.com). They lead programs that combine outdoor adventures with arts and cultural experiences, with spa treatments massaged in for good measure. You might start the day with fly fishing or white-water rafting, and then in the afternoon take a cooking or pottery-making class. Families especially enjoy the guided "geocaching" adventure, a scavenger hunt using a global positioning device. Prices range from $99 to $120 per day, depending on the length of participation and whether you stay at one of their "partner hotels."

704 Kathryn St. © **505/984-8236.** 4-hour tours for 2 people $135. Additional person $30 per hour, and discounted group rates available.

Recursos de Santa Fe/Royal Road Tours ★   This organization is a full-service destination management company, emphasizing custom-designed itineraries to meet the interests of any group. They specialize in the archaeology, art, literature, spirituality, architecture, environment, food, and history of the Southwest. Call or visit the website for a calendar and information about their annual writers' conferences.

826 Camino de Monte Rey. © **505/982-9301.** www.recursos.org.

Rojo Tours & Services   Customized and private tours are arranged to pueblos, cliff dwellings, and ruins, and can include hot-air ballooning, backpacking, or white-water rafting. Rojo also provides planning services for groups.

P.O. Box 15744. © **505/474-8333.** Fax 505/474-2992. www.rojotours.com.

Santa Fe Detours ★   Santa Fe's most extensive tour-booking agency accommodates almost all travelers' tastes, from bus and rail tours to river rafting, backpacking, and cross-country skiing. The agency can also facilitate hotel reservations, from budget to high end.

54½ E. San Francisco St. (summer tour desk, 107 Washington Ave.). © **800/338-6877** or 505/983-6565. www.sfdetours.com.

Southwest Safaris ★★   This tour is one of the most interesting Southwestern experiences available. You'll fly in a small plane 1,000 feet off the ground to various destinations while pilot Bruce Adams explains millions of years of geologic history. En route to the Grand Canyon, for instance, you may pass by the ancient ruins of Chaco Canyon and over the vivid colors of the Painted Desert, and then, of course, over the spectacular Grand Canyon itself. Trips to many Southwestern destinations are available, including Monument Valley, Mesa Verde, Canyon de Chelly, and Arches/Canyonlands, as well as a trip to Capulin Volcano and the ruins at Aztec, New Mexico. Local half-hour, 1- and 2-hour scenic flights are available as well, to places such as the Rio Grande Gorge, the back route in to Acoma Pueblo, and Abiquiu Valley—Georgia O'Keeffe country.

Departs from Santa Fe Airport. © **800/842-4246** or 505/988-4246. www.southwestsafaris.com. Tours $89–$799 per person.

OUTDOOR ACTIVITIES

Set between the granite peaks of the Sangre de Cristo Mountains and the subtler volcanic Jemez Mountains, and with the Rio Grande flowing through, the Santa Fe area offers outdoor enthusiasts many opportunities to play. This is the land of high desert, where temperatures vary with the elevation, allowing for a full range of activities throughout the year.

Ballooning

New Mexico is renowned for its spectacular Balloon Fiesta, which takes place annually in Albuquerque (p. 35). If you want to take a ride, you'll probably have to go to Albuquerque or Taos, but you can book your trip in Santa Fe through **Santa Fe Detours**, 54½ E. San Francisco St. (tour desk for summer, 107 Washington Ave.; ✆ **800/338-6877** or 505/983-6565; www.sfdetours.com). Flights take place early in the day. Rates begin at around $175 a flight. If you have your heart set on a balloon flight, I suggest that you reserve a time early in your trip because flights are sometimes canceled due to bad weather. That way, if you have to reschedule, you'll have enough time to do so.

Biking

You can cycle along main roadways and paved country roads year-round in Santa Fe, but be aware that traffic is particularly heavy around the plaza—and all over town, motorists are not particularly attentive to bicyclists, so you need to be especially alert. Mountain-biking interest has blossomed here and is especially popular in the spring, summer, and fall; the high-desert terrain is rugged and challenging, but mountain bikers of all levels can find exhilarating rides. The Santa Fe Convention and Visitors Bureau can supply you with bike maps.

I recommend the following trails: West of Santa Fe, the **Caja del Rio** area has nice dirt roads and some light-to-moderate technical biking; the **railroad tracks south of Santa Fe** provide wide-open biking on beginner-to-intermediate technical trails; and the **Borrego Trail** up toward the Santa Fe Ski Area is a challenging technical ride that links in with the **Windsor Trail,** a nationally renowned technical romp with plenty of verticality.

In Santa Fe bookstores, or online at sites like Amazon.com, look for *Mountain Biking Northern New Mexico: A Guide to Taos, Santa Fe, and Albuquerque Areas' Greatest Off-Road Bicycle Rides* by Bob D'Antonio. The book details 40 rides ranging in difficulty from beginning to advanced. **Santa Fe Mountain Sports,** 1221 Flagman Way (✆ **505/988-3337;** www.santafemountainsports.com), rents hard-tail mountain bikes for $20 per half-day and $25 per full day, or full-suspension bikes for $35 per full day. **Mellow Velo Bikes,** 638 Old Santa Fe Trail (✆ **505/982-8986;** www.mellowvelo.com), rents front-suspension mountain bikes for $23 per half-day and $30 per full day. Town cruisers run $23 per half-day and $30 per full day. Full-suspension bikes run $55 per day. Add $7, and Mellow Velo will deliver to and pick up from your hotel (in the Santa Fe area). Price per day charges decrease with multiday rentals. Both shops supply accessories such as helmets, locks, maps, and trail information, usually at an additional cost.

If you want to see Santa Fe's downtown the old-fashioned way, check out the '50s retro cruisers at Mellow Velo Bikes. These reproduction bicycles come with a basket on the front, so shoppers can cruise the plaza and Canyon Road and have a place to stash their goods. If you rent one, take a spin through some of Santa Fe's old neighborhoods on Acequia Madre and Garcia Street. Town cruisers run $23 for a half-day and $30 for a full day. Contact **Mellow Velo Bikes,** 638 Old Santa Fe Trail (✆ **505/982-8986;** www.mellowvelo.com).

Bird-Watching

Bird-watchers flock to the **Randall Davey Audubon Center** ★ (see "Parks & Refuges," earlier in this chapter), 1800 Upper Canyon Rd. (✆ **505/983-4609**), to see more than 100 species of birds and many other animals. For guided bird-watching tours all over the region, contact **Wings West** (✆ **800/583-6928;** wingswestnm.com). Bill West guides half-day tours to local spots such as the Santa Fe Mountains and Cochiti Lake ($105 for one to two people) and full-day ones farther afield ($195 for one to two people).

Fishing

In the lakes and waterways around Santa Fe, anglers typically catch trout (there are five varieties in the area). Other local fish include bass, perch, and kokanee salmon. The most popular fishing holes are Cochiti and Abiquiu lakes, as well as the Rio Chama, Pecos River, and the Rio Grande. A world-renowned fly-fishing destination, the **San Juan River,** near Farmington, is worth a visit and can make for an exciting 2-day trip in combination with a tour around **Chaco Culture National Historic Park** (see chapter 11). Check with the **New Mexico Game and Fish Department** (✆ **505/476-8000;** www.wildlife.state.nm.us) for information (including maps of area waters), licenses, and fishing proclamations. **High Desert Angler,** 460 Cerrillos Rd. (✆ **505/988-7688;** www.highdesertangler. com), specializes in fly-fishing gear and guide services.

Golf

There are three courses in the Santa Fe area: the 18-hole **Santa Fe Country Club,** on Airport Road (✆ **505/471-2626;** www.santafecountryclub.com); the often-praised 18-hole **Cochiti Lake Golf Course,** 5200 Cochiti Hwy., Cochiti Lake, about 35 miles southwest of Santa Fe via I-25 and NM 16 and 22 (✆ **505/465-2239;** www.pueblodecochiti.org); and Santa Fe's newest 18-hole course, **Marty Sanchez Links de Santa Fe,** 205 Caja del Rio (✆ **505/955-4400;** www.linksdesantafe.com). Both the Santa Fe Country Club and the Marty Sanchez Links offer driving ranges as well. North of Santa Fe on Pojoaque Pueblo land, the **Towa Golf Resort,** Buffalo Thunder Resort, 12 miles north of Santa Fe on US 285/84 (✆ **877/465-3489** or 505/455-9000; www.buffalothunderresort.com), offers 36 holes, 27 of them designed by Hale Irwin and William Phillips, set with views of the Jemez and Sangre de Cristo Mountains.

Hiking

It's hard to decide which of the 1,000 miles of nearby national forest trails to tackle. Four wilderness areas are nearby, most notably **Pecos Wilderness,** with 223,000 acres east of Santa Fe. Also visit the 58,000-acre **Jemez Mountain National Recreation Area.** Information on these and other wilderness areas is available from the **Santa Fe National Forest,** P.O. Box 1689 (1474 Rodeo Rd.), Santa Fe, NM 87504 (© **505/438-7840;** www. fs.fed.us). If you're looking for company on your trek, contact the Santa Fe branch of the **Sierra Club,** 1807 Second St. (© **505/983-2703;** www.riogrande.sierraclub.org). A hiking schedule can be found in the local newsletter; you can pick one up outside the office. Some people enjoy taking a chairlift ride to the summit

Trail Closures

The drought that has spread across the Southwest in recent years has caused the U.S. Forest Service to close trails in many New Mexico mountains during the summer in order to reduce fire hazard. Before you head out in this area, contact the **Santa Fe National Forest** (© **505/438-5300**).

of the **Santa Fe Ski Area** (© **505/982-4429;** www.skisantafe.com) and hiking around up there during the summer. A popular guide with Santa Feans is *Day Hikes in the Santa Fe Area,* put out by the local branch of the Sierra Club.

The most popular hiking trails are the **Borrego Trail,** a moderate 4-mile jaunt through aspens and ponderosa pines, ending at a creek, and **Aspen Vista,** an easy 1- to 5-mile hike through aspen forest with views to the east. Both are easy to find; simply head up Hyde Park Road toward Ski Santa Fe. The Borrego Trail is 8¼ miles up, while Aspen Vista is 10 miles. In recent years an energetic crew has cut the **Dale Ball Trails** (© **505/955-6977;** www.santafenm.gov), miles of hiking/biking trails throughout the Santa Fe foothills. The easiest access is off Hyde Park Road toward Ski Santa Fe. Drive 2 miles from Bishop's Lodge Road and watch for the trail head on the left. If you're looking for "outspiration" (versus inspiration) on a guided day-hiking experience, call **Outspire** (© **505/660-0394;** www.outspire.com). They'll set you up with a guide and design the hike just for your ability level and interest. A 3- to 4-hour hike begins at $150. Outspire also guides snowshoeing trips.

Horseback Riding

Trips ranging in length from a few hours to overnight can be arranged by **Santa Fe Detours,** 54½ E. San Francisco St. (summer tour desk, 107 Washington Ave.; © **800/338-6877** or 505/983-6565; www.sfdetours.com). You'll ride with "experienced wranglers" and they can even arrange a trip that includes a cookout or brunch. Rides are also major activities at the **Bishop's Lodge** (p. 79). The **Broken Saddle Riding Company** (© **505/424-7774**) offers rides through the stunning Galisteo Basin south of Santa Fe.

Hunting

Elk and mule deer are taken by hunters in the Pecos Wilderness and Jemez Mountains, as are occasional black bears and bighorn sheep. Wild turkeys and grouse are frequently bagged in the uplands, geese and ducks at lower elevations. Check with the **New Mexico Game and Fish Department** (© **505/476-8000;** www.wild life.state.nm.us) for information and licenses.

River Rafting & Kayaking

Although Taos is the real rafting center of New Mexico, several companies serve Santa Fe during the April-to-August white-water season. They include **New Wave Rafting,** 2110 Hwy. 68, Embudo, NM 87531 (© **800/984-1444** or 505/579-0075; www.newwaverafting.com), and **Santa Fe Rafting Co.,** 1000 Cerrillos Rd., Santa Fe, NM 87505 (© **888/988-4914** or 505/988-4914; www.santaferafting. com). You can expect the cost of a full-day trip to range from about $110 to $125 per person before tax and the 3% federal land-use fee. The day of the week (weekdays are less expensive) and group size may also affect the price.

Running

Despite its elevation, Santa Fe is popular with runners and hosts numerous competitions, including the annual **Old Santa Fe Trail Run** on Labor Day. The **Santa Fe Striders** website (www.santafestriders.org) lists various runs during the year, as well as weekly runs. This is a great opportunity for travelers to find their way and to meet some locals.

Skiing

There's something available for every ability level at **Ski Santa Fe,** about 16 miles northeast of Santa Fe via Hyde Park (Ski Basin) Road. Lots of locals ski here, particularly on weekends; if you can, go on weekdays. It's a good family area and fairly small, so it's easy to split off from and later reconnect with your party. Built on the upper reaches of 12,000-foot Tesuque Peak, the area has an average annual snowfall of 225 inches and a vertical drop of 1,725 feet. Seven lifts, including a 5,000-foot triple chair and a quad chair, serve 69 runs and 660 acres of terrain, with a total capacity of 7,800 riders an hour. Base facilities, at 10,350 feet, center on **La Casa Mall,** with a cafeteria, lounge, ski shop, and boutique. A restaurant, **Totemoff's,** has a midmountain patio.

The ski area is open daily from 9am to 4pm; the season often runs from Thanksgiving to early April, depending on snow conditions. Rates for all lifts are $58 for adults, $46 for those ages 13 to 20, $40 for children 12 and under and seniors; half-day (a.m. or p.m.) tickets run $42. Tickets are free for kids less than 46 inches tall (in their ski boots), and for seniors 72 and older. For more information, contact **Ski Santa Fe,** 2209 Brothers Rd., Ste. 220 (© **505/982-4429;** www.skisantafe.com). For 24-hour reports on snow conditions, call © **505/983-9155.** Ski packages are available through **SantaFeHotels.com** (© **800/745-9910**).

Cross-country skiers find seemingly endless miles of snow to track in the **Santa Fe National Forest** (© **505/438-5300;** www.fs.fed.us). A favorite place to start is at the Black Canyon campground, about 9 miles from downtown en route to Ski Santa Fe. In the same area are the **Borrego Trail** (high intermediate), **Aspen Vista Trail,** and the **Norski Trail,** all en route to Ski Santa Fe as well. Other popular activities at the ski area in winter include snowshoeing, snowboarding, sledding, and inner tubing. Ski, snowboard, and snowshoe rentals are available at a number of downtown shops and the ski area.

8

WHAT TO SEE & DO IN SANTA FE

Outdoor Activities

GETTING PAMPERED: THE spa SCENE

If traveling, skiing, or other activities have left you weary, Santa Fe has a number of relaxation options. **Absolute Nirvana Spa & Gardens ★★** (© 866/585-7942; www.absolutenirvana.com) offers imaginative Indo-Asian spa "experiences" as well as massages and facials. Their signature treatment, the Javanese Lulur, includes a full-body massage with jasmine oil, a sandlewood/rice powder exfoliation and yogurt/honey wrap, followed by a steam shower and decadent rose petal bath, all accompanied by tea, fruit, and a house-made truffle. The spa is open Sunday to Thursday 10am to 6pm and Friday and Saturday 10am to 8pm. Prices range from $105 to $240. Another option with a more Japanese bent is **Ten Thousand Waves ★★**, a spa about 3 miles northeast of Santa Fe on Hyde Park Road (© 505/982-9304; www.tenthousand waves.com). This serene retreat, nestled in a grove of *piñons*, offers hot tubs, saunas, and cold plunges, plus a variety of massage and other bodywork techniques. Bathing suits are optional in both the communal hot tub (during the day) and the women's communal tub, where you can stay as long as you want for $19. Nine private hot tubs cost $30 to $40 an hour, with discounts for seniors and children. A premium bath is offered at $49 for 90 minutes. You can also arrange therapeutic massage, hot-oil massage, in-water *watsu*

massage, herbal wraps, salt glows, facials, dry brush aromatherapy treatments, Ayurvedic treatments, and the much-praised Japanese Hot Stone Massage. If you call far enough in advance, you may be able to find lodging at Ten Thousand Waves as well (p. 76). The spa is open Monday, Wednesday, and Thursday from 10:30am to 10:30pm; Tuesday from noon to 10:30pm; and Friday through Sunday from 9am to 10:30pm (winter hours are shorter, so be sure to call). Reservations are recommended, especially on weekends.

Decorated in Southwestern-cum-Asian style, with clean lines and lots of elegant stone, Santa Fe's chicest option is **Rock Resorts Spa ★★** at La Posada de Santa Fe Resort and Spa (© 505/986-0000; www.laposada.rockresorts.com). A full-service spa offering a range of treatments from massage to salt glows, this spot may initially seem expensive (about $135 for 60 min.), but treatments come with full use of the steam room, hot tub, and grass-surrounded pool.

Another south-of-town option, **Sunrise Springs Inn and Retreat,** 242 Los Pinos Rd. (© 505/466-4400; www.sunrise springs.com), offers spa stays in a lovely pond-side setting. Even if you don't stay here, plan a meal at the inn's **Blue Heron Restaurant ★★**, where you'll feast on delectable New American cuisine with a healthy flair.

Swimming

There's a public pool at the **Fort Marcy Complex** (© 505/955-2500; www.santafenm.gov) on Camino Santiago, off Bishop's Lodge Road. In summer, the public **Bicentennial Pool,** 1121 Alto St. (© 505/955-4778), offers outdoor swimming. Admission to both is less than $2 for all ages.

Tennis

Santa Fe has 44 public tennis courts and 4 major private facilities. The **City Recreation Department** (© 505/955-2602; www.santafenm.gov) can help you locate indoor, outdoor, and lighted public courts.

SANTA FE SHOPPING

Santa Fe offers a broad range of art, from very traditional Native American crafts and Hispanic folk art to extremely innovative contemporary work. Some call Santa Fe one of the top art markets in the world. Galleries speckle the downtown area, and as an artists' thoroughfare, Canyon Road is preeminent. The greatest concentration of Native American crafts is displayed beneath the portal of the Palace of the Governors.

Any serious arts aficionado should try to attend one or more of the city's great arts festivals—the Spring Festival of the Arts in May, the Spanish Market in July, the Indian Market in August, and the Fall Festival of the Arts in October.

THE SHOPPING SCENE

Few visitors to Santa Fe leave the city without acquiring at least one item from the Native American artisans at the Palace of the Governors. When you are thinking of making such a purchase, keep the following pointers in mind.

Silver jewelry should have a harmony of design, clean lines, and neatly executed soldering. Navajo jewelry typically features large stones, with designs shaped around the stone. Zuni jewelry usually has patterns of small or inlaid stones. Hopi jewelry rarely uses stones; it's usually a silver-on-silver overlay, darkly oxidized so the image stands out.

Turquoise of a deeper color is usually higher quality, so long as it hasn't been color treated (undesirable because the process adds false color to the stone). Often, turquoise is "stabilized," which means it has resin baked into the stone. This makes the stone less fragile but also prevents it from changing color with age and contact with body oils. Many people find the aging effect desirable. Beware of "reconstituted turquoise." In this process, the stone is disassembled and reassembled; it usually has a uniformly blue color that looks very unnatural.

Pottery is traditionally hand-coiled and made of natural clay, not thrown on a potter's wheel using commercial clay. It is hand-polished with a stone, hand-painted, and fired in an outdoor oven (usually an open fire pit) rather than an electric kiln. Look for an even shape; clean, accurate painting; a high polish (if it's a polished piece); and an artist's signature.

Navajo rugs are appraised according to tightness and evenness of weave, symmetry of design, and whether natural (preferred) or commercial dyes have been used.

The value of **katsina dolls** (also known as *kachinas*) depends on the detail of their carving: fingers, toes, muscles, rib cages, feathers, and so on. Elaborate costumes are also desirable. Oil staining is preferred to the use of bright acrylic paints.

Sand paintings should display clean, narrow lines; even colors; balance; an intricacy of design; and smooth craftsmanship.

Local museums, particularly the Wheelwright Museum and the Institute of American Indian Arts Museum, can give you a good orientation to contemporary craftsmanship.

Contemporary artists are mainly painters, sculptors, ceramists, and fiber artists, including weavers. Peruse one of the outstanding **gallery catalogs** for an introduction to local dealers. They're available for free in many galleries and hotels. They include *The Collector's Guide to Art in Santa Fe and Taos* by Wingspread Incorporated (www.collectorsguide.com), *The Essential Guide to Santa Fe & Taos* by Essential Guides, LLC (www.essentialguide.com), and others. For a current listing of gallery openings, with recommendations on which ones to attend, purchase a copy of the monthly magazine the *Santa Fean* by Santa Fean, LLC, 466 W. San Francisco St., Santa Fe, NM 87501 (www.santafean.com). Also check in the "Pasatiempo" section of the local newspaper, the *New Mexican* (www.santafenewmexican.com), every Friday.

Business hours vary quite a bit among establishments, but most are open at least Monday through Friday from 10am to 5pm, with mall stores open until 8 or 9pm. Most shops are open similar hours on Saturday, and many also open on Sunday afternoon during the summer. Winter hours tend to be more limited.

After the high-rolling 1980s, during which art markets around the country prospered, came the penny-pinching 1990s and the fearful 2000s. Many galleries in Santa Fe have been forced to shut their doors. Those that remain tend to specialize in particular types of art, a refinement process that has improved the gallery scene here. Some locals worry that the lack of serious art buyers in the area leads to fewer good galleries and more T-shirt and trinket stores. The plaza has its share of those, but still has a good number of serious galleries appealing to those buyers whose interests run to accessible art—Southwestern landscapes and the like. On Canyon Road, the art is often more experimental and diverse.

THE TOP GALLERIES
Contemporary Art

Adieb Khadoure Fine Art   Featuring contemporary artists Steven Boone, Robert Anderson, and Barry Lee Darling, the works here are shown in the gallery daily from 10am to 6pm. Adieb Khadoure also sells elegant rugs, furniture, and pottery from around the world. 613 Canyon Rd. ℭ **505/820-2666.** www.akhadourefineart.com.

Bellas Artes   Though a bit on the stuffy side, this lovely gallery down a side street near the Compound Restaurant sells art that stretches the imagination. You'll find works in many mediums by nationally known artists. Look for "architectural tapestries" by Olga de Amaral and inventive sculpture by Ruth Duckworth. 653 Canyon Rd. ✆ **505/983-2745.** www.bellasartesgallery.com.

Cafe Pasqual's Gallery 🎁 Head upstairs from the lively Cafe Pasqual's (see p. 90) to this fun shop full of the same whimsical passion as its namesake. Here you'll find art ranging from papier-mâché bowls to micaceous cookware to silver jewelry, much of it with food-related themes. Look for Rick Phelps's hanging fish plates and Leovigildo Martinez Torres's paintings (the artists who painted the restaurant's murals). Also look for Pasqual's T-shirts and cookbooks. 103 E. Water St., Ste. G. (find the elevator and stairs next to the Atomic Grill). ✆ **505/983-9340.** www.pasquals.com.

Canyon Road Contemporary Art This gallery represents some of the finest emerging U.S. contemporary artists, as well as internationally known artists. You'll find figurative, landscape, and abstract paintings, as well as raku pottery. 403 Canyon Rd. ✆ **505/983-0433.** www.crcainc.com.

Chiaroscuro Gallery This gallery presents contemporary fine art and photography. Especially look for Willy Heeks's lovely textured paintings. 702 and 708 Canyon Rd. ✆ **505/992-0711.** www.chiaroscurogallery.com.

Hahn Ross Gallery Owners Tom Ross and Elizabeth Hahn, a children's book illustrator and surrealist painter, respectively, specialize in representing artists who create colorful, fantasy-oriented works. Check out the sculpture garden here. 409 Canyon Rd. ✆ **505/984-8434.** www.hahnross.com.

Jean Jack Gallery Antique Americana folk art fills this gallery, coupled with Jean Jack's paintings of open spaces and farmhouses. 1521 Upper Canyon Rd. ✆ **505/995-9701.** www.jeanjack.com.

La Mesa of Santa Fe ★ 🎁 Step into this gallery and let your senses dance. Dramatically colored ceramic plates, bowls, and other kitchen items fill one room. Contemporary *katsinas* by Gregory Lomayesva—a real buy—line the walls, accented by steel lamps and rag rugs. 225 Canyon Rd. ✆ **505/984-1688.** www.lamesaofsantafe.com.

LewAllen Galleries ★★ 🎁 This is one of Santa Fe's most prized galleries. You'll find bizarre and beautiful contemporary works in a range of media, from granite to clay to twigs. There are always exciting works on canvas. They have a second location at the railyard on 1613 Paseo del Peralta. 129 W. Palace Ave. ✆ **505/988-8997.** www. lewallencontemporary.com.

Linda Durham Contemporary Art ★ Linda Durham has devoted more than 30 years to representing New Mexico-based artists in a range of mediums including painting, sculpture, photography, and others. These are often daring and always soulful works from a strong roster of talent, including Greg Erf. 1807 2nd St., no. 107. © **505/466-6600.** www.lindadurham.com.

Manitou Galleries ★ This expansive space just off the plaza presents bold contemporary images of the Southwest and beyond through a variety of mediums, including paintings, prints, sculpture, glass, and jewelry. Look for the work of Miguel Martinez and Roger Hayden Johnson. 123 W. Palace Ave. © **800/283-0440** or 505/986-0440. www.manitougalleries.com.

Patina Gallery 🎁 Selling functional objects and sculptural art, including jewelry, fiber, clay and wood pieces, this gallery exhibits the work of more than 100 leading American and European artists. Look for silver work by Harold O'Connor. 131 W. Palace Ave. © **877/877-0827.** www.patina-gallery.com.

Peyton Wright Gallery ★ Housed within the Historic Spiegelberg House (a refurbished Victorian adobe), this excellent gallery offers contemporary, American Modernism, Spanish Colonial, Russian, and 18th-century New Mexico *bultos* and *santos*. In addition to representing such artists as Orlando Leyba, Roni Stretch, and Tim Murphy, the gallery features monthly exhibitions—including contemporary paintings, sculptures, and works on paper. 237 E. Palace Ave. © **800/879-8898** or 505/989-9888. www.peytonwright.com.

Shidoni Foundry, Gallery, and Sculpture Gardens ★★ 📷 Shidoni Foundry is one of the area's most exciting spots for sculptors and sculpture enthusiasts. At the foundry, visitors may take a tour through the facilities to view casting processes. In addition, Shidoni Foundry includes a 5,000-square-foot contemporary gallery, a bronze gallery, and a wonderful sculpture garden—a great place for a picnic. Bishop's Lodge Rd., Tesuque. © **505/988-8001.** www.shidoni.com.

Waxlander Gallery Primarily featuring the whimsical acrylics and occasional watercolors of Phyllis Kapp, this is the place to browse if you like bold color. 622 Canyon Rd. © **800/342-2202** or 505/984-2202. www.waxlander.com.

Native American & Other Indigenous Art

Andrea Fisher Fine Pottery ★ This expansive gallery is a wonderland of authentic Southwestern Indian pottery. You'll find real showpieces here, including the work of renowned San Ildefonso Pueblo potter Maria Martinez. 100 W. San Francisco St. © **505/986-1234.** www.andreafisherpottery.com.

Frank Howell Gallery If you've never seen the wonderful illustrative hand of the late Frank Howell, you'll want to visit this gallery. You'll find a variety of works by contemporary American Indian artists. The gallery also features sculpture, jewelry, and graphics. 103 Washington Ave. © **505/984-1074.** www.frankhowellgallery.com.

Michael Smith Gallery ★ This gallery's namesake has made his mark through the years by finding and displaying some of the region's most exciting rugs, baskets, jewelry, and paintings. It's a small shop with a big heart. 526 Canyon Rd. © **505/995-1013.** www.michaelsmithgallery.com

Morning Star Gallery ★★ 🎁 This is one of my favorite places to browse. Throughout the rambling gallery are American Indian art masterpieces, all elegantly displayed. You'll see a broad range of works, from late-19th-century Navajo blankets to 1920s Zuni needlepoint jewelry. 513 Canyon Rd. © **505/982-8187.** www.morningstargallery. com.

Ortega's on the Plaza   A hearty shopper could spend hours here, perusing inventive turquoise and silver jewelry and especially fine-strung beadwork, as well as rugs and pottery. An adjacent room showcases a wide array of clothing, all with a hip Southwestern flair. 101 W. San Francisco St. © **505/988-1866.** www.ortegasontheplaza.net.

Sherwoods ★   Set in the historic Bandelier House, this gallery features museum-quality Plains Indians antiquities such as an 1870 Nez Perce beaded dress and a Crow war shirt. Some paintings hang here as well, including works by Santa Fe masters such as J. H. Sharp and Gene Kloss. Firearm buffs will go ballistic over the gun room here. 1005 Paseo de Peralta. © **505/988-1776.** www.sherwoodsspirit.com.

Photography

Andrew Smith Gallery ★   I'm always amazed when I enter this gallery and notice works I've seen reprinted in major magazines for years. There they are, photographic prints, large and beautiful, hanging on the wall. Here, you'll see famous works by Edward Curtis, Henri Cartier-Bresson, Ansel Adams, Annie Leibovitz, and others. A new gallery at the corner of Grant and Johnson streets extends this collection. 122 Grant Ave. © **505/984-1234.** www.andrewsmithgallery.com.

Lisa Kristine Gallery ★★   With galleries here in Santa Fe and in California, Lisa Kristine's work gets around, and it's no wonder. These richly colored portraits and landscapes of Asian and African culture will have you gaping in wonderment. 204 W. San Francisco St. © **505/820-6330.** www.lisakristine.com.

Photo-Eye Gallery   You're bound to be surprised each time you step into this gallery a few blocks off Canyon Road. Dealing in contemporary photography, the gallery represents both internationally renowned and emerging artists. 370 Garcia St. © **505/988-5152.** www.photoeye.com.

Spanish & Hispanic Art

Montez Gallery   This shop is rich with New Mexican (and Mexican) art, decorations, and furnishings such as *santos, retablos, bultos,* and *trasteros.* Sena Plaza Courtyard, 125 E. Palace Ave., Ste. 33. © **505/982-1828.** www.montezsantafe.com.

Traditional Art

Altermann Galleries   This is a well of interesting traditional art, mostly 19th-, 20th-, and 21st-century American paintings and sculpture. The gallery represents Remington and Russell, in addition to Taos founders, Santa Fe artists, and members of the Cowboy Artists of America and the National Academy of Western Art. Stroll through the sculpture garden among whimsical bronzes of children and dogs. 225 Canyon Rd. © **505/983-1590.** www.altermann.com.

Gerald Peters Gallery ★★   Displayed throughout a graceful Pueblo-style building, the works here are so fine you'll feel as though you're in a museum. You'll find 19th-, 20th-, and 21st-century American painting and sculpture, featuring the art of Georgia O'Keeffe, William Wegman, and the founders of the Santa Fe and Taos artist colonies, as well as more contemporary works. 1011 Paseo de Peralta. © **505/954-5700.** www.gpgallery.com.

The Mayans Gallery Ltd.   Established in 1977, this is one of the oldest galleries in Santa Fe. You'll find 20th-century American and Latin American paintings, photography, prints, and sculpture. 601 Canyon Rd. © **505/983-8068.**

Nedra Matteucci Galleries ★★   As you approach this gallery, note the elaborately crafted stone and adobe wall that surrounds it, merely a taste of what's to come. The gallery specializes in 19th-, 20th-, and 21st-century American art. Inside, you'll find a lot of high-ticket works such as those of early Taos and Santa Fe painters, as well as classic American Impressionism, historical Western modernism, and contemporary Southwestern landscapes and sculpture. Another excellent gallery, Nedra Matteucci Fine Art, is located at 555 Canyon Rd. There look for the fabulous impressionist works by Evelyne Boren. 1075 Paseo de Peralta. © **505/982-4631.** www.matteucci.com.

Owings-Dewey Fine Art ★   These are treasure-filled rooms. You'll find 19th-, 20th-, and 21st-century American painting and sculpture, including works by Georgia O'Keeffe, Robert Henri, Maynard Dixon, Fremont Ellis, and Andrew Dasburg, as well as antique works such as Spanish colonial *retablos, bultos,* and tin works. Look for the exciting bird sculptures by Peter Woytuk. There's a second shop at 120 E. Marcy St. 76 E. San Francisco St., upstairs. © **505/982-6244.** www.owingsgallery.com.

Zaplin Lampert Gallery ★★   Art aficionados as well as those who just like a nice landscape will enjoy this gallery, one of Santa Fe's classics. Hanging on old adobe walls are works by some of the region's early masters, including Bert Phillips, Gene Kloss, and Gustauve Baumann. 651 Canyon Rd. © **505/982-6100.** www.zaplinlampert.com.

MORE SHOPPING A TO Z

Belts

Desert Son of Santa Fe ★ 📷   From belts to mules, everything in this narrow little shop is hand-tooled, hand-carved, and/or hand-stamped. As well as leather items, look for cowboy hats and exotic turquoise jewelry. It's a slip of a shop with lots of character, presided over by the artist herself, Mindy Adler. 725 Canyon Rd. © **505/982-9499.**

Books

Borders   With close to 200 stores nationwide, this chain provides a broad range of books, music, and videos, and it hosts in-store appearances by authors, musicians, and artists. 500 Montezuma Ave. © **505/954-4707.** www.borders.com.

Collected Works Bookstore ★★   This is an excellent downtown book source, with carefully recommended books up front, in case you're not sure what you want, and shelves of Southwest, travel, nature, and other books. The shop includes a coffeehouse and hosts weekly readings and talks by notable authors. 202 Galiseo St. © **505/988-4226.** www.cwbookstore.com.

Garcia Street Books ★   One of Santa Fe's best shops for perusing, this gem stocks a broad range of titles on the Southwest and collectibles. Not sure what to read? The knowledgeable staff here will help you decide. 376 Garcia St. © **866/986-0151** or 505/986-0151. www.garciastreetbooks.com.

ARCADE SHOPPING ON THE Plaza

Opened in 2004, the **Santa Fe Arcade,** 60 E. San Francisco St. (② **505/988-5792**), on the south side of the plaza, offers three stories of shops in a sleek, glassy European-style space. It's a far cry from the Woolworth's that once lived there. Showy Western wear, fine Indian jewelry, and hip clothing fill the display windows of some 60 spaces in the mall. To pamper yourself with natural products, many made in northern New Mexico, step into **Sombria,** Ste. 222 (② **888/480-5554** or 505/982-7383). Look for their margarita salt glow, made with salt from Utah's Great Salt Lake. Prima Fine Jewelry's **Oro Fino,** Ste. 218 (② **505/983-9699**), sells contemporary and Southwestern inlaid jewelry in silver, gold, and platinum. After all the shopping, if you find yourself hungry, head to the **Rooftop Pizzeria** ★, top floor (② **505/984-0008;** www.rooftoppizzeria. com), for some of the city's best pizza. Two types of crust, an "artisan" or a blue corn, are topped with imaginative concoctions such as smoked duck and roasted garlic or wild mushroom and Alfredo sauce. Salads, pasta dishes, and beer and wine are also available. It's open Sunday through Thursday 11am to 10pm and Friday and Saturday 11am to 11pm.

Children

Gypsy Baby   This shop sells bright clothes, beaded slippers, and mustang rocking horses, all mindful of the slogan "Born to be spoiled." 318 S. Guadalupe St. ② **505/820-1898.** www.gypsybabies.com.

Crafts

Davis Mather Folk Art Gallery   This small shop is a wild-animal adventure. You'll find New Mexican animal woodcarvings in shapes of lions, tigers, and bears—even chickens—as well as other folk and Hispanic arts. 141 Lincoln Ave. ② **505/983-1660.** www.santafefolkartgallery.com.

Nambe ★ 🎁   The cooking, serving, and decorating pieces here are fashioned from an exquisite sand-cast and handcrafted alloy. These items are also available at the Nambe stores at 104 W. San Francisco St. (② 505/988-3574) and in Taos at 109 North Plaza (② 575/758-8221). 924 Paseo de Peralta. ② **988-5528.** www.nambe.com.

Fashions

Back at the Ranch ★   This shop has chic Western wear and what it calls the "largest selection of handmade cowboy boots in the country." 209 E. Marcy St. ② **888/962-6687** or 505/989-8110. www.backattheranch.com.

Origins ★ 📷   A little like a Guatemalan or Turkish marketplace, this store is packed with wearable art, folk art, and the work of local designers. Look for good buys on ethnic jewelry. Throughout the summer there are trunk shows, which offer opportunities to meet the artists. 135 W. San Francisco St. ② **505/988-2323.** www.originssantafe.com.

Overland Sheepskin Company   The rich smell of leather will draw you in the door, and possibly hold onto you until you purchase a coat, blazer, hat, or other finely made leather item. 74 E. San Francisco St. ② **505/983-4727.** www.overland.com.

🎁 Gypsy TIME

Even if you don't shop, you'll want to wander down Gypsy Alley, one of Canyon Road's older artist enclaves. Though the once-crooked shops and studios have been replaced by sleek galleries, it still retains a row of whimsically painted mailboxes—a great photo op. **Emilia Poochle,** 708 Canyon Rd., no. 3 (⟨*ℂ*⟩ **505/438-9663;** www.emiliapoochie. com), likes to "pamper your pooch," and they're not kidding. If you take your doggie in with you, he or she will get treats and water, and can choose from an array of designer beds, dog houses, and games. Monopoly fans should check out the Dog-opoly. Across the alley, **Cielo,** 322 S. Guadalupe St. (⟨*ℂ*⟩ **505/ 820-2151;** www.cielohome.com), offers an eclectic selection of furniture, tableware, and bath and beauty items that's great fun perusing.

Food

The Chile Shop   This store has too many cheap trinketlike items for me, but many people find some novelty items to take back home. You'll find everything from salsas to cornmeal and tortilla chips. The shop also stocks cookbooks and pottery items. 109 E. Water St. ⟨*ℂ*⟩ **505/983-6080.** www.thechileshop.com.

Señor Murphy Candy Maker   Unlike any candy store you'll find in other parts of the country—everything here is made with local ingredients. The chile–*piñon* nut brittle is a taste sensation! Señor Murphy has another shop in the Santa Fe Place mall (⟨*ℂ*⟩ **505/471-8899**). 100 E. San Francisco St. (La Fonda Hotel). ⟨*ℂ*⟩ **505/982-0461.** www. senormurphy.com.

Furniture

Asian Adobe   This shop marries the warmth of Southwestern decor with the austere grace of Asian. You'll find weathered wood tables and *trasteros,* colorful wall hangings, and moody rugs. 310 Johnson St. ⟨*ℂ*⟩ **505/992-6846.** www.asianadobe.com.

Carpinteros   Here you'll find classic Southwestern furnishings handcrafted in solid ponderosa pine—both contemporary and traditional. Prices are a little better here than in downtown shops. 217 Galisteo St. ⟨*ℂ*⟩ **800/443-3448** or 505/988-1229. www.southwestspanish craftsmen.com.

Casa Nova   Also in the Santa Fe Railyard district, this colorful shop offers everything from dishware to furniture, all in bold and inventive colors. Those with whimsical natures will get happily lost here. 530 S. Guadalupe St. (in the Gross Kelly Warehouse). ⟨*ℂ*⟩ **505/983-8558.** www.casanovagallery.com.

El Paso Import Company ★   Whenever I'm in the vicinity of this shop, I always stop in. It's packed—and I mean packed—with colorful, weathered colonial and ranchero furniture. The affordable home furnishings and folk art here are imported from Mexico, India, and Romania. 418 Sandoval St. ⟨*ℂ*⟩ **505/982-5698.** www.elpasoimportco. com.

Jackalope ★ ☺ ⚑   Spread over 7 acres of land, this is a wild place to spend a morning or an afternoon browsing through exotic furnishings from India and Mexico,

More Than Dinosaurs

A timeless adventure tucked into a small space, **Dinosaurs & More,** 137 W. San Francisco St., upstairs in Ste. 5 (✆ 505/988-3299; www.meteoritefossil gallery.com), caters to children of all ages, even those simply young at heart. Rockhound Charlie Snell has been hunting and collecting fossils, minerals, and meteorites for 25 years. He displays and sells them here, with special attention to children's curiosity. At the back of the shop, kids can participate in the archaeology by brushing and scraping away rock and dust from real dinosaur bones.

as well as imported textiles, pottery, jewelry, and clothing. It's a great place to find gifts. Kids will love the prairie-dog village. 2820 Cerrillos Rd. ✆ **505/471-8539.** www.jackalope.com.

Southwest Spanish Craftsmen　The Spanish colonial and Spanish provincial furniture, doors, and home accessories in this store are a bit too elaborate for my tastes, but if you find yourself dreaming of carved wood, this is your place. 314 S. Guadalupe St. ✆ **505/982-1767.** www.nussbaumerfineart.com.

Gifts & Souvenirs

El Nicho 🔖　If you want to take a little piece of Santa Fe home with you, you'll likely find it at this shop. You'll find handcrafted Navajo folk art as well as jewelry and other items by local artisans, including woodcarvings (watch for the *santos!*) by the renowned Ortega family. 227 Don Gaspar Ave. ✆ **505/984-2830.**

Hats

Montecristi Custom Hat Works ★　This fun shop hand-makes fine Panama and felt hats in a range of styles, from Australian outback to Mexican bolero. 322 McKenzie St. ✆ **505/983-9598.** www.montecristihats.com.

Jewelry

Packards ★　Opened by a notable trader, Al Packard, and later sold to new owners, this store on the plaza is worth checking out to see some of the best jewelry available. You'll also find exquisite rugs and pottery. 61 Old Santa Fe Trail. ✆ **505/983-9241.** www.packards-santafe.com.

Tresa Vorenberg Goldsmiths　You'll find some wildly imaginative designs in this jewelry store, where more than 40 artisans are represented. All items are handcrafted, and custom commissions are welcomed. 656 Canyon Rd. ✆ **505/988-7215.** www. tvgoldsmiths.com.

Malls & Shopping Centers

De Vargas Center　There are approximately 50 merchants and restaurants in this mall just northwest of downtown. This is Santa Fe's small, more intimate mall, with anchors Ross and Office Depot; it's open Monday to Friday 10am to 7pm, Saturday 10am to 6pm, and Sunday noon to 5pm. N. Guadalupe St. and Paseo de Peralta. ✆ **505/982-2655.** www.devargascenter.com.

Fashion Outlets of Santa Fe   Outlet shopping fans will enjoy this open-air mall on the south end of town. Anchors include Brooks Brothers, Jones New York, and Coach. 8380 Cerrillos Rd. ℂ **505/474-4000.** www.fashionoutletssantafe.com.

Sanbusco Market Center ★   Unique shops and restaurants occupy this remodeled warehouse near the old Santa Fe Railyard. Many of the shops are overpriced, but it's a fun place to window-shop. Borders (see above) is here as well. It's open Monday to Saturday 10am to 6pm, Sunday noon to 5pm. 500 Montezuma St. ℂ **505/989-9390.** www.sanbusco.com.

Santa Fe Place   Santa Fe's largest mall is near the southwestern city limits, not far from the I-25 on-ramp. If you're from a major city, you'll probably find shopping here very provincial. Anchors include JCPenney, Sears, Dillard's, and Mervyn's. Hours are Monday to Saturday 10am to 9pm, Sunday noon to 6pm. 4250 Cerrillos Rd. (at Rodeo Rd.). ℂ **505/473-4253.** www.shopsantafeplace.com.

Markets

Santa Fe Farmers' Market ★★ 🎁   This farmers' market has everything from fruits, vegetables, and flowers to cheeses, cider, and salsas. Great local treats! If you're an early riser, stroll through and enjoy good coffee, excellent breakfast burritos, and music ranging from flute to fiddle. In 2008, the market moved into a beautiful new building in the railyard district. It's open April to mid-November Tuesday and Saturday 7am to noon. In winter, an abbreviated version takes place indoors. In the Santa Fe Railyard, off Paseo de Peralta. ℂ **505/983-4098.** www.santafefarmersmarket.com.

Tesuque Flea Market ★ 📷   If you're a flea-market hound, you'll be happy to discover this one. More than 500 vendors sell everything from used cowboy boots (you might find some real beauties) to clothing, jewelry, books, and furniture, all against a big northern New Mexico view. The flea market runs March to late November Friday to Sunday. Vendors start selling at about 7:30am and stay open until about 6:30pm, weather permitting. US 84/285 (about 8 miles north of Santa Fe). No phone. www.pueblooftesuquefleamarket.com.

Natural Art

Mineral & Fossil Gallery of Santa Fe ★   You'll find ancient artwork here, from fossils to geodes in all sizes and shapes. Natural mineral jewelry and decorative items for the home, including lamps, wall clocks, furniture, art glass, and carvings are also on hand. Mineral & Fossil also has galleries in Taos, and in Scottsdale and Sedona, Arizona. 127 W. San Francisco St. ℂ **800/762-9777** or 505/984-1682. www.mineralgallery.net.

Stone Forest ★★ 🎁   Proprietor Michael Zimber travels to China and other Asian countries every year to collaborate with the stone carvers who create the fountains, sculptures, and bath fixtures that fill this inventive shop and garden not far from the plaza. 213 St. Francis Dr. ℂ **505/986-8883.** www.stoneforest.com.

Pottery & Tiles

Artesanos Imports Company ★ 📷   Coming here is like taking a trip south of the border, with all the scents and colors you'd expect on such a journey. You'll find a wide selection of Talavera tile and pottery, as well as light fixtures and many other accessories for the home. 1414 Maclovia St. ℂ **505/471-8020.** www.artesanos.com.

Santa Fe Pottery at Double Take   The work of more than 120 master potters from New Mexico and the Southwest is on display here; you'll find everything from mugs and lamps to home furnishings. 323 S. Guadalupe St. ✆ **505/989-3363.**

Rugs

Seret & Sons Rugs, Furnishings, and Architectural Pieces ★   If you're like me and find Middle Eastern decor irresistible, you'll want to wander through this shop. You'll find *kilims* and Persian and Turkish rugs, as well as some of the Moorish-style ancient doors and furnishings that you see around Santa Fe. 224 Galisteo St. ✆ **505/988-9151** or 505/983-5008. www.seretandsons.com.

SANTA FE AFTER DARK

S anta Fe is a city committed to the arts, so it's no surprise that the Santa Fe night scene is dominated by highbrow cultural events, beginning with the world-famous Santa Fe Opera. The club and popular music scene runs a distant second.

Information on all major cultural events can be obtained from the **Santa Fe Convention and Visitors Bureau** (© 800/777-2489 or 505/955-6200) or from the **City of Santa Fe Arts Commission** (© 505/955-6707). Current listings are published each Friday in the "Pasatiempo" section of *The New Mexican* (www.santafenewmexican.com), the city's daily newspaper, and in the *Santa Fe Reporter* (www.sfreporter.com), published every Wednesday.

You can also order tickets to events by phone from **Ticketmaster** (© 800/745-3000). Discount tickets may be available on the night of a performance; for example, the opera offers standing-room tickets on the day of the performance. Sales start at 10am.

A variety of free concerts, lectures, and other events are presented in the summer, cosponsored by the City of Santa Fe and the Chamber of Commerce. Many of these musical and cultural events take place on the plaza; check in the "Pasatiempo" section for current listings and information.

THE PERFORMING ARTS

Many performing-arts groups flourish in this city of 72,000. Some of them perform year-round, while others are seasonal. The acclaimed Santa Fe Opera, for instance, has a 2-month summer season: late June to August.

Note: Many companies noted here perform at locations other than their listed addresses, so check the site of the performance you plan to attend.

Major Performing Arts Companies

CHORAL GROUPS

Desert Chorale This 28-member vocal ensemble recruits members from all over the United States. It's nationally recognized for its eclectic blend of Renaissance melodies and modern avant-garde compositions.

During summer months, the chorale performs classical concerts at various locations, including the Cathedral Basilica of St. Francis and Loretto Chapel, as well as settings throughout Santa Fe and Albuquerque. The chorale also performs a popular series of Christmas concerts during December. Most concerts begin at 8pm. 811 St. Michael's Dr., Ste. 208. ℂ **800/244-4011** or 505/988-2282. www.desertchorale.org. Tickets $20–$100 adults, half-price for students 17 and under.

Sangre de Cristo Chorale   This 34-member ensemble has a repertoire ranging from classical, baroque, and Renaissance works to more recent folk music and spirituals, much of it presented a cappella. The group gives concerts in Santa Fe, Los Alamos, and Albuquerque. The Christmas dinner concert is extremely popular. P.O. Box 4462. ℂ **505/455-3707.** www.sdcchorale.org. Tickets $20–$60, depending on the season.

Santa Fe Women's Ensemble   This choral group of 13 semiprofessional singers offers classical works sung a cappella as well as with varied instrumental accompaniment during February, March, and December. The "Spring Offering" concert (Feb–Mar) is held at the Santuario de Guadalupe, 100 S. Guadalupe St., and the "Christmas Offering" concert (mid-Dec) is held in the Loretto Chapel, Old Santa Fe Trail at Water Street. Call for tickets. 424 Kathryn Place. ℂ **505/954-4922.** www.sfwe.org. Tickets $25–$35, $16 students.

OPERA & CLASSICAL MUSIC

Santa Fe Opera ★★★   Many rank the Santa Fe Opera second only to the Metropolitan Opera of New York in the United States. Established in 1957, it consistently attracts famed conductors, directors, and singers. At the height of the season, the company is 500 strong. It's noted for its performances of the classics, little-known works by classical European composers, and American premieres of 21st-century works. The theater, completed for the 1998 season, sits on a wooded hilltop 7 miles north of the city, off US 84/285. It's partially open air, with open sides. A controversial structure, this new theater replaced the original, built in 1968, but preserved the sweeping curves attuned to the contour of the surrounding terrain. At night, the lights of Los Alamos can still be seen in the distance under clear skies.

The 8-week, 40-performance opera season runs from late June through late August. Highlights for 2011 include the first major U.S. production of Vivaldi's *Griselda,* Gian Carlo Menotti's *The Last Savage,* Gounod's *Faust,* and Puccini's *La Bohême.* All performances begin at 9pm, until the end of July when performances start at 8:30pm, and the last week of the season when performances begin at 8pm. A small screen in front of each seat shows the libretto during the performance. A gift shop has been added, as has additional parking. The entire theater is wheelchair accessible. P.O. Box 2408. ℂ **800/280-4654** or 505/986-5900. www.santafeopera.org. Tickets $28–$180; standing room $10; Opening Night Gala $1,750–$3,000. Backstage tours June–Aug Mon–Sat at 9am; $5 adults, free for children 5–17.

ORCHESTRAL & CHAMBER MUSIC

Santa Fe Pro Musica Chamber Orchestra & Ensemble ★   Nominated in 2008 for a Grammy Award, this chamber ensemble performs everything from Bach to Vivaldi to contemporary masters. During Holy Week, the Santa Fe Pro Musica presents its annual Mozart and Hayden Concert at the St. Francis Cathedral. Christmas brings candlelight chamber ensemble concerts. Pro Musica's season runs September to May. Students and teachers get half off ticket prices. 1405 Luisa St., Ste. 10. ℂ **505/988-4640.** www.santafepromusica.com. Tickets $15–$70.

A HOME FOR THE Arts

The Santa Fe arts scene's best venue, the **Lensic Performing Arts Center,** 211 W. San Francisco St. ((C) **505/988-7050**), hosts many of the city's major performances, including the Santa Fe Chamber Music Festival and the Santa Fe Symphony Orchestra and Chorus, among others. The setting is wonderfully atmospheric; a multimillion-dollar face-lift brought out the 1931 movie palace's *Arabian Nights* charm.

Santa Fe Symphony Orchestra and Chorus ★ This 60-piece professional symphony orchestra has grown rapidly in stature since its founding in 1984. Matinee and evening performances of classical and popular works are presented in a subscription series at the Lensic Performing Arts Center from August to May. There's a preconcert lecture before each performance. During the spring, the orchestra presents music festivals (call for details). P.O. Box 9692. (C) **800/480-1319** or 505/983-1414. www.santafesymphony.org. Tickets $20–$75.

Serenata of Santa Fe ★ This professional chamber-music group specializes in bringing an eclectic mix of classic contemporary works to the stage. Concerts are presented September to May at the Scottish Rite Center, 463 Paseo de Peralta. P.O. Box 8410. (C) **505/989-7988.** Tickets $25 general admission, $20 seniors, $10 youth, $5 students, and $1 for children 5 and under.

Music Festivals & Concert Series

Santa Fe Chamber Music Festival ★★ An extraordinary group of international artists comes to Santa Fe every summer for this festival. Its 6-week season runs mid-July to mid-August and is held in the St. Francis Auditorium and the Lensic Performing Arts Center. Each festival features chamber-music masterpieces, new music by a composer in residence, jazz, free youth concerts, preconcert lectures, and open rehearsals. Performances are Monday, Tuesday, Thursday, and Friday at 8pm; Saturday at various evening times; and Sunday at 6pm. Open rehearsals, youth concerts, and preconcert lectures are free to the public. 239 Johnson St., Ste. B (P.O. Box 2227). (C) **505/983-2075** or 505/982-1890 for box office (after the 3rd week of June). www.sfcmf.org. Tickets $10–$62.

Santa Fe Concert Association ★ Founded in 1937, this oldest musical organization in northern New Mexico has a September-to-May season that includes a six-performance series. Among them are a "Great Performances" series and an "Adventures" series, which feature renowned instrumental and vocal soloists and chamber ensembles. The association also hosts special holiday concerts around Christmas and New Year's. Performances are held at the Lensic Performing Arts Center; tickets are available at the Lensic box office. 210 E. Marcy St., Ste. 15. (C) **505/988-1234,** 800/905-3315 (www.tickets.com), or 505/984-8759. www.santafeconcerts.org. Tickets $20–$175.

Theater Companies

Greer Garson Theater Center In this graceful, intimate theater, the College of Santa Fe's Performing Arts Department produces and performs plays and musicals

October and May. The college also sponsors studio productions and various contemporary music concerts. College of Santa Fe, 1600 St. Michael's Dr. ✆ **505/473-6511.** www.csf.edu. Tickets $10–$20 adults, $5 students.

Santa Fe Playhouse ★ Founded in the 1920s, this is the oldest extant theater group in New Mexico. Still performing in a historic adobe theater in the Barrio de Analco, it attracts thousands for its dramas, avant-garde theater, and musical comedy. Its popular one-act melodramas call on the public to boo the sneering villain and swoon for the damsel in distress. 142 E. de Vargas St. ✆ **505/988-4262.** www.santafeplayhouse. org. Tickets "pay what you wish" to $20, depending on the show.

Theater Grottesco ★★ 🎁 This troupe combines the best of comedy, drama, and dance in its original productions performed each spring, summer, or fall, at whatever venue suits the performance. Expect to be romanced, shocked, intellectually stimulated, and, above all, struck silly with laughter. Look for upcoming winter shows as well. 551 W. Cordova Rd., no. 8400. ✆ **505/474-8400.** www.theatergrottesco.org. Tickets $10–$25.

Theaterwork Studio ★ This community theater goes out of its way to present refreshing, at times risky, plays. In an intimate space on the south end of town, Theaterwork offers seven main-stage productions a year, a broad variety including new plays and classics by regional and national playwrights. Expect to see works by such names as Brecht, Shakespeare, and Victor Hugo. 1336 Rufina Circle. ✆ **505/471-1799.** www. theaterwork.org. Tickets $10–$18.

Dance Companies

Aspen Santa Fe Ballet ★ In its second decade, the Aspen Santa Fe Ballet brings classically trained dancers to Santa Fe and Aspen. Performances are an eclectic repertoire by some of the world's foremost choreographers. The season is year-round, with performances at the Lensic Performing Arts Center. 550-B St. Michael's Dr. ✆ 505/983-5591. www.aspensantafeballet.com. Purchase tickets at the Lensic (✆ **505/988-1234**). Tickets $20–$72.

María Benitez Teatro Flamenco ★ 🎁 True flamenco is one of the most thrilling of dance forms, displaying the inner spirit and verve of the gypsies of Spanish Andalusia. María Benitez, trained in Spain, choreographs a troupe of vibrant young dancers called Flamenco's Next Generation. Their summer series holds matinee performances from mid-July to mid-August on Sundays at 2pm. The María Benitez Theater at the Lodge at Santa Fe is modern and showy, and yet it's intimate enough so you're immersed in the art. Institute for Spanish Arts, P.O. Box 8418. ✆ **505/470-7828.** www. mariabenitez.com. Tickets $5–$15.

Major Concert Halls & All-Purpose Auditoriums

Center for Contemporary Arts and Cinematheque ★ CCA presents the work of internationally, nationally, and regionally known contemporary artists in art exhibitions, dance, music concerts, poetry readings, performance-art events, theater, and video screenings. The Cinematheque screens films from around the world nightly, with special series presented regularly. CCA's galleries are open daily noon to 7:30pm. 1050 Old Pecos Trail. ✆ **505/982-1338.** www.ccasantafe.org. Film tickets $8. Art exhibitions are free; performances range broadly in price.

St. Francis Auditorium This atmospheric music hall, patterned after the interiors of traditional Hispanic mission churches, is noted for its excellent acoustics. The hall hosts a wide variety of musical events, including the Santa Fe Chamber Music Festival in July and August. Museum of Fine Arts, Lincoln and Palace aves. ✆ **505/476-5072.** Ticket prices vary; see above for specific performing-arts companies.

THE CLUB & MUSIC SCENE

In addition to the clubs and bars listed below, there are a number of hotels whose bars and lounges feature some type of entertainment (see chapter 6.)

Country, Jazz & Latin

Chispa! ★ A tapas bar with the *chispa* or "spark" of fun entertainment and dancing, this hot spot next to the dining room at El Meson (p. 93) draws locals of all types. Music ranges from guitar duos to jazz combos and Brazilian music, with flamenco dancers performing on some Saturday nights. On Tango Tuesdays, locals turn out in their tightest dance clothes to party. The tapas are excellent. It's open Tuesday to Saturday. 213 Washington Ave. ✆ **505/983-6756.** www.elmeson-santafe.com. Cover charge for select performances.

Cowgirl Hall of Fame ★ It's difficult to categorize what goes on in this bar and restaurant, but there's live entertainment nightly. Some nights there's blues guitar, others folk music; you might also find progressive rock, comedy, reggae, karaoke, or cowboy poetry. In the summer, this is a great place to sit under the stars and listen to music. 319 S. Guadalupe St. ✆ **505/982-2565.** No cover for music Sun–Mon and Wed; Tues and Thurs–Sat $3–$5 cover. Special performances $10.

Eldorado Hotel ★ In a grand lobby-lounge full of fine art, classical guitarists and pianists perform nightly. 309 W. San Francisco St. ✆ **505/988-4455.** www.eldoradohotel.com.

El Farol ★ This original neighborhood bar of the Canyon Road artists' quarter (its name means "the lantern") is the place to head for local ambience. Its cozy interior is home to Santa Fe's largest and most unusual selection of tapas. Jazz, swing, folk, and most notably, salsa and flamenco musicians (and dancers)—some of national note—perform most nights. On Friday nights the Flamenco Dinner Show starts at 7pm for $25. 808 Canyon Rd. ✆ **505/983-9912.** www.elfarolsf.com. Cover $5.

La Fiesta Lounge ★ Set in the notable La Fonda hotel on the plaza, this night-club offers excellent country bands on weekends, with old- and new-timers two-stepping across the floor. This lively lobby bar offers cocktails, an appetizer menu, and live entertainment nightly. It's a great authentic Santa Fe spot. La Fonda Hotel, 110 E. San Francisco St. ✆ **505/982-5511.** www.lafondasantafe.com.

Snub Out the Smokes

In 2006, smoking in Santa Fe bars and restaurants, including outdoor-dining areas, became illegal. The law was instituted mainly to protect entertainment and hospitality workers from secondhand smoke, but it will likely protect many others as well.

Rock & Disco

Catamount Bar and Grille   The postcollege crowd hangs out at this bar, where live rock and blues music play on weekends. Food is served until 11pm, and there is also a billiards room. 125 E. Water St. © **505/988-7222.**

THE BAR SCENE

The Dragon Room ★   A number of years ago, *International Newsweek* named the Dragon Room at the Pink Adobe (p. 95) one of the top 20 bars in the world. The reason is its spirited but comfortable ambience, which draws students, artists, politicians, and even an occasional celebrity. The decor theme is dragons, which you'll find carved on the front doors as well as depicted on the walls, all within low-lit, aged elegance akin to the Pink Adobe's interior. Live trees also grow through the roof. In addition to the tempting lunch and bar menu, there's always a complimentary bowl of popcorn close at hand. 406 Old Santa Fe Trail. © **505/983-7712.**

El Paseo Bar and Grill   You can almost always catch live music at this casual, unpretentious place. The crowd here is somewhat younger than at most other downtown establishments, and on certain nights, the bar is completely packed. In addition to the open mic night on Tuesdays, a variety of local bands play here regularly—cranking out many types of music, from blues to rock to jazz to bluegrass. Friday happy hour is from 4 to 6pm. 208 Galisteo St. © **505/992-2848.** www.elpaseobar.com. Cover $3–$5 Fri-Sat.

Evangelo's   A popular downtown hangout, with tropical decor and a mahogany bar, this place can get raucous at times. It's a bit seedy, but more than 200 varieties of imported beer are available, and pool tables are an added attraction. On Friday and Saturday nights starting at 9pm and Wednesdays at 7:30pm, live bands play (jazz, rock, or reggae). Evangelo's has reached new fame as one of the bars where Jeff Bridges sang in the 2009 movie *Crazy Heart.* You'll find your share of business people, artists, and even bikers here. The bar downstairs attracts a younger crowd and music. It's open Monday to Saturday noon to 1:30am and Sundays until midnight. 200 W. San Francisco St. © **505/982-9014.** Cover for special performances only.

Milagro 139   This restaurant and lounge that opened in 2010 transports the flavor and feel of New Orleans to the desert. After dinner hours the lounge becomes a dance spot in a courtyard with climbing bougainvilleas and a live tree growing in the middle. A broad range of ages shows up to sip martinis and margaritas and to enjoy live music on Thursday through Saturday nights. Hours are daily 4pm to midnight, later on weekends. 139 W. San Francisco St. © **505/995-0139.** www.milagro139.com.

Vanessie of Santa Fe ★   This is unquestionably Santa Fe's most popular piano bar. The talented Doug Montgomery and Charles Tichenor have a loyal local following. Their repertoire ranges from Bach to Billy Joel, Gershwin to Barry Manilow. They play nightly from 8pm until closing, which could be anywhere from midnight to 2am. There's an extra microphone, so if you're daring (or drunk), you can stand up and accompany the piano and vocals (though this is not a karaoke scene). National celebrities have even joined in—including Harry Connick, Jr. Vanessie's offers a great bar menu. 434 W. San Francisco St. © **505/982-9966.** www.vanessiesantafe.com.

EXCURSIONS FROM SANTA FE

Native American pueblos and ruins, a national monument and national park, Los Alamos (the A-bomb capital of the U.S.), and the scenic and fascinating High Road to Taos are all easy day trips from Santa Fe. A longer drive will take you to Chaco Culture National Historic Park (well worth the time) and to Chama, home of the Cumbres & Toltec Scenic Railroad.

EXPLORING THE NORTHERN PUEBLOS

Of the eight northern pueblos, Tesuque, Pojoaque, Nambe, San Ildefonso, San Juan, and Santa Clara are within about 30 miles of Santa Fe. Picuris (San Lorenzo) is on the High Road to Taos (see section 3, below), and Taos Pueblo is just outside the town of Taos (p. 214).

The six pueblos described in this section can easily be visited in a single day's round-trip from Santa Fe, though I suggest visiting just the two that really give a feel of the ancient lifestyle: San Ildefonso, with its broad plaza, and San Juan, the birthplace of Pope (Poh-*pay*), who led the Pueblo Revolt of 1680. In an easy day trip from Santa Fe you can take in both, with some delicious New Mexican food in Española en route. If you're in the area at a time when you can catch certain rituals, try to see some of the other pueblos as well.

Tesuque Pueblo

Tesuque (Te-*soo*-keh) Pueblo is about 9 miles north of Santa Fe on US 84/285. You'll know that you're approaching the pueblo when you see a large store near the highway. If you're driving north and you get to the unusual Camel Rock and a large roadside casino, you've missed the pueblo entrance.

The 800 pueblo dwellers at Tesuque are faithful to their traditional religion, rituals, and ceremonies. Excavations confirm that a pueblo has existed here at least since the year A.D. 1200; accordingly, this pueblo is

Indian Pueblos & Ancient Cultures

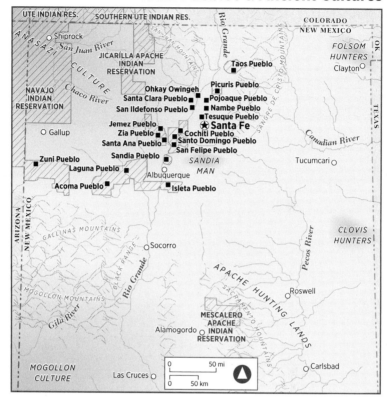

now on the National Register of Historic Places. When you come to the welcome sign at the pueblo, turn right, go a block, and park on the right. You'll see the plaza off to the left. There's not a lot to see; in recent years renovation has brought a new look to some of the homes around it. There's a big open area where dances are held

Pueblo Etiquette

There are personal dwellings and/or important historic sites at pueblos that must be respected as such. Don't climb on the buildings or peek into doors or windows. Don't enter sacred grounds, such as cemeteries and kivas. If you attend a dance or ceremony, remain silent while it is taking place and refrain from applause when it's over. Many pueblos prohibit photography or sketches; others require you to pay a fee for a permit. If you don't respect the privacy of the Native Americans who live at the pueblo, you'll be asked to leave.

and the **San Diego Church,** completed in 2004 on the site of an 1888 structure that burned down. It's the fifth church on the pueblo's plaza since 1641. Visitors are asked to remain in this area.

Some Tesuque women are skilled potters; Ignacia Duran's black-and-white and red micaceous pottery and Teresa Tapia's miniatures and pots with animal figures are especially noteworthy. You'll find many crafts at a gallery on the plaza's southeast corner. The **San Diego Feast Day,** which may feature harvest, buffalo, deer, flag, or Comanche dances, is November 12.

The Tesuque Pueblo's address is Route 42, Box 360-T, Santa Fe, NM 87501 (© **505/983-2667**). Admission to the pueblo is free; however, there is a $20 charge for use of still cameras; special permission is required for filming, sketching, and painting. The pueblo is open daily from 8am to 5pm. **Camel Rock Casino** (© **505/984-8414;** www.camelrockcasino.com) is open Sunday to Wednesday from 8am to 4am, and Thursday to Saturday for 24 hours; it has a snack bar on the premises.

Pojoaque Pueblo

About 6 miles farther north of Tesuque Pueblo on US 84/285, at the junction of NM 502, Pojoaque (Po-*hwa*-keh) Pueblo provides a roadside peek into Pueblo arts. Though small (pop. 2,712) and without a definable village (more modern dwellings exist now), Pojoaque is important as a center for traveler services; in fact, Pojoaque, in its Tewa form, means "water-drinking place." The historical accounts of the Pojoaque people are sketchy, but we do know that in 1890 smallpox took its toll on the Pojoaque population, forcing most of the pueblo residents to abandon their village. Since the 1930s, the population has gradually increased, and in 1990, a war chief and two war captains were appointed. Today, visitors won't find a historic village, but the **Poeh Cultural Center and Museum,** on US 84/285, operated by the pueblo, features a museum, a cultural center, and artists' studios. It's situated within a complex of adobe buildings, including the three-story Sun Tower. There are frequent artist demonstrations, exhibitions, and, in the warmer months, traditional ceremonial dances. Indigenous pottery, embroidery, silverwork, and beadwork are available for sale at the Pojoaque Pueblo Visitor Center nearby.

If you leave US 84/285 and travel on the frontage road back to where the pueblo actually was, you'll encounter lovely orchards and alfalfa fields backed by desert and mountains. There's a modern community center near the site of the old pueblo and church. On December 12, the annual feast day of **Our Lady of Guadalupe** features a buffalo dance.

The pueblo's address is Route 11, Box 71, Santa Fe, NM 87506 (© **505/455-2278**). The pueblo is open every day during daylight hours. The Poeh Center is at 78 Cities of Gold Rd. (© **505/455-3334;** www.poehcenter.com). Admission is free, and it's open daily 8am to 5pm. Sketching, photography, and filming are prohibited.

WHERE TO STAY & DINE

Hilton Santa Fe Golf Resort & Spa at Buffalo Thunder ★★★ Twenty minutes north of Santa Fe, this lively resort offers luxury accommodations and plenty to do for those seeking fun. The structure itself is gigantic, though designers have managed to impart an intimate feel. The rooms pay special attention to details and texture, with carved headboards, Native American art, and granite counter tops. The suites are spacious and have sleeper sofas—a good option for small families. Most rooms have balconies.

Owned by the Pueblo of Pojoaque, the resort features a number of restaurants and lounges, and a contemporary nightclub. Most notable is **Red Sage Restaurant,** featuring Southwest cuisine with Native American accents. The resort offers duffers 36 holes at the Towa Golf Course, Gamblers test their luck with 1,200 slots, a variety of table games, poker and simulcast horse and dog racing. Spa fans enjoy 16,000 square feet of relaxation. In artful treatment rooms, staff members provide a full range of massages and salt glows.

20 Buffalo Thunder Trail, Pojoaque, NM, 87506 🕜 **505/455-5555.** Fax 505/455-0200. www.buffalo thunderresort.com. 395 units. $149–$189 double; $209–$389 suite. AE, DISC, MC, V. Free parking. **Amenities:** 6 restaurants; lounge; casino; children's center; concierge; executive-level rooms; exercise room; golf course; Jacuzzi; 2 pools; room service; sauna; spa; tennis courts. *In room:* A/C, TV, CD player, hair dryer, minibar, Wi-Fi.

Nambe Pueblo

If you're still on US 84/285, continue north from Pojoaque about 3 miles until you come to NM 503; turn right, and travel until you see the Bureau of Reclamation sign for Nambe Falls; turn right on NP 101. Approximately 2 miles farther is Nambe ("mound of earth in the corner"), a 700-year-old Tewa-speaking pueblo (pop. 500), with a solar-powered tribal headquarters, at the foot of the Sangre de Cristo range. Only a few original pueblo buildings remain, including a large round kiva, used today in ceremonies. Pueblo artisans make woven belts, beadwork, and brown micaceous pottery. One of my favorite reasons for visiting this pueblo is to see the small herd of bison that roams on 179 acres set aside for them.

Nambe Falls make a stunning three-tier drop through a cleft in a rock face about 4 miles beyond the pueblo. You can reach the falls via a 15-minute hike on a rocky, clearly marked path that leaves from the picnic area. A recreational site at the reservoir offers fishing, boating (nonmotor boats only), hiking, camping, and picnicking. The **Waterfall Dances** on July 4 and the **Saint Francis of Assisi Feast Day** on October 4, which has buffalo and deer dances, are observed at the pueblo. Recent dry weather has caused cancellations; before setting out, call the pueblo.

The address is Route 1, Box 117-BB, Santa Fe, NM 87506 (🕜 **505/455-2036,** or 505/455-2304 for the Ranger Station). Admission to the pueblo is free, and no photography is allowed. Filming and sketching are prohibited. The pueblo is open daily 8am to 5pm. The recreational site is open 8am to noon and 1 to 5pm April to October.

San Ildefonso Pueblo ★★

Pox Oge, as San Ildefonso Pueblo is called in its own Tewa language, means "place where the water cuts down through," possibly named such because of the way the Rio Grande cuts through the mountains nearby. At Pojoaque, head west on NM 502 and drive about 6 miles to the turnoff. This pueblo has a broad, dusty plaza, with a kiva on one side, ancient dwellings on the other, and a church at the far end. It's nationally famous for its matte-finish, black-on-black pottery, developed by tribeswoman María Martinez in the 1920s. One of the most visited pueblos in northern New Mexico (pop. 1,524), San Ildefonso attracts more than 20,000 visitors a year.

The San Ildefonsos could best be described as rebellious because this was one of the last pueblos to succumb to the reconquest spearheaded by Don Diego de Vargas in 1692. Within view of the pueblo is the volcanic Black Mesa, a symbol of the San Ildefonso people's strength. Through the years, each time San Ildefonso felt itself threatened by enemy forces, the residents, along with members of other pueblos, would hide out up on the butte, returning to the valley only when starvation set in. Today, a visit to the pueblo is valuable mainly in order to see or buy rich black pottery. A few shops surround the plaza, and there's the **San Ildefonso Pueblo Museum** tucked away in the governor's office beyond the plaza. I especially recommend visiting during ceremonial days. **San Ildefonso Feast Day,** on January 23, features the buffalo and Comanche dances in alternate years. **Corn dances,** held in late August or early September, commemorate a basic element in pueblo life, the importance of fertility in all creatures—humans as well as animals—and plants.

The pueblo has a 4½-acre fishing lake that is surrounded by *bosque* (Spanish for "forest"), open April to October. Picnicking is encouraged, though you may want to look at the sites before you decide to stay; some are nicer than others. Camping is not allowed.

The pueblo's address is Route 5, Box 315A, Santa Fe, NM 87506 (© **505/455-3549**). The admission charge is $7 per car. The charge for taking photographs is $10; you'll pay $20 to film and $25 to sketch. If you plan to fish, the charge is $10 for adults and $5 for seniors and children 11 and under, but you'll want to call to be sure the lake is open. The pueblo is open in the summer daily 8am to 5pm; call for weekend hours. In the winter, it's open Monday to Friday 8am to 4:30pm. It's closed for major holidays and tribal events.

Ohkay Owinge (San Juan Pueblo) ★

If you continue north on US 84/285, you will reach Ohkay Owinge, via NM 74, a mile off NM 68, about 4 miles north of Española.

The largest (pop. 6,748) and northernmost of the Tewa-speaking pueblos and headquarters of the Eight Northern Indian Pueblos Council, San Juan is on the east side of the Rio Grande—opposite the 1598 site of San Gabriel, the first Spanish settlement west of the Mississippi River and the first capital of New Spain. In 1598, the Spanish, impressed with the openness and helpfulness of the people of San Juan, decided to establish a capital there (it was moved to Santa Fe 10 years later), making San Juan Pueblo the first to be subjected to Spanish colonization. The Indians were generous, providing food, clothing, shelter, and fuel—they even helped sustain the settlement when its leader Conquistador Juan de Oñate became preoccupied with his search for gold and neglected the needs of his people.

The past and present cohabit here. Though many of the tribe members are Catholics, most of the San Juan tribe still practice traditional religious rituals. Thus, two rectangular kivas flank the church in the main plaza, and *caciques* (pueblo priests) share power with civil authorities. The annual **San Juan Fiesta** is held June 23 and 24; it features buffalo and Comanche dances. Another annual ceremony is the **turtle dance** on December 26. The **Matachine dance,** performed here Christmas Day, vividly depicts the subjugation of the Native Americans by the Catholic Spaniards (p. 24).

THE GREAT PUEBLO Revolt

By the 17th century, the Spanish subjugation of the Native Americans in the region had left them virtual slaves, forced to provide corn, venison, cloth, and labor. They were also forced to participate in Spanish religious ceremonies and to abandon their own religious practices. Under no circumstances were their ceremonies allowed; those caught participating in them were severely punished. In 1676, several Puebloans were accused of sorcery and jailed in Santa Fe. Later they were led to the plaza, where they were flogged or hanged. This incident became a turning point in Indian-Spanish relations, generating an overwhelming feeling of rage in the community. One of the accused, a San Juan Pueblo Indian named Pope, became a leader in the Great Pueblo Revolt of 1680, which led to freedom from Spanish rule for 12 years.

The address of the pueblo is P.O. Box 1099, San Juan Pueblo, NM 87566 (© 505/852-4400 or 505/852-4210). Admission is free. Photography or sketching may be allowed for a fee with prior permission from the governor's office. For information, call the number above. The charge for fishing is $8 for adults and $5 for children and seniors. The pueblo is open every day during daylight hours.

The **Eight Northern Indian Pueblos Council** (© 505/747-1593) is a sort of chamber of commerce and social-service agency.

Fishing and picnicking are encouraged at the **San Juan Tribal Lakes,** open year-round. **Ohkay Casino** (© 505/747-1668; www.ohkay.com) offers table games and slot machines, as well as live music nightly Tuesday through Saturday. It's open 24 hours on weekends.

Santa Clara Pueblo

Close to Española (on NM 5), Santa Clara, with a population of 1,944, is one of the largest pueblos. You'll see the village sprawling across the river basin near the beautiful Black Mesa, rows of tract homes surrounding an adobe central area. Although it's in an incredible setting, the pueblo itself is not much to see; however, a trip through it will give a real feel for the contemporary lives of these people. Though stories vary, the Santa Clarans teach their children that their ancestors once lived in cliffside dwellings named Puye and migrated down to the river bottom in the 13th century. This pueblo is noted for its language program. Artisan elders work with children to teach them their native Tewa language, on the brink of extinction because so many now speak English. This pueblo is also the home of noted potter Nancy Youngblood, who comes from a long line of famous potters and now does alluring contemporary work.

Follow the main route to the old village, where you come to the visitor center, also known as the neighborhood center. There you can get directions to small shops that sell distinctive black incised Santa Clara pottery, red burnished pottery, baskets, and other crafts. One stunning sight here is the cemetery. Stop on the west side of the church and look over the 4-foot wall. It's a primitive site, with plain wooden crosses and some graves adorned with plastic flowers.

There are corn and harvest dances on **Santa Clara Feast Day** (Aug 12); information on other special days (including the corn or harvest dances, as well as children's dances) can be obtained from the pueblo office.

The famed **Puye Cliff Dwellings** (see below) are on the Santa Clara reservation. The pueblo's address is P.O. Box 580, Española, NM 87532 (© **505/753-7326**). A permit is required from the governor's office to enter the pueblo. The fee is $5 and includes permission for photography; filming and sketching are not allowed. The pueblo is open every day from 8am to 4:30pm.

PUYE CLIFFS ★★

The Puye Cliff Dwellings offer a view of centuries of culture so well preserved you can almost hear ancient life clamoring around you. You'll first visit the Harvey House and exhibit hall, which tells some of the history of the site. Next, with a guide, you'll take a fairly steep hike up to a 200-foot cliff face where you'll see caves that were once part of dwellings believed to have been built around 1450. Next, either by bus or ladder, you will travel to the mesa top to see stone dwellings dating from 1200. By 1540, this community's population was at its height, and Puye was the center for a number of villages of the Pajarito Plateau. The guides, ancestors of this culture, help interpret the site.

Unfortunately, Santa Clara Pueblo, which owns Puye, is currently charging a steep price for a visit, as you'll see below. For this reason, I would recommend a visit to Bandelier National Monument (see below) instead. But if you have money and plenty of time (the guided tours—the only way to see the ruins—take upwards of 2 hours), then by all means go. Your best bet is to check the website or call to make sure tours are available.

From the Monday after Easter to Labor Day, the site is open daily 8:30am to 6pm, with tours on the hour from 9am to 5pm. After Labor Day to the week before Easter, daily hours are 9:30am to 3pm, with tours on the hour from 10am to 2pm. The site is closed the week before Easter, June 13, August 12, Christmas Day, and during inclement weather.

In the spring and fall, the site is open from 8:30am to 6pm, and during winter from 9:30am to 4pm, weather permitting. In those off seasons, tours run intermittently, so be sure to call in order to time your visit properly. Admission is $35 per person for adults, $33 for children ages 5 to 14, free for ages 4 and under. To reach Puye from Santa Fe, on US 285, drive 28 miles to Española. Turn left onto US 84 and travel just under a mile. You will cross the Rio Grande. Turn left onto NM 30 and travel south 2 miles to the Puye Cliffs Welcome Center. From there you will travel on Indian Route 601 for 7 miles to Puye. Call © **888/320-5008** (www.puyecliffs.com).

LOS ALAMOS & BANDELIER NATIONAL MONUMENT

Pueblo tribes lived in the rugged Los Alamos area for well over 1,000 years, and an exclusive boys' school operated atop the 7,300-foot plateau from 1918 to 1943. Then, the **Los Alamos National Laboratory** was established here in secrecy, code-named Site Y of the Manhattan Project, the hush-hush wartime program that developed the world's first atomic bombs.

Monument Project director J. Robert Oppenheimer, later succeeded by Norris E. Bradbury, worked along with thousands of scientists, engineers, and technicians in research, development, and production of those early weapons. Today, with an annual budget of $2 billion, the lab operates more than 2,100 facilities and employs about 11,000 people, making it the largest employer in northern New Mexico. The lab is operated by Los Alamos National Security, currently under a contract through the U.S. Department of Energy.

The laboratory is one of the world's foremost scientific institutions. It primarily focuses on nuclear weapons research—the Trident and Minuteman strategic warheads were designed here, for example—and has many other interdisciplinary research programs, including international nuclear safeguards and nonproliferation, space, and atmospheric studies; supercomputing; theoretical physics; biomedical and materials science; and environmental restoration.

Currently Los Alamos National Laboratory is building a limited number of replacement plutonium pits for use in the enduring U.S. nuclear weapons stockpile. The lab has the only plutonium-processing facility in the United States that is capable of producing those components.

An unusual town, Los Alamos has the highest per capita Ph.D. population in the nation—22 percent. If you listen closely you may hear people talk of such complexities as quantum cryptography, trapdoor functions of polynomial integers, reciprocal space, and heterogeneous multicores. With researchers convening here from all over the world, the accents range from Russian to French to Japanese and even a Texas twang or two.

Orientation/Useful Information

Los Alamos is about 35 miles west of Santa Fe and about 65 miles southwest of Taos. From Santa Fe, take US 84/285 north approximately 16 miles to the Pojoaque junction, then turn west on NM 502. Driving time is only about 50 minutes.

Los Alamos is a town of 18,000, spread over the colorful, fingerlike mesas of the Pajarito Plateau, between the Jemez Mountains and the Rio Grande Valley. As NM 502 enters Los Alamos from Santa Fe, it follows Trinity Drive, where accommodations, restaurants, and other services are located. Central Avenue parallels Trinity Drive and has restaurants, galleries, and shops, as well as the **Los Alamos Historical Museum,** 1921 Juniper St. (© **505/662-4493;** free admission) and the **Bradbury Science Museum,** 15th Street and Central Avenue (© **505/667-4444;** free admission). In the spring of 2000, the town was evacuated due to a forest fire that destroyed 400 families' homes. Though no lives were lost, the appearance of Los Alamos and particularly the forest surrounding it—47,000 acres of which burned—were forever changed.

The **Los Alamos Chamber of Commerce,** P.O. Box 460, Los Alamos, NM 87544 (© **505/662-8105;** fax 505/662-8399; www.losalamoschamber.com), runs a visitor center that is open Monday to Saturday 9am to 5pm and Sunday 10am to 3pm. It's at 109 Central Park Sq. (across from the Bradbury Science Museum).

Events

The Los Alamos events schedule includes a **Sports Skiesta** in mid-March; **arts-and-crafts fairs** in May, August, and November; a **county fair, rodeo,** and **arts festival** in August; and a **triathlon** in August/September.

What to See & Do

Aside from the sights described below, Los Alamos offers the **Pajarito Mountain ski area,** Camp May Road (P.O. Box 155), Los Alamos, NM 87544 (✆ 505/662-5725; www.skipajarito.com), with five chairlifts—it's only open on Friday through Sunday and federal holidays. It's an outstanding ski area that rarely gets crowded; many trails are steep and have moguls. Los Alamos also offers the **Los Alamos Golf Course,** 4250 Diamond Dr. (✆ 505/662-8139; www.losalamosgolf.org), where greens fees are around $28 for 18 holes and $17 for 9 holes; and the **Larry R. Walkup Aquatic Center,** 2760 Canyon Rd. (✆ 505/662-8170; www.losalamosnm.us), the highest-altitude indoor Olympic-size swimming pool in the United States. Not far from downtown is the outdoor **Los Alamos County Ice Rink,** with a snack bar and skate rentals, open Thanksgiving to late February (✆ 505/662-4500; www.losalamosnm.us). It's at 4475 West Rd. (take Trinity Dr. to Diamond St., turn left, and watch for the sign on your right). There are no outstanding restaurants in Los Alamos, but if you get hungry, you can stop at the **Central Avenue Grill & Quark Bar ★,** 1789 Central Ave., Ste. 8 (✆ 505/662-2005), a festive gathering place at the center of town that serves salads, sandwiches, pasta dishes and sushi. Science-minded folks gather here in the evenings over drinks. Another option is **Hill Diner,** 1315 Trinity Dr. (✆ 505/662-9745), which serves diner-style fare in a relaxed atmosphere. The chamber of commerce has maps for self-guided historical walking tours, and you can find self-guided driving-tour tapes at stores and hotels around town.

The Art Center at Fuller Lodge   This is a public showcase for work by visual artists from northern New Mexico and the surrounding region. Two annual arts-and-crafts fairs are also held here in August and October. The gallery shop sells local crafts at good prices.

In the same building is the **Los Alamos Arts Council** (✆ 505/663-0477), a multidisciplinary organization that sponsors an art fair in May, as well as evening and noontime cultural programs.

2132 Central Ave., Los Alamos. ✆ **505/662-9331.** www.artfulnm.org. Free admission. Mon–Sat 10am–4pm.

Black Hole 📖   This store/museum is an engineer's dream world, a creative photographer's heaven, and a Felix Unger nightmare. Created by the late Edward Grothus and now run by his children, it's an old grocery store packed to the ceiling with the remains of the nuclear age, from Geiger counters to giant Waring blenders. The Black Hole has been written about in *Wired* magazine and has supplied props for the movies *Silkwood, Earth II,* and *The Manhattan Project.*

4015 Arkansas Ave., Los Alamos. ✆ **505/662-5053.** Free admission. Mon–Sat 10am–5pm.

Bradbury Science Museum ★   This is a great place to get acquainted with what goes on at a weapons production facility after nuclear proliferation. Although the museum is run by Los Alamos National Laboratory, which definitely puts a positive spin on the business of producing weapons, it's a fascinating place to learn about—through dozens of interactive exhibits—the lab's many contributions to science.

Begin in the History Gallery, where you'll learn about the evolution of the site from the Los Alamos Ranch School days through the Manhattan Project to the present, including a 1939 letter from Albert Einstein to President Franklin D. Roosevelt, suggesting research into uranium as a new and important source of energy. Next, move into the Research and Technology Gallery, where you can see work that's been done on the Human Genome Project, including a computer map of human DNA. You can try out a laser and learn about the workings of a particle accelerator. Meanwhile, listen for announcement of the film *The Town That Never Was,* a 16-minute presentation on this community that grew up shrouded in secrecy (shown in the auditorium). Further exploration will take you to the Defense Gallery, where you can test the heaviness of plutonium against that of other substances, see an actual 5-ton Little Boy nuclear bomb (like the one dropped on Hiroshima), and see firsthand how Los Alamos conducts worldwide surveillance of nuclear explosions. The museum also has an exhibit on national defense. It presents issues related to nuclear weapons: why we have them, how they work, how scientists ensure that aging weapons will still work, what treaties govern them, and what environmental-problem sites resulted from their production.

15th St. and Central Ave., Los Alamos. © **505/667-4444.** www.lanl.gov/museum. Free admission. Tues–Sat 10am–5pm; Sun–Mon 1–5pm. Closed New Year's Day, Thanksgiving, Christmas.

Los Alamos Historical Museum ★   Start your visit to this museum next door at Fuller Lodge, a massive vertical-log building built by John Gaw Meem in 1928. The log work is intricate and artistic, and the feel of the old place is warm and majestic. It once housed the dining and recreation hall for the Los Alamos Ranch School for boys and is now a National Historic Landmark. Its current occupants include the museum office and research archives and the Art Center at Fuller Lodge (see above). The museum, located in the small log-and-stone building to the north of Fuller Lodge, depicts area history from prehistoric cliff dwellers to the present. Exhibits range from Native American artifacts to school memorabilia and an excellent Manhattan Project exhibit that offers a more realistic view of the devastation resulting from use of atomic bombs than is offered at the Bradbury Science Museum.

1921 Juniper St., Los Alamos. © **505/662-4493.** www.losalamoshistory.org. Free admission. Summer Mon–Sat 9:30am–4:30pm, Sun 1–4pm; winter Mon–Sat 10am–4pm, Sun 1–4pm. Closed New Year's Day, Easter, Thanksgiving, Christmas.

NEARBY

Bandelier National Monument ★★★   Less than 15 miles south of Los Alamos along NM 4, this site contains stunningly preserved ruins of the ancient cliff-dwelling ancestral Puebloan (Anasazi) culture within 46 square miles of canyon-and-mesa wilderness. The national monument is named after the Swiss-American archaeologist Adolph Bandelier, who explored here in the 1880s. During busy summer months, head out early—there can be a waiting line for cars to park.

After an orientation stop at the visitor center and museum to learn about the culture that flourished here between 1100 and 1550, most visitors follow a trail along Frijoles Creek to the principal ruins. The pueblo site, including an underground kiva, has been stabilized. The biggest thrill for most folks is climbing hardy ponderosa pine ladders to visit an alcove—140 feet above the canyon floor—that was once home to prehistoric people. Tours are self-guided or led by a National Park Service ranger. Be aware that dogs are not allowed on trails.

On summer nights, rangers offer campfire talks about the history, culture, and geology of the area. During the day, nature programs are sometimes offered for

INSIDE A Volcano

While you're in the area, check out the **Valles Caldera National Preserve,** past Bandelier National Monument on NM 4, beginning about 15 miles from Los Alamos. The reserve is all that remains of a volcanic caldera created by a collapse after eruptions nearly a million years ago. When the mountain spewed ashes and dust as far away as Kansas and Nebraska, its underground magma chambers collapsed, forming this great valley—one of the largest volcanic calderas in the world. Lava domes that pushed up after the collapse obstruct a full view across the expanse, but the beauty of the place is still within grasp. Visitors have many guided options for exploring the preserve, from sleigh rides and snowshoeing in winter to fly-fishing and horseback riding in summer. For more information, contact ✆ **866-382-5537** (www.valles caldera.gov).

adults and children. The small museum at the visitor center displays artifacts found in the area.

Elsewhere in the monument area, 70 miles of maintained trails lead to more ruins, waterfalls, and wildlife habitats. However, a number of years ago a fire decimated parts of this area, so periodic closings take place in order to allow the land to reforest.

The separate **Tsankawi** section, reached by an ancient 2-mile trail close to **White Rock,** has a large unexcavated ruin on a high mesa overlooking the Rio Grande Valley. The town of White Rock, about 10 miles southeast of Los Alamos on NM 4, offers spectacular panoramas of the river valley in the direction of Santa Fe; the **White Rock Overlook** is a great picnic spot. Within Bandelier, areas have been set aside for picnicking and camping.

NM 4 (HCR 1, Box 1, Ste. 15, Los Alamos). ✆ **505/672-3861,** ext 517. www.nps.gov/band. Admission $12 per vehicle. Daily during daylight hours. No pets allowed on trails. Closed New Year's Day, Christmas. From Santa Fe take US 84/285 north to Pojoaque. Exit west onto NM 502 toward Los Alamos. Bear right onto NM 4 toward White Rock and continue for 12 miles. Bandelier is on the left. Travel time is approximately 1 hr.

ALONG THE HIGH ROAD TO TAOS ★★

Unless you're in a hurry to get from Santa Fe to Taos, the High Road—also called the Mountain Road or the King's Road—is by far the most fascinating route between the two cities. It begins in lowlands of mystically formed pink and yellow stone, passing by apple and peach orchards and chile farms in the weaving village of **Chimayo.** Then it climbs toward the highlands to the village of **Cordova,** known for its woodcarvers, and higher still to **Truchas,** a renegade arts town where Hispanic traditions and ways of life continue much as they did a century ago. Though I've described this tour from south to north, the most scenic way to see it is from north to south, when you travel down off the mountains rather than up into them. This way, you see more expansive views.

Chimayo

About 28 miles north of Santa Fe on NM 76/285 is the historic weaving center of Chimayo. It's approximately 16 miles past the Pojoaque junction, at the junction of NM 520 and NM 76 via NM 503. In this small village, families still maintain the tradition of crafting hand-woven textiles initiated by their ancestors seven generations ago, in the early 1800s. One such family is the Ortegas, and **Ortega's Weaving Shop** (℃ **505/351-4215;** www.ortegasweaving.com) and **Galeria Ortega** ★ (℃ **505/351-2288;** www.galeriaortegainc.com), both at the corner of NM 520 and NM 76, are fine places to take a close look at this ancient craft. A more humble spot is **Trujillo Weaving Shop** (℃ **505/351-4457**) on NM 76. If you're lucky enough to find the proprietors in, you might get a weaving history lesson. You can see a 100-year-old loom and an even older shuttle carved from apricot wood. The weavings you'll find are some of the best of the Rio Grande style, with rich patterns, many made from naturally dyed wool. Also on display are some fine Cordova woodcarvings. Also check out **Centinela Traditional Arts,** 946 NM 76 (℃ **505/351-2180;** www.chimayoweavers.com), for a good selection of rugs made by weavers from up and down the Rio Grande Valley. Watch for the chenille shawls by Lore Wills.

One of the best places to shop in Chimayo, **Chimayo Trading and Mercantile** ★ (℃ **505/351-4566**), on NM 76, is a richly cluttered store carrying Pueblo pottery, Navajo weavings, and local arts and crafts as well as select imports. It has a good selection of *katsinas* and Hopi corn maidens. Look for George Zarolinski's fused glass.

Many people come to Chimayo to visit **El Santuario de Nuestro Señor de Esquipulas (The Shrine of Our Lord of Esquipulas)** ★★ (℃ **505/351-4360;** holyfamily@cybermesa.com), better known simply as El Santuario de Chimayo. Ascribed with miraculous powers of healing, this church has attracted thousands of pilgrims since its construction in 1816. Up to 30,000 people participate in the annual Good Friday pilgrimage, many of them walking from as far away as Albuquerque. Although only the earth in the anteroom beside the altar is presumed to have the gift of healing powers, the entire shrine radiates true serenity. A National Historic Landmark, the church has five beautiful *reredos* (panels of sacred paintings)— one behind the main altar and two on each side of the nave. Each year during the fourth weekend in July, the military exploits of the 9th-century Spanish saint Santiago are celebrated in a weekend fiesta, including games and music. The Santuario is open daily March to September 9am to 6pm and October to February 9am to 5pm. Please remember that this is a place of worship, so quiet is always appreciated.

A good place to stop for a quick bite, **Leona's Restaurante de Chimayo** (℃ **505/351-4569**) is right next door to the Santuario de Chimayo. Leona herself presides over this little taco and burrito stand with plastic tables inside and, during warm months, out. Burritos and soft tacos made with chicken, beef, or veggie-style with beans will definitely tide you over en route to Taos or Santa Fe. Open Thursday through Monday 11am to 5pm. Right next door to the Santuario, look for **El Portrero Trading Post** (℃ **505/351-4112**), a great place to buy rosary beads and votive candles, and, most notably, local woodcarvings. During a recent visit there, I found the owners roasting *piñon* nuts, the scent blending with that of the local red chile they sell. I bought a bag of nuts to crunch on as I headed higher into the mountains.

Nearby **Santa Cruz Lake** provides water for Chimayo Valley farms and also offers a recreation site for trout fishing and camping at the edge of the Pecos Wilderness. During busy summer months, trash might litter its shores. To reach the lake from Chimayo, drive 2 miles south on NM 520, then turn east on NM 503 and travel 4 miles.

WHERE TO STAY

Casa Escondida ★ On the outskirts of Chimayo, this inn is a good home base for exploring the Sangre de Cristo Mountains and their many soulful farming villages. Decor is simple and classic, with Mission-style furniture lending a colonial feel. The breakfast room is a sunny atrium with French doors that open out in summer to a grassy yard spotted with apricot trees. The rooms are varied; all of my favorites are within the main house. The Sun Room catches all that passionate northern New Mexico sun upon its red brick floors and on its private flagstone patio as well. It has an elegant feel and connects with a smaller room, so it's a good choice for families. The Vista is on the second story. It has a wrought-iron queen-size bed as well a twin, and it opens out onto a large deck offering spectacular sunset views. The casita adjacent to the main house has a kiva fireplace, a stove, and a minifridge, as well as nice meadow views.

P.O. Box 142, Chimayo, NM 87522. **✆ 800/643-7201** or 505/351-4805. Fax 505/351-2575. www. casaescondida.com. 8 units. $99–$159 double. Rates include full breakfast. MC, V. Pets welcome in four rooms for a small fee; prearrangement required. **Amenities:** Jacuzzi. *In room:* Kitchenette (in 1 room), no phone.

WHERE TO DINE

Restaurante Rancho de Chimayo ★★ NEW MEXICAN For as long as I can remember, my family and many of my friends' families have scheduled trips into northern New Mexico to coincide with lunch or dinner at this atmospheric restaurant. In an adobe home built by Hermenegildo Jaramillo in the 1880s, it's now run as a restaurant by his descendants. Over the years the restaurant has become so famous that tour buses now stop here. However, the food is still delicious. In the warmer months, request a spot on the terraced patio. During winter, you'll be seated in the atrium or one of a number of cozy rooms with thick viga ceilings. The food is native New Mexican, prepared from generations-old Jaramillo family recipes. You can't go wrong with the chicken enchiladas with green chile. For variety you might want to try the *combinación picante* (*carne adovada*, tamale, enchilada, beans, and *posole*). Each plate comes with a fluffy *sopaipilla*. With a little honey, who needs dessert? The full bar serves tasty margaritas.

300 CR 98 (¼ mile west of the Santuario), Chimayo, NM 87522. **✆ 505/984-2100.** www.ranchodechimayo.com. Reservations recommended. Main courses $7–$10 lunch, $9–$21 dinner. AE, DC, DISC, MC, V. May–Oct daily 11:30am–9pm, Sat–Sun breakfast 8:30–10:30am; Nov–Apr Tues–Sun 11:30am–8:30pm.

Cordova

Just as Chimayo is famous for its weaving, the village of Cordova, about 7 miles east on NM 76, is noted for its woodcarving. It's easy to whiz by this village, nestled below the High Road, but don't. Just a short way through this truly traditional northern New Mexico town is a gem: **The Castillo Gallery ★** (**✆ 505/351-4067**), a mile into the village of Cordova, carries moody and colorful acrylic paintings by Paula Castillo, as well as her metal welded sculptures. It also carries the work of

HIGH ON Art

If you really like art and want to meet artists, check out one of the **Art Studio Tours** held in the fall in the region. Artists spend months preparing their best work, and then open their doors to visitors. Wares range from pottery and paintings to furniture and woodcarvings to *ristras* and dried-flower arrangements. The most notable tour is the **High Road Studio Art Tour** (www.high roadnewmexico.com) in mid- to late September. If you're not in the region during that time, watch the newspapers (such as the *Santa Fe New Mexican*'s Friday edition, "Pasatiempo") for notices of other art-studio tours. Good ones are held in **Galisteo** (in mid-Oct; www.galisteostudiotour.com); **Abiquiu** (early Sept; www.abiquiustudiotour.org); **El Rito** (mid-Oct; www.elritostudiotour. org); and **Dixon** (early Nov; www.dixon arts.org). If you're not here during those times, you can still visit many of the galleries listed on the websites.

Terry Enseñat Mulert, whose contemporary woodcarvings are treasures of the high country. En route to the Castillo, you may want to stop in at two other local carvers' galleries. The first you'll come to is that of **Sabinita Lopez Ortiz;** the second belongs to her cousin, **Gloria Ortiz.** Both are descendants of the noted José Dolores Lopez. Carved from cedar wood and aspen, their works range from simple *santos* (statues of saints) to elaborate scenes of birds.

Truchas

Robert Redford's 1988 movie *The Milagro Beanfield War* featured the town of Truchas (which means "trout"). A former Spanish colonial outpost built on top of an 8,000-foot mesa, 4 miles east of Cordova, it was chosen as the site for the film in part because traditional Hispanic culture is still very much in evidence. Subsistence farming is prevalent here. The scenery is spectacular: 13,101-foot Truchas Peak dominates one side of the mesa, and the broad Rio Grande Valley dominates the other.

Look for the **High Road Marketplace ★** (© 866/343-5381 or 505/689-2689), an artists' co-op gallery with a variety of offerings ranging from jewelry to landscape paintings to a broad range of crosses made from tin, rusted metal, and nails. Be sure to find your way into the **Cordovas' Handweaving Workshop** (© 505/689-1124). In the center of town, this tiny shop is run by Harry Cordova, a fourth-generation weaver with a unique style. His works tend to be simpler than many Rio Grande weavings, utilizing mainly stripes in the designs.

Just down the road from Cordovas' is **Hand Artes Gallery** (© 800/689-2441 or 505/689-2443), a definite surprise in this remote region. Here you'll find an array of contemporary as well as representational art from noted regional artists. Look for Sheila Keeffe's worldly painted panels, and Norbert Voelkel's colorful paintings and monoprints.

About 6 miles east of Truchas on NM 76 is the small town of **Las Trampas,** noted for its 1780 **San José de Gracia Church,** which, with its thick walls and elegant lines, might possibly be the most beautiful of all New Mexico churches built during the Spanish colonial period.

11 Picuris (San Lorenzo) Pueblo & Peñasco

Not far from the regional education center of Peñasco, about 24 miles from Chimayo, near the intersection of NM 75 and NM 76, is the Picuris (San Lorenzo) Pueblo (© 575/587-2519; www.indianpueblo.org/19pueblos/picuris.html). The 375 citizens of this 15,000-acre mountain pueblo, native Tewa speakers, consider themselves a sovereign nation: Their forebears never made a treaty with any foreign country, including the United States. Thus, they observe a traditional form of tribal council government. A few of the original mud-and-stone houses still stand, as does a lovely church. A striking aboveground ceremonial kiva called "the Roundhouse," built at least 700 years ago, and some historic excavated kivas and storerooms are on a hill above the pueblo and are open to visitors. The **annual feast days** at San Lorenzo Church are August 9 and 10.

The people here are modern enough to have fully computerized their public showcase operations as Picuris Tribal Enterprises. Besides running the Hotel Santa Fe in the state capital, they own the **Picuris Pueblo Museum and Visitor's Center,** where weaving, beadwork, and distinctive reddish-brown clay cooking pottery are exhibited daily 8am to 5pm. Self-guided tours through the old village ruins begin at the museum and cost $5; the camera fee is $6; sketching and video camera fees are $25. There's also an information center, crafts shop, and restaurant. Fishing permits ($11 for all ages) are available, as are permits to camp ($8) at Tu-Tah Lake, which is regularly stocked with trout.

You might want to plan your High Road trip to include a visit to **Sugar Nymphs Bistro ★★**, 15046 NM 75 (© 575/587-0311), for some inventive food. Inside a vintage theater in the little farming village of Peñasco, Kai Harper, former executive chef at Greens in San Francisco, prepares contemporary bistro cuisine, using local and seasonal ingredients. Lunch brings imaginative pizza, salads, and burgers, while dinner includes a full range of entrees. Some of my favorites include a goat-cheese salad and a chicken breast with green-chile cream. All breads and desserts are baked in-house by Kai's partner Ki Holste, including a delectable chocolate-pecan pie. It goes great with a range of coffee drinks, including a perfect latte. The Bistro also sponsors family-oriented events in the theater. On a recent visit they were screening *The Milagro Beanfield War,* but they also have trapeze and puppet shows. Call ahead of time to find out when you can partake in these; they usually occur on and around weekends. In summer, the cafe is open Tuesday to Saturday 11:30am to 3pm and Thursday to Saturday 5:30 to 7:30 or 8pm, with Sunday brunch 10am to 2pm. In winter, spring, and fall, the schedule is abbreviated. Call ahead to be sure it's open.

About a mile east of Peñasco on NM 75 is **Vadito,** the former center for a conservative Catholic brotherhood, the Penitentes, early in the 20th century. You'll see a small adobe chapel on the left. Also watch for Penitente crosses scattered about the area, often on hilltops.

Dixon & Embudo

Taos is about 24 miles north of Peñasco via NM 518, but day-trippers from Santa Fe can loop back to the capital by taking NM 75 west from Picuris Pueblo. Dixon, approximately 12 miles west of Picuris, and its twin village Embudo, a mile farther on NM 68 at the Rio Grande, are home to many artists and craftspeople who exhibit their works during the annual **autumn show** sponsored by the Dixon Arts

Lowriders: CAR ART

While cruising Española's main drag, don't drop your jaw if you see the front of a car rise up off the ground and then sink down again, or if you witness another that appears to be scraping its underbelly on the pavement. These novelties are part of a car culture that thrives in northern New Mexico. Traditionally, the owners use late-model cars, which they soup up with such novelties as elaborate chrome, metal chain steering wheels, even portraits of Our Lady of Guadalupe painted on the hood. If you're interested in seeing the Custom Car and Truck Show put on by local car clubs (and often cosponsored by local casinos), call the Española Valley Chamber of Commerce for information (✆ **505/753-2831;** www.espanola nmchamber.com).

Association. If you get to Embudo at mealtime, stop in at **Embudo Station** (✆ **505/852-4707;** www.embudostation.com), a restaurant right on the banks of the Rio Grande. From mid-April to October—the only time it's open—you can sit on the patio under giant cottonwoods and sip the restaurant's own microbrewed beer (try the green-chile ale, its most celebrated) and signature wines while watching the peaceful Rio flow by. The specialty here is Southwestern food, but you'll find other tantalizing tastes as well. Try the rainbow trout roasted on a cedar plank. The restaurant is generally open Tuesday to Sunday noon to 9pm, but call before making plans. It's especially known for its jazz on Sunday, an affair that PBS once featured.

To taste more of the local grape, follow signs to **La Chiripada Winery** (✆ **505/579-4437;** www.lachiripada.com), whose product is quite good, especially to those who don't know that New Mexico has a long winemaking history. Local pottery is also sold in the tasting room. The winery is open Monday to Saturday 10am to 5pm, Sunday noon to 5pm.

Two more small villages lie in the Rio Grande Valley at 6-mile intervals south of Embudo on NM 68. **Velarde** is a fruit-growing center; in fall, the road here is lined with stands selling fresh fruit or crimson chile *ristras* and wreaths of native plants. **Alcalde** is the site of Los Luceros, a restored early-17th-century home that will soon house a school for Native American and Hispanic filmmakers. The school is a collaboration of efforts between the state of New Mexico and actor Robert Redford. The unique **Dance of the Matachines,** a Moorish-style ritual brought from Spain, is performed here on holidays and feast days (p. 24).

Española

The commercial center of Española (pop. 9,688) no longer has the railroad that led to its establishment in the 1880s, but it may have New Mexico's greatest concentration of **lowriders.** These are late-model customized cars, so called because their suspension leaves them sitting quite close to the ground. For details, see the box below.

Sights of interest in Española include the **Bond House Museum** (✆ **505/747-8535**), a Victorian-era adobe home that exhibits local history and art, and the **Santa Cruz Church,** built in 1733 and renovated in 1979, which houses many fine

GEORGIA O'KEEFFE & NEW MEXICO: A DESERT romance

In June 1917, during a short visit to the Southwest, the painter Georgia O'Keeffe (born 1887) visited New Mexico for the first time. She was immediately enchanted by the stark scenery; even after her return to the energy and chaos of New York City, her mind wandered frequently to New Mexico's arid land and undulating mesas. However, it wasn't until coaxed by the arts patron and "collector of people" Mabel Dodge Luhan 12 years later that O'Keeffe returned to the multihued desert of her daydreams.

O'Keeffe was reportedly ill, both physically and emotionally, when she arrived in Santa Fe in April 1929. New Mexico seemed to soothe her spirit and heal her physical ailments almost magically. Two days after her arrival, Luhan persuaded O'Keeffe to move into her home in Taos. There, she would be free to paint and socialize as she liked.

In Taos, O'Keeffe began painting what would become some of her best-known canvases—close-ups of desert flowers and objects such as cow and horse skulls. "The color up there is different . . . the blue-green of the sage and the mountains, the wildflowers in bloom," O'Keeffe once said of Taos. "It's a different kind of color from any I've ever seen—there's nothing like that in north Texas or even in Colorado." Taos transformed not only her art, but her personality as well. She bought a car

and learned to drive. Sometimes, on warm days, she ran naked through the sage fields. That August, a new, rejuvenated O'Keeffe rejoined her husband, photographer Alfred Stieglitz, in New York.

The artist returned to New Mexico year after year, spending time with Luhan as well as staying at the isolated Ghost Ranch. She drove through the countryside in her snappy Ford, stopping to paint in her favorite spots along the way. Until 1949, O'Keeffe always returned to New York in the fall. Three years after Stieglitz's death, though, O'Keeffe relocated permanently to New Mexico, spending each winter and spring in Abiquiu and each summer and fall at Ghost Ranch. Georgia O'Keeffe died in Santa Fe in 1986.

A great way to see Ghost Ranch is on a hike that climbs above the mystical area. Take US 84 north from Española about 36 miles to Ghost Ranch and follow the road to the Ghost Ranch office. The ranch is owned by the Presbyterian Church, and the staff will supply you with a primitive map for the **Kitchen Mesa** and **Chimney Rock** hikes. If you hike there, be sure to check in at the front desk, which is open Monday to Saturday from 8am to 5pm. For more information, contact **Ghost Ranch,** 401 Old Taos Hwy., Santa Fe (℃ **505/685-4333;** www. ghostranch.org).

examples of Spanish colonial religious art. The **Convento,** built to resemble a colonial cathedral, on the Española Plaza (at the junction of NM 30 and US 84), houses a variety of shops, including a trading post and an antiques gallery, as well as a display room for the Historical Society. Major events include the July **Fiesta de Oñate,** commemorating the valley's founding in 1596; the October **Tri-Cultural Art Festival** on the Northern New Mexico Community College campus; the week-long **Summer Solstice** celebration staged in June by the nearby Hacienda de Guru

Ram Das (☎ 888/346-2420); and **Peace Prayer Day,** an outdoor festival in mid-June—featuring art, music, food, guest speakers, and more—in the Jemez Mountains (☎ 877/707-3221; www.peaceprayerday.org).

Complete information on Española and the vicinity can be obtained from the **Española Valley Chamber of Commerce,** no. 1 Calle de Las Espanolas, NM 87532 (☎ 505/753-2831; www.espanolanmchamber.com).

If you admire the work of Georgia O'Keeffe, try to plan a short trip to **Abiquiu,** a tiny town at a bend of the Rio Chama, 14 miles south of Ghost Ranch and 22 miles north of Española on US 84. When you see the surrounding terrain, it will be clear that this was the inspiration for many of her startling landscapes. **O'Keeffe's adobe home ★** (where she lived and painted) is open for public tours. However, a reservation must be made in advance; the fee for adults is $30 (some discounts apply) for a 1-hour tour. A number of tours are given each week—on Tuesday, Thursday, and Friday (mid-Mar to late Nov only)—and a limited number of people are accepted per tour. Visitors are not permitted to take pictures. Fortunately, O'Keeffe's home remains as it was when she lived there (until 1986). Call several months in advance for reservations (☎ 505/685-4539; www.okeeffemuseum.org).

If you're in the area and need gas for your car, a snack for yourself, or goodies for a picnic, stop in at **Bode's** on US 84 in Abiquiu (☎ 505/685-4422). The general store for the area, this place has shovels and irrigation boots, and better yet, cold drinks, gourmet sandwiches, and other deli items—even a hearty green-chile stew.

WHERE TO STAY & DINE

A fun side trip while in the area is the village of **El Rito.** One of the state's best chile spots is there, at the family-owned restaurant **El Farolito ★★** at 1212 Main St. (☎ 575/581-9509). The remote place has been written about in *Gourmet* and *Travel + Leisure,* and it's no wonder—their enchiladas are some of the best in the state. The hours vary, so call ahead.

El Paragua ★ NORTHERN NEW MEXICAN   Every time I enter El Paragua (which means "the umbrella"), with its red-tile floors and colorful Saltillo-tile trimmings, I feel as though I've stepped into Mexico. The restaurant opened in 1958 as a small taco stand owned by two brothers, and through the years it has received praise from many sources, including *Gourmet* magazine and N. Scott Momaday, writing for the *New York Times.* You can't go wrong ordering the enchilada suprema, a chicken-and-cheese enchilada with onion and sour cream. Also on the menu are fajitas and a variety of seafood dishes and steaks, including the *churrasco Argentino.* Served at your table in a hot brazier, it's cooked in a green-herb salsa chimichurri. There's a full bar from which you may want to try Don Luis's Italian coffee, made with a coffee-flavored liquor called Tuaca. For equally excellent but faster food, skip next door to the kin restaurant **El Parasol ★** and order a guacamole chicken taco—the best in the region.

603 Santa Cruz Rd., Española (off the main drag; turn east at Long John Silver's). ☎ **505/753-3211.** www.elparagua.com. Reservations recommended. Main courses $11–$22. AE, DISC, MC, V. Mon–Fri 11am–9pm; Sat 9am–9pm; Sun 9am–8pm.

Ojo Caliente Mineral Springs Resort & Spa ★★ 📷   This newly renovated retreat offers fine lodging and quality soaks and spa treatments. A National Historic Site, no other hot spring in the world has Ojo Caliente's combination of minerals, and these are split into separate pools so visitors can partake of the healing qualities of each. If the weather is warm enough, the outdoor mud bath is a treat.

The lodging options range from posh cliffside rooms with fireplaces and their own mineral soaking tubs on a patio to very basic ones with a shared shower. Lodging rates include access to all mineral pools for both the day of arrival and the day of departure.

The pools are open daily 8am to 10pm. Children 12 and under are welcome in the springs from 10am to 6pm in the large pool only and with adult supervision. Mineral springs entry Monday to Thursday costs $16 adult and $12 for children 12 and under; Friday to Sunday and holidays, it's $24 adult and $18 children, with reduced rates after 6pm. Private pools are available.

50 Los Baños Dr., Ojo Caliente, NM 87549. (C) **800/222-9162**. Fax 505/583-9198. www.ojospa.com. 48 units. $119–$329 double; $399–$449 house for 4 guests. Additional person $50. AE, DISC, MC, V. **Amenities:** Restaurant; lounge; bikes; concierge; pool; sauna; spa; steam room. *In room:* A/C, TV, fridge, hair dryer, Wi-Fi. On US 285, 45 miles northwest of Santa Fe and 50 miles southwest of Taos.

Rancho de San Juan Country Inn & Three Forks Restaurant ★★★   Thirty eight miles from Santa Fe, between Española and Ojo Caliente, this inn set on 225 acres provides an authentic northern New Mexico desert experience with the comforts of a luxury hotel. The original part of the inn comprises four recently renovated and enlarged rooms around a central courtyard, all with fireplaces. Additional casitas with kitchens are in the outlying hills. Rooms here are open, bright, and decorated with a creative mix from the owners' personal art collections. From private patios, you'll enjoy spectacular views of desert landscapes and distant, snow-capped peaks. The Kiva Suite is the most innovative, with a round bedroom and a skylight just above the bed, perfect for stargazing.

Meals at the **Three Forks Restaurant** are delicious, served in a room with contemporary decor that looks out on the desert. The weekly seasonal menus often take a French-inspired twist on Southwest ingredients and include such selections as Gruyère-stuffed avocado croquets with almond cream for an appetizer, a sautéed halibut with lemon-parsley butter and bacon mashed potatoes for an entree ($35), and a chocolate mousse tart with whipped cream for dessert. The restaurant also has an impressive wine list that includes more than 250 selections; it has won *Wine Spectator*'s "Award of Excellence" since 1999. **Note:** I've received comments that the prices both at the inn and restaurant are too expensive.

US 285 (en route to Ojo Caliente), P.O. Box 4140, Fairview Station, Española, NM 87533. (C) **505/753-6818**. www.ranchodesanjuan.com. 13 units. $285–$485 double. AE, MC, V. **Amenities:** Restaurant; concierge; spa treatments. *In room:* A/C (in most), CD player, fridge, hair dryer.

PECOS NATIONAL HISTORIC PARK

About 15 miles east of Santa Fe, I-25 meanders through **Glorieta Pass,** site of an important Civil War skirmish. In March 1862, volunteers from Colorado and New Mexico, along with Fort Union regulars, defeated a Confederate force marching on Santa Fe, thereby turning the tide of Southern encroachment in the West.

Follow NM 50 east to **Pecos** for about 7 miles. This quaint town, well off the beaten track since the interstate was constructed, is the site of a noted **Benedictine** monastery. About 26 miles north of here on NM 63 is the village of **Cowles,** gateway to the natural wonderland of the **Pecos Wilderness.** There are many camping, picnicking, and fishing locales en route.

Pecos National Historical Park ★★ (ⓒ **505/757-7200;** www.nps.gov/peco), about 2 miles south of the town of Pecos off NM 63, contains the ruins of a 15th-century pueblo and 17th- and 18th-century missions that jut up spectacularly from a high meadow. Coronado mentioned Pecos Pueblo in 1540: "It is feared through the land," he wrote. The approximately 2,000 Native Americans here farmed in irrigated fields and hunted wild game. Their pueblo had 660 rooms and many kivas. By 1620, Franciscan monks had established a church and convent. Military and natural disasters took their toll on the pueblo, and in 1838, the 20 surviving Pecos went to live with relatives at the Jemez Pueblo.

The **E. E. Fogelson Visitor Center** tells the history of the Pecos people in a well-done, chronologically organized exhibit, complete with dioramas. A 1.5-mile loop trail begins at the center and continues through Pecos Pueblo and the **Misión de Nuestra Señora de Los Angeles de Porciuncula** (as the church was formerly called). This excavated structure—170 feet long and 90 feet wide at the transept—was once the most magnificent church north of Mexico City.

Pecos National Historical Park is open daily 8am to 6pm (until 5pm Labor Day to Memorial Day). It's closed January 1 and December 25. Admission is $3 per person age 17 and over.

CHACO CULTURE NATIONAL HISTORIC PARK ★★★

A combination of a stunning setting and well-preserved ruins makes the long drive to **Chaco Culture National Historic Park,** often referred to as Chaco Canyon, worth the trip. Whether you come from the north or south, you drive in on a dusty (and sometimes muddy) road that seems to add to the authenticity and adventure of this remote New Mexico experience.

When you finally arrive, you walk through stark desert country that seems perhaps ill suited as a center of culture. However, the ancestral Puebloan (Anasazi) people successfully farmed the lowlands and built great masonry towns, which connected with other towns over a wide-ranging network of roads crossing this desolate place.

What's most interesting here is how changes in architecture—beginning in the mid-800s, when the Anasazi started building on a larger scale than they had previously—chart the area's cultural progress. The Anasazi used the same masonry techniques that tribes had used in smaller villages in the region (walls one stone thick, with generous use of mud mortar), but they built stone villages of multiple stories with rooms several times larger than in the previous stage of their culture. Within a century, six large pueblos were underway. This pattern of a single large pueblo with oversize rooms, surrounded by conventional villages, caught on throughout the region. New communities built along these lines sprang up. Old villages built similarly large pueblos. Eventually there were more than 75 such towns, most of them closely tied to Chaco by an extensive system of roads. Aerial photos show hundreds of miles of roads connecting these towns with the Chaco pueblos, one of the longest running 42 miles straight north to Salmon Ruins and the Aztec Ruins. It is this road network that leads some scholars to believe that Chaco was the center of a unified Anasazi society.

This progress led to Chaco becoming the economic center of the San Juan Basin by A.D. 1000. As many as 5,000 people may have lived in some 400 settlements in and around Chaco. As masonry techniques advanced through the years, walls rose more than four stories in height. Some of these are still visible today.

Chaco's decline after 1½ centuries of success coincided with a drought in the San Juan Basin between A.D. 1130 and 1180. Scientists still argue vehemently over why the site was abandoned and where the Chacoans went. Many believe that an influx of outsiders may have brought new rituals to the region, causing a schism among tribal members. Most agree, however, that the people drifted away to more hospitable places in the region and that their descendants are today's Pueblo people.

This is an isolated area, and there are **no services** available within or close to the park—no food, gas, auto repairs, firewood, lodging (besides the campground), and drinking water (other than at the visitor center) are available. Overnight camping is permitted year-round. If you're headed toward Santa Fe after a day at the park and looking for a place to spend the night, one nice option is the **Cañon del Rio–A Riverside Inn,** 16445 Scenic Hwy. 4, Jemez Springs, NM 87025 (© **505/829-4377;** www.canondelrio.com; p. 288).

Essentials

GETTING THERE To get to Chaco from Santa Fe, take I-25 south to Bernalillo, then US 550 northwest. Turn off US 550 at CR 7900 (3 miles southeast of Nageezi and about 50 miles west of Cuba at mile 112.5). Follow the signs from US 550 to the park boundary (21 miles). This route includes 8 miles of paved road (CR 7900) and 13 miles of rough dirt road (CR 7950). This is the recommended route. NM 57 from Blanco Trading Post is closed. The trip takes 3½ to 4 hours. Farmington is the nearest population center, a 1½-hour drive away. The park can also be reached from Grants via I-40 west to NM 371, which you follow north to Indian Route 9, east, and north again on NM 57 (IR 14), with the final 19 miles ungraded dirt. This route is rough to impassable and is not recommended for RVs.

Whichever way you come, call ahead to inquire about **road conditions** (© **505/827-5100;** www.nmroads.com) before leaving the paved highways. The dirt roads can get extremely muddy and dangerous after rain or snow, and afternoon thunderstorms are common in late summer. Roads often flood when it rains.

VISITOR INFORMATION Ranger-guided walks and campfire talks are available in the summer at the visitor center where you can get self-guiding trail brochures and permits for the overnight campground (see "Camping," below). If you want information before you leave home, write to the Superintendent, Chaco Culture National Historical Park, 1808 CR 7950, Nageezi, NM 87037 (© **505/786-7014;** www.nps.gov/chcu).

ADMISSION FEES & HOURS Admission is $8 per car; a campsite is $10 extra. The visitor center is open daily from 8am to 5pm. Trails are open from sunrise to sunset.

Seeing the Highlights

Exploring the ruins and hiking are the most popular activities here. A series of pueblo ruins stand within 5 or 6 miles of each other on the broad, flat, treeless canyon floor. Plan to spend at least 3 to 4 hours here driving to and exploring the different pueblos. A one-way road from the visitor center loops up one side of the canyon and down the other. Parking lots are scattered along the road near the various pueblos; from most, it's only a short walk to the ruins.

You may want to focus your energy on seeing **Pueblo Bonito,** the largest prehistoric Southwest Native American dwelling ever excavated. It contains giant kivas and 800 rooms covering more than 3 acres. Also, the **Pueblo Alto Trail** is a nice hike that takes you up on the canyon rim so that you can see the ruins from above—in the afternoon, with thunderheads building, the views are spectacular. If you're a cyclist, stop at the visitor center to pick up a map outlining rideable trails

Camping

Gallo Campground, within the park, is quite popular with hikers. It's about 1 mile east of the visitor center; fees are $10 per night. The campground has 49 sites (group sites are also available). The campgrounds have fire grates (bring your own wood or charcoal), central toilets, and nonpotable water. Drinking water is available only at the visitor center. The campground cannot accommodate trailers over 30 feet.

Remember, there is no place to stock up on supplies once you start the arduous drive to the canyon, so if you're camping, make sure to be well supplied, especially with water, before you leave home base.

CHAMA

Some of my best outdoor adventuring has taken place in the area surrounding this pioneer village of 1,250 people at the base of the 10,000-foot Cumbres Pass. With backpack on, I cross-country skied high into the mountains and stayed the night in a yurt (Mongolian hut), the next day waking to hundreds of acres of snowy fields to explore. Another time, I headed down **Rio Chama,** an official wild and scenic river, on rafts and in kayaks following the course that Navajos, Utes, and Comanches once traveled to raid the Pueblo Indians down river. The campsites along the way were pristine, with mule deer threading through the trees beyond our tents. In a more recent visit to the village, it was summertime, and I'd just come from Durango, which was packed with tourists, to hike, raft, and ride the train. Chama was still quiet, and I realized Chama is New Mexico's undiscovered Durango, without the masses.

Bordered by three wilderness areas, the Carson, Rio Grande, and Santa Fe national forests, the area is indeed prime for hunting, fishing, cross-country skiing, snowmobiling, snowshoeing, and hiking.

Another highlight here is America's longest and highest narrow-gauge coal-fired steam line, the **Cumbres & Toltec Scenic Railroad,** which winds through valleys and mountain meadows 64 miles between Chama and Antonito, Colorado. The village of Chama boomed when the railroad arrived in 1881. A rough-and-ready frontier town, the place still maintains that flavor, with lumber and ranching making up a big part of the economy.

Landmarks to watch for are the **Brazos Cliffs** and waterfall and **Heron and El Vado lakes.** Tierra Amarilla, the Rio Arriba County seat, is 14 miles south, and is at the center—along with Los Ojos and Los Brazos—of a wool-raising and weaving tradition where local craftspeople still weave masterpieces. Dulce, governmental seat of the Jicarilla Apache Indian Reservation, is 27 miles west.

Essentials

GETTING THERE From Santa Fe, take US 84 north (2 hr.). From Taos, take US 64 west (2½ hr.). From Farmington, take US 64 east (2¼ hr.).

VISITOR INFORMATION The **New Mexico Visitor Information Center,** P.O. Box 697, Chama, NM 87520 (② **575/756-2235**), is at 2372 US 17. It's open daily from 8am to 6pm in the summer, and from 8am to 5pm in the winter. At the same address is the **Chama Valley Chamber of Commerce** (② **800/477-0149** or 575/756-2306; www.chamavalley.com).

All Aboard the Historic C&T Railroad

Cumbres & Toltec Scenic Railroad ★★ 📷 If you have a passion for the past and for incredible scenery, climb aboard America's longest and highest narrow-gauge steam railroad, the historic C&T. It operates on a 64-mile track between Chama and Antonito, Colorado. Built in 1880 as an extension of the Denver and Rio Grande line to serve the mining camps of the San Juan Mountains, it is perhaps the finest surviving example of what once was a vast network of remote Rocky Mountain railways.

The C&T passes through forests of pine and aspen, past striking rock formations, and over the magnificent Toltec Gorge of the Rio de los Pinos. It crests at the 10,015-foot Cumbres Pass, the highest in the United States used by scheduled passenger trains.

Halfway through the route, at Osier, Colorado, the *New Mexico Express* from Chama meets the *Colorado Limited* from Antonito. They stop to exchange greetings, engines, and through passengers. A lunch of roast turkey, mashed potatoes, gravy, and other offerings is served in a big, barnlike dining hall in Osier. From there, through passengers continue on to Antonito and return by van, while round-trip passengers return to their starting point. Be aware that both trips are nearly full-day events. Those who find it uncomfortable to sit for long periods may instead want to opt for hiking or skiing in the area. Ask about their Parlor Car, a more luxurious alternative to coach seating.

A walking-tour brochure, describing 23 points of interest in the Chama railroad yards, can be picked up at the 1899 depot in Chama. These yards are a living, working museum. A registered National Historic Site, the C&T is owned by the states of Colorado and New Mexico. Special cars with lifts for people with disabilities are available with a 7-day advance reservation.

500 Terrace Ave., Chama, NM 87520. ② **888/286-2737** or 575/756-2151. Fax 575/756-2694. www. cumbrestoltec.com. Lunch included with all fares. Round-trip to Osier: adults $75, children age 11 and under $38. Through trip to Antonito, return by van (or to Antonito by van, return by train): adults $91, children $50. Reservations highly recommended. Memorial Day to mid-Oct, trains leave Chama daily at 10am; vans depart for Antonito at 8:30am.

Where to Stay

Most accommodations in this area are found on NM 17 or south of the US 64/84 junction, known as the "Y."

HOTELS/LODGES

Chama Station Inn ★ Set in downtown Chama, right across the street from the Cumbres & Toltec Scenic Railroad station, this inn offers clean, atmospheric rooms in a 1920s building. Wood floors, high ceilings, and quilts on the comfortable beds

Steam Power Shopping

After sitting on the steam train, you may want to stroll for a while, hitting a few of the shops in Chama. One of note is the **Local Color Gallery,** 567 Terrace Ave. (📞 **888/756-2604** or 575/756-2604) in the center of town. Here you'll find all kinds of locally made arts and crafts, from pottery to moody candles painted with petroglyph symbols to picturesque watercolors of the Chama area. Nearby, the **Trackside Emporium,** 611 Terrace Ave. (📞 **575/756-1848**), offers train books and videos and model cars.

create a cozy atmosphere. Bathrooms are small, with only a shower, but functional. A portal on the two-story building allows a nice place to lounge next to an elaborate garden. Best of all, you can climb out of bed and walk to the train. The only drawback here is that the inn is only open from late May to mid-October, when the train is running. Two of the rooms have kiva fireplaces. Next door, a coffee shop offers breakfast. I'd give its name but it seems to change hands every year, so your guess is as good as mine.

423 Terrace Ave. Chama, NM 87520. 📞 **888/726-8150** or 575/756-2315. www.chamastationinn.com. 9 units. $75–$85 double. AE, DISC, MC, V. *In room:* TV, hair dryer.

River Bend Lodge   Set on a bend of the Chama River, this lodge offers the best cabins in town and clean motel rooms. Though they're prefab cabins, they're better than some of the more authentic and overly rustic ones nearby. If you can reserve cabin no. 40, 50, or 60 at the back of the property, you'll have a sweet riverside stay. Some of these are split level, with a queen-size sleeping loft and a bedroom—not great for privacy, but good for a family that doesn't mind sharing space. Others are similar, but without the loft. Every cabin has a fold-out futon in the living room, an efficient little kitchen, and a small bathroom. The motel rooms are medium-size, with basic furnishing and a long portal to relax on in the afternoons.

2625 US 84/64, Chama, NM 87520. 📞 **800/288-1371** or 575/756-2264. Fax 575/756-2664. www.chamariverbendlodge.com. 21 units. Motel $68–$89 double; cabins $115–$135 double. Children 12 and under stay free in parent's room. AE, DC, DISC, MC, V. Pets accepted with $10 fee. **Amenities:** Jacuzzi; river for fishing and wading. *In room:* A/C, TV, fridge, hair dryer, Wi-Fi.

CAMPING

At **Rio Chama RV Campground** (📞 **575/756-2303**), you're within easy walking distance of the Cumbres & Toltec Scenic Railroad depot. This shady campground with 100 sites along the Rio Chama is ideal for RVers and tenters who plan to take train rides. The campground also offers great photo opportunities of the old steam trains leaving the depot. Hot showers, a dump station, and complete hookups are available. It's open May to mid-October only. The campground is 2¼ miles north of the US 84/64 junction on NM 17.

   Twin Rivers Trailer Park (📞 **575/756-2218**) has 50 sites and 40 full hookups; phone hookups are offered. Tenting is available, as are laundry facilities and ice and picnic tables. River swimming and fishing are popular activities; other sports facilities include basketball, volleyball, badminton, and horseshoes. Twin Rivers is open from April 15 to November 1 and is 100 yards west of the junction of NM 17 and US 84/64.

Where to Dine

High Country Restaurant and Saloon ★ STEAKS/SEAFOOD/NEW MEXI-CAN   This is definitely a country place, with functional furniture, orange vinyl chairs, brown carpet, and a big stone fireplace. But it's *the* place innkeepers recommend. The steaks are a big draw here. More sophisticated appetites may like the *trucha con piñon*, trout dusted in flour and cooked with pine nuts, garlic, and shallots. Meals are served with a salad and choice of potato. The New Mexican food is also good. Sunday brunch offers a buffet with biscuits and gravy as well as egg dishes and pancakes. The attached saloon has a full bar and bustles with people eating peanuts and throwing the shells on the floor.

Main St. (⁷⁄₁₀ mile north of the Y), Chama. ℂ **575/756-2384.** Main courses $5–$20 lunch, $7–$20 dinner; Sun breakfast buffet $10. AE, DISC, MC, V. Mon–Sat 11am–10pm; Sun 8am–10pm. Closed Easter, Thanksgiving, Christmas.

On the Road: What to See & Do on US 84 South

Distinctive yellow earth provided a name for the town of **Tierra Amarilla,** 14 miles south of Chama at the junction of US 84 and US 64. Throughout New Mexico, this name is synonymous with a continuing controversy over the land-grant rights of the descendants of the original Hispanic settlers. But the economy of this community of 1,000 is dyed in the wool—literally.

The organization Ganados del Valle (Livestock Growers of the Valley) is at work to save the longhaired Spanish churro sheep from extinction, to introduce other unusual wool breeds to the valley, and to perpetuate a 200-year-old tradition of shepherding, spinning, weaving, and dyeing. Many of the craftspeople work in conjunction with **Tierra Wools** ★, 91 Main St. Los Ojos, NM 87551 (ℂ **505/588-7231;** www.handweavers.com), which has a showroom and workshop in a century-old mercantile building just north of Tierra Amarilla. One-of-a-kind blankets and men's and women's apparel are among the products displayed and sold.

Just down the street, across from the Los Ojos General Store, is an interesting little art studio worth checking out. **Yellow Earth Studio** (ℂ **575/588-7807**) is a great place to see and purchase enchanting scenes of the Los Ojos area in the form of paintings and monotype, woodcut, and metal engraving prints.

Two state parks are a short drive west from Tierra Amarilla. **El Vado Lake State Park,** 14 miles southwest on NM 112 (ℂ **575/588-7247;** www.nmparks.com), offers boating and water-skiing, fishing, and camping in summer, and cross-country skiing and ice fishing in winter. **Heron Lake State Park,** 11 miles west on US 64 and NM 95 (ℂ **575/588-7470;** www.nmparks.com), has a no-wake speed limit for motor vessels, adding to its appeal for fishing, sailing, windsurfing, canoeing, and swimming. The park has an interpretive center, plus camping, picnic sites, hiking trails, and cross-country skiing in the winter. The 5½-mile Rio Chama trail connects the two lakes.

East of Tierra Amarilla, the Rio Brazos cuts a canyon through the Tusas Mountains and around 11,403-foot Brazos Peak. Just north of Los Ojos, NM 512 heads east 7½ miles up the **Brazos Box Canyon.** High cliffs that rise straight from the valley floor give it a Yosemite-like appearance—which is even more apparent from an overlook on US 64, 18 miles east of Tierra Amarilla en route to Taos. **El Chorro,** an impressive waterfall at the mouth of the canyon, usually flows only from early May to mid-June. Several resort lodges are in the area.

About 37 miles south of Tierra Amarilla on US 84, and 3 miles north of Ghost Ranch, is **Echo Canyon Amphitheater** (© **575/684-2486**), a U.S. Forest Service campground and picnic area. The "theater," hollowed out of sandstone by thousands of years of erosion, is a natural work of art with layers of stone ranging from pearl-color to blood red. The walls send back eerie echoes and even clips of conversations. It's just a 10-minute walk from the parking area. The fee is $2 per car. Some 13 miles west of here, via the dirt Forest Service Road 151 into the Chama River Canyon Wilderness, is the isolated **Monastery of Christ in the Desert** (www.christdesert.org), built in 1964 by Benedictine monks. The brothers produce crafts, sold at a small gift shop, and operate a guesthouse.

Along the same road (FS 151) is access to the Chama River, a good place to hike, mountain bike, kayak, and camp. The **Rim Vista Trail** will take you to the top of the rim, with vast views out across Abiquiu Lake and Ghost Ranch. Primitive campsites can be found all along the river.

A 3-mile drive from there is **Ghost Ranch,** a collection of adobe buildings that make up an adult study center maintained by the United Presbyterian Church. A number of hauntingly memorable hikes originate from this place, which gets its name from the *brujas,* or witches, said to inhabit the canyons. Most popular among the hikes is spectacular **Chimney Rock,** but even more notable in my opinion is **Kitchen Mesa.** Directions for the hikes can be obtained at the visitor center. Georgia O'Keeffe spent time at Ghost Ranch painting these canyons and other land formations. Eventually she bought a portion of the ranch and lived in a humble adobe house there. The ranch now offers seminars on a variety of topics, ranging from art to literature to religion, that are open to all. For information, contact **Ghost Ranch,** 401 Old Taos Hwy., Santa Fe (© **877/804-4678** or 505/982-8539; www. ghostranch.org).

As a part of Ghost Ranch, the **Florence Hawley Ellis Museum of Anthropology** has interpretive exhibits of a Spanish ranch house and Native American anthropology, and the **Ruth Hall Paleontology Museum** (both museums © **505/685-4333;** www.ghostranch.org) displays fossils of the early dinosaur named coelophysis found on the ranch. A lightly built creature, it was very fast when chasing prey. It roamed the area 250 million years ago, making it the oldest dinosaur found in New Mexico.

Many dinosaur skeletons have been found in rocks along the base of cliffs near **Abiquiu Reservoir** (© **505/685-4371**), a popular boating and fishing spot formed by the Abiquiu Dam.

A good place to stay and dine in the area is the **Abiquiu Inn ★**, a small country inn, restaurant, art gallery, and gift shop, ½ mile north of the village of Abiquiu (© **505/685-4378;** www.abiquiuinn.com). The casitas are especially nice. Rates are $139 to $199.

Heading south from Abiquiu, watch for **Dar al Islam** (© **505/685-4515**), a spiritual center with a circular Middle Eastern–style mosque made of adobe; the small community of **Mendanales,** is the home of renowned weaver Cordelia Coronado; and **Hernandez,** the village immortalized in Ansel Adams's famous 1941 photograph *Moonrise, Hernandez, New Mexico.* **Rancho de San Juan** (p. 174) is a wonderful nearby place to stay and dine.

GETTING TO KNOW TAOS

12

New Mexico's favorite arts town sits in a masterpiece setting. It's wedged between the towering peaks of the Rocky Mountains and the plunging chasm of the Rio Grande Gorge.

Located about 70 miles north of Santa Fe, this town of 5,000 residents combines 1960s hippiedom (thanks to communes set up in the hills back then) with the ancient culture of Taos Pueblo (some people still live without electricity and running water, as their ancestors did 1,000 years ago). It can be an odd place, where some completely eschew materialism and live "off the grid" in half-underground houses called earthships. But there are plenty of more mainstream attractions as well—Taos boasts some of the best restaurants in the state, a hot and funky arts scene, and incredible outdoors action, including world-class skiing.

Its history is rich. Throughout the Taos valley, ruins and artifacts attest to a Native American presence dating back 5,000 years. The Spanish first visited this area in 1540, colonizing it in 1598. In the last 2 decades of the 17th century, they put down three rebellions at Taos Pueblo. During the 18th and 19th centuries, Taos was an important trade center: New Mexico's annual caravan to Chihuahua, Mexico, couldn't leave until after the annual midsummer **Taos Fair.** French trappers began attending the fair in 1739. Even though the Plains tribes often attacked the pueblos at other times, they would attend the market festival under a temporary annual truce. By the early 1800s, Taos had become a meeting place for American mountain men, the most famous of whom, Kit Carson, made his home in Taos from 1826 to 1868.

Taos remained loyal to Mexico during the U.S.–Mexican War of 1846. The town rebelled against its new U.S. landlord in 1847, even killing newly appointed Governor Charles Bent in his Taos home. Nevertheless, the town was eventually incorporated into the Territory of New Mexico in 1850. During the Civil War, Taos fell into Confederate hands for 6 weeks; afterward, Carson and two other men raised the Union flag over Taos Plaza and guarded it day and night. Since that time, Taos has had the honor of flying the flag 24 hours a day.

Taos's population declined when the railroad bypassed it in favor of Santa Fe. In 1898, two East Coast artists—Ernest Blumenschein and Bert Phillips—discovered the dramatic, varied effects of sunlight on the natural environment of the Taos valley and depicted them on canvas. By

Downtown Taos & Environs

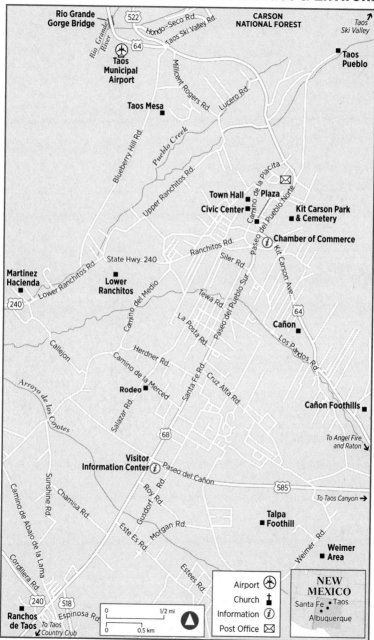

Rio Grande Gorge Bridge

522

Hondo–Seco Rd.

Taos Ski Valley Rd.

CARSON NATIONAL FOREST

Taos Ski Valley

64

Rio Grande River

Taos Municipal Airport

Millicent Rogers Rd.

Taos Pueblo

Taos Mesa

Lucero Rd.

Blueberry Hill Rd.

Pueblo Creek

Upper Ranchitos Rd.

Camino de la Placita

Town Hall
Plaza

Civic Center

Camino del Pueblo Norte

Kit Carson Park & Cemetery

Paseo del Pueblo Norte

Chamber of Commerce

State Hwy. 240

Ranchitos Rd.

Siler Rd.

Kit Carson Ave.

Martinez Hacienda

240

Lower Ranchitos Rd.

Lower Ranchitos

Camino del Medio

Tewa Rd.

Paseo del Pueblo Sur

64

Cañon

Callejon

La Posta Rd.

Los Pandos Rd.

Herdner Rd.

Camino de la Merced

Arroyo de los Cootes

Salazar Rd.

Rodeo

Santa Fe Rd.

Cruz Alta Rd.

Cañon Foothills

To Angel Fire and Raton

68

Visitor Information Center

Paseo del Cañon

585

To Taos Canyon →

Sunshine Rd.

Camino de Abajo de la Lama

Chamisa Rd.

Roy Rd.

Gusdorf Rd.

Este Es Rd.

Morgan Rd.

Talpa Foothill

Weimer Rd.

Weimer Area

Cordillera Rd.

240

518

Estees Rd.

Espinosa Rd.

Ranchos de Taos

To Taos Country Club

0   1/2 mi
0   0.5 km

Airport ✈
Church ✝
Information ⓘ
Post Office ✉

NEW MEXICO

Santa Fe • Taos

• Albuquerque

1912, thanks to the growing influence of the **Taos Society of Artists,** the town had gained a worldwide reputation as a cultural center. Today, it is estimated that more than 15% of the population are painters, sculptors, writers, or musicians, or in some other way earn their income from artistic pursuits.

The town of Taos is merely the focal point of rugged 2,200-square-mile Taos County. Two features dominate this sparsely populated region: the high desert mesa, split in two by the 650-foot-deep chasm of the **Rio Grande;** and the **Sangre de Cristo** range, which tops out at 13,161-foot Wheeler Peak, New Mexico's highest mountain. From the forested uplands to the sage-carpeted mesa, the county is home to a large variety of wildlife. The human element includes Native Americans who are still living in ancient pueblos and Hispanic farmers who continue to irrigate their farmlands using centuries-old methods.

Taos is also inhabited by many people who have chosen to retreat from, or altogether drop out of, mainstream society. There's a laid-back attitude here, even more pronounced than the general *mañana* attitude for which New Mexico is known. Most Taoseños live here to play here—and that means outdoors. Many work at the ski area all winter (skiing whenever they can) and work for raft companies in the summer (to get on the river as much as they can). Others are into rock climbing, mountain biking, and backpacking. That's not to say that Taos is just a resort town. With the Hispanic and Native American populations' histories in the area, there's a richness and depth here that most resort towns lack.

Taos's biggest task these days is to try to stem the tide of overdevelopment that is flooding northern New Mexico. In "Northern New Mexico Today" (p. 10), I address the city's success in battling back airport expansion and some housing developments. A grass-roots community program has been implemented that gives neighborhoods a say in how their area is developed.

ORIENTATION

Arriving

BY PLANE The **Taos Regional Airport** (℡ 575/758-4995) is about 8 miles northwest of town on US 64. Most people opt to fly into Albuquerque International Sunport, rent a car, and drive up to Taos from there. The drive takes approximately 2½ hours. If you'd rather be picked up at Albuquerque International Sunport, call **Faust's Transportation, Inc.** (℡ 575/758-3410), which offers daily service, as well as taxi service between Taos and Taos Ski Valley.

BY BUS/TRAIN Besides Faust's Transportation (above) the only way to arrive in Taos by bus is via Rail Runner. The **New Mexico Rail Runner Express** train service connects Santa Fe to Taos via the Taos Express Shuttle Service on Fridays through Sundays. Contact ℡ 866/799-7245 or www.nmrailrunner.com/bus_santafe_depot. asp. For more information on this and other bus services to and from Albuquerque and Santa Fe, see "Getting There & Around," in chapter 3.

BY CAR Most visitors arrive in Taos via either NM 68 or US 64. Northbound travelers should exit I-25 at Santa Fe, follow US 285 as far as Española, and then continue on the divided highway when it becomes NM 68. Taos is about 79 miles from the I-25 junction. Southbound travelers from Denver on I-25 should exit about 6 miles south of

Raton at US 64 and then follow it about 95 miles to Taos. Another major route is US 64 from the west (214 miles from Farmington).

Visitor Information

The **Taos County Chamber of Commerce,** at 108 Kit Carson Rd., Taos, NM 87571 (℃ **575/751-8800;** www.taoschamber.com), is open Monday to Friday 9am to 5pm in summer and 1 to 5pm in winter. It's closed on major holidays.

City Layout

The **plaza** is a short block west of Taos's major intersection—where US 64 (Kit Carson Rd.) from the east joins NM 68, **Paseo del Pueblo Sur.** US 64 proceeds north from the intersection as **Paseo del Pueblo Norte. Camino de la Placita (Placita Rd.)** circles the west side of downtown, passing within a block of the other side of the plaza. Many of the streets that join these thoroughfares are winding lanes lined by traditional adobe homes, many of them over 100 years old.

Most of the art galleries are located on or near the plaza, which was paved over with bricks several years ago, and along neighboring streets. Others are in the **Ranchos de Taos** area, a few miles south of the plaza.

MAPS   To find your way around town, pick up a free Taos map from the **Town of Taos Visitor Center,** 1139 Paseo del Pueblo Sur (℃ **800/732-8267** or 575/758-3873). Good, detailed city maps can be found at area bookstores as well (see "Shopping," in chapter 15). **Carson National Forest** information and maps are available in the same building.

GETTING AROUND

By Car

With offices at the Taos airport, **Enterprise** (℃ **575/751-7490)** is reliable and efficient. Other car-rental agencies are available out of Albuquerque. See "Getting Around," in chapter 16, for details.

PARKING   Parking can be difficult during the summer rush, when the stream of tourists' cars moving north and south through town never ceases. If you can't find parking on the street or in the plaza, check out some of the nearby roads (Kit Carson Rd., for instance); there are plenty of metered and unmetered lots in Taos.

ROAD CONDITIONS   Information on highway conditions throughout the state can be obtained from the **State Highway Department** (℃ **800/432-4269).**

Warning for Drivers

En route to many recreation sites, reliable paved roads often give way to poorer forest roads, where gas stations and cafes are scarce. Four-wheel-drive vehicles are recommended on snow and much of the unpaved terrain of the region. If you're doing some off-road adventuring, it's wise to go with a full gas tank, extra food and water, and warm clothing—just in case. At the higher-than-10,000-foot elevations of northern New Mexico, sudden summer snowstorms can occur.

By Bus & Taxi

If you're in Taos without a car, you're in luck because there's local bus service, provided by **Chile Line Town of Taos Transit** (© **575/751-4459;** www.taosgov.com). It operates on the half-hour Monday to Saturday 7am to 7pm in summer, 7am to 6pm in winter, and on the hour Sunday 8am to 5pm year-round. Two simultaneous routes run southbound from Taos Pueblo and northbound from the Ranchos de Taos Post Office. Each route makes stops at the casino and various hotels in town, as well as at Taos RV Park. Bus fares are 50¢ one-way, $1 round trip, $5 for a 7-day pass, and $20 for a 31-day pass.

In addition, **Faust's Transportation** (© **575/758-3410**) has a taxi service linking town hotels and Taos Ski Valley. Faust's Transportation also offers shuttle service and on-call taxi service daily from 8am to 5pm (special arrangements made for after hours; Sun by appointment only), with fares of about $10 anywhere within the city limits for up to two people. Bus service to and from the mountain is 50¢ one-way, exact change only.

By Bicycle

Bicycle rentals are available from **Gearing Up Bicycle Shop,** 129 Paseo del Pueblo Sur (© **575/751-0365;** www.gearingupbikes.com); daily rentals run $35 for a full day and $25 for a half-day for a mountain bike with front suspension. From April to October, **Native Sons Adventures,** 1334 Paseo del Pueblo Sur (© **800/753-7559** or 575/758-9342; www.nativesonsadventures.com), also rents front-suspension bikes for $35 for a full day and $25 for a half-day. It also rents car racks for $5. Each shop supplies helmets and water bottles with rentals.

[FastFACTS] Taos

Airport See "Orientation," above.

Area Code The telephone area code for Taos is **575.**

ATMs You can find ATMs all over town, at supermarkets, banks, and drive-throughs.

Business Hours Most **businesses** are open at least Monday to Friday 10am to 5pm, though some may open an hour earlier and close an hour later. Many **tourist-oriented shops** are also open on Saturday morning, and some **art galleries** are open all day Saturday and Sunday, especially during peak tourist seasons. **Banks** are generally open

Monday to Thursday 9am to 5pm and often for longer hours on Friday. Some may be open Saturday morning. Most branches have cash machines available 24 hours. Call establishments for specific hours.

Car Rentals See "Getting Around," in chapter 3, or "Getting Around," above.

Climate Taos's climate is similar to that of Santa Fe. Summer days are dry and sunny, except for frequent afternoon thunderstorms. Winter days are often bracing, with snowfalls common but rarely lasting too long. Average **summer**

temperatures range from 50° to 87°F (10°–31°C). **Winter temperatures** vary between 9° and 40°F (–13° to 4°C). **Annual rainfall** is 12 inches; annual snowfall is 35 inches in town and as much as 300 inches at Taos Ski Valley, where the elevation is 9,207 feet. (A foot of snow is equal to an inch of rain.)

Currency Exchange Foreign currency can be exchanged at the **Centinel Bank of Taos,** 512 Paseo del Pueblo Sur (© **575/758-6700**) for a $35 fee.

Dentists If you need dental work, try **Dr. Walter Jakiela,** 1392 Weimer Rd. (© **575/758-8654**); **Dr.**

Michael Rivera, 107 Plaza Garcia, Ste. E (☏ **575/758-0531**); or **Dr. Tom Simms,** 1392 Weimer Rd. (☏ **575/758-8303**).

Doctors Members of the **Taos Medical Group,** on Weimer Road (☏ **575/758-2224**), are highly respected. Also recommended are **Family Practice Associates of Taos,** 630 Paseo del Pueblo Sur, Ste. 150 (☏ **575/758-3005**).

Emergencies Dial ☏ **911** for police, fire, and ambulance.

Hospital Holy Cross Hospital, 1397 Weimer Rd., off Paseo del Canyon (☏ **575/758-8883**), has 24-hour emergency service. Serious cases are transferred to Santa Fe or Albuquerque.

Hot Lines The **crisis hot line** (☏ **575/758-9888**) is available for emergency counseling.

Information See "Visitor Information," above.

Internet Access You can retrieve your e-mail via Wi-Fi or the cafe's computers at **Sustaining Cultures,** 114 Doña Luz (☏ **575/613-3490;** www. sustainingcultures.org). It's located 1 block west of the plaza. And the Taos County Chamber of Commerce, 108 Kit Carson Rd., Ste. F (☏ **575/751-8800;** www.taoschamber.com), just off the plaza, offers free access. As well, the **Taos Public Library** offers free access.

Library The **Taos Public Library,** 402 Camino de la Placita (☏ **575/758-3063** or 575/737-2590; www. taoslibrary.org), has a general collection for Taos residents, a children's library, and special collections on the Southwest and Taos art.

Lost Property Check with the **Taos police** at ☏ **575/758-2216.**

Newspapers & Magazines *The Taos News* (☏ **575/758-2241;** www. taosnews.com) and the *Sangre de Cristo Chronicle* (☏ **575/377-2358;** www. sangrechronicle.com) are published every Thursday. *Taos Magazine* is also a good source of local information. The *Albuquerque Journal* (www.abqjournal. com) and Santa Fe's *New Mexican* (www.santafenew mexican.com) are easily obtained at book and convenience stores.

Pharmacies There are several full-service pharmacies in Taos. **Sav-on Drug** (☏ **575/758-1203**), **Smith's Pharmacy** (☏ **575/758-4824**), and **Wal-Mart Pharmacy** (☏ **575/758-2743**) are all on Pueblo Sur and are easily seen from the road.

Police In case of emergency, dial ☏ **911.** All other inquiries should be directed to the **Taos police,** Civic Plaza Drive (☏ **575/758-2216**). The **Taos County Sheriff,** with jurisdiction outside the city limits, is in the county

courthouse on Paseo del Pueblo Sur (☏ **575/758-3361**).

Post Offices The main **Taos post office** is at 318 Paseo del Pueblo Norte (☏ **575/758-2081**), a few blocks north of the plaza traffic light; it's open Monday to Friday 8:30am to 5pm. There are smaller offices in **Ranchos de Taos** (☏ **575/758-3944;** Mon-Fri 8:30am–5pm, Sat 9am-noon) and at **El Prado** (☏ **575/758-4810;** Mon–Fri 8am–4:30pm, Sat 8:30–11:30am). The zip code for Taos is 87571.

Radio A local station is **KTAOS-FM** (101.9), which broadcasts an entertainment calendar daily (☏ **575/758-5826**); National Public Radio can be found on **KUNM-FM** (98.5) from Albuquerque.

Road Conditions For **emergency road service** in the Taos area, call the state police at ☏ **575/758-8878;** for **road conditions** dial ☏ **800/432-4269** (within New Mexico) for the state highway department.

Taxes Gross receipts tax for the city of Taos is 8.06%, and for Taos County it's 7%. There is an additional lodgers' tax of 5% in both the city of Taos and in Taos County.

Taxis See "Getting Around," above.

Television Channel 2, the local access station, is available in most hotels.

For a few hours a day it shows local programming. Cable networks carry Santa Fe and Albuquerque stations.

Time As is true throughout New Mexico, Taos is on **Mountain Standard Time.** It's 2 hours earlier than New York, 1 hour earlier than Chicago, and 1 hour later than Los Angeles. Clocks change the second Sunday in March and the first Sunday in November.

Weather Taos has no number to call for weather forecasts, but you can log on to **www.taosnews.com/ weather**.

WHERE TO
STAY IN TAOS

A tiny town with a big tourist market, Taos has thousands of rooms in hotels, motels, condominiums, and bed-and-breakfasts. In the slower seasons—January through early February and April through early May—when competition for travelers is steep, you may even want to try bargaining your room rate down. Most of the hotels and motels are on Paseo del Pueblo Sur and Norte, with a few scattered just east of the town center, along Kit Carson Road. The condos and bed-and-breakfasts are generally scattered throughout Taos's back streets.

During peak seasons, visitors without reservations may have difficulty finding vacant rooms. **Taos Chamber of Commerce,** 108 S. Kit Carson Rd. (© **575/751-8800**), might be able to help.

Rocky Mountain Tours (© **800/233-2300,** ext. 3442; www.rocky mountaintours.com) will help you find accommodations ranging from bed-and-breakfasts to home rentals, hotels, and cabins throughout Taos, Taos Ski Valley, and the rest of northern New Mexico. It'll also help you arrange package trips for outdoor activities such as skiing, horseback riding, hot-air ballooning, and snowmobiling.

There are two high seasons in Taos: winter (the Christmas-to-Easter ski season, except for Jan, which is notoriously slow) and June through September. Spring and fall are shoulder seasons, often with lower rates. The period between Easter and Memorial Day is also slow in the tourist industry here, and many proprietors of restaurants and other businesses take their annual vacations at this time. Book well ahead for ski holiday periods (especially Christmas) and for the annual arts festivals (late May to mid-June and late Sept to early Oct).

THE TAOS AREA Hotels/Motels
EXPENSIVE

El Monte Sagrado ★★★ 📷   New to Taos in 2003, this resort near the center of town offers a feast for the senses. Water running over falls, lush landscaping, and delicious food and drink all lull guests into a state of relaxation. Rooms range in theme from the Caribbean casita, a medium-size room that evokes the feel of an African jungle, to the Argentina global suite, a huge two-bedroom decorated in cowboy-contemporary style with wood floors, leather furniture, and two large bathrooms featuring mosaic-decorated shower and tub. In 2007, the inn nearly doubled in size with a series of more reasonably priced rooms. All rooms are serene, with patios or balconies and views. In line with the resort's commitment to responsible development, the resort recycles its water, using it to irrigate the cottonwood-shaded Sacred Circle, at the resort's center. The intimate spa offers a full range of treatments and free classes such as yoga and tai chi. The **Anaconda Bar** (p. 232) and **De La Tierra** restaurant (p. 201) combine a contemporary feel with elegant Asian touches.

317 Kit Carson Rd., Taos, NM 87571. ☎ **800/828-8267** or 575/758-3502. www.elmontesagrado.com. 84 units. $169–$229 1-bedroom casita; $199–$519 suites. AE, DC, DISC, MC, V. Valet parking $12. **Amenities:** Restaurant; bar; concierge; health club; Jacuzzi; indoor pool; spa. *In room:* A/C, TV, CD player, minibar (stocked on request), hair dryer, Wi-Fi.

The Historic Taos Inn ★ Here, you'll be surrounded by 21st-century luxury without ever forgetting that you're within the thick walls of 19th-century homes. It's listed on the State and National Registers of Historic Places. The lobby doubles as the popular **Adobe Bar,** which surrounds a wishing well that was once the old town well. A number of rooms open onto a balcony that overlooks this area. I don't recommend these rooms, as they can be noisy. All the other rooms sit among a number of "houses" separated by walkways and grass. Some have modest style, with lower ceilings and Spanish Colonial furnishings, while others are more chic. My favorites are no. 204 in the Sandoval House, decorated with antiques, and any room in the recently built **Helen House** ★★. These rooms, with Saltillo tile floors and kiva fireplaces, will appeal to travelers who don't appreciate the whims of an older building, but still enjoy character. **Doc Martin's** (p. 201) is a good bet for any meal.

125 Paseo del Pueblo Norte, Taos, NM 87571. ☎ **800/826-7466** or 575/758-2233. Fax 575/758-5776. www.taosinn.com. 44 units. $75–$120 double; $195–$275 suite. AE, DISC, MC, V. **Amenities:** Restaurant; lounge; Jacuzzi; room service; Wi-Fi in lobby. *In room:* A/C, TV, hair dryer.

Hotel La Fonda de Taos ★ Taos now has a recommendable hotel on the plaza. A $3-million renovation to this historic property built in 1880 has turned it into a comfortable, fun spot with a stellar location. The charismatic Taos figure Saki Kavaras put this hotel on the society map in the 1930s, when, most notably, British author D. H. Lawrence frequented it. His legacy is preserved in a unique museum, where some of his risqué paintings hang—a must-see even if you don't stay here (free for guests; $3 for nonguests). Rooms are set off broad hallways, each styled in earth tones, Southwestern furnishings, and tile bathrooms. Standards are small, each with a queen-size bed. Your better bet is to reserve a plaza or deluxe plaza room, or a suite. These are larger, with king beds. My favorite rooms are nos. 201 and 301, which overlook the plaza. Groups can rent the whole top floor (or the whole hotel), which includes a full kitchen suite.

108 South Plaza, Taos, NM 87571. ☎ **800/833-2211** or 575/758-2211. Fax 575/758-8508. www.lafonda taos.com. 25 units. $119–$179 standard double; $129–$249 plaza and deluxe plaza double; $179–$229 suite. AE, DISC, MC, V. Free parking. **Amenities:** Restaurant; coffee shop; lounge. *In room:* A/C, TV, hair dryer, high-speed Internet.

Taos Area Accommodations

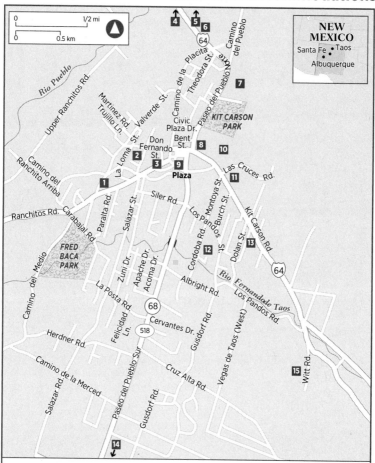

Abominable Snowmansion Skiers' Hostel **5**
Adobe & Pines Inn **14**
Adobe and Stars Bed and Breakfast Inn **5**
Best Western Kachina Lodge **7**
Carson National Forest **4**
Casa del las Chimeneas **12**
El Monte Sagrado **11**
Hacienda del Sol **6**
The Historic Taos Inn **8**
Hotel La Fonda de Taos **9**
Inger Jirby's Guest Houses **3**

Inn on La Loma Plaza **1**
Inn on the Rio **13**
La Posada de Taos **2**
Little Tree Bed & Breakfast **5**
Mabel Dodge Luhan House **10**
Old Taos Guesthouse **15**
Questa Lodge & RV Park **5**
Sagebrush Inn **14**
Taos Hampton Inn **14**
Taos Valley RV Park &
   Campground **14**

Inger Jirby's Guest Houses ★★ Two blocks from the plaza, between the R.C. Gorman Gallery and the Ernest L. Blumenschein Museum, this inn provides a stay in an artistic ancient adobe. Painter Inger Jirby has chosen this for her gallery space as well as a home for travelers. From the remains of a 400-year-old adobe, she's carved and added these lively dwellings and adorned them with her unique style. Full of rich Mexican and Balinese art, and then accented by her own vivid landscapes of the Southwest and beyond, the casitas are artsy as well as comfortable. Both have a full kitchen, flagstone floors, large windows, and sleeping lofts. (Very large or elderly people might have trouble maneuvering the spiral staircases in these.) They also have fold-out couches, so they're a great option for families. Both are equipped with stereos and robes. More than anywhere else in town, these casitas provide a real home away from home. The attached Inger Jirby Gallery provides Internet access for guests.

207 Ledoux St., Taos, NM 87571. ✆ **575/758-7333.** www.jirby.com. 2 units. $175–$225 double (up to $275 during holidays). Additional person $25–$35. *In room:* TV/DVD, hair dryer, kitchen.

MODERATE

Inn on the Rio ★ ☺ Once a Route 66 motel, this inn will still appeal to road warriors who like a comfortable but simple night's rest. It sits just off Kit Carson Road, with rooms in two buildings painted with murals and shaded by portals. The lobby, in a 250-year-old structure where breakfast is served, offers an elaborate hand-sculpted adobe fireplace. The simple rooms have whimsical Southwestern furnishings. Each comes with a queen-size bed and a couch and hand-painted accents in the small bathrooms. Kids enjoy the outdoor pool in summer.

910 Kit Cason Rd., Taos, NM 87571. ✆ **800/859-6572** or 575/758-7199. Fax 575/751-1816. www.innon therio.com. 12 units. $125–$145 double (seasonal specials available). Rates include full breakfast. AE, DISC, MC, V. Pets welcome by prior arrangement, one-time $20–$25 fee. **Amenities:** Jacuzzi; outdoor pool; Wi-Fi in lobby and on grounds. *In-room:* TV.

Sagebrush Inn Three miles south of Taos, surrounded by acres of sage, this sprawling inn provides reasonably priced rooms for travelers who don't mind dated furnishings. The hotel is most noted for when Georgia O'Keeffe lived and worked here for 10 months in the late 1930s.

The treasure of this place is the large grass courtyard dotted with elm trees, where visitors relax in the warm months. Be aware that some of the rooms added in the '50s through '70s have a tackiness not overcome by the vigas and tile work. The rooms are dark and need updating. More recent additions (to the west) are more skillful; these suites away from the hotel proper are spacious and full of amenities, but they, too, with their heavy Spanish colonial furnishings feel dated.

The lobby-cum-cantina has an Old West feel that is a venue for country/western dancing and one of Taos's most active nightspots for live music (see "Taos After Dark," in chapter 15).

1508 Paseo del Pueblo Sur, Taos, NM 87571. ✆ **800/428-3626** or 575/758-2254. Fax 575/758-5077. www.sagebrushinn.com. 97 units. $70–$95 double; $95–$165 deluxe or small suite; $130–$185 executive suite. Additional person $10. Children 16 and under stay free in parent's room. Rates include full break-fast. AE, DC, DISC, MC, V. Pets welcome in most rooms, $7 per night. **Amenities:** 2 restaurants; bar; executive-level rooms; 2 Jacuzzis; outdoor pool. *In room:* A/C, TV, hair dryer, Wi-Fi.

Taos Hampton Inn ★ ☺ The most reliable moderately priced hotel in town, the Hampton is about 5 minutes (by car) from the plaza. Rooms are medium size with either two queens or one king bed, a few with Jacuzzis and mountain views. All have nice pine furnishings, quality bedding, and a hint of Southwestern decor, some with desks, others with a table and chair. The beds are comfortable and the medium-size bathrooms very clean and functional. The medium-size indoor pool keeps kids entertained year-round.

1515 Paseo del Pueblo Sur, Taos, NM 87571. **800/426-7866** or 575/737-5700. Fax 575/737-5701. www. hampton.com. 71 units. $109–$149 double. Rates include full hot breakfast and afternoon snack. AE, DC, DISC, MC, V. **Amenities:** Exercise room; Jacuzzi; indoor pool. *In room:* A/C, TV, hair dryer, free Wi-Fi.

INEXPENSIVE

Abominable Snowmansion Skiers' Hostel
Set in the quaint village of Arroyo Seco, about 8 miles north of Taos and 10 miles from Taos Ski Valley, this hostel offers clean beds (in dorm rooms or private ones) for reasonable prices, and a nice community experience. The common room has a pool table, piano, and circular fireplace. A full kitchen is available to guests, as is a kitchen garden in summer. Best of all are the tepees that sit out around a grassy yard. They each sleep two to four people; an outdoor kitchen, showers, and toilets are nearby. The owners/managers, natives of the area, offer excellent advice about what to do nearby.

476 Taos Ski Valley Rd. (Hwy. 150), Arroyo Seco (P.O. Box GG), Taos, NM 87571. ⓒ **575/776-8298.** www. abominablesnowmansion.com. 80 beds. $15–$22 bed; $40–$56 double, depending on size of accommodations and season; $34 cabins and tepees; $12 camping. MC, V. **Amenities:** Communal kitchen; Wi-Fi in common area. *In room:* A/C, TV, hair dryer, free Wi-Fi. *In room:* No phone.

Best Western Kachina Lodge & Meeting Center ☺
Built in the early 1960s, this lodge on the north end of town, within walking distance of the plaza, has a lot of charm despite the fact that it's a motor hotel. Unfortunately, it's in need of a major remodel. It does receive periodic minor ones, such as new linens and painted trim. If you don't mind crumbling sidewalks and frayed carpeting, the place will suit you fine. Some of the Southwestern-style rooms have couches and most have Taos-style *trasteros* (armoires) that hold the TVs. Rooms sit around a grassy courtyard studded with huge blue spruce trees, allowing kids room to run. In the center is a stage where a family from Taos Pueblo builds a bonfire and dances nightly in the summer and explains the significance of the dances—a real treat for anyone intrigued by the Pueblo rituals.

413 Paseo del Pueblo Norte (P.O. Box NM), Taos, NM 87571. ⓒ **800/522-4462** or 575/758-2275. Fax 575/758-9207. www.kachinalodge.com. 118 units. $69–$149 double. Rates includes half-price breakfast and half-price cocktail. Additional person $15. Children 11 and under stay free in parent's room. AE, DISC, MC, V. **Amenities:** 2 restaurants; lounge; outdoor pool (summer only). *In room:* A/C, TV, hair dryer, Wi-Fi.

Bed & Breakfasts

EXPENSIVE

Adobe & Pines Inn ★★
This inn occupies a 180-year-old adobe directly off NM 68, less than half a mile south of St. Francis Plaza (about a 10-min. drive from Taos Plaza). The inn is set around a courtyard marked by an 80-foot-long grand portal and surrounded by pine and fruit trees. Each room has a private entrance and fireplace (three in their bathrooms!), and each is uniquely decorated. Colors are richly displayed on the walls and in the furnishings. Puerta Azul, a good value, is cozy with blue accents and thick adobe walls, and Puerto Roja has bold maroon walls, a comfortable couch, and kitchenette. Many rooms have Jacuzzi tubs, including three with private outdoor hot tubs. Because this inn is near the highway, at times cars can be heard on the grounds, but the rooms themselves are quiet. Morning brings a delicious full gourmet breakfast in the atrium. Guests also enjoy a labyrinth and Zen garden.

NM 68, Ranchos de Taos, NM 87557. © **800/723-8267** or 575/751-0947. Fax 575/758-8423. www. adobepines.com. 8 units. $98–$225 double; $215–$225 suite. $25 for additional person. Rates include full gourmet breakfast. MC, V. Pets accepted with prior arrangement, one-time $25 fee. *In room:* A/C, TV, kitchenette (in some), Wi-Fi (in some), no phone.

Adobe and Stars Bed and Breakfast Inn ★★

This inn sitting on the mesa between Taos town and Taos Ski Valley offers chic Southwestern-style rooms with a focus on fine detail in a quiet country setting. The breakfast area and common room are sunny, with large windows facing the mountains. A few rooms are upstairs, such as La Luna, my favorite, with views in every direction and a heart-shaped Jacuzzi tub for two. All rooms have kiva fireplaces and private decks or patios. Most of the downstairs rooms open onto a portal. All are decorated with hand-crafted Southwestern-style furniture, and many have Jacuzzi tubs. As well, guests enjoy an outdoor hot tub under the stars, reserved by the half-hour. The full breakfast may vary from New Mexican dishes such as breakfast burritos with green chile to gingerbread waffles with whipped cream. In the afternoons, a glass of New Mexico wine is served with a snack. A courtesy computer with Internet is available for guest use.

At the corner of State Hwy. 150 and Valdez Rim Rd. (P.O. Box 2285), Taos, NM 87571. © **800/211-7076** or 575/776-2776. Fax 575/776-2872. www.taosadobe.com. 8 units. $95–$180 double. Rates include full breakfast and refreshments. AE, MC, V. Pets accepted with $15 per-pet fee and $50 damage deposit. **Amenities:** Jacuzzi. *In room:* A/C, TV, CD player, hair dryer, Wi-Fi.

Casa de las Chimeneas ★★★

This 82-year-old adobe home set on spacious grounds has, since its opening as a luxury inn in 1988, been a model of Southwestern elegance. Adding to its appeal is a spa with a small fitness room and sauna, as well as complete massage and facial treatments for an additional charge. I recommend the Sombraje Room; with old-world elegance, it has high ceilings, a gas fireplace, and two queen beds. The Rio Grande has tile floors, handcrafted furniture, and a large jetted tub. Each room in the inn is decorated with original works of art and has elegant bedding, a private entrance, and robes. All rooms have kiva fireplaces, and most look out on flower and herb gardens. Breakfasts are delicious. Specialties include an artichoke-heart and mushroom omelet or ricotta cream-cheese blintz. In the evenings the inn offers a full dinner, which may include corn-crusted tilapia or roasted chicken served with vegetables from a local organic farm. End the day at the large hot tub in the courtyard.

405 Cordoba Rd., at Los Pandos Rd. (5303 NDCBU), Taos, NM 87571. © **877/758-4777** or 575/758-4777. Fax 575/758-3976. www.visittaos.com. 8 units. $195–$290 double; $325 suite. Rates include breakfast and light evening supper. AE, DC, DISC, MC, V. **Amenities:** Concierge; small exercise room; Jacuzzi; sauna; spa. *In room:* TV/VCR/DVD, hair dryer, free stocked nonalcoholic minibar, MP3 docking station, Wi-Fi.

Hacienda del Sol ★★ ☺

This inn offers spectacular views of Taos Mountain and elegant comfort in both modern and historic rooms. The 1¼-acre property borders Taos Pueblo, providing a rural feel. The inn was once owned by arts patron Mabel Dodge Luhan, and it was here that Frank Waters wrote *The People of the Valley.* You'll find bold splashes of color from the gardens—where in summer tulips, pansies, and flax bloom—to the rooms themselves—where woven bedspreads and original art lend a Mexican feel. The main house is 204 years old, so it has the wonderful curves of adobe as well as thick vigas. My favorite is the Mabel's Salon, with wood floors and a kiva fireplace. Other guestrooms are newer and yet also atmospheric. The Cowgirl and

Cowboy suites have adjoining rooms, perfect for children. Most rooms have fireplaces, three have private Jacuzzis, and four have private steam showers. A delicious breakfast, with favorites such as a mushroom frittata with bacon and toast, is served in the Spanish-hacienda-style dining area. The outdoor hot tub has a mountain view.

109 Mabel Dodge Lane (P.O. Box 177), Taos, NM 87571. © **866/333-4459** or 575/758-0287. Fax 575/758-5895. www.taoshaciendadelsol.com. 11 units. $135–$325 double; $190–$305 suite. Additional person $25. Rates include full breakfast and evening sweets. AE, DISC, MC, V. **Amenities:** Concierge; privileges at nearby health club; Jacuzzi. *In room:* CD player, fridge (in some), hair dryer, Wi-Fi.

Inn on La Loma Plaza ★★   Named by *American Historic Inns* as one of the 10 most romantic inns in America, this inn is on a historic neighborhood plaza, complete with dirt streets and a tiny central park. A 10-minute walk from Taos Plaza, the inn is in a 200-year-old home, complete with aged vigas and maple floors, decorated tastefully with comfortable furniture and Middle Eastern rugs. Three new rooms offer Southwest style and modern convenience. These are spacious, with viga ceilings and elaborate baths. Each room is unique, most with sponge-painted walls and Talavera tile in the bathrooms to provide an eclectic ambience. All have robes, slippers, lighted makeup mirrors, bottled water, and fireplaces, and most have balconies or terraces and views. The Happy Trails Room features knotty pine paneling, a brass bed, old chaps, and decorative hanging spurs. Guests dine on such delights as breakfast burritos or green-chile casserole in a plant-filled sunroom or on the patio.

315 Ranchitos Rd., Taos, NM 87571. © **800/530-3040** or 575/758-1717. Fax 575/751-0155. www.vacationtaos.com. 10 units. $155–$240 double; $275–$325 artist's studio; $425–$590 suite. Additional person $25. Children 12 and under stay free in parent's room. Discounts available. Rates include full breakfast. AE, DISC, MC, V. **Amenities:** Concierge; Internet; Jacuzzi; pool and spa privileges at nearby Taos Spa. *In room:* TV/VCR/DVD, hair dryer, kitchenette (in some), Wi-Fi.

Little Tree Bed & Breakfast ★★ 🐾   Little Tree is one of my favorite Taos bed-and-breakfasts. It's in a beautiful, secluded setting, and constructed with real adobe that's been left in its raw state, lending the place an authentic hacienda feel. Two miles down a country road, about midway between Taos and the ski area, it's surrounded by sage and *piñon*. The charming rooms have radiant heat under the floors, queen-size beds (one with a king-size), and access to the portal and courtyard garden, at the center of which is the little tree for which the inn is named. The Piñon (my favorite) and Juniper rooms are equipped with fireplaces and private entrances. The Piñon and Aspen rooms offer sunset views. The Spruce Room has a private patio and outdoor hot tub. In the main building, the living room has *tierra blanca* adobe (adobe that's naturally white; if you look closely at it, you can see little pieces of mica and straw). Visiting hummingbirds enchant guests as they enjoy a scrumptious breakfast on the portal during warmer months.

County Rd. B-143 (P.O. Box 509), Arroyo Hondo, NM 87513. © **800/334-8467** or 575/776-8467. www.littletreebandb.com. 4 units. $135–$175 double. Rates include breakfast and afternoon snack. MC, V. *In room:* TV/VCR, Wi-Fi.

Mabel Dodge Luhan House   This National Historic Landmark is also called "Las Palomas de Taos" because of the throngs of doves *(palomas)* that live on the property. Like so many other free spirits, they were attracted by the flamboyant Mabel Dodge (1879–1962), who came to Taos in 1916. A familiar figure in these parts, she and her fourth husband, a full-blooded Pueblo named Tony Luhan, enlarged this 200-year-old home to its present size in the 1920s. If you like history and don't mind the curves and undulations it brings to a building, this is a good choice, but it doesn't quite compete with the other B&Bs in town because the rooms have very basic furnishings and are quite rustic. The place evokes images of the glitterati of the 1920s—writers, artists, adventurers—sitting on the terrace under the cottonwoods, drinking margaritas.

All rooms in the main house have thick vigas, arched pueblo-style doorways, hand-carved doors, kiva fireplaces, and dark hardwood floors. Eight newer guest rooms are also equipped with fireplaces, but they lack character so I don't recommend them.

240 Morada Lane, Taos, NM 87571. ℂ **800/846-2235** or 575/751-9686. www.mabeldodgeluhan.com. 18 units. $98–$245 double. Additional person $20. During holiday season add $35. Rates include full breakfast. AE, MC, V. **Amenities:** Internet. *In room:* No phone.

MODERATE

La Posada de Taos ★ ☺ This cozy inn just a few blocks from the plaza rests within the thick adobe walls of a 1905 home and is decorated with a combination of Mexican tile and country antiques. The three rooms off the common area are the coziest. All the rooms except one have fireplaces and private patios. El Solecito and the Beutler Room have Jacuzzi tubs. The place lights with special touches, such as old Mexican doors opening onto a patio in the Lino, a view of Taos Mountain from the Taos Room, and a skylight over the bed in La Casa de la Luna Miel, the honeymoon suite, which is set in a cottage separate from the rest of the inn. A renovated house is also available and a good choice for families. Expect such breakfast treats as *atole* (blue corn) *piñon* pancakes, along with fresh baked goods and house-made granola, served community style at a big table inside or on the patio. Under new ownership, the inn is undergoing many positive changes.

309 Juanita Lane (P.O. Box 1118), Taos, NM 87571. ℂ **800/645-4803** or 575/758-8164. www.laposadade taos.com. 7 units. $129–$239 double. Discounts available, except during holidays. Additional person $20. Rates include full breakfast and homemade afternoon snack. AE, DISC, MC, V. **Amenities:** Concierge. *In room:* A/C (in some), TV, DVD, hair dryer, Wi-Fi.

Old Taos Guesthouse ★ ☺ This 190-year-old adobe hacienda has been extensively restored but maintains its country charm: Mexican tile in the bathrooms, vigas on the ceilings, and kiva-style fireplaces in most of the rooms. Each room has an entrance from the outside, some off the broad portal that shades the front of the hacienda, some from a grassy lawn in the back, with a view toward the mountains. Some rooms are more utilitarian, some quainter, so make a request depending on your needs. One of my favorites is the Taos Suite, with a king-size bed, a big picture window, and a full kitchen. Less than 2 miles from the plaza, this inn sits on 7½ acres and provides a cozy northern New Mexico rural experience, complete with birds galore and a healthy breakfast. Kids enjoy the inn's dogs and plenty of space to run free.

1028 Witt Rd., Taos, NM 87571. ℂ **800/758-5448** or 575/758-5448. www.oldtaos.com. 10 units. $90–$185 double. Rates include a full breakfast. Ask about seasonal rates. DISC, MC, V. Pets accepted in some rooms with one-time $25 fee. **Amenities:** Babysitting; concierge; Jacuzzi; Wi-Fi (in some). *In room:* TV (in some rooms), hair dryer, kitchen (in some).

TAOS SKI VALLEY

For information on the skiing and the facilities offered at Taos Ski Valley, see "Skiing" in chapter 15.

Lodges
EXPENSIVE

The Bavarian Lodge ★ ☺ At an elevation of 10,200 feet, this mountain-get-away lodge with interesting accommodations and excellent food offers the quintessence of Bavaria at the base of Taos Ski Valley's back bowls. The first-floor restaurant/reception area is crafted with aged-pine paneling accented by an antler chandelier. Upstairs, the rooms combine antique and modern elements—not always successfully, but with good intent. All are fairly spacious, with large bathrooms, most with lofts to accommodate kids. The rooms aren't cozy, and some have odd configurations, but they all utilize faux painting to evoke old Europe; some have kitchenettes and balconies. The sun deck is the place to be on sunny ski days, and the Bavarian Restaurant (p. 210) is worth visiting even if you aren't a guest. The lodge offers nature hikes in summer.

100 Kachina Rd. (P.O. Box 653), Taos Ski Valley, NM 87525. ℂ **888/205-8020** or 575/776-8020. Fax 888/304-5301. www.thebavarian.com. 4 units. Christmas holiday–New Year and spring break $400–$455; Nov–Christmas holiday and mid-Jan to Feb $305–$355; June–Sept $185–$205. MC, V. Free parking. Closed Oct, Apr–May. **Amenities:** Restaurant; bar. *In room:* TV, fridge, kitchenette (in some), no phone, Wi-Fi.

Powderhorn Suites and Condominiums ★ 🦅 A homelike feel and Euro-Southwestern ambience make this condo-inn one of the best buys in Taos Ski Valley, just a 2-minute walk from the lift. You'll find consistency and quality here, with clean medium-size rooms, mountain views, vaulted ceilings, well-planned bathrooms, and comfortable beds. The larger suites have stoves, balconies, and fireplaces. Adjoining rooms are good for families. As with almost all of the accommodations in Taos Ski Valley, this one has been condo-ized so each suite has a distinct owner; thus the service isn't what you would find at a full-service hotel, though it is still conscientious. There's no elevator, so if stairs are a problem for you, make sure to ask for a room on the ground floor.

5 Ernie Blake Rd. (P.O. Box 69), Taos Ski Valley, NM 87525. ℂ **800/776-2346** or 575/776-2341. Fax 575/776-2341. www.taospowderhorn.com. 16 units. Ski season $199–$245 double, $259–$290 suite, $309–$370 condo; summer $89–$169 all room options. 2- to 6-person occupancy. MC, V. Valet parking. **Amenities:** 2 Jacuzzis. *In room:* TV, kitchenette (in some), Wi-Fi.

MODERATE

Alpine Village Suites ★★ Alpine Village is a small village within Taos Ski Valley, a few steps from the lift. The complex also houses a ski shop and bar/restaurant. The owners began with seven rooms, still nice rentals, above their ski shop. Each has a sleeping loft, for the agile who care to climb a ladder, as well as sunny windows. The newer section has elegantly decorated rooms, with attractive touches such as Mexican furniture and inventive tile work. Like most other accommodations at Taos Ski Valley, the rooms are not especially soundproof. Fortunately, most skiers go to bed early. In the newer building, rooms have fireplaces and private balconies. Request a south-facing room for a view of the slopes. The Jacuzzi sits below a lovely mural, and has a fireplace and a view of the slopes.

100 Thunderbird Rd. (P.O. Box 98), Taos Ski Valley, NM 87525. ℂ **800/576-2666** or 575/776-8540. Fax 575/776-8542. www.alpine-suites.com. 31 units. Ski season $150–$215 suite for 2, $216–$347 suite for 4, $216–$391 suite for up to 6; summer $90 suite for 2, $102–$132 suite for 4, $120–$270 suite for up to 6. Continental breakfast only in summer. AE, DISC, MC, V. Covered valet parking $15 per night. **Amenities:** Jacuzzi; massage; sauna. *In room:* TV, DVD and VCR (in some), kitchenette, Wi-Fi (in most).

Condominiums

EXPENSIVE

Edelweiss Lodge & Spa ★★ Opened in 2005, this lodge at the base of the mountain took the place of a 1960s classic chalet. Now, it's a brand-new condohotel. The condominiums are upscale, each with a flagstone fireplace and full kitchen with marble countertops, stainless-steel appliances, and many with nice views of the slopes. All have luxury furnishings decorated in earth tones. For those looking for an upscale stay, this is your choice. Hotel rooms follow with the same luxury as the condos. Rooms are medium size with comfortable beds and medium-size baths. Underground parking, a full spa, an excellent restaurant, and valet service for your skis add to the appeal.

106 Sutton Place, Taos Ski Valley, NM 87525. ℂ **800/458-8754** or 575/737-6900. Fax 575/737-6995. www.edelweisslodgeandspa.com. 31 units. Winter $220–$440 double, $275–$1,156 condo; summer $100 double, $160–$335 condo. AE, DISC, MC, V. Free parking. **Amenities:** Restaurant; bar; concierge; health club and full spa; Jacuzzi; sauna. *In room:* TV/DVD, CD player, hair dryer, kitchen, Wi-Fi.

Sierra del Sol Condominiums ★ I have wonderful memories of these condominiums, which are just a 2-minute walk from the lift; family friends used to invite me to stay with them when I was young. I'm happy to say that the units, built in the 1960s, with additions through the years, have been well maintained. Though they're privately owned, and therefore decorated at the whim of the owners, management does inspect them every year and make suggestions. They're smartly built and come in a few sizes: studio, one-bedroom, and two-bedroom. The one- and two-bedroom units have big living rooms with fireplaces and porches that look out on the ski runs. The bedrooms are spacious, and some have sleeping lofts. Two-bedroom units sleep up to six. Grills and picnic tables on the grounds sit near a mountain river.

13 Thunderbird Rd. (P.O. Box 84), Taos Ski Valley, NM 87525. ℂ **800/523-3954** or 575/776-2981. Fax 575/776-2347. www.sierrataos.com. 32 units. From $79 for studio in summer to $471 for 2-bedroom condo in high season. DISC, MC, V. Free parking. **Amenities:** Babysitting; 2 Jacuzzis; 2 saunas. *In room:* TV/DVD, hair dryer (upon request), kitchen, Wi-Fi.

Snakedance Condominiums and Spa ★★ The original structure that stood on this site was known as the Hondo Lodge. Before there was a Taos Ski Valley, Hondo Lodge served as a refuge for fishermen, hunters, and artists. A $3.5-million renovation has transformed the rooms of this once-time hotel into elegant condominiums. Skiers appreciate the inn's location, just steps from the lift, as well as amenities such as ski storage and boot dryers. The Snakedance Condominiums today are privately owned units, so each may differ some, though they are consistent in quality. All are bright, comfortable spaces with balconies with French doors, and kitchens with granite counters and a range, fridge, dishwasher, and microwave. All have gas fireplaces. The Hondo Restaurant and Bar offers dining and entertainment daily during the ski season (schedules vary off season) and also sponsors wine tastings and wine dinners. The hotel also offers shuttle service to and from nearby shops and restaurants, and, at certain times, to Albuquerque and Santa Fe.

110 Sutton Place (P.O. Box 89), Taos Ski Valley, NM 87525. ℂ **800/322-9815** or 575/776-2277. Fax 575/776-1410. www.snakedancecondos.com. 33 units. Winter $272–$450 1-bedroom condo, $380–$700 2-bedroom condo for 4 people, $460–$800 2-bedroom loft condo for 6 people; summer $95 1-bedroom condo, $120 2-bedroom condo, $150 2-bedroom loft condo. Extra person $30 in winter, $10 in summer. Rates include continental breakfast. AE, DC, DISC, MC, V. Free parking at Taos Ski Valley parking lot.

Closed mid-Apr to Memorial Day and mid-Oct to mid-Nov. **Amenities:** Restaurant; bar; free airport transfers; exercise room; Jacuzzi; sauna; spa. *In room:* Satellite TV/DVD, hair dryer, kitchen, Wi-Fi.

MODERATE

Taos Mountain Lodge ⚡ These loft suites (which can each accommodate up to six) provide airy, comfortable lodging for a good price. Built in 1990, about a mile west of Taos Ski Valley on the road from Taos, the place has undergone some renovation over the years. Don't expect a lot of privacy in these condominiums, but they're good for a romping ski vacation. The beds are comfortable and the baths are small but functional. Each unit has a small bedroom downstairs and a loft bedroom upstairs, as well as a foldout or futon couch in the living room. Regular rooms have kitchenettes, with minifridges and stoves, and deluxe rooms have full kitchens, with full refrigerators, stoves, and ovens.

Taos Ski Valley Rd. (P.O. Box 202), Taos Ski Valley, NM 87525. © **866/320-8267** or 575/776-2229. Fax 575/776-3982. www.taosmountainlodge.net. 10 units. Ski season $120–$275 suite; May–Oct $85–$100 suite. AE, DISC, MC, V. *In room:* TV, hair dryer, kitchen or kitchenette.

RV PARKS & CAMPGROUNDS

Carson National Forest There are nine national forest camping areas within 20 miles of Taos; these developed areas are open from Memorial Day to Labor Day. They range from woodsy, streamside sites on the road to Taos Ski Valley to open lowlands with lots of sage. Call the Forest Service to discuss the best location for your needs.

208 Cruz Alta Rd., Taos, NM 87571. © **575/758-6200.** www.fs.fed.us/r3/carson. $7–$15 per night. No credit cards.

Questa Lodge & RV Park On the banks of the Red River, this RV camp is just outside the small village of Questa. It's a nice pastoral setting near the river and with a little pond. The cabins aren't in the best condition and are usually rented out long term (see website for pricing options), but the RV and camping accommodations are pleasant—all with amazing mountain views.

Lower Embargo Rd. no. 8 (P.O. Box 155), Questa, NM 87556. © **575/586-9913.** www.questalodge.com. 28 sites. Full RV hookup $32 per day, $400 per month. 5 cabins for rent. MC, V.

Taos Valley RV Park and Campground ★ Just 2½ miles south of the plaza, this lovely, well-maintained campground is surrounded by sage and offers views of the surrounding mountains. Each site has a picnic table and grill. The place has a small store, a laundry room, a playground, and tent shelters, as well as a dump station and very clean restrooms. Pets are welcome. Wireless Internet access is available throughout the park.

120 Este Rd., off NM 68 (7204 NDCBU), Taos, NM 87571. © **800/999-7571** or 575/758-4469. Fax 575/758-4469. www.taosrv.com. 91 spaces. $22 without RV hookup; $30–$39 with RV hookup. AE, DISC, MC, V.

WHERE TO DINE IN TAOS

Taos has some of the region's most inventive and fun restaurants. The creativity of the town flourishes in the flavors here. It's also a comfortable place to dine. Informality reigns; at a number of restaurants you can eat world-class food while wearing jeans or even ski pants. Nowhere is a jacket and tie mandatory. This informality doesn't extend to reservations, however; especially during the peak season, it's important to make reservations well in advance and keep them or else cancel. Also, be aware that Taos is not a late-night place; most restaurants finish serving at about 9pm.

14

RESTAURANTS BY CUISINE

AMERICAN
Caffé Renato ★★ ($$, p. 205)
Eske's Brew Pub and Eatery ★
($, p. 208)
Michael's Kitchen ($, p. 209)
Old Blinking Light ★ ($$, p. 206)

ASIAN
Sushi a la Hattori ★★ ($$, p. 207)

BAVARIAN
The Bavarian Restaurant ★
($, p. 210)

CONTINENTAL
Stakeout Grill & Bar ★★ ($$$,
p. 204)

DELI/CAFE
Bent Street Cafe & Deli ($$, p. 204)
Café Loka ★★ ($, p 208)
Lula's ★★ ($, p. 209)
Taos Cow ★ ($, p. 210)

DESSERT
Taos Cow ★ ($, p. 210)

FRENCH/SPANISH FUSION
Gutiz ★★ ($, p. 209)

INTERNATIONAL
Bent Street Cafe & Deli ($$, p. 204)
El Meze ★★ ($$$, p. 202)

KEY TO ABBREVIATIONS:
$$$$** = Very Expensive   **$$$** = Expensive   **$$** = Moderate   **$ = Inexpensive

Graham's Grille ★★ ($$, p. 205)
Trading Post Café ★★ ($$, p. 207)

ITALIAN
Caffé Renato ★★ ($$, p. 205)
Taos Pizza Out Back ★ ($$, p. 207)
Trading Post Café ★★ ($$, p. 207)

MEDITERRANEAN
El Meze ★★ ($$$, p. 202)
Sabroso ★★ ($$$, p. 202)

MEXICAN
Antonio's ★★ ($$, p. 204)
Guadalajara Grill ★ ($, p. 208)
Old Blinking Light ★ ($$, p. 206)

NEW AMERICAN
Chef Damon's ★★ ($$, p. 205)
De La Tierra ★★★ ($$$, p. 201)
Doc Martin's ★ ($$$, p. 201)
Graham's Grille ★★ ($$, p. 205)
Gutiz ★★ ($, p. 209)

Lambert's of Taos ★★★ ($$$, p. 202)
The Love Apple ★★★ ($$, p. 206)
Sabroso ★★ ($$$, p. 202)

NEW MEXICAN
Antonio's ★★ ($$, p. 204)
Chef Damon's ★★ ($$, p. 205)
Doc Martin's ★ ($$$, p. 201)
Eske's Brew Pub and Eatery ★ ($, p. 208)
The Love Apple ★★★ ($$, p. 206)
Michael's Kitchen ($, p. 209)
Orlando's New Mexican Café ★ ($, p. 209)

PIZZA
Taos Pizza Out Back ★ ($$, p. 207)

STEAK/SEAFOOD
Sabroso ★★ ($$$, p. 202)
Stakeout Grill & Bar ★★ ($$$, p. 204)

SUSHI
Sushi a la Hattori ★★ ($$, p. 207)

EXPENSIVE

De La Tierra ★★★ NEW AMERICAN Located in the eco-resort El Monte Sagrado (p. 202), this restaurant offers delectably inventive American cuisine in an old-world ambience, with a high ceiling, comfortable black silk chairs, and elegant contemporary art on the walls. Service is excellent, even down to the master sommelier overseeing the wine selections. The chef utilizes seasonal and local ingredients, including organic ones when he can. For starters, you might try the buffalo ravioli with green-chile alfredo and cilantro pesto. For a main course, the Prairie Farms elk tenderloin with chestnut mashed potatoes and green-chile Brussels sprouts is delicious, as is the Kessler Canyon mountain trout with mint and green-pea potatoes and lemon caper sauce. Excellent food, including Sunday brunch, is served during the day at the Gardens, a more casual spot, with lots of exotic plants and a lovely patio. Meals are also served at the Anaconda Bar (p. 232).

In the El Monte Sagrado Hotel, 317 Kit Carson Rd. © **800/828-8267** or 575/758-3502. www.elmonte sagrado.com/dining/dining.asp. Reservations recommended. The Gardens main courses $7–$14 breakfast, $8–$16 lunch; De La Tierra $19–$39 dinner. AE, DC, DISC, MC, V. The Gardens daily 7am–3pm; De La Tierra daily 6–9:30pm.

Doc Martin's ★ NEW AMERICAN/NEW MEXICAN Doc Martin's serves innovative food in a historic setting. The restaurant comprises Dr. Thomas Paul Martin's former home, office, and delivery room. In 1912, painters Bert Philips and Ernest Blumenschein hatched the concept of the Taos Society of Artists here.

The chef uses local and organic ingredients and wild game when available. The wine list has received numerous "Awards of Excellence" from *Wine Spectator* magazine. In the rich atmosphere of a thick-walled adobe home with a kiva fireplace, diners feast on breakfast fare such as a grilled organic buffalo patty and eggs, with wild mushroom gravy and home fries; or blue-corn and blueberry hotcakes. Lunch might include Doc's *chile relleno,* or a turkey, avocado, bacon, and green-chile sandwich. For dinner, a good bet is the grilled buffalo steak with a red chile–and–roasted tomatillo sauce, served with beans, rice, and vegetables. If you have room, there's always a nice selection of desserts. The Adobe bar has live music with no cover charge.

In the Historic Taos Inn, 125 Paseo del Pueblo Norte. ✆ **575/758-1977.** www.taosinn.com. Reservations recommended. Main courses $5–$10 breakfast, $7–$15 lunch, $18–$30 dinner. AE, DISC, MC, V. Daily 5–9:30pm; Mon–Fri 7:30–11am and 11:30am–2:30pm; brunch Sat–Sun 7:30am–2:30pm.

El Meze ★★ 🏛 INTERNATIONAL/MEDITERRANEAN   Meaning "table" in Arabic, El Meze offers delicious Spanish/Mediterranean food with Moroccan influences. The setting is an 1847 hacienda with vigas, walls painted orange and green, a gold fireplace, and bright contemporary art on the walls. The classically trained chef puts much thought into his food and its preparation. Service is helpful and efficient. Dinner might begin with grilled prawns with lemon and Moroccan spices, or a butternut squash–and–chicken tortilla soup with avocado and feta. For an entree, I've enjoyed a tuna carpaccio with fresh grated horseradish, capers, lemon, and Spanish olive oil. Another excellent offering is the grilled bone-in rib-eye steak. For dessert, the chocolate truffle soufflé is as good as it sounds. A thoughtful beer and wine list accompanies the menu.

1017 Paseo del Pueblo Norte. ✆ **575/751-3337.** www.elmeze.com. AE, DISC, MC, V. Reservations recommended. Main courses $18–$32. AE, DISC, MC, V. Summer Mon–Sat 5:30–9:30pm; winter hours vary, call ahead.

Lambert's of Taos ★★★ NEW AMERICAN   Open since 1989 in the historic Randall Home near Los Pandos Road, this restaurant serves flavorful contemporary food in an elegant setting. Wood floors, lightly sponge-painted walls, and crisp tablecloths set the scene for imaginative food utilizing seasonal and local ingredients whenever possible. The meal begins with good crusty bread served with a head of roasted garlic and your choice of olive oil or butter. For an appetizer you might try the Maryland-style crab cakes with roasted garlic remoulade. For an entree, the pepper-crusted lamb loin served with ravioli is a signature dish, but you might opt for one of the fresh fish specials, such as Scottish salmon with chard cream sauce, fingerling potatoes, and asparagus. For dessert, try the warm apple-and-almond crisp with white-chocolate ice cream or Zeke's chocolate truffle mousse. A full bar, with an interesting wine and beer list and espresso, is available. The restaurant also has a cozy lounge with its own menu—a real locals hangout.

309 Paseo del Pueblo Sur. ✆ **575/758-1009.** www.lambertsoftaos.com. Reservations recommended. Main courses $22–$38. AE, DC, DISC, MC, V. Daily 5–9pm or so.

Sabroso ★★ NEW AMERICAN/STEAK/SEAFOOD/MEDITERRANEAN Housed in the classic hacienda-style building of what once was the Casa Cordova—a popular après-ski spot in the '60s, when my parents used to come to drink martinis—this new restaurant, about 10 minutes north of town in Arroyo Seco, offers quality food in a cozy northern New Mexico ambience. Viga ceilings and candle sconces create an old-world mood, while the food is quite innovative. The service is conscientious. You might start with gulf oysters, with bacon and Parmesan, served over a wedge of grilled romaine lettuce with a spicy vinaigrette. Wood-grilled items top the entree list. The

Taos Area Dining

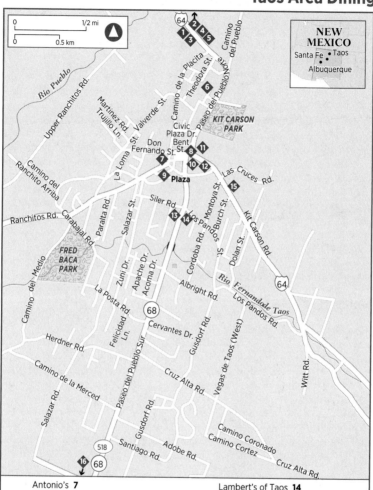

NEW MEXICO

Santa Fe • • Taos

Albuquerque

Antonio's **7**
The Bavarian Restaurant **2**
Bent Street Cafe & Deli **8**
Café Loka **9**
Caffé Renato **11**
Chef Damon's **16**
De La Tierra **15**
Doc Martin's **11**
El Meze **4**
Eske's Brew Pub and Eatery **12**
Graham's Grill **8**
Guadalajara Grill **3**, **16**
Gutiz **3**

Lambert's of Taos **14**
The Love Apple **5**
Lula's **13**
Michael's Kitchen **6**
Old Blinking Light **2**
Orlando's New Mexican Café **1**
Rellenos **10**
Sabroso **2**
Stakeout Grill & Bar **16**
Sushi a la Hattori **2**
Taos Pizza Out Back **3**
Taos Cow **2**
Trading Post Café **16**

beef is quality, as is the wild salmon. There's also a vegetarian ravioli. My recent lamb chops came with roasted potatoes and fresh vegetables. The waiter characterizes the wine list as "big, bold, and seasonal." The attached bar offers comfy couches and a less formal menu with a notable buffalo chile and wood-grilled burgers.

470 NM 150, Arroyo Seco. ℗ **575/776-3333.** www.sabrosotaos.com. Reservations recommended. Main courses $16–$32; bar menu $9–$18. AE, DISC, MC, V. Daily 5–9pm; bar 4:30–10pm.

Stakeout Grill & Bar ★★ CONTINENTAL/STEAK/SEAFOOD   This is one of northern New Mexico's most adventurous dining experiences. You drive about a mile up a dirt road toward the base of the Sangre de Cristo Mountains to reach the restaurant, and dine looking down on the Taos gorge while the sun sets over the Jemez Range. The warm, rustic decor of this sprawling hacienda with a broad patio (a great place to sit in summer) includes creaking hardwood floors—and a crackling fireplace in the winter. The fare, which focuses on steak and seafood, is fresh and thoughtfully prepared. Start with baked brie with sliced almonds and apples, or green-chile crab cakes with citrus aioli. Move on to a filet mignon served with béarnaise sauce, or sample one of the chef's excellent pasta specials. Recently, I had shrimp over linguini with goat cheese that was a bowl of pure joy. This is also the place to come if you have a craving for lobster. Try to time your reservation so you can see the sunset. A full bar, an extensive wine list, and cigars are available.

101 Stakeout Dr. (9 miles south of Taos, just off Hwy. 68). ℗ **575/758-2042.** www.stakeoutrestaurant. com. Reservations recommended. Main courses $20–$72. AE, DC, DISC, MC, V. Daily 5–9:30pm.

MODERATE

Antonio's ★★ 📷 MEXICAN/NEW MEXICAN   A summer afternoon on the patio of this new restaurant, with a fountain flowing and sun shining on flowers in garden beds, could just transport you to an idyllic Mexico. Add in a margarita and a plate of enchiladas or tacos, and you may never return. Just a block from the plaza, the food at this fun cafe is spirited, though the service could pay more attention. Start your meal with guacamole mixed at your table and move on to Rellenos en Nogada, a roasted poblano pepper stuffed with beef, pear, apple, raisins, onion, tomato, and spices, and smothered with walnut brandy cream sauce. Too rich for you? Try the beef, chicken, cheese, or spinach enchiladas with a red- or green-chile sauce. Finish with *tres leches*—cake in rich, whipped milk. A bar inside bustles at cocktail hour, as does the whole place during busy summer days. Under the same ownership, just a few blocks away at 135 Paseo del Pueblo Sur, **Rellenos Café** also serves the same delicious Mexican food but in a more modest setting (℗ **575/758-7001;** Mon–Sat 11am–3pm).

122-B Doña Luz. ℗ **575/751-4800.** www.antoniosoftaos.com. Reservations recommended Fri–Sat. Main courses $8.50–$23. MC, V. Mon–Sat 11am–9pm.

Bent Street Cafe & Deli DELI/CAFE/INTERNATIONAL   This popular cafe, a short block north of the plaza, serves decent food in a country-home atmosphere. Outside, a flower box surrounds sidewalk seating that is heated in winter. Inside, wood floors and lots of windows provide a country diner feel. The menu features breakfast burritos, egg dishes, and homemade granola; for lunch—the best meal to eat here—you can choose from 18 deli sandwiches, plus a "create-your-own" column, as well as a variety of salads. Their dark-brown bread matched with a changing selection of soups is one of their best offerings. Though the deli meats here are fresh, the vegetables sometimes aren't. Real sandwich aficionados will prefer those at Lula's (p. 209). The restaurant has resumed serving dinner, with such offerings as burgers and pasta dishes. A Sunday brunch favorite is banana-bread French toast. If you'd like a picnic to go, their deli offers carryout service.

120 Bent St. © **575/758-5787.** Reservations accepted. Breakfast $4–$8.50; lunch $3.50–$11; dinner $8–$12. MC, V. Mon–Sat 8am–9pm; Sun 10am–3pm.

Caffé Renato ★★ 🍴 AMERICAN/ITALIAN   You can't miss this cafe decked out with bright red umbrellas on its patio. Diners enjoy the cool Taos air while feasting on tasty food prepared with fine ingredients. A back patio is quieter, and inside, a kitchen-side dining room provides a comfortable ambience with wood floors and white tablecloths. Service is friendly but may be understaffed. The lunch menu offers a variety of sandwiches and salads. The Angus burger is stellar, as is the Caprese, with mozzarella, basil, tomato, and pesto mayo grilled on focaccia. For dinner, the classic spaghetti with meatballs is easy on the wallet, while the grilled salmon with a lemon-tarragon aioli is equally delicious. Finish with red pear, cranberry, and ginger cobbler so good the recipe was published in *Bon Appetit* magazine. A selection of beers, wines, and coffee drinks accompanies the menu.

133 Paseo del Pueblo N. © **575/758-0244.** Reservations recommended Fri–Sat night. Main courses lunch $8.50–$15, dinner $12–$18. AE, DISC, MC, V. Daily 11am–9pm.

Chef Damon's ★★ NEW AMERICAN/NEW MEXICAN   This new restaurant toward the south end of town serves thoughtfully prepared food in a warm contemporary ambience, with diamond-finished walls, glazed glass art on the windows, and hardwood floors. Chef Damon, a Best Chef Southwest semifinalist in 2009, uses local, seasonal ingredients to create some interesting twists on New Mexico favorites, such as a spicy lamb green-chile stew and lamb enchiladas, both delightful. He also serves excellent fish specials such as the grouper with saffron buerre blanc over mashed potatoes with kale and carrots. The wine list is selected to pair with the chef's offerings, including a number of Spanish vintages. For dessert, try the Kahlua chocolate torte—it's gluten-free.

1041 Paseo del Pueblo Sur. © **575/737-0140.** Reservations recommended Fri–Sat. Main courses $18–$30. MC, V. Wed–Sun 5–9:30pm.

Graham's Grille ★★ INTERNATIONAL/NEW AMERICAN   Opened in 2007, this restaurant offers comfort food with a Southwestern flair. It's set in a long, narrow space just off the plaza, a cozy urban atmosphere with hanging halogen lamps and a long *banco* along one wall. Meals start with delectable flour tortilla crisps. The must-have appetizer is the baked mac and cheese with green chile and bacon, but if that sounds too rich, the artichoke-and-fennel fritti will also please. Lunches offer soup, salad, and sandwich combinations, if you'd like. The town is buzzing about the salmon BLT, which is just what it sounds, salmon with good bacon, lettuce, and tomato. Burritos, tamale pie, and burgers—even veggie, buffalo, and lamb ones—come on house-made buns. For dinner, the cherry chipotle-grilled salmon is the most popular dish here. For dessert, the chocolate nachos are a real novelty, but my favorite is the mango coconut cake. A select beer and wine list accompanies the menu.

Lula's (p. 209)   A relaxed atmosphere and lots of sandwich choices, as well as soups, are sure to please here.

Michael's Kitchen (p. 209)   With a broad menu, comfy booths, and a very casual, diner-type atmosphere, Michael's Kitchen makes both kids and their parents feel at home.

Orlando's New Mexican Café (p. 209)   The relaxed atmosphere and playfully colorful walls will please the kids almost as much as the tacos and quesadillas made especially for them.

Sushi a la Hattori (p. 207)   *"Raw fish, no way!"* That might be your kids'

response to this idea, but if you can coax them through the door, you'll find a relaxed atmosphere and a children's dinner of tempura shrimp, beef, or chicken, with ice cream for dessert.

Taos Cow (p. 210)   Potpies and sandwiches will fill kids up before they dive into the all-natural ice cream at this cafe north of town.

Taos Pizza Out Back (p. 207)   The pizza will please both parents and kids, and so will all the odd decorations, such as the chain with foot-long links hanging over the front counter.

106 Paseo del Pueblo Norte. ☏ **575/751-1350.** www.grahamstaos.com. AE, MC, V. Reservations recommended at dinner. Main courses $7–$13 lunch, $13–$32 dinner. Mon–Sat 11am–2:30pm and 5–9pm.

The Love Apple ★★★ 🎁 NEW AMERICAN/NEW MEXICAN   Set in the mid-1800s Placitas Chapel, this new restaurant serves inventive food in a warm and cozy atmosphere. The soulful setting includes candlelight, aged wood floors, thick adobe walls, and vigas adorning the ceiling. Service is attentive and intuitive. Diners feast on seasonal and often organic produce and meats in all the dishes. Good appetizer choices include a sautéed apple and roasted squash quesadilla; or a beet, pear, and mozzarella salad. The main course might bring a grilled lamb sausage with *posole* (hominy) or a ruby rainbow trout cooked in corn husks and served with a quinoa-*piñon* fritter. An eclectic list of wines accompanies the menu, with many value options. The seasons drive the dessert creations. My favorite thus far is hot apple pie á la mode. Be aware that this is a cash- or check-only establishment.

803 Paseo del Pueblo Norte, Taos, NM 87571. ☏ **575/751-0050.** Reservations recommended. Main courses $13–$18. No credit cards. Tues–Sat 5:30–9:30pm.

Old Blinking Light ★ AMERICAN/MEXICAN   This restaurant on the Ski Valley Road provides tasty American food in a casual atmosphere. It's named for the blinking yellow light that was once the marker Taoseños used to give directions ("turn left at the blinking light," and so on), now replaced by a stoplight. Decorated with Spanish colonial furniture and an excellent art collection, this restaurant is a good place to stop after skiing or for a romping night of music. The service is friendly and efficient. To accompany the free chips and homemade salsa, order a margarita—preferably their standard, made with Sauza Gold Tequila—and sip it next to the patio bonfire, open evenings year-round. The menu ranges from salads and burgers to steaks, seafood, and Mexican food. I say head straight for the fajitas, especially the jumbo shrimp wrapped in bacon and stuffed with poblano peppers and jack cheese. Leave room for the Old Blinking Light Mud Pie, made with local Taos Cow Ice Cream. Live music plays on Monday and Friday nights.

US 150, mile marker 1. © **575/776-8787.** www.oldblinkinglight.com. Reservations recommended Fri–Sat and Mon night. Main courses $9–$20. AE, MC, V. Restaurant daily 5–10pm. Bar opens at 4pm for happy hour. Wine shop daily noon–10pm.

Sushi a la Hattori ★★ ☺ ASIAN/SUSHI

Set north of town in the aged-wood Overland Sheepskin complex, this popular locals' spot serves fresh sushi and Japanese meals in a modest atmosphere, with stunning views of meadows and Taos Mountain. The food is authentic, the fish flown in from Japan. The setting is basic, with Formica tables, a sushi bar, and Japanese art on the walls. Service is efficient. All the sushi favorites are available here. My best choice is the Sunset Roll, with eel, cucumber and avocado, but the locals' favorite here is the Rainbow Roll, with five different fish and avocado. Lunch brings specials such as a tempura box that contains shrimp, salmon, and various veggies along with miso soup, cabbage salad, and rice. Dinner entrees include such tasty items as beef teriyaki and broiled Chilean sea bass served with miso soup and rice. A children's dinner is available, as is a select beer and wine list, and, of course, sake.

1405 Paseo del Pueblo Norte, Bldg. 3, Ste. 6. © **575/737-5123.** Sushi $3–$13 per selection. Main courses lunch and dinner $7.50–$20. AE, DISC, MC, V. Tues–Sat noon–2pm and 5–9pm.

Taos Pizza Out Back ★ ☺ ITALIAN/PIZZA

My kayaking buddies always go here after a day on the river. That will give you an idea of the level of informality (very), as well as the quality of the food and beer (great), and the size of the portions (large). It's a raucous old hippie-decorated adobe restaurant, with a friendly and eager waitstaff. What to order? I have one big word here: PIZZA. Sure the spicy Greek pasta is good, as is the Veggie Zone (a calzone filled with stir-fried veggies and two cheeses)—but, why? The pizzas are incredible. All come with a delicious thin crust that's folded over on the edges and sprinkled with sesame seeds. The sauce is unthinkably tasty, and the variations are broad. There's the Killer, with sun-dried tomatoes, Gorgonzola, green chile, and black olives; and my favorite, pizza Florentine (spinach, basil, sun-dried tomatoes, chicken breast, mushrooms, capers, and garlic). Don't leave without trying the house-made carrot cake. Check out the selection of wines and large selection of microbrews.

712 Paseo del Pueblo Norte (just north of Allsup's). © **575/758-3112.** Reservations recommended Fri–Sat and holidays. Pizzas $13–$28; pastas and calzones $10–$13. MC, V. Daily 11am–10pm (winter Sun–Thurs until 9pm).

Trading Post Café ★★ 📷 NORTHERN ITALIAN/INTERNATIONAL

One of my tastiest writing assignments was when I did a profile of this restaurant for the *New York Times*. Chef/owner René Mettler served course after course prepared especially for me. But if you think this might color my opinion, just ask anyone in town where he or she most likes to eat. Don't expect quiet romance here: The place bustles. A bar encloses an open-exhibition kitchen. If you're dining alone or don't feel like waiting for a table, the bar is a fun place to sit. Diners can feel comfortable here, even if trying three appetizers and skipping the main course. The outstanding Caesar salad has an interesting twist—garlic chips. The *fettuccine alla carbonara* is tasty, as is the seafood pasta. Heartier appetites might like the New Zealand lamb chops with tomato-mint sauce. There's also a fresh fish of the day and usually some nice soups at very reasonable prices. A good list of beers and wines rounds out the experience. For dessert, try the tarts.

4179 Paseo del Pueblo Sur, Ranchos de Taos. © **575/758-5089.** www.tradingpostcafe.com. Reservations accepted. Menu items $8–$30. AE, DC, DISC, MC, V. Tues–Sat 11:30am–9:30pm; Sun 5–9pm.

INEXPENSIVE

Café Loka ★★ DELI/CAFE   With a background in urban planning, owner Dave Hardy designed this contemporary new cafe with the intention of uniting the Ledoux Street neighborhood. It appears he has succeeded. Locals come to the bright, open space, with hardwood floors and viga ceilings, or to the courtyard patio to meet with friends, write poetry, view art hanging on the indoor walls, and eat delectable baked goods, sandwiches, and soups. Service here is courteous. You might start the day with an espresso or latte accompanied by a buttermilk blueberry muffin or a breakfast burrito with cilantro and jalapeño salsa. For lunch, I've enjoyed a turkey-and-havarti sandwich with green-chile sweet potato soup, and my friend raved about the artichoke, tomato, mushroom, and havarti quiche. Special sandwiches and salads dress the menu each day. For dessert, try the carrot cake. This is a Wi-Fi hot spot.

112-E Camino de la Placita. © **575/758-4204.** www.cafeloka.com. All menu items under $9. AE, DISC, MC, V. Mon–Sat 8am–3pm.

Eske's Brew Pub and Eatery ★ AMERICAN/NEW MEXICAN   This is brew pub Taos style. Diners sit on tall chairs at tall tables and sample such comfort food as Wanda's green-chile turkey stew, or, for the really hungry, the Fatty (a whole-wheat tortilla filled with beans, mashed potatoes, onions, cheeses, and smothered in green-chile turkey stew). Eske's also serves bratwurst, burgers, and vegetarian dishes. The beers change with the season, the darker ones more prevalent in winter. For a real local treat, try the Taos Green Chile Beer. Service is friendly and informal. The crowd is local, with people sitting at the bar to watch the beer-pouring and food preparation. At times it can be rowdy, but mostly it's just fun, with ski patrollers and mountain guides showing up to swap stories. In summer, you can eat on picnic tables outside, where live music plays on Friday and Saturday nights.

106 DesGeorges Lane. © **575/758-1517.** All menu items under $10. MC, V. Mar–Sept and peak times (spring and winter breaks) daily 11:30am–10pm; rest of year Fri–Sun 11:30am–9pm.

Guadalajara Grill ★ MEXICAN   This bustling restaurant set in a plain building on the south side serves authentic Mexican food in a casual setting. Glass-topped tables and wooden benches are highlighted by a mural of the plaza in the town of Teocuitatlan, the owner's original home. During warm months a wrap-around patio offers a great place to sip *cerveza*. The food is Mexican rather than New Mexican, a refreshing treat. I recommend the tacos, particularly pork or chicken, served in soft homemade corn tortillas, the meat artfully seasoned and grilled. The enchiladas and burritos are large and smothered in chile. *Platos* are served with rice and beans, and half orders are available for smaller appetites. The seafood dishes also offer real flavor—try the *mojo de ajo* (shrimp cooked with garlic), served with rice, beans, and guacamole. Beer and wine accompany the menu. Equally popular, and casual, is their north-side location, at 822 Paseo del Pueblo Norte (© **575/737-0816**).

1384 Paseo del Pueblo Sur. © **575/751-0063.** Main courses $5–$15. MC, V. Sun–Thurs 10:30am–9pm (winter until 8:30pm); Fri–Sat 10:30am–9:30pm (winter until 9pm).

Gutiz ★★ 🍴 FRENCH/SPANISH/NEW AMERICAN   Between purple and apricot walls hung with bright contemporary art, this restaurant, recently under new ownership, serves unique and flavorful cuisine. The recipes combine flavors from Spain, France, Peru, and Bolivia and use organic greens and fresh meats and fish, and a broad variety of chile peppers. Service is friendly and efficient. Breakfast brings delicacies such as my favorite, the Taoseño—rice, potatoes, chile, cheese, and fresh herbs topped with scrambled eggs. The French toast is thick, made with home-baked bread. Lunch might begin with a niçoise salad made with fresh tuna, French beans, veggies, potatoes, and olives. The many varied sandwiches come on homemade bread. Alongside the great food, sip from a variety of coffees and chai tea.

812-B Paseo del Pueblo Norte. © **575/758-1226.** Main courses $7–$18. MC, V. Tues–Sun 8am–3pm.

Lula's ★★ 😊 DELI/CAFE   A few blocks south of the plaza, this deli offers gourmet soups and sandwiches and diner-style meals between sun-colored walls or to go. The tables here, tall and glass, with stools, don't quite match the comfort level of the food, so diners tend to grab the few regular wooden ones. You order at a counter and the food is served at your table. The soups are gourmet, especially the vegetable stew, which has a rich broth and is served with a baguette. Paninis are a big draw here, the one with roasted eggplant, roasted red bell peppers, zucchini, spinach, provolone, and pesto a real favorite. The nightly blue-plate specials served after 4pm on weekdays and all day Saturday may include chicken alfresco—chicken in broth seasoned with garlic, tomato, and basil over linguini. A kids' menu pleases the tots. Don't leave without sampling a coconut macaroon with whipped ganache dipped in chocolate. Sample from the small select beer and wine list.

316 Paseo del Pueblo Sur. © **575/751-1280.** Main courses $7.50–$14. MC. V. Mon–Sat 11am–9pm (winter until 8pm).

Michael's Kitchen 😊 NEW MEXICAN/AMERICAN   A couple blocks north of the plaza, this eatery provides big portions of rib-sticking food in a relaxed atmosphere. Between its hardwood floor and viga ceiling are various knickknacks: an antique wood stove here, a Tiffany lamp there. Seating is at booths and tables. Breakfast is the meal to eat here, with a large selection of pancakes and egg preparations served all day. Lunch brings sandwiches, including a Philly cheesesteak, a tuna melt, and a veggie option. Some people like the generically (and facetiously) titled "Health Food" meal, a double order of fries with red or green chile and cheese. If you're in a hurry, try one of the excellent doughnuts served from Michael's bakery.

304-C Paseo del Pueblo Norte. © **575/758-4178.** No reservations. Breakfast $4–$16; lunch $6–$10. AE, DISC, MC, V. Mon–Thurs 7am–2:30pm; Fri–Sun 7am–8pm. Closed major holidays.

Orlando's New Mexican Café ★ 😊 NEW MEXICAN   Festivity reigns in this spicy little cafe on the north end of town. Serving some of northern New Mexico's best chile, this place has colorful tables set around a bustling open kitchen and airy patio dining during warmer months. Service is friendly but minimal. Try the Los Colores, their most popular dish, with three enchiladas (chicken, beef, and cheese) smothered in chile and served with beans and *posole*. The taco salad is another favorite. Portions are big here, and you can order a Mexican or microbrew beer, or a New Mexican or California wine.

114 Don Juan Valdez Lane (1¾ miles north of the plaza, off Paseo del Pueblo Norte). ☏ **575/751-1450.** Reservations not accepted. Main courses under $12. MC, V. Daily 10:30am-3pm and 5-9pm.

North of Town

The Bavarian Restaurant ★ 🍴 BAVARIAN   This restaurant, sitting high above Taos Ski Valley at an elevation of 10,200 feet, feels both rustic and elegant. Beamed ceilings, aged pine paneling, 300-year-old castle doors, and an antler chandelier all set around an authentic *kachelofen* (a Bavarian-style stove), help create the atmospheric scene. Service is uneven but well intentioned. At lunch, the porch fills with sun-worshipers and menu choices include traditional foods such as goulash and *spätzle* (Bavarian-style pasta). Dinnertime brings classic dishes such as Wiener schnitzel (Viennese veal cutlet) and sauerbraten (beef roast). Most entrees come with a potato dish and fresh vegetable. For dessert, try the apple strudel. Accompany your meal with a selection from the well-chosen European wine list or with a beer, served in an authentic stein. The road to the Bavarian is easily drivable in summer. In winter, most diners ski here or call to arrange for a shuttle to pick them up at the Taos Ski Valley parking lot.

In the Bavarian Lodge, Taos Ski Valley. ☏ **888/205-8020** or 575/776-8020. Reservations recommended at dinner. Main courses $7.50-$17 lunch, $18-$35 dinner. AE, MC, V. Ski season daily 11:30am-3:30pm and 5:30-9pm; summer Thurs-Sun 11:30am-4:30pm and 5:30pm-closing.

Taos Cow ★ ☺ DELI/DESSERT   Located about 10 minutes north of town in Arroyo Seco, Taos Cow offers fun breakfast and lunch fare in a relaxed atmosphere—and, of course, ice cream! Diners order and pick up at a counter. A unique item here is the potpies in chicken, buffalo, beef, or veggie, all with rich sauce and lots of vegetables. Village residents like to wake up to the breakfast tacos, made with fresh local eggs and lots of green chile. A different quiche special, such as a veggie with quinoa, tops the menu each day, and a variety of sandwiches are made with fresh ingredients ranging from black forest ham to portobello mushrooms. All that said, the real reason to come here is the hormone-free ice cream in a variety of flavors. My all-time favorite is the Cherry Ristra, with *piñon* nuts and chocolate chunks. Kids love their shakes. On chillier afternoons, there are espresso, cappuccino, and hot chocolate to warm you after a day on the slopes.

485 NM 150, Arroyo Seco. ☏ **575/776-5640.** All menu items under $12. AE, DISC, MC, V. Daily 7am-7pm (winter until 6pm).

WHAT TO SEE & DO IN TAOS

With a history shaped by pre-Columbian civilization, Spanish colonialism, and the Wild West; outdoor activities that range from ballooning to world-class skiing; and a clustering of artists, writers, and musicians, Taos has something to offer almost everybody. Its pueblo is the most accessible in New Mexico, and its museums represent a world-class display of regional history and culture.

THE TOP ATTRACTIONS

Millicent Rogers Museum of Northern New Mexico ★★ This museum will give you a glimpse of some of the finest Southwestern arts and crafts anywhere, but it's small enough to avoid being overwhelming. It was founded in 1953 by Millicent Rogers's family members after her death. Rogers was a wealthy Taos émigré who, in 1947, began acquiring a magnificent collection of beautiful Native American arts and crafts. Included are Navajo and Pueblo jewelry, Navajo textiles, Pueblo pottery, Hopi and Zuni *katsina* dolls, paintings from the Rio Grande Pueblo people, and basketry from a wide variety of Southwestern tribes. The museum also presents exhibitions of Southwestern art, crafts, and design.

Since the 1970s, the scope of the museum's permanent collection has been expanded to include Anglo arts and crafts and Hispanic religious and secular arts and crafts, from Spanish and Mexican colonial to contemporary times. Included are *santos*, furniture, weavings, *colcha* embroideries, and decorative tinwork. Agricultural implements, domestic utensils, and tools dating from the 17th and 18th centuries are also displayed.

The museum gift shop has a fine collection of superior regional art. Classes, workshops, lectures, and field trips are held throughout the year.

Off US 64, 4 miles north of Taos Plaza, on Millicent Rogers Rd. © **575/758-2462.** www.millicentrogers.org. Admission $10 adults, $6 students, $8 seniors, $2 children 6-16, $18 family rate. Daily 10am–5pm. Closed Mon Nov–Mar, Easter, Thanksgiving, Christmas, New Year's Day.

A Tip for Museumgoers

If you'd like to visit five museums that comprise the Museum Association of Taos—Blumenschein Home, Martinez Hacienda, Harwood Museum, Millicent Rogers Museum, and Taos Art Museum—you'll save money by purchasing a combination ticket for $25. The ticket allows one-time entry to each museum during a 1-year period and is fully transferable to other people. You may purchase the pass at any of the five museums. For more information, call ℂ **575/758-0505.**

San Francisco de Asis Church ★★   On NM 68, about 4 miles south of Taos, this famous church appears as a modern adobe sculpture with no doors or windows, an image that has often been photographed and painted, most notably by Ansel Adams and Georgia O'Keeffe. Visitors must walk through the garden on the east side to enter the two-story church and get a full perspective of its massive walls, authentic adobe plaster, and beauty.

A video presentation is given in the church office every half-hour. Also, displayed on the wall is an unusual painting, *The Shadow of the Cross,* by Henri Ault (1896). Under ordinary light, it portrays a barefoot Christ at the Sea of Galilee; in darkness, however, the portrait becomes luminescent, and the perfect shadow of a cross forms over the left shoulder of Jesus' silhouette. The artist reportedly was as shocked as everyone else to see this. The reason for the illusion remains a mystery. A few crafts shops surround the square.

Ranchos de Taos Plaza. ℂ **575/758-2754.** Admission $3 for video and mystery painting. Mon–Sat 9am–4pm. Visitors may attend Mass Mon–Wed and Fri 6:45am; Sat 6pm (Mass rotates from this church to the 3 mission chapels); Sun 7 (Spanish), 9, and 11:30am. Closed to the public 1st 2 weeks in June, when repairs are done; however, services still take place.

Taos Art Museum ★ 🏛   Set in the home of Russian artist Nicolai Fechin (Fehshin), this collection displays works of the Taos Society of Artists, which give a sense of what Taos was like in the late 19th and early 20th centuries. The works are rich and varied, including panoramas and images of the Native American and Hispanic villagers. The setting in what was Fechin's home from 1927 until 1933 is truly unique. The historic building commemorates his career. Born in Russia in 1881, Fechin came to the United States in 1923, already acclaimed as a master of painting, drawing, sculpture, architecture, and woodwork. In Taos, he renovated the home and embellished it with hand-carved doors, windows, gates, posts, fireplaces, and other features of a Russian country home. Fechin died in 1955. If you don't care to pay the admission, you can see just Fechin's studio, which is attached to the gift shop, for free. Also, bear in mind that this museum is privately funded, so your dollars are a real help.

227 Paseo del Pueblo Norte. ℂ **575/758-2690.** www.taosartmuseum.org. Admission $8 adults, $7 seniors, $5 students $4 children 6–12, free for 5 and under. Summer Tues–Sun 10am–5pm; call for winter hours.

Taos Historic Museums ★★   Two historical homes are operated as museums, affording visitors a glimpse of early Taos lifestyles. The Martinez Hacienda and Ernest Blumenschein home each has unique appeal.

The Top Attractions

WHAT TO SEE & DO IN TAOS

Taos Attractions

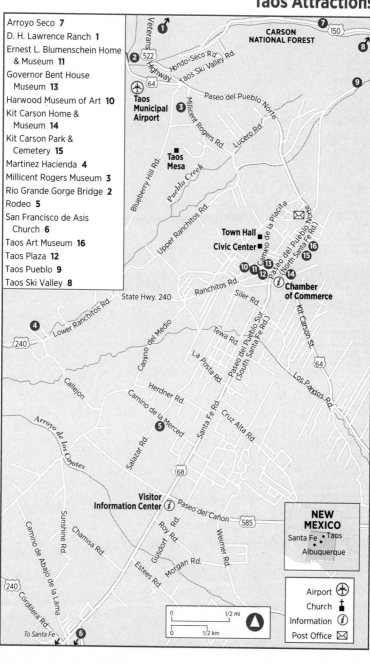

Arroyo Seco **7**
D. H. Lawrence Ranch **1**
Ernest L. Blumenschein Home
 & Museum **11**
Governor Bent House
 Museum **13**
Harwood Museum of Art **10**
Kit Carson Home &
 Museum **14**
Kit Carson Park &
 Cemetery **15**
Martinez Hacienda **4**
Millicent Rogers Museum **3**
Rio Grande Gorge Bridge **2**
Rodeo **5**
San Francisco de Asis
 Church **6**
Taos Art Museum **16**
Taos Plaza **12**
Taos Pueblo **9**
Taos Ski Valley **8**

CARSON
NATIONAL FOREST

Taos
Municipal
Airport

Taos
Mesa

Town Hall
Civic Center

Chamber
of Commerce

State Hwy. 240

NEW
MEXICO

Santa Fe • Taos

Albuquerque

Visitor
Information Center

To Santa Fe

0   1/2 mi
0   1/2 km

Airport
Church
Information
Post Office

The **Martinez Hacienda,** Lower Ranchitos Road, Highway 240 (© **575/758-1000**), is one of the only Spanish colonial haciendas in the United States that's open to the public year-round. This was the home of the merchant, trader, and *alcalde* (mayor) Don Antonio Severino Martinez, who bought it in 1804 and lived here until his death in 1827. His eldest son was Padre Antonio José Martinez, northern New Mexico's controversial spiritual leader from 1826 to 1867. Located on the west bank of the Rio Pueblo de Taos, about 2 miles southwest of the plaza, the museum is remarkably beautiful, with thick, raw adobe walls. The hacienda has no exterior windows—this was to protect against raids by Plains tribes.

Twenty-one rooms were built around two *placitas,* or interior courtyards. They give you a glimpse of the austerity of frontier lives, with only a few pieces of modest period furniture in each. You'll see bedrooms, stables, a kitchen, and a large fiesta room. Exhibits tell the story of the Martinez family and life in Spanish Taos between 1598 and 1821, when Mexico gained control.

Taos Historic Museums has developed the Martinez Hacienda into a living museum with weavers, blacksmiths, and woodcarvers. Demonstrations are scheduled daily, and during the **Taos Trade Fair** (held in late Sept) they run virtually nonstop. The Trade Fair commemorates the era when Native Americans, Spanish settlers, and mountain men met here to trade with each other.

The **Ernest L. Blumenschein Home & Museum,** 222 Ledoux St. (© **575/758-0505**), 1½ blocks southwest of the plaza, re-creates the lifestyle of one of the founders of the Taos Society of Artists. An adobe home with garden walls and a courtyard, parts of which date from the 1790s, it became the home and studio of Blumenschein (1874–1960) and his family in 1919. Period furnishings include European antiques and handmade Taos furniture in Spanish colonial style.

Blumenschein was born and raised in Cincinnati. In 1898, after training in New York and Paris, he and fellow painter Bert Phillips were on assignment for *Harper's* and *McClure's* magazines of New York when a wheel of their wagon broke 30 miles north of Taos. Blumenschein drew the short straw and thus was obliged to bring the wheel by horseback to Taos for repair. He later recounted his initial reaction to the valley he entered: "No artist had ever recorded the New Mexico I was now seeing. No writer had ever written down the smell of this air or the feel of that morning sky. I was receiving . . . the first great unforgettable inspiration of my life. My destiny was being decided."

That spark later led to the foundation of Taos as an art colony. An extensive collection of works by early-20th-century Taos artists, including some by Blumenschein's wife, Mary, and daughter, Helen, are on display in several rooms of the home.

222 Ledoux St. © **575/758-0505** (information for both museums can be obtained at this number). www.taosmuseums.org. Admission for each museum $8 adults, $4 children 6-16, free for children 5 and under. Summer daily 9am–5pm; call for winter hours.

Taos Pueblo ★★★   This home to some 100 residents offers a peak into the traditional Pueblo culture. When you enter this UNESCO World Heritage Site, you'll see two large buildings, both with rooms piled on top of each other, forming structures that echo the shape of Taos Mountain (which sits to the northeast). Here, a portion of Taos residents lives without electricity and running water. The remaining 2,000 residents of Taos Pueblo live in conventional homes on the pueblo's 100,000 acres.

The main buildings' distinctive flowing lines of shaped mud, with a straw-and-mud exterior plaster, are typical of Pueblo architecture throughout the Southwest.

It's architecture that blends in with the surrounding land. Bright blue doors are the same shade as the sky that frames the brown buildings.

The northernmost of New Mexico's 19 pueblos, Taos Pueblo has been home to the Tiwa-speaking people for more than a millennium. Many residents here still practice ancestral rituals. The center of their world is still nature; women use *hornos* to bake bread, and most still drink water that flows down from the sacred Blue Lake. Meanwhile, arts and crafts and other tourism-related businesses support the economy, along with government services, ranching, and farming.

The village looks much the same today as it did when a regiment from Coronado's expedition first came upon it in 1540. Though the Tiwa were essentially a peaceful agrarian people, they are perhaps best remembered for spearheading the most successful revolt by Native Americans. Launched by Pope (Poh-*pay*) in 1680, the uprising drove the Spanish from Santa Fe until 1692 and from Taos until 1698.

As you explore the pueblo, you can visit the residents' studios, sample homemade bread, look into the **San Geronimo Chapel,** and wander past the fascinating ruins of the old church and cemetery. You're expected to ask permission from individuals before taking their photos; some will ask for a small payment. Do not trespass into kivas (ceremonial rooms) and other areas marked as restricted.

The **Feast of San Geronimo** (the patron saint of Taos Pueblo), on September 29 and 30, marks the end of the harvest season. The feast day is reminiscent of an ancient trade fair for the Taos Indians, when tribes from as far south as South America and as far north as the Arctic would come and trade for wares, hides, clothing, and harvested crops. The day is filled with foot races, pole climbing done by traditional Indian clowns, and artists and craftspeople dressed like early traders. Dance ceremonies are held the evening of September 29. Other annual events include a **turtle dance** on New Year's Day, **buffalo** or **deer dances** on Three Kings Day (Jan 6), and **corn dances** on Santa Cruz Day (May 3), San Antonio Day (June 13), San Juan Day (June 24), Santiago Day (July 25), and Santa Ana Day (July 26). The annual **Taos Pueblo Powwow** (www.taospueblopowwow.com), a dance competition and parade that brings together tribes from throughout North America, is held the second weekend of July on tribal lands off NM 522 (see "Northern New Mexico Calendar of Events," in chapter 3). The pueblo Christmas celebration begins on Christmas Eve, with bonfires and a procession of the Blessed Mother. On Christmas Day, a variety of dances take place. These may include the **deer dance,** in which dancers act out a hunt, or the **Matachine dances,** which depicts the blending of the native and Spanish traditions (p. 24).

During your visit to the pueblo you will have the opportunity to purchase traditional fried and oven-baked bread as well as a variety of arts and crafts. If you would like to try traditional feast-day meals, the **Tiwa Kitchen,** near the entrance to the pueblo, is a good place to stop.

As with many of the other pueblos in New Mexico, Taos Pueblo has opened a casino. The nonsmoking **Taos Mountain Casino** (ⓒ **888/946-8267;** www.taosmountaincasino.com) is on the main road to Taos Pueblo and features slot machines, blackjack, and poker.

Note: To learn more about the pueblo and its people, I recommend taking a 15-minute guided tour. Ask upon arrival when the next one will be given and where you should meet your guide.

Veterans Hwy. (P.O. Box 1846), Taos Pueblo. ⓒ **575/758-1028.** www.taospueblo.com. $10 adults, $5 students, children 10 and under free. Camera, video, and sketching fees subject to change on a yearly basis; be sure to ask about telephoto lenses and tripods, as the pueblo may not allow them; photography not permitted on feast days. Daily 8am–4:30pm in summer, 8am–4pm in winter, with a few exceptions. Guided tours available. Closed for 6 weeks every year late winter or early spring (call ahead). Because this is a living community, you can expect other periodic closures. From Paseo del Pueblo Norte, travel north 2 miles on Veterans Hwy.

MORE ATTRACTIONS

D. H. Lawrence Ranch   A trip to this ranch north of Taos leads you into odd realms of devotion for the controversial early-20th-century author who lived and wrote in the area in the early 1920s. A short uphill walk from the ranch home (not open to visitors) is the D. H. Lawrence Memorial, a small stucco structure that is said to have Lawrence's ashes mixed in with the cement. The guest book is interesting: One couple wrote of trying for 24 years to get here from England.

Lawrence lived in Taos on and off between 1922 and 1925. The ranch was a gift to his wife, Frieda, from the art patron Mabel Dodge Luhan. Lawrence repaid Luhan the favor by giving her the manuscript of *Sons and Lovers*. When Lawrence died in southern France in 1930 of tuberculosis, his ashes were returned here for burial. The grave of Frieda, who died in 1956, is outside the memorial. The memorial is the only public building at the ranch, which is operated today by the University of New Mexico as an educational and recreational retreat.

NM 522, San Cristobal. ✆ **575/776-2245.** Free admission. Daily 8am–6pm. To reach the site, head north from Taos about 15 miles on NM 522, then another 6 miles east into the forested Sangre de Cristo Range via a well-marked dirt road.

Governor Bent House Museum ☺   This residence of Charles Bent, New Mexico Territory's first American governor, offers an interesting peek into the region's at-times brutal history. Bent, a former trader who established Fort Bent, Colorado, was murdered during the 1847 Native American and Hispanic rebellion, while his wife and children escaped by digging through an adobe wall into the house next door. The hole is still visible. Period art and artifacts are on display at the museum, just a short block north of the plaza. Owned by the same family since the 1950s, the museum also has a charming gift shop with historic memorabilia.

117 Bent St. ✆ **575/758-2376.** Admission $3 adults, $1 children 8–15, free for children 7 and under. MC, V. Daily 9:30am–5pm (winter from 10am). Closed Easter, Thanksgiving, Christmas, New Year's Day. Street parking.

Harwood Museum of Art of the University of New Mexico ★★   With its high ceilings and broad wood floors, this museum is a lovely place to wander among New Mexico–inspired images. A cultural and community center since 1923, the museum displays paintings, drawings, prints, sculpture, and photographs by Taos-area artists from 1800 to the present. Featured are paintings from the early days of the art colony by members of the Taos Society of Artists, including Oscar Berninghaus, Ernest Blumenschein, Herbert Dunton, Victor Higgins, Bert Phillips, and Walter Ufer. Also included are works by Emil Bisttram, Andrew Dasburg, Agnes Martin, Larry Bell, and Thomas Benrimo.

Upstairs are 19th-century pounded-tin pieces, *bultos* (carved statues) and *retablos* (religious paintings of saints that have traditionally been used for decoration and inspiration in the homes and churches of New Mexico). The permanent collection

WHAT TO SEE & DO IN TAOS   More Attractions

Art Classes

If you'd like to pursue an artistic adventure of your own in Taos, check out the weeklong classes in such media as painting, Native American pottery making, and weaving offered by **Taos Art School ★** (℃ **575/758-0350;** www.taosartschool. org). Open since 1989, the school is a virtual campus in which classes are held wherever they need to be. For instance, a painting class on Georgia O'Keeffe is held in Abiquiu, a Pueblo pottery class at Taos Pueblo, and a painting class on churches in New Mexico is held at five different churches in the region. The fees vary from class to class and usually don't include the cost of materials.

includes sculptures by Patrociño Barela, one of the leading Hispanic artists of 20th-century New Mexico. It's well worth seeing, especially his 3-foot-tall "Death Cart," a rendition of Doña Sebastiána, the bringer of death.

The museum also schedules six or more changing exhibitions a year, many of which feature works by celebrated artists currently living in New Mexico. A new addition holds more space for changing exhibitions and an auditorium.

238 Ledoux St. ℃ **575/758-9826.** www.harwoodmuseum.org. Admission $8 adults, $7 seniors, free for children 11 and under. Tues–Sat 10am–5pm; Sun noon–5pm (winter until 4pm).

Kit Carson Home and Museum If you want a glimpse into the modest lifestyle of Taos's frontiersmen, head to this three-room adobe home, a block east of the plaza. Built in 1825 and purchased in 1843 by Carson—the famous mountain man, Indian agent, and scout—it was a wedding gift for his young bride, Josefa Jaramillo. It remained their home for 25 years, until both died (exactly a month apart) in 1868. Rooms have sparse displays such as buffalo hide and sheepskin bedding, a wooden chest, basic kitchen utensils, and a cooking fireplace. The treasure of the museum is interpreter Natívídad Mascarenas-Gallegos, a distant relative of Carson, who can tell you plenty about the family. The museum also includes a film on Carson produced by the History Channel. The price of a visit here is a bit steep for what you see, but if you decide to come, plan on spending about a half-hour. If you'd like to see more of Carson's possessions, visit the Martinez Hacienda (see above).

113 Kit Carson Rd. ℃ **575/758-4945.** www.kitcarsonhomeandmuseum.com. Admission $5 adult, $4 seniors 65 years and older, $3 children 13–18, $2 children 6–12. Daily 9am–6pm.

Kit Carson Park and Cemetery Major community events are held in the park in summer. The cemetery, established in 1847, contains the graves of Carson, his wife, Governor Charles Bent, the Don Antonio Martinez family, Mabel Dodge Luhan, and many other noted historical figures and artists. Their lives are described briefly on plaques.

211 Paseo del Pueblo Norte. ℃ **575/758-8234.** Free admission. Daily 24 hr.

Rio Grande Gorge Bridge ★ ☺ This impressive bridge, west of the Taos airport, spans the Southwest's greatest river. At 650 feet above the canyon floor, it's one of America's highest bridges. If you can withstand the vertigo, it's interesting to come more than once, at different times of day, to observe how the changing light plays

15

WHAT TO SEE & DO IN TAOS

More Attractions

tricks with the colors of the cliff walls. A curious aside is that the wedding scene in the movie *Natural Born Killers* was filmed here.

US 64, 10 miles west of Taos. Free admission. Daily 24 hr.

ORGANIZED TOURS

An excellent opportunity to explore the historic downtown area of Taos is offered by **Taos Historic Walking Tours** (© 575/758-4020). Tours cost $12 and take 1½ to 2 hours, leaving from the Kit Carson Cemetery at 10am Monday to Saturday (June–Aug; closed holidays). Call to make an appointment.

If you'd really like a taste of Taos history and drama, call **Enchantment Dreams Walking Tours** ★ (© 575/776-2562; storytel1@yahoo.com). Roberta Courtney Meyers, a theater artist, dramatist, and composer, will tour you through Taos's history while performing a number of characters, such as Georgia O'Keeffe and Kit Carson. Walking tours cost $25 per person.

SKIING ★★★
Downhill

Five alpine resorts are within an hour's drive of Taos; all offer complete facilities, including equipment rentals. Although exact opening and closing dates vary according to snow conditions, the season usually begins around Thanksgiving and continues into early April.

Ski clothing can be purchased, and ski equipment can be rented or bought, from several Taos outlets. Among them are **Cottam's Ski & Outdoor Shops,** with four locations (call © 800/322-8267 or 575/758-2822; www.cottamsoutdoor.com), and **Taos Ski Valley Sportswear, Ski & Boot Co.,** in Taos Ski Valley (© 575/776-2291).

Taos Ski Valley ★★★, P.O. Box 90, Taos Ski Valley, NM 87525 (© 575/776-2291; www.skitaos.org), is the preeminent ski resort in the southern Rocky Mountains. It was founded in 1955 by a Swiss-German immigrant, Ernie Blake. According to local legend, Blake searched for 2 years in a small plane for the perfect location for a ski resort comparable to what he was accustomed to in the Alps. He found it at the abandoned mining site of Twining, high above Taos. Today, under the management of two younger generations of Blakes, the resort has become internationally renowned for its light, dry powder (as much as 300 in. annually), its superb ski school, and its personal, friendly service.

Taos Ski Valley can best be appreciated by the more experienced skier and snowboarder. It offers steep, high-alpine, high-adventure skiing. The mountain is more intricate than it might seem at first glance, and it holds many surprises and challenges—even for the expert. The *London Times* called the valley "without any argument the best ski resort in the world. Small, intimate, and endlessly challenging, Taos simply has no equal." The quality of the snow here (light and dry) is believed to be due to the dry Southwestern air and abundant sunshine. ***Note:*** In 2008, Taos Ski Valley began allowing snowboarders onto its slopes.

Between the 11,819-foot summit and the 9,207-foot base, there are 72 trails and bowls, more than half of them designated for expert and advanced skiers. Most of the remaining trails are suitable for advanced intermediates; there is little flat terrain

Skiing with Kids

With its children's ski school, Taos Ski Valley has always been an excellent choice for skiing families, but with the 1994 addition of an 18,000-square-foot children's center (Kinderkäfig Center), skiing with your children in Taos is even better. Kinderkäfig offers many services, from equipment rental for children to babysitting services. Call ahead for more information.

for novices to gain experience and mileage. However, many beginning skiers find that after spending time in lessons they can enjoy the **Kachina Bowl,** which offers spectacular views as well as wide-open slopes.

The area has an uphill capacity of 15,000 skiers per hour on its five double chairs, one triple, four quads, and one surface tow. Full-day lift tickets, depending on the season, cost $45 to $69 for adults, $30 to $58 for ages 13 to 17, $20 to $41 for children 12 and under, $35 to $58 for seniors 65 to 79, and are free for seniors over 80 and for children 6 and under with an adult ticket purchase. Full rental packages are $29 for adults and $20 for children. Taos Ski Valley is open daily 9am to 4pm from Thanksgiving to around the second week of April. *Note:* Taos Ski Valley has one of the best ski schools in the country, specializing in teaching people how to negotiate steep and challenging runs.

Taos Ski Valley has many lodges and condominiums, with nearly 1,500 beds. (See "Taos Ski Valley," in chapter 13, for details on accommodations.) All offer ski-week packages; three of them have restaurants. There are three restaurants on the mountain in addition to the many facilities of Village Center at the base. Call the **Taos Ski Valley** (© 800/776-1111 or 575/776-2233).

Not far from Taos Ski Valley is **Red River Ski & Snowboard Area,** P.O. Box 900, Red River, NM 87558 (© 800/331-7669 for reservations; 575/754-2223 for information; www.redriverskiarea.com). One of the bonuses of this ski area is that lodgers at Red River can walk out their doors and be on the slopes. Two other factors make this 40-year-old, family-oriented area special: First, most of its 58 trails are geared toward the intermediate skier, though beginners and experts also have some trails, and second, good snow is guaranteed early and late in the year by snowmaking equipment that can work on 87% of the runs, more than any other in New Mexico. However, be aware that this human-made snow tends to be icy, and the mountain is full of inexperienced skiers, so you really have to watch your back. Locals in the area refer to this as "Little Texas" because it's so popular with Texans and other Southerners. A very friendly atmosphere, with a touch of redneck attitude, prevails.

There's a 1,600-foot vertical drop here to a base elevation of 8,750 feet. Lifts include four double chairs, two triple chairs, and a surface tow, with a capacity of 7,920 skiers per hour. The cost of a ticket for all lifts is $59 for adults for a full day, $44 half-day; $48 for ages 13 to 19 for a full day, $35 half-day; and $39 for children 4 to 12 and seniors 60 through 69 for a full day, $32 half-day (free for seniors 70 and over). All rental packages start at $25 for adults, $17 for children. Lifts run daily 9am to 4pm approximately Thanksgiving through March. Ask about their lesson packages.

Also quite close to Taos (approx. 20 miles) is **Angel Fire Resort ★**, P.O. Drawer B, Angel Fire, NM 87710 (© 800/633-7463 or 575/377-6401; www.angelfireresort. com). If you (or your kids) don't feel up to skiing steeper Taos Mountain, Angel Fire is a good choice. The 73 trails are heavily oriented to beginner and intermediate skiers and snowboarders, with a few runs for more advanced skiers and snowboarders. The mountain has received over $7 million in improvements in past years. This is not an old village like you'll find at Taos and Red River. Instead, it's a Vail-style resort, built in 1960, with a variety of activities other than skiing (see "A Driving Tour of the Enchanted Circle," later in this chapter). The snowmaking capabilities here are excellent, and the ski school is good, though I hear it's so crowded that it's difficult to get in during spring break. Two high-speed quad lifts whisk you to the top quickly. There are also three double lifts and one surface lift. A large snowboard park contains a banked slalom course, rails, jumps, and other obstacles. Cross-country skiing, snowshoeing, and snowbiking are also available. All-day lift tickets cost $59 for adults, $52 for ages 13 to 17, and $39 for children 7 to 12. Kids 6 and under and seniors 70 and over ski free. It's open daily 9am to 4pm from approximately mid-December to March 29 (depending on the weather).

The oldest ski area in the Taos region, founded in 1952, **Sipapu Ski and Summer Resort,** Hwy. 518, Rte. Box 29, Vadito, NM 87579 (© **505/587-2240;** www.sipapu nm.com), is 25 miles southeast of Taos, on NM 518 in Tres Ritos Canyon. It prides itself on being a small local ski area, especially popular with schoolchildren. It has two triple chairs and two surface lifts, with a vertical drop of 1,025 feet to the 8,200-foot base elevation. There are 31 trails, half classified as intermediate, and two terrain park trails have been added. It's a nice little area, tucked way back in the mountains, with excellent lodging rates. Be aware that because the elevation is fairly low, runs can be icy. Lift tickets are $39 for adults for a full day, $29 for half-day; $34 for ages 13 through 20 full day, $26 for half-day; $29 for children 12 and under full day, $22 for half day; $29 for seniors 60 to 69 full day, $22 for half-day; free for seniors 70 and over and children 5 and under. A package including lift tickets, equipment rental, and a lesson costs $53 for adults and $42 for children. Also check out their lodging/skiing packages. Sipapu is open from about the end of November to March, and lifts run daily from 9am to 4pm.

Cross-Country

Numerous popular Nordic trails traverse **Carson National Forest.** If you call or write ahead, the ranger will send you a booklet titled *Where to Go in the Snow,* which gives cross-country skiers details about the maintained trails. One of the more popular trails is **Amole Canyon,** off NM 518 near the Sipapu Ski Area, where the Taos Nordic Ski Club maintains set tracks and signs along a 3-mile loop. It's closed to snowmobiles, a comfort to lovers of serenity.

Just east of Red River, with 16 miles of groomed trails (in addition to 6 miles of trails strictly for snowshoers) in 400 acres of forestlands atop Bobcat Pass, is the **Enchanted Forest Cross Country Ski Area ★** (© **575/754-6112;** www.enchantedforestxc. com). Full-day trail passes, good from 9am to 4:30pm, are $15 for adults, $12 for teens 13 to 17 and seniors 62 to 69, $7 for children 7 to 12, and free for seniors 70 and over, as well as for children 6 and under. In addition to cross-country ski and snowshoe rentals, the ski area also rents pulk sleds—high-tech devices in which children are pulled by their skiing parents. The ski area offers a full ski shop and snack bar. Instruction in cross-country classic as well as freestyle skating is available. A new yurt (Mongolian-style hut) is also available for a ski-in accommodation.

Taos Mountain Outfitters, 114 S. Plaza (© **575/758-9292;** www.taosmountain outfitters.com), offers telemark and cross-country sales and rentals. **Southwest Nordic Center ★** (© **575/758-4761;** www.southwestnordiccenter.com) offers rental of five yurts, four of which are in the Rio Grande National Forest near Chama. The fifth one is located outside the Taos Ski Valley (offering access to high-alpine terrain) and is twice as big as the others. Skiers trek into the huts, carrying their clothing and food in backpacks. Guide service is provided, or people can go in on their own, following directions on a map. The yurts are rented by the night and range from $70 to $125 per group. Call for reservations as much in advance as possible as they do book up. The season is mid-November through April, depending on snow conditions.

MORE OUTDOOR ACTIVITIES

Taos County's 2,200 square miles embrace a great diversity of scenic beauty, from New Mexico's highest mountain, 13,161-foot **Wheeler Peak,** to the 650-foot-deep chasm of the **Rio Grande Gorge ★★. Carson National Forest,** which extends to the eastern city limits of Taos and cloaks a large part of the county, contains several major ski facilities as well as hundreds of miles of hiking trails through the **Sangre de Cristo Range.**

Recreation areas are mainly in the national forest, where pine and aspen provide refuge for abundant wildlife. Forty-eight areas are accessible by road, including 38 with campsites. There are also areas on the high desert mesa, carpeted by sagebrush, cactus, and, frequently, wildflowers. Two beautiful areas within a short drive of Taos are the **Valle Vidal Recreation Area,** north of Red River, and the **Wild Rivers Recreation Area** near Questa (see "A Driving Tour of the Enchanted Circle," later in this chapter). For complete information, contact **Carson National Forest,** 208 Cruz Alta Rd. (© **575/758-6200;** www.fs.fed.us/r3/carson), or the **Bureau of Land Management,** 226 Cruz Alta Rd. (© **575/758-8851;** www.blm.gov/nm).

ALONG A green shore

A sweet spot en route to Taos from Santa Fe, the **Orilla Verde** (Green Shore) **Recreation Area** offers just what its name implies: lovely green shores along the Rio Grande. It's an excellent place to camp or to simply have a picnic. If you're adventurous, the flat water in this section of the river makes for scenic canoeing, kayaking, rafting, and fishing. Hiking trails thread through the area as well. Along them, you may come across ancient cultural artifacts, but be sure to leave them as you find them.

While traveling to the area, you'll encounter two places of note. The village of **Pilar ★** is a charming farming village, home to apple orchards, cornfields, and artists. The **Rio Grande Gorge Visitor Center** (at the intersection of NM 570 and NM 68; © **575/751-4899**) provides information about the gorge and has very clean restrooms. It's open May to October daily 8:30am to 4:30pm (also Nov–Apr daily 10am to 2pm, if they can secure volunteer staff).

The day-use fee for Orilla Verde is $3 per day, camping is $7 per night, and RV camping is $15 per night. All campsites have picnic tables, grills, and restrooms. For information, contact the **Orilla Verde Visitor Station** (© **575/751-4899;** www.blm.gov/nm), at the campground. To reach the recreation area, travel north from Santa Fe 50 miles or southwest from Taos 15 miles on NM 68; turn north on NM 570 and travel 1 mile.

Ballooning

As in many other towns throughout New Mexico, hot-air ballooning is a top attraction. Recreational trips over the Taos Valley and Rio Grande Gorge are offered by **Paradise Hot Air Balloon Adventure** (✆ **575/751-6098;** www.taosballooning. com). The company also offers ultralight rides.

Biking

Even if you're not an avid cyclist, it won't take long for you to realize that getting around Taos by bike is preferable to driving. You won't have the usual parking problems, and you won't have to sit in the line of traffic as it snakes through the center of town. If you feel like exploring the surrounding area, Carson National Forest rangers recommend several biking trails in the greater Taos area. Head to the **West Rim Trail** for a scenic and easy ride. To reach the trail, travel US 64 to the Taos Gorge Bridge, cross it, and find the trail head on your left, or head south on NM 68 for 17 miles to Pilar; turn west onto NM 570. Travel along the river for 6¼ miles, cross the bridge, and drive to the top of the ridge. Watch for the trail marker on your right. For a more technical and challenging ride, go to **Devisadero Loop.** From Taos, drive out of town on US 64 to your first pullout on the right, just as you enter the canyon at El Nogal Picnic Area. To ride the notorious **South Boundary Trail,** a 20-mile romp for advanced riders, contact **Native Sons Adventures** (✆ **800/753-7559** or 575/758-9342; www.nativesonsadventures.com). Native Sons can arrange directions, a shuttle, and a guide, if necessary. The **U.S. Forest Service** office, 208 Cruz Alta Rd. (✆ **575/758-6200**), has excellent trail information. Also look for the *Taos Trails* map (created jointly by Carson National Forest, Native Sons Adventures, and Trails Illustrated) at area bookstores.

Bicycle rentals are available from the **Gearing Up Bicycle Shop,** 129 Paseo del Pueblo Sur (✆ **575/751-0365;** www.gearingupbikes.com); daily rentals run $35 for a mountain bike with front suspension.

Annual touring events include Red River's **Enchanted Circle Century Bike Tour** (✆ **575/754-2366**) on the weekend following Labor Day.

Fishing

In many of New Mexico's waters, fishing is possible year-round, though, due to conditions, many high lakes and streams are fishable only during the warmer months. Overall, the best fishing is in the spring and fall. Naturally, the Rio Grande is a favorite fishing spot, but there is also excellent fishing in the streams around Taos. Taoseños favor the Rio Hondo, Rio Pueblo (near Tres Ritos), Rio Fernando (in Taos Canyon), Pot Creek, and Rio Chiquito. Rainbow, cutthroat, German brown trout, and kokanee (a freshwater salmon) are commonly stocked and caught. Pike and catfish have been caught in the Rio Grande as well. Jiggs, spinners, or woolly worms are recommended as lure, or worms, corn, or salmon eggs as bait; many experienced anglers prefer fly-fishing.

Licenses are required, and are sold, along with tackle, at several Taos sporting-goods shops. For backcountry guides, try **Deep Creek Wilderness Outfitters and Guides,** P.O. Box 721, El Prado, NM 87529 (✆ **575/776-8423** or 575/776-5901), or **Taylor Streit Flyfishing Service,** 405 Camino de la Placita (✆ **575/751-1312;** www.streitflyfishing.com).

Fitness Facilities

The **Taos Spa and Tennis Club,** 111 Dona Ana Dr. (across from Sagebrush Inn; *©* **575/758-1980;** www.taosspa.com), is a fully equipped fitness center that rivals any you'd find in a big city. It has a variety of cardiovascular machines, bikes, and weight-training machines, as well as saunas, indoor and outdoor Jacuzzis, a steam room, and indoor and outdoor pools. Classes range from yoga to Pilates to water fitness. In addition, it has tennis and racquetball courts. Therapeutic massage, facials, and physical therapy are available daily by appointment. Children's programs include a tennis camp and swimming lessons, and babysitting programs are available in the morning and evening. The spa is open Monday to Thursday 5am to 9pm, Friday 5am to 8pm, and Saturday and Sunday 7am to 8pm. Monthly memberships are available for individuals and families, as are summer memberships. For visitors, there's a daily rate of $12.

The **Northside Health and Fitness Center,** at 1307 Paseo del Pueblo Norte (*©* **575/751-1242;** www.taosnorthsidespa.com), is also a full-service facility, featuring top-of-the-line Cybex equipment, free weights, and cardiovascular equipment. Aerobics classes are scheduled daily (Jazzercise classes weekly), and there are indoor/outdoor pools and four tennis courts, as well as children's and seniors' programs. The center is open weekdays 5am to 9pm and weekends 8am to 8pm. The daily visitors' rate is $8. Also of note, with classes daily, is **Taos Pilates Studio,** 1103 Paseo del Pueblo Norte (*©* **575/758-7604;** www.taospilates.net).

Golf

Since the summer of 1993, the 18-hole golf course at the **Taos Country Club,** 54 Golf Course Dr., Ranchos de Taos (*©* **575/758-7300;** www.taoscountryclub.com), has been open to the public. Located off CR 110, just 6 miles south of the plaza, it's a first-rate championship golf course designed for all levels of play. It has open fairways and no hidden greens. The club also features a driving range, practice putting and chipping green, and instruction by PGA professionals. Greens fees are seasonal and start at $62; cart and club rentals are available. The country club has also added a clubhouse, featuring a restaurant and full bar. It's always advisable to call ahead for tee times 1 week in advance, but it's not unusual for people to show up unannounced and still manage to find a time to tee off.

The par-72, 18-hole course at the **Angel Fire Resort Golf Course** (*©* **800/633-7463** or 575/377-3055; www.angelfireresort.com/summer) is PGA endorsed. Surrounded by stands of ponderosa pine, spruce, and aspen, at 8,500 feet, it's one of the highest regulation golf courses in the world. It also has a driving range and putting green. Carts and clubs can be rented at the course, and the club pro provides instruction. Greens fees range from $47 to $99.

Hiking

There are hundreds of miles of hiking trails in Taos County's mountain and high-mesa country. The trails are especially well traveled in the summer and fall, although nights turn chilly and mountain weather may be fickle by September.

Free materials and advice on all **Carson National Forest** trails and recreation areas can be obtained from the **Forest Service Building,** 208 Cruz Alta Rd. (*©* **575/758-6200;**

www.fs.fed.us/r3/carson), open Monday to Friday 8am to 4:30pm. Detailed USGS topographical maps of backcountry areas can be purchased from **Taos Mountain Outfitters,** 114 S. Plaza (© **575/758-9292;** www.taosmountainoutfitters.com).

One of the easiest hikes to access is the **West Rim Trail,** aptly named because it runs along the rim of the Rio Grande Gorge. Access this 9-mile-long trail by driving west from Taos on US 64, crossing the Rio Grande Gorge Bridge, and turning left into the picnic area. The 19,663-acre **Wheeler Peak Wilderness** is a wonderland of alpine tundra, encompassing New Mexico's highest peak (13,161 ft.). A favorite (though rigorous) hike to Wheeler Peak's summit (15 miles round-trip with a 3,700-ft. elevation gain) makes for a long but fun day. The trail head is at Taos Ski Valley. For year-round hiking, head to the **Wild Rivers Recreation Area** ★ (© **575/770-1600**), near Questa (see "A Driving Tour of the Enchanted Circle," later in this chapter).

Trail Closures

The drought that has spread across the Southwest in recent years has caused the U.S. Forest Service to close trails in many New Mexico mountains during the summer in order to reduce fire hazard. Before you head out in this area, contact the **Carson National Forest** (© **575/758-6200;** www.fs.fed.us/r3/carson).

Horseback Riding

The sage meadows and pine-covered mountains around Taos make it one of the West's most romantic places to ride. **Taos Indian Horse Ranch** ★★, on Pueblo land off Ski Valley Road, just before **Arroyo Seco** (© **575/758-3212;** www.taosindianhorseranch.com), offers a variety of guided rides. Open by appointment, the ranch provides horses for all types of riders (English, Western, Australian, and bareback) and ability levels. Call ahead to reserve and for prices, which will likely run about $100 for a 2-hour trail ride.

Horseback riding is also offered by **Rio Grande Stables,** P.O. Box 2122, El Prado (© **575/776-5913;** www.lajitasstables.com), with rides taking place during the summer months at Taos Ski Valley. Most riding outfitters offer lunch trips and overnight trips. Call for prices and further details.

Hunting

Hunters in **Carson National Forest** bag deer, turkey, grouse, band-tailed pigeons, and elk by special permit. Hunting seasons vary year to year, so it's important to inquire ahead with the New Mexico **Game and Fish Department** in Santa Fe (© **505/476-8000;** www.wildlife.state.nm.us).

Jogging

The paved paths and grass of Kit Carson Park (p. 217) provide a quiet place to stretch your legs.

Llama Trekking

For a taste of the unusual, you might want to try letting a llama carry your gear and food while you walk and explore, free of any heavy burdens. They're friendly, gentle animals that have keen senses of sight and smell. Often, other animals, such as elk, deer, and mountain sheep, are attracted to the scent of the llamas and will venture closer to hikers if the llamas are present.

Wild Earth Llama Adventures ★★ (② 800/758-5262 or 575/586-0174; www.llamaadventures.com) offers a "Take a Llama to Llunch" day hike—a full day of hiking into the Sangre de Cristo Mountains, complete with a gourmet lunch for $99. Wild Earth also offers a variety of custom multiday wilderness adventures tailored to trekkers' needs and fitness levels for $165 per person per day. Children 11 and under receive discounts. Camping gear and food are provided. On the trips, experienced guides provide information about native plants and local wildlife, as well as natural and regional history of the area. The head guide has doubled as a chef in the off season, so the meals on these treks are quite tasty. **El Paseo Llama Expeditions ★** (② 800/455-2627 or 575/758-3111; www.elpaseollama.com) utilizes U.S. Forest Service–maintained trails that wind through canyons and over mountain ridges. The llama expeditions are scheduled March through November. The rides are for all ages, so kids can ride too. Gourmet meals are provided. Half-day hikes cost $74 and $84, day hikes $94, and 2- to 5-day hikes run $299 to $749.

River Rafting

Half- or full-day white-water rafting trips down the Rio Grande and Rio Chama originate in Taos and can be booked through a variety of outfitters in the area. The wild **Taos Box ★★★**, a steep-sided canyon south of the Wild Rivers Recreation Area, offers a series of class IV rapids that rarely let up for some 17 miles. The water drops up to 90 feet per mile, providing one of the most exciting 1-day white-water tours in the West. May and June, when the water is rising, is a good time to go. Experience is not required, but you will be required to wear a life jacket (provided), and you should be willing to get wet.

Most of the companies listed run the **Taos Box** ($104–$115 per person) and **Pilar Racecourse** ($45–$56 per person for a half-day) on a daily basis.

I highly recommend **Los Rios River Runners ★** in Taos, P.O. Box 2734 (② 800/544-1181 or 575/776-8854; www.losriosriverrunners.com). Other safe bets are **Native Sons Adventures,** 1335 Paseo del Pueblo Sur (② 800/753-7559 or 575/758-9342; www.nativesonsadventures.com), and **Far Flung Adventures,** P.O. Box 707, El Prado (② 800/359-2627 or 575/758-2628; www.farflung.com).

Safety warning: Only experienced river runners should attempt these waters without a guide. Check with the **Bureau of Land Management** (② 575/758-8851; www.blm.gov/nm) to make sure that you're fully equipped to go white-water rafting. Have them check your gear to make sure that it's sturdy enough—this is serious rafting and kayaking!

Rock Climbing

Mountain Skills, P.O. Box 206, Arroyo Seco, NM 87514 (② 575/776-2222; www.climbingschoolusa.com), offers rock-climbing instruction for all skill levels, from beginners to more advanced climbers who would like to fine-tune their skills or just find out about the best area climbs.

Skateboarding

Try your board at **Taos Youth Family Center,** 407 Paseo del Cañon, 2 miles south of the plaza and about ¾ mile off Paseo del Pueblo Sur (② 505/758-4160;

www.taosyouth.com). There is an in-line-skate and skateboarding park, open when there's no snow or ice. Admission is free.

Snowmobiling & ATV Riding

Native Sons Adventures, 1335 Paseo del Pueblo Sur (© **800/753-7559** or 575/758-9342; www.nativesonsadventures.com), runs fully guided tours in the Sangre de Cristo Mountains. Rates run $65 to $130. Advance reservations required.

Swimming

The indoors **Taos Swimming Pool,** Civic Plaza Drive at Camino de la Placita, opposite the Convention Center (© **575/758-4160;** www.taosyouth.com), admits swimmers 8 and over without adult supervision.

Tennis

Taos Spa and Tennis Club has four courts, and the **Northside Health and Fitness Center** has three tennis courts (see both under "Fitness Facilities," above). In addition, there are four free public courts in Taos—two at **Kit Carson Park,** on Paseo del Pueblo Norte, and two at **Fred Baca Memorial Park,** on Camino del Medio, south of Ranchitos Road.

SHOPPING

Given the town's historical associations with the arts, it isn't surprising that many visitors come to Taos to buy fine art. Some 50-odd galleries are within walking distance of the plaza, and a couple dozen more are just a short drive from downtown. Galleries and shops are generally open 7 days a week during summer and closed Sundays during winter. Hours vary but generally run from 10am to 5 or 6pm. Some artists show their work by appointment only.

The best-known artist in modern Taos is the late R. C. Gorman, a Navajo from Arizona who made his home in Taos for more than 2 decades. He was internationally acclaimed for his bright, somewhat surrealistic depictions of Navajo women. His **Navajo Gallery,** at 210 Ledoux St. (© **575/758-3250;** www.rcgormangallery. com), is a showcase for his widely varied work: acrylics, lithographs, silk screens, bronzes, tapestries, hand-cast ceramic vases, etched glass, and more.

My favorite spots to shop are the **Plaza and Bent Street** areas and the village of **Arroyo Seco** ★ on NM 150, about 5 miles north of Taos en route to Taos Ski Valley. At the village you'll find a lovely 1834 church, La Santísima Trinidad, along with a few cute little shops lining the winding lane through town. A few of my favorites there are **Arroyo Seco Mercantile** ★ (𝓒 **575-776-8806**) at 488 NM 150, which is full of cowboy hats, antiques, and country home items; and **Jack Leustig Imaging** ★ (𝓒 **800/670-6651** or 575/776-3899; www.jliprints. com), which carries quality reproductions of fine artworks along with hundreds of art greeting cards.

Art

Act I Gallery   This gallery has a broad range of works in a variety of media. You'll find watercolors, *retablos*, furniture, paintings, Hispanic folk art, pottery, jewelry, and sculpture. 218 Paseo del Pueblo Norte. 𝓒 877/228-1278 or 575/758-7831. www.actonegallery.com.

Envision Gallery ★   Offering contemporary art with an elaborate sculpture garden, this is a fun place to browse for works on paper and of clay. Bold colors and innovative designs mark this work, with wind sculptures by Lyman Whitaker the real prize. 1405 Paseo del Pueblo Norte (in the Overland Sheepskin Complex), El Prado. 𝓒 505/751-1344. www.envisiongallery.net.

Inger Jirby Gallery ★ 🎒   The word *expressionist* could have been created to define the work of internationally known artist Inger Jirby. Full of bold color and passionate brush strokes, Jirby's oils record the lives and landscapes of villages from the southwestern U.S. to Guatemala to Bali. This gallery, which meanders back through a 400-year-old adobe house, is a feast for the eyes and soul. 207 Ledoux St. 𝓒 575/758-7333. www.jirby.com.

Lumina Contemporary Art ★★ 🎒   North of Taos (about 8 min.) outside the village of Arroyo Seco, this gallery, a new version of the notable gallery that was in Taos, offers a tranquil museum-quality experience. Set within a 3-acre Japanese garden, it has a water cascade and Buddhist teahouse accented with large stone sculptures. Inside, works offer a refreshing look at the world. Watch for Chacha's gold- and copper-leaf works on metal, and Annell Livingston's geometric paintings on handmade paper. It's open in summer Thursday to Monday 11am to 6:30pm; winter Friday to Monday 11am to 5pm. 11 NM 230, Arroyo Seco. 𝓒 877/5-558-6462 or 575/776-0123. www.luminagallery.com.

sipping WHILE SHOPPING

While slipping in and out of shops in the plaza area, be sure to stop in at **La Chiripada Winery & Vineyards,** 103 Bent St. (𝓒 **575-751-1311;** www.lachiripada.com). Their tasting room offers a variety of samples that may include a rich pinot noir or chardonnay. The wine is grown in Dixon, south of Taos, and offers a taste of the 400-year-old winemaking tradition in the region. While tasting, check out the ceramics and paintings made by the vintners themselves. La Chiripada also has a tasting room at the vineyard in Dixon (NM 75, 2.5 miles from NM 68) itself, well worth a visit.

Michael McCormick Gallery ★ 🎁 Nationally renowned artists dynamically play with Southwestern themes in the works hanging at this gallery, steps from the plaza. Especially notable are the bright portraits by Miguel Martinez. If the gallery's namesake is in, strike up a conversation about art or poetry. 106C Paseo del Pueblo Norte. ✆ 800/279-0879 or 575/758-1372. www.mccormickgallery.com.

Nichols Taos Fine Art Gallery Here you will find traditional works in all media, including Western and cowboy art. 403 Paseo del Pueblo Norte. ✆ 575/758-2475.

Parks Gallery ★ Some of the region's finest contemporary art decks the walls of this gallery just off the plaza. Some of the top artists here include the late Melissa Zink, Jim Wagner, Susan Contreres, and Erin Currier. 127 Bent St. ✆ 575/751-0343. www.parksgallery.com.

Philip Bareiss Gallery The works of some 30 leading Taos artists, including sculptor and painter Ron Davis, and painter Norbert Voelke, are exhibited here, along with early Taos modernists. 15 NM 150. ✆ 800/458-2284 or 575/776-2284. www.taosartappraisal.com.

R. B. Ravens A trader for many years, including 25 years on the Ranchos Plaza, R. B. Ravens is skilled at finding incredible period artwork. Here, you'll find Navajo rugs and pottery, all in the setting of an old home with raw pine floors and hand-sculpted adobe walls. 4146 NM 68 (across from the St. Francis Church Plaza), Ranchos de Taos. ✆ 800/758-7322 or 575/758-7322. www.rbravens.com.

Robert L. Parsons Fine Art ★★ This gallery set in the 1859 Ferdinand Maxwell home carries works of the early Taos and Santa Fe artists, including Nicolai Fechin, Joseph Sharp, and O.E. Berninghaus. Fine Pueblo pottery and antique Navajo blankets dress the space as well. 131 Bent St. ✆ 575/751-0159. www.parsonsart.com.

Books

Brodsky Bookshop Come here for the exceptional inventory of fiction, nonfiction, Southwestern and Native American–studies books, children's books, used books, cards, tapes, and CDs. 226A Paseo del Pueblo Norte. ✆ 888/223-8730 or 575/758-9468. www.taosbooks.com.

Moby Dickens Bookshop ★ This is Taos's best bookstore, with comfortable places to sit and read. You'll find children's and adults' collections of Southwest, Native American, and out-of-print books. 124A Bent St. ✆ 888/442-9980 or 575/758-3050. www.mobydickens.com.

Children

Twirl ★ ☺ As well as a fun place to shop, this is an adventure. A play structure, hobbit home, and fountain keep kids occupied while those of all ages hunt for musical instruments, toys, and clothing. 225 Camino de la Placita. ✆ 575/751-1402. www.twirlhouse.com.

Crafts

Taos Artisans Cooperative Gallery 🖌 This 10-member cooperative gallery, owned and operated by local artists, sells local handmade jewelry, wearables, clay work, glass, leather work, and garden sculpture. You'll always find an artist in the shop. 107C Bent St. ✆ 575/758-1558. www.taosartisansgallery.com.

Taos Blue   This gallery has fine Native American and contemporary handcrafts. 101A Bent St. ✆ 575/758-3561. www.taosblue.com.

Weaving Southwest   Contemporary tapestries by New Mexico artists, as well as one-of-a-kind rugs, blankets, and pillows, are the woven specialties found here. 106-A Paseo del Pueblo Norte. ✆ 575/758-0433. www.weavingsouthwest.com.

Fashion

Artemisia ★   Advertising "one-of-a-kind artwear and accessories," this shop delivers, with wearable art in bold colors, all hand-woven or hand-sewn, all for women. 115 Bent St. ✆ 575/737-9800. www.artemisiataos.com.

Blue Fish   Selling handblock-printed, unique organic and natural fiber clothing for women, this shop is full of surprises. The colors are dreamy and the fashions for the untailored but fashion conscious. 1405 Paseo del Pueblo Norte (in the Overland Sheepskin Complex), El Prado. ✆ 575/758-7474. www.barclaystudio.com.

Mariposa Boutique   What first caught my eye in this little shop were bright fiesta skirts for girls. Closer scrutiny brought me to plenty of finds for myself, such as suede broomstick skirts and peasant blouses, most handmade by the shop owner, perfect for showing off turquoise jewelry. 120-F Bent St. ✆ 575/758-9028.

Overland Sheepskin Company ★ 🎒   You can't miss the romantically weathered barn sitting on a meadow north of town. Inside, you'll find anything you can imagine in leather: coats, gloves, hats, and slippers. The coats here are exquisite, from oversize ranch styles to tailored blazers in a variety of leathers from sheepskin to buffalo hide. NM 522 (a few miles north of town). ✆ 575/758-8820. www.overland.com.

Food

Cid's Food Market   This store has the best selection of natural and gourmet foods in Taos. It's a great place to stock your picnic basket with such items as roasted chicken and barbecued brisket, or with lighter fare, such as sushi, Purple Onion–brand sandwiches, black-bean salad, and fresh hummus and tabbouleh. 623 Paseo del Pueblo Norte. ✆ 575/758-1148. www.cidsfoodmarket.com.

Furniture & Home

At Home in Taos ★ 🎒   If you're looking to brighten your abode, head to this brilliant shop just off the plaza. You'll find colorful, handmade placemats and bowls as well as bags made from recycled materials. 117 S. Plaza. ✆ 575/751-1486.

Country Furnishings of Taos   Here, you'll find unique hand-painted folk-art furniture. The pieces are as individual as the styles of the local folk artists who make them. There are also home accessories, unusual gifts, clothing, and jewelry. 534 Paseo del Pueblo Norte. ✆ 575/758-4633.

Mineral & Fossil Gallery ★   This fine showroom offers an adventure into an ancient world of stunning geodes and fossils, both decorative and functional. Look for jewelry and fetishes here as well. 110 S. Plaza. ✆ 575-737-5001.

Nambé ★   This company made a name for itself producing serving platters, picture frames, and candlesticks from a metal alloy. Over the years, Nambé has expanded into production of crystal and wood designs, all lovely for the home. 109 N. Plaza. ✆ 575/758-8221. www.nambe.com.

Gifts & Souvenirs

Chimayo Trading del Norte   Specializing in Navajo weavings, pueblo pottery, and other types of pottery, this is a fun spot to peruse on the Ranchos de Taos Plaza. Look especially for the Casas Grandes pottery from Mexico. 1 Ranchos de Taos Plaza. ✆ 575/758-0504.

El Rincón Trading Post 🎁   This shop has a real trading-post feel. It's a wonderful place to find turquoise jewelry, whether you're looking for contemporary or antique. In the back of the store is a museum full of Native American and Western artifacts. 114 Kit Carson Rd. ✆ 575/758-9188.

San Francisco de Asis Gift Shop   Local devotional art fills this funky little shop behind the San Francisco de Asis church. *Retablos* (altar paintings), rosary beads, and hand-carved wooden crosses appeal to a range of visitors, from the deeply religious to the pagan power shopper. 58 Ranchos de Taos Plaza. ✆ 575/758-2754.

Two Graces Gallery   For a wild range of devotional and kitschy art, don't miss this place on the Ranchos de Taos Plaza. In this 250-year-old building, you'll find antique curios, Southwest collectibles, books, and antiques. 66 St. Francis Church Plaza, Ranchos de Taos. ✆ 575/758-4639.

Jewelry

Artwares Contemporary Jewelry   The gallery owners here call their contemporary jewelry "a departure from the traditional." True to this slogan, each piece here offers a new twist on traditional Southwestern and Native American design, by artists such as Roberto Coin, John Hardy, Diane Malouf, Judith Ripka, and Alex Sepkus. 129 N. Plaza. ✆ 800/527-8850 or 575/758-8850. www.artwaresjewelry.com.

Musical Instruments

Taos Drum Company ★   Taos Drums has one of the largest selections of Native American log and hand drums in the world. In addition to drums, the showroom displays Southwestern and wrought-iron furniture, cowboy art, more than 60 styles of rawhide lampshades, and an array of other items as well. To find Taos Drum Company, look for the tepees and drums off NM 68. Ask about the tour that demonstrates the drum-making process. 5 miles south of Taos Plaza (off NM 68). ✆ 800/424-3786 or 575/758-3796. www.taosdrums.com.

Pottery & Tiles

Stephen Kilborn Pottery   Visiting this shop in town is a treat, but for a real adventure, go 17 miles south of Taos toward Santa Fe to Stephen Kilborn's studio in Pilar, open daily 10am to 5pm June to October (shorter hours off season). There, you can watch how the pottery is made. 136A Paseo del Pueblo Norte. ✆ 800/853-2519 or 575/758-5760. www.kilbornpottery.com.

Vargas Tile Co.   Vargas Tile has a great little collection of hand-painted Mexican tiles at good prices. You'll find ceramic pots with bright Mexican designs on them and colorful cabinet doorknobs, as well as inventive sinks. South end of town on NM 68. ✆ 575/758-5986. www.vargastile.com.

TAOS AFTER DARK

For a small town, Taos has its share of top entertainment. The resort atmosphere and the arts community attract performers, and the city enjoys annual programs in music and literary arts. State troupes, such as the New Mexico Repertory Theater and New Mexico Symphony Orchestra, make regular visits.

Many events are scheduled by the **Taos Center for the Arts (TCA),** 133 Paseo del Pueblo Norte (℃ **575/758-2052;** www.tcataos.org), at the Taos Community Auditorium. The TCA imports local, regional, and national performers in theater, dance, and concerts (Robert Mirabal, among others, has performed here). Also, look for a weekly film series offered year-round.

You can obtain information on current events in the *Taos News,* published every Thursday. The **Taos County Chamber of Commerce** (℃ **800/732-8267** or 575/751-8800; www.taoschamber.com) is also a good resource. Taos Visitors Center (℃ **575/758-3873**) publishes semiannual listings of *Taos County Events,* as well as the annual *Taos Country Vacation Guide* that also lists events and happenings around town.

The Performing Arts

Fort Burgwin   This historic site (of the 1,000-year-old Pot Creek Pueblo), located about 10 miles south of Taos, is a summer campus of Dallas's Southern Methodist University. From mid-May through mid-August, the SMU-in-Taos curriculum (including studio arts, humanities, and sciences) includes courses in music and theater. There are regularly scheduled orchestral concerts, guitar and harpsichord recitals, and theater performances available to the community, without charge, throughout the summer. 6580 NM 518, Ranchos de Taos. ℃ 575/758-8322. www.smu.edu/taos.

Music from Angel Fire   This acclaimed program of chamber music begins in mid-August, with weekend concerts, and continues up to Labor Day. Based in the small resort community of Angel Fire (located about 21 miles east of Taos, off US 64), it also presents numerous concerts in Taos, Las Vegas, and Raton. P.O. Box 502, Angel Fire. ℃ 575/377-3233 or 888/377-3300. www.musicfromangelfire.org.

Taos School of Music ★   Founded in 1963, this music summer school located at the Hotel St. Bernard in Taos Ski Valley offers excellent concerts by notable artists. From mid-June to mid-August there is an intensive 8-week study and performance program for advanced students of violin, viola, cello, and piano. The 8-week **Chamber Music Festival,** an important adjunct of the school, offers 16 concerts and seminars for the public; performances are given by pianist Robert McDonald, the Borromeo, St. Lawrence, and Brentano String Quartets, and the Young Artists International orchestra. Performances are held at the Taos Community Auditorium

THE MAJOR concert & performance halls

Taos Convention Center, 121 Civic Plaza Dr. (℃ **575/758-5792**). This convention space has an exhibit center where presentations, lectures, and concerts are held.

Taos Community Auditorium, Kit Carson Memorial State Park (℃ **575/758-4677**). A comfortable, small-town space, this community auditorium makes a nice venue for films, concerts, and lectures.

and the Hotel St. Bernard. P.O. Box 1879. © 575/776-2388. www.taosschoolofmusic.com. Tickets for chamber music concerts $20 for adults, $10 for children 16 and under.

The Club & Music Scene

Adobe Bar ★   A favorite gathering place for locals and visitors, the Adobe Bar is known for its live music series (nights vary) devoted to the eclectic talents of Taos musicians. The schedule offers a little of everything—classical, jazz, folk, flamenco, and world music. The Adobe Bar features a wide selection of international beers, wines by the glass, light New Mexican dining, desserts, and an espresso menu. Their margarita consistently wins the "Best of Taos" competition in *Taos News*. It's open daily 11:30am to 10pm. In the Historic Taos Inn, 125 Paseo del Pueblo Norte. © 575/758-2233. www.taosinn.com.

Alley Cantina ★ 🔘   This bar that touts its location as the oldest house in Taos has become the hot late-night spot. The focus is on interaction, as well as TV sports, but there's also a cozy outdoor patio. Patrons playing shuffleboard, pool, chess, and backgammon listen to live music 4 to 5 nights a week. Burgers, fish and chips, and other informal dishes are served until 11pm. 121 Teresina Lane. © 575/758-2121. www.alley cantina.com. Cover for live music only.

Anaconda Bar ★★   Set in the eco-resort El Monte Sagrado, this is Taos's most happening nightspot, with live entertainment—jazz, blues, Native American flute, or country—playing Thursday through Saturday. An anaconda sculpture snaking across the ceiling and an 11,000-gallon fish tank set the contemporary tone of the place, where a variety of the hotel's signature dishes are served. In the El Monte Sagrado hotel, 317 Kit Carson Rd. © 575/758-3502. www.elmontesagrado.com.

Caffe Tazza ★   This cozy three-room cafe, with a summer patio, attracts local community groups, artists, performers, and poets. Plays, films, comedy, and musical performances are given here on weekends (and some weeknights in summer). You can read one of the assorted periodicals available (including the *New York Times*) while sipping a cappuccino or *café Mexicano* (espresso with steamed milk and Mexican chocolate), made from organic coffee beans. The food—soups and sandwiches—is quite good. Pastries, which are imported from many bakeries around the region, are almost as big a draw here as the Taos Cow ice cream. Choose from 15 flavors. 122 Kit Carson Rd. © 575/758-8706.

Hideaway Lounge   This hotel lounge, built around a large adobe fireplace, offers live entertainment and an extensive hors d'oeuvre buffet. Call for schedule. Don Fernando de Taos, 1005 Paseo del Pueblo Sur. © 575/758-4444. www.donfernandodetaos.com.

Sagebrush Inn ★   This is a real hot spot for locals. The atmosphere is Old West, with a rustic wooden dance floor and plenty of rowdiness. Live country or rock music generally plays Thursdays to Saturdays from 8:30 to 11:30pm. Paseo del Pueblo Sur (P.O. Box 557). © 575/758-2254.

A DRIVING TOUR OF THE ENCHANTED CIRCLE ★★

If you're in the mood to explore, take this 90-mile loop north of Taos, through the old Hispanic villages of Arroyo Hondo and Questa, into a pass that the Apaches,

Taos & Environs

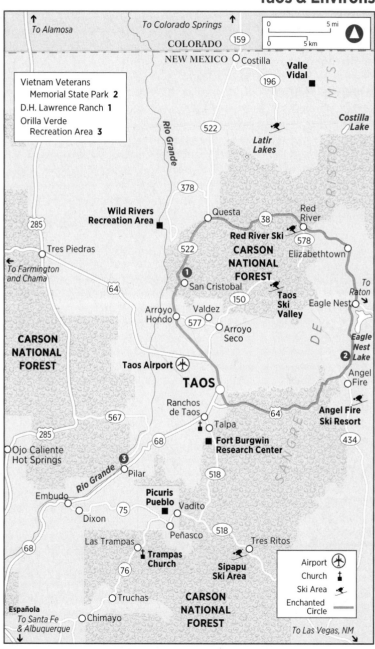

Vietnam Veterans
  Memorial State Park **2**
D.H. Lawrence Ranch **1**
Orilla Verde
  Recreation Area **3**

To Alamasa

To Colorado Springs

COLORADO   159

NEW MEXICO   Costilla

Valle
Vidal

196

Rio Grande

522

Latir
Lakes

Costilla
Lake

SANGRE DE CRISTO MTS.

378

Wild Rivers
Recreation Area

Questa

Red
River

38

Red River Ski

578

285

522

Tres Piedras

To Farmington
and Chama

64

San Cristobal

CARSON
NATIONAL
FOREST

Elizabethtown

To
Raton

Arroyo
Hondo

Valdez

577

Arroyo
Seco

150

Taos
Ski
Valley

Eagle Nest

Taos Airport

TAOS

Eagle
Nest
Lake

Angel
Fire

Ranchos
de Taos

Talpa

64

Angel Fire
Ski Resort

567

285

68

Fort Burgwin
Research Center

434

Ojo Caliente
Hot Springs

Rio Grande

Pilar

518

Embudo

Picuris
Pueblo

Vadito

75

Dixon

Peñasco

518

Tres Ritos

Las Trampas

Trampas
Church

76

Sipapu
Ski Area

Airport

Church

Ski Area

Enchanted
Circle

Truchas

CARSON
NATIONAL
FOREST

Española
To Santa Fe
& Albuquerque

Chimayo

To Las Vegas, NM

0   5 mi
0   5 km

15

WHAT TO SEE & DO IN TAOS | Enchanted Circle Driving Tour

Kiowas, and Comanches once used to cross the mountains to trade with the Taos Indians. You'll come to the Wild West mining town of Red River, pass through the expansive Moreno Valley, and travel along the base of some of New Mexico's tallest peaks. Then, you'll skim the shores of a high mountain lake at Eagle Nest, pass through the resort village of Angel Fire, and head back to Taos along the meandering Rio Fernando de Taos. Although one can drive the entire loop in 2 hours from Taos, most folks prefer to take a full day, and many take several days.

Arroyo Hondo

Traveling north from Taos via NM 522, it's a 9-mile drive to this village, the remains of an 1815 land grant along the Rio Hondo. Along the dirt roads that lead off NM 522, you may find a windowless *morada* or two, marked by plain crosses in front—places of worship for the still-active Penitentes, a religious order known for self-flagellation. This is also the turnoff point for trips to the Rio Grande Box, an awesome 1-day, 17-mile white-water run for which you can book trips in Santa Fe, Taos, Red River, and Angel Fire. (See the "Outdoor Activities" sections in chapter 8 and earlier in this chapter for booking agents in Santa Fe and Taos, respectively.)

Arroyo Hondo was also the site of the New Buffalo commune in the 1960s. Hippies flocked here, looking to escape the mores of modern society. Over the years, the commune members have dispersed throughout northern New Mexico, bringing an interesting creative element to the food, architecture, and philosophy of the state. En route north, the highway passes near **San Cristobal,** where a side road turns off to the **D. H. Lawrence Ranch** (see "More Attractions," earlier in this chapter) and **Lama,** site of an isolated spiritual retreat.

Questa

Next, NM 522 passes through Questa, most of whose residents are employed at a molybdenum mine about 5 miles east of town. Mining molybdenum (an ingredient in light bulbs, television tubes, and missile systems) in the area has not been without controversy. The process has raked across hillsides along the Red River, and though the mine's owner treats the water it uses before returning it to the river, studies show that it has adversely affected the fish life. Still, the mine is a major employer in the area, and locals are grateful for the income it generates.

If you turn west off NM 522 onto NM 378 about 3 miles north of Questa, you'll travel 8 miles on a paved road to the Bureau of Land Management–administered **Wild Rivers Recreation Area ★★** (© **575/586-1150;** www.blm.gov/nm). Here, where the Red River enters the gorge, you'll find 22 miles of trails, some suited for biking and some for hiking, a few trails traveling 800 feet down into the gorge to the banks of the Rio Grande. Forty-eight miles of the Rio Grande, which extend south from the Colorado border, are protected under the national Wild and Scenic River Act of 1968. Information on geology and wildlife, as well as hikers' trail maps, can be obtained at the visitor center here. The stunning La Junta Trail (1.2 miles) is difficult, but travels into the canyon at the convergence of the Red River and Rio Grande. The Big Arsenic Springs Trail (1 mile) is moderate and offers a self-guided interpretive trail. Both are excellent ways to get down into the canyon.

The village of **Costilla,** near the Colorado border, is 20 miles north of Questa. This is the turnoff point for four-wheel-drive jaunts and hiking trips into **Valle Vidal,** a huge U.S. Forest Service–administered reserve with 42 miles of roads and many hiking trails. A day hike in this area can bring you sightings of hundreds of elk.

Red River

To continue on the Enchanted Circle loop, turn east at Questa onto NM 38 for a 12-mile climb to Red River, a rough-and-ready 1890s gold-mining town that has parlayed its Wild West ambience into a pleasant resort village that's especially popular with families from Texas and Oklahoma.

This community, at 8,750 feet, is a center for skiing, snowmobiling, fishing, hiking, off-road driving, horseback riding, mountain biking, river rafting, and other outdoor pursuits. Frontier-style celebrations, honky-tonk entertainment, and even staged shootouts on Main Street are held throughout the year.

Though it can be a charming and fun town, Red River's food and accommodations are mediocre at best. Its patrons are down-home folks, happy with a bed and a diner-style meal. If you decide to stay, try the **Lodge at Red River,** 400 E. Main St. (© **800/915-6343** or 575/754-6280; www.lodgeatredriver.com), in the center of town. It offers hotel rooms ranging in price from $84 to $225. Knotty pine throughout, the accommodations are clean and comfortable. Downstairs, **Texas Reds Steak House** ★ serves steaks, burgers, and chicken dishes in a country-diner atmosphere. It's open in summer and winter daily from 4:30 to 9pm. During the shoulder seasons in spring and fall, it's open on Friday and Saturday nights.

If you're passing through and want a tasty meal, **Mountain Treasures** ★, 121 E. Main St. (© **575/754-2700**), a gallery, bistro, and espresso bar, offers excellent sandwiches. Go straight for the muffulettas or "muffys," Italian sandwiches made popular in New Orleans. Salami, turkey, provolone, cheddar, and olive spread are set within homemade Sicilian round bread and heated until the outside is crusty, the inside gooey rich. For dessert try the Czech pastry *kolache* in a variety of fruits, including peach and cherry. Summer and winter ski season the cafe is open daily 6am to 8pm, and other times Monday to Saturday 7am to 2pm.

The **Red River Chamber of Commerce,** P.O. Box 870, Red River, NM 87558 (© **800/348-6444** or 575/754-2366; www.redrivernewmexico.com), lists more than 40 accommodations, including lodges and condominiums. Some are open winters or summers only.

Eagle Nest

About 16 miles southeast of Red River, on the other side of 9,850-foot Bobcat Pass, is the village of Eagle Nest, resting on the shore of Eagle Nest Lake in the Moreno Valley. Gold was mined in this area as early as 1866, starting in what is now the ghost town of **Elizabethtown,** about 5 miles north; Eagle Nest itself (pop. 200) wasn't incorporated until 1976. The 4-square-mile **Eagle Nest Lake State Park** (© **888/667-2757** or 575/377-1594; www.emnrd.state.nm.us) stretches out below the village. Currently facilities include restrooms, a boat ramp, and visitor center. The lake is considered one of the top trout producers in the United States and attracts ice fishermen in winter as well as summer anglers. It's too cold for swimming, but sailboaters and windsurfers ply the waters.

One of New Mexico's more atmospheric country bars, the **Laguna Vista Saloon,** resides here, on US 64 at the center of Eagle Nest (© **800/821-2093** or 575/377-6522; www.lagunavistalodge.com).

ghosts OF ELIZABETHTOWN

Although only a few trodden clues remain, the gold-mining Elizabethtown once boasted 7,000 residents and was the first seat of Colfax County. It was called Virginia City when founded in 1865, but the name was changed to honor Elizabeth Moore, daughter of a leading citizen. What has become known as E-town had plenty of gold-town perks: five stores, two hotels, seven saloons, and three dance halls. By the early 1900s, much of the gold had run out, and in 1903 fire blazed through the town, leveling much of it. Today, visitors can still see a few foundations and remnants of a cemetery. It's on the west side of NM 38, about 10 miles east of Red River.

If you're heading to Cimarron or Denver, proceed east on US 64 from Eagle Nest. But if you're circling back to Taos, continue southwest on NM 38 and US 64 to Agua Fría and Angel Fire.

Shortly before the Agua Fría junction, you'll see the **Vietnam Veterans Memorial State Park,** C.R. B-4, Angel Fire (𝄞 **575/377-6900;** www.angelfirememorial.com). It's a stunning structure with curved white walls soaring high against the backdrop of the Sangre de Cristo Range. Consisting of a chapel and an underground visitor center, it was built by Dr. Victor Westphall in memory of his son, David, a marine lieutenant killed in Vietnam in 1968. The 6,000-square-foot memorial houses exhibits, videos, and memorabilia. It also has a changing gallery of photographs of Vietnam veterans who lost their lives in the Southeast Asian war, but no photo is as poignant as this inscription written by young David Westphall, a promising poet:

> *Greed plowed cities desolate.*
> *Lusts ran snorting through the streets.*
> *Pride reared up to desecrate*
> *Shrines, and there were no retreats.*
> *So man learned to shed the tears*
> *With which he measures out his years.*

Angel Fire

If you like the clean efficiency of a resort complex, you may want to plan a night or two here—at any time of year. Angel Fire is approximately 150 miles north of Albuquerque and 21 miles east of Taos. Opened in the late 1960s, this resort offers a hotel, condominiums, and cabins. Winter is the biggest season. This medium-size beginner and intermediate mountain is an excellent place for families to roam about (see "Skiing," earlier in this chapter). Two high-speed quad lifts zip skiers to the top quickly, while allowing them a long ski down. The views of the Moreno Valley are awe inspiring. Fourteen miles of Nordic trail have been added at the top of the mountain; visitors can also snowmobile and take sleigh rides, including one out to a sheepherder's tent with a plank floor and a wood stove where you can eat dinner cooked over an open fire. Contact **Roadrunner Tours** (𝄞 **575/377-6416** or 575/377-1811).

During spring, summer, and fall, **Angel Fire Resort ★** offers golf, tennis, hiking, mountain biking (you can take your bike up on the quad lift), fly-fishing, river rafting,

15

Enchanted Circle Driving Tour

WHAT TO SEE & DO IN TAOS

and horseback riding. There are other fun family activities, such as a video arcade, a miniature golf course, theater performances, and, throughout the year, a variety of festivals, including a hot-air balloon festival, Winterfest, and concerts of both classical and popular music.

The unofficial community center is the **Angel Fire Resort,** 10 Miller Lane (P.O. Box 130), Angel Fire, NM 87710 (© **800/633-7463** or 575/377-6401; www.angel fireresort.com), a 155-unit hotel with spacious, comfortable rooms, some with fireplaces and some with balconies. The resort is in the process of remodeling, so be sure to request one of their updated rooms. Rates range from $92 to $200.

If you'd like a good meal while in the area, stop in at the **Roasted Clove** ★, 48 N. Angel Fire Rd. (© **575/377-0636;** www.roastedclove.com), a fine-dining restaurant that serves contemporary American cuisine. Your best bet here is the filet-mignon tacos served with fresh guacamole, chile sauce, and lime crema. It's open during ski season and in summer Monday to Wednesday, Thursday, and Sunday from 5 to 8:30pm, and Friday to Saturday 5 to 9pm.

For more information on the Moreno Valley, including full accommodations listings, contact the **Angel Fire Chamber of Commerce,** P.O. Box 547, Angel Fire, NM 87710 (© **800/446-8117** or 575/377-6661; fax 575/377-3034; www.angelfirechamber.org).

A fascinating adventure you may want to try here is a 1-hour, 1-day, or overnight horseback trip with **Roadrunner Tours,** P.O. Box 274, Angel Fire, NM 87710 (© **575/377-6416;** www.rtours.com). One-and-a-half-hour rides run year-round for $70, but if you'd like a little more adventure, try an overnight. From Angel Fire, Nancy Burch guides adventurers on horseback through private ranchland of ponderosa forests and meadows of asters and sunflowers, often including wildlife sightings. Once at camp, riders bed down in an authentic mountain cowboy cabin. Call for prices.

ALBUQUERQUE

Albuquerque is the gateway to northern New Mexico, the portal through which most domestic and
international visitors pass before traveling on to
Santa Fe and Taos. But it's worth stopping here for a day
or two in order to get a feel for the history of this area.

From the rocky crest of Sandia Peak at sunset, one can see the lights of
this city of more than a half million people spread out across 16 miles of
high desert grassland. As the sun drops beyond the western horizon, it
reflects off the Rio Grande River, flowing through Albuquerque more
than a mile below.

This waterway is the bloodline for the area, what allowed a city to
spring up in this vast desert, and it continues to be at the center of the
area's growth. Farming villages that line its banks are being stampeded
by expansion. As the west side of the city sprawls, more means for
transporting traffic across the river have been built.

The railroad, which set up a major stop here in 1880, prompted much
of Albuquerque's initial growth, but that economic explosion was nothing
compared with what happened since World War II. Designated a major
national center for military research and production, Albuquerque
became a trading center for New Mexico, whose populace is spread
widely across the land. Look closely, and you'll see ranchers, Native
Americans, and Hispanic villagers stocking up on goods to take back to
the New Mexico boot heel or the Texas panhandle.

Climbing out of the valley is **Route 66,** well worth a drive, if only to
see the rust that time has left. Old court motels still line the street,
many with their funky '50s signage. One enclave on this route is the
University of New Mexico and Nob Hill district, with a number
of fun cafes and shops.

Farther downhill, you come to **downtown Albuquerque.** During
the day, this area is all suits and heels, but at night it boasts a hip nightlife scene. People from all over the state come to Albuquerque to check
out the live music and dance clubs, most within walking distance from
each other.

The section called **Old Town** is worth a visit. Though it's the most
touristy part of town, it's also a unique Southwestern village with a
beautiful and intact plaza. Also in this area are Albuquerque's aquarium
and botanical gardens, as well as its zoo.

Greater Albuquerque

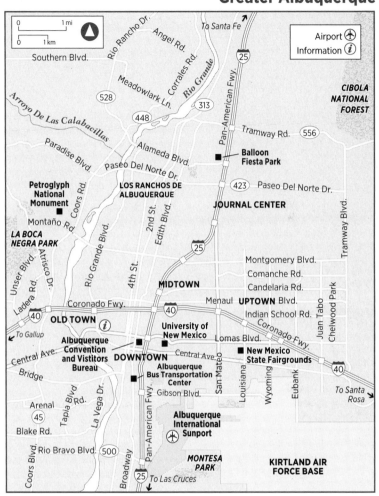

Southern Blvd.

Rio Rancho Dr.

Angel Rd.

To Santa Fe

Airport ⊕
Information ⓘ

528

Meadowlark Ln.

Corrales Rd.

Rio Grande

313

448

Pan-American Fwy.

25

CIBOLA
NATIONAL
FOREST

Arroyo De Las Calabacillas

Paradise Blvd.

Alameda Blvd.

Paseo Del Norte Dr.

Tramway Rd. 556

Petroglyph
National
Monument

LOS RANCHOS DE
ALBUQUERQUE

Balloon
Fiesta Park

423 Paseo Del Norte Dr.

JOURNAL CENTER

Coors Rd.

2nd St.

Edith Blvd.

Montaño Rd.

LA BOCA
NEGRA PARK

Rio Grande Blvd.

4th St.

MIDTOWN

Montgomery Blvd.

Comanche Rd.

Candelaria Rd.

Tramway Blvd.

Unser Blvd.

Atrisco Dr.

Ladera Rd.

Coronado Fwy.

40

OLD TOWN ⓘ

Menaul **UPTOWN** Blvd.

Indian School Rd.

Juan Tabo

Chelwood Park

To Gallup

Albuquerque
Convention
and Vistitors
Bureau

Central Ave.

Bridge

University of
New Mexico

DOWNTOWN

Central Ave.

Lomas Blvd.

Coronado Fwy.

40

New Mexico
State Fairgrounds

San Mateo

Louisiana

Wyoming

Eubank

To Santa
Rosa

Albuquerque
Bus Transportation
Center

Gibson Blvd.

Arenal

Tapia Blvd.

La Vega Dr.

45

Blake Rd.

Albuquerque
International
Sunport ⊕

Coors Blvd.

Rio Bravo Blvd. 500

Broadway

Pan-American Fwy.

25 To Las Cruces

MONTESA
PARK

KIRTLAND AIR
FORCE BASE

0   1 mi
0   1 km

ORIENTATION
Arriving

Albuquerque is the transportation hub for New Mexico, so getting in and out of town
is easy. For more detailed information, see "Getting There & Around," in chapter 3.

BY PLANE The **Albuquerque International Sunport** (✆ 505/842-4366; www.cabq.gov/airport) is in the southcentral part of the city, between I-25 on the west and Kirtland Air Force Base on the east, just south of Gibson Boulevard. Sleek and efficient, the airport is served by most national airlines and two local ones.

Most hotels have courtesy vans to meet their guests and take them to their respective destinations. In addition, **Sunport Shuttle** (✆ 866/505-4966; www.sunportshuttle. com) runs services to and from city hotels. **ABQ Ride** (✆ 505/243-7433; www.cabq. gov/transit), Albuquerque's public bus system, also makes airport stops. There is efficient taxi service to and from the airport, and there are numerous car-rental agencies.

BY TRAIN Amtrak's *Southwest Chief* arrives and departs daily to and from Los Angeles and Chicago. The station is at the Alvarado Transportation Center, 300 2nd St. SW (at the corner of Lead and Second; ✆ 800/872-7245 or 505/842-9650; www.amtrak.com). The **New Mexico Rail Runner Express** (✆ 866/795-7245; www.nmrailrunner.com) runs trains daily from various points in Albuquerque to various ones in Santa Fe, with connecting busses to the Albuquerque International Sunport and to Taos.

BY BUS Greyhound/Trailways (✆ 800/231-2222; www.greyhound.com) arrives and departs from the Alvarado Transportation Center, 300 2nd St. SW (at the corner of Lead and Second).

BY CAR If you're driving, you'll probably arrive via either the east-west I-40 or the north-south I-25. Exits are well marked. For information and advice on driving in New Mexico, see "Getting There & Around," in chapter 3.

Visitor Information

The main office of the **Albuquerque Convention and Visitors Bureau** is at 20 First Plaza NW (✆ 800/284-2282 or 505/842-9918; www.itsatrip.org). It's open Monday to Friday 8am to 5pm. There are information centers at the airport, on the lower level at the bottom of the escalator, open daily 9:30am to 8pm; and in Old Town at 303 Romero St. NW, Ste. 107, open daily 10am to 5pm. Tape-recorded information about current local events is available from the bureau after 5pm weekdays and all day Saturday and Sunday. Call ✆ 800/284-2282.

City Layout

The city's sprawl takes a while to get used to. A visitor's first impression is of a grid of arteries lined with shopping malls and fast-food eateries, with residences tucked behind on side streets.

If you look at a map of Albuquerque, you'll notice that it lies at the crossroads of I-25 north-south and I-40 east-west. Focus your attention on the southwest quadrant: Here, you'll find both downtown Albuquerque and Old Town, site of many tourist attractions. Lomas Boulevard and Central Avenue, the old Route 66 (US 66), flank downtown on the north and south. They come together 2 miles west of downtown near Old Town Plaza, the historical and spiritual heart of the city. Lomas and Central continue east across I-25, staying about half a mile apart as they pass by the University of New Mexico and the Expo New Mexico fairgrounds. The airport is directly south of the UNM campus, about 3 miles via Yale Boulevard. Kirtland Air Force Base—site of Sandia National Laboratories—is an equal distance south of the fairgrounds, on Louisiana Boulevard.

Roughly paralleling I-40 to the north is Menaul Boulevard, the focus of midtown and uptown shopping, as well as the hotel districts. As Albuquerque expands northward, the Journal Center business park area, about 4½ miles north of the freeway interchange, is expanding. Near there is home to the Albuquerque International Balloon Fiesta and the new Balloon Museum. East of Eubank Boulevard lie the Sandia Foothills, where the alluvial plain slants a bit more steeply toward the mountains.

When looking for an address, it is helpful to know that Central Avenue divides the city into north and south, and the railroad tracks—which run just east of First Street downtown—comprise the dividing line between east and west. Street names are followed by a directional: NE, NW, SE, or SW.

MAPS   The most comprehensive Albuquerque street map is distributed by the Convention and Visitors Bureau, 20 First Plaza NW (© **800/284-2282** or 505/842-9918).

GETTING AROUND

Albuquerque is easy to get around, thanks to its wide thoroughfares and grid layout, combined with its efficient transportation systems.

BY PUBLIC TRANSPORTATION   ABQ Ride (© **505/243-7433**) cloaks the arterials with its city bus network. Call for information on routes and fares.

BY TAXI   **Yellow Cab** (© **505/247-8888**) serves the city and surrounding area 24 hours a day.

BY CAR   The Yellow Pages list more than 30 car-rental agencies in Albuquerque. Among them are the following well-known national firms: **Alamo,** 3400 University Blvd. SE (© **505/842-4057;** www.alamo.com); **Avis,** at the airport (© **505/842-4080;** www.avis.com); **Budget,** at the airport (© **505/247-3443;** www.budget.com); **Hertz,** at the airport (© **505/842-4235;** www.hertz.com); **Rent-A-Wreck,** 2001 Ridegecrest Dr. SE (© **505/232-7552;** www.rentawreck.com/nm.htm); and **Thrifty,** 2039 Yale Blvd. SE (© **505/842-8733;** www.thrifty.com). Those not located at the airport itself are close by and can provide rapid airport pickup and delivery service.

Parking is generally not difficult in Albuquerque. Meters operate weekdays 8am to 6pm and are not monitored at other times. Only the large downtown hotels charge for parking. Traffic is a problem only at certain hours. Avoid I-25 and I-40 at the center of town around 8am and 5pm.

[FastFACTS] ALBUQUERQUE

Airport   See "Orientation," above.

Area Code   For the northwestern section of New Mexico, including Santa Fe and Albuquerque, the area code is **505,** while the rest of the state is **575.**

ATMs   You can find ATMs all over town, at supermarkets, banks, and drive-throughs.

Business Hours

Offices and **stores** are generally open Monday to Friday, 9am to 5pm, with many stores also open Friday

night, Saturday, and Sunday in the summer season. Most **banks** are also open Monday to Friday, 9am to 5pm. Some may be open Saturday morning. Most branches have ATMs available 24 hours. Call establishments for specific hours.

Car Rentals See "Getting Around Northern New Mexico," in chapter 3, or "Getting Around," above.

Climate See "When to Go," in chapter 3.

Currency Exchange Foreign currency can be exchanged at any of the branches of **Bank of America** (its main office is at 303 Roma NW; ✆ **505/282-2450**).

Dentists Contact **Emergency Dental USA of Albuquerque** at ✆ 505/296-9911 (www.albuquerque emergencydental.com).

Doctors Call the **Greater Albuquerque Medical Association,** at ✆ **505/821-4583,** for information.

Emergencies For police, fire, or ambulance, dial ✆ **911.**

Hospitals The major hospital facilities are **Presbyterian Hospital,** 1100 Central Ave. SE (✆ **505/841-1234,** or 505/841-1111 for emergency services), and **University of New Mexico Hospital,** 2211 Lomas Blvd. NE (✆ **505/272-2111,** or 505/272-2411 for emergency services).

Hot Lines The following hot lines are available in Albuquerque: rape crisis (✆ **505/266-7711**), poison control (✆ **800/432-6866**), suicide (✆ **505/247-1121**), and Psychiatric Emergency Services (✆ **505/272-2920**).

Information See "Visitor Information," under "Orientation," above.

Internet Access **FedEx Office** provides high-speed Internet access at five locations throughout the city. Two convenient ones are 6220 San Mateo Blvd. NE at Academy Boulevard (✆ **505/821-2222**) and 2706 Central Ave. SE at Princeton Boulevard (✆ **505/255-9673**).

Library The Albuquerque/Bernalillo County Public Library's **main branch** is at 501 Copper Ave. NW, between Fifth and Sixth streets (✆ **505/768-5140**). You can find the locations of the 17 other library facilities in the area by checking online at **www.cabq.gov/library**.

Liquor Laws The legal drinking age is 21 throughout New Mexico. Bars may remain open until 2am Monday to Saturday and until midnight on Sunday. Wine, beer, and spirits are sold at licensed supermarkets and liquor stores. It is illegal to transport liquor through most Native American reservations.

Lost Property Contact the city police at ✆ **505/768-2229.**

Newspapers & Magazines The daily newspaper is the **Albuquerque Journal** (✆ **505/823-7777;** www.abqjournal.com). You can pick up the **Alibi** (✆ **505/346-0660;** www.alibi.com), Albuquerque's alternative weekly, for free at newsstands all over town, especially around the University of New Mexico.

It offers entertainment listings and alternative views on a variety of subjects.

Pharmacies **Walgreens** (www.walgreens.com) has many locations throughout Albuquerque. To find one near you, call ✆ **800/925-4733.** Two centrally located ones, which are open both 24 hours, are 8011 Harper Dr. NE at Wyoming Boulevard (✆ **505/858-3134**) and 5001 Montgomery Blvd. NE at San Mateo (✆ **505/881-5210**).

Police For emergencies, call ✆ **911.** For other business, contact the **Albuquerque City Police** (✆ **505/242-COPS** [2677]) or the **New Mexico State Police** (✆ **505/841-9256**).

Post Offices To find the nearest U.S. Post Office, dial ✆ **800/275-8777.** The service will ask for your zip code and give you the closest post office address and hours.

Radio The local AM station **KKOB** (770) broadcasts news and events. FM band stations include **KUNM** (89.9), the University of New Mexico station, which broadcasts Public Radio programming and a variety of music; **KPEK** (100.3), which plays adult contemporary music; and **KHFM** (95.5), which broadcasts classical music.

Taxes In Albuquerque, the sales tax is 6.25%. An additional hotel tax of 6% will be added to your bill.

Taxis See "Getting Around," above.

Television There are five Albuquerque network affiliates: **KOB-TV** (Channel 4, NBC), **KOAT-TV** (Channel 7, ABC), **KQRE-TV** (Channel 13, CBS), **KASA-TV** (Channel 2, FOX), and **KNME-TV** (Channel 5, PBS).

Time As is true throughout New Mexico, Albuquerque is on **Mountain Standard Time.** It's 2 hours earlier than New York, 1 hour earlier than Chicago, and 1 hour later than Los Angeles. Daylight saving time is in effect from mid-March to early November.

Transit Information **ABQ Ride** is the public bus system. Call ☎ **505/243-7433** for schedules and information.

Useful Telephone Numbers For **road information,** call ☎ **800/432-4269;** for **emergency road service** (AAA), call ☎ **505/291-6600.**

Weather For **time** and **temperature,** call ☎ **505/821-1111.** To get **weather forecasts** on the Internet, check **www.accuweather.com** and use the Albuquerque zip code, 87104.

WHERE TO STAY

Albuquerque's hotel glut is good news for travelers looking for quality rooms at a reasonable cost. Except during peak periods—specifically, the New Mexico Arts and Crafts Fair (late June), the New Mexico State Fair (Sept), and the Albuquerque International Balloon Fiesta (early Oct)—most of the city's hotels have vacant rooms, so guests can frequently request and get lower room rates than the ones posted.

A tax of approximately 12.25% is added to every hotel bill. All hotels and bed-and-breakfasts listed offer rooms for nonsmokers and travelers with disabilities.

Hotels/Motels

EXPENSIVE

Albuquerque Marriott Pyramid North ★★ About a 15-minute drive from Old Town and downtown, this Aztec pyramid–shaped structure provides well-appointed rooms in an interesting environment. The 10 guest floors are grouped around a skylit atrium. Vines drape from planter boxes on the balconies, and water falls five stories to a pool between the two glass elevators. The rooms are spacious, all with picture windows and ample views. The third stage of a $10-million renovation was completed in 2008. With lots of convention space at the hotel, you're likely to encounter name-tagged conventioneers here. Overall, the service seems to be good enough to handle the crowds, but there are only two elevators, so guests often must wait.

5151 San Francisco Rd. NE, Albuquerque, NM 87109. ☎ **800/262-2043** or 505/821-3333. Fax 505/822-8115. www.marriott.com/abqmc. 310 units. $109–$185 double; $185 and up suite. Ask about special weekend and package rates. AE, DC, DISC, MC, V. Free parking. **Amenities:** Restaurant; lounge; concierge; exercise room; Jacuzzi; indoor/outdoor pool; room service. *In room:* A/C, TV, hair dryer, Wi-Fi.

Embassy Suites Albuquerque Hotel & Spa ★★ This newer addition to Albuquerque's hotel scene, opened in 2005, boasts nine floors of suites set around a grand atrium. Its location between the university and downtown offers easy access to the freeway as well, and is just 10 minutes from Old Town. It's an elegant place frequented by business people and conventioneers, but it can also prove a nice stay for travelers, especially families who enjoy the two-room suites. The elegant rooms, which are fairly large, have comfortable beds, large baths with granite counter tops, and many other amenities. A fold-out bed in the second room allows for plenty of space. The Spa Botanica offers a full range of treatments.

Evenings bring a manager's reception, where hors d'oeuvres and drinks are served. Service here is friendly and efficient.

1000 Woodward Place NE, Albuquerque, NM 87102. ✆ **800/362-2779** or 505/245-7100. Fax 505/247-1083. www.embassysuites.com. 261 units. $129–$214 double. AE, DC, DISC, MC, V. Free parking. **Amenities:** 2 restaurants; lounge; concierge; exercise room; Jacuzzi; indoor pool; room service. *In room:* A/C, TV, fridge, hair dryer, Wi-Fi.

Hotel Albuquerque at Old Town ★★ ✒ This hotel, just a 5-minute walk from Old Town, offers artfully decorated rooms with views and excellent service. No Albuquerque hotel is closer to top tourist attractions than the Hotel Albuquerque. The cathedral-style lobby has Spanish colonial furnishings and art, a theme that carries into the guest rooms. They're medium size, with handcrafted furniture, comfortable beds, and medium-size baths with outer vanities. Request a south-side room, and you'll get a balcony with a view over Old Town. A north-side room yields mountain views but no balconies (this is the side to request during the Balloon Fiesta). The lovely grounds have a long trellis portal and a quaint chapel. One of the prettiest pools in town offers a great place to cool off after touring the city. The Q Bar is one of Albuquerque's chicest night spots, with a good tapas menu and a dance floor.

800 Rio Grande Blvd. NW, Albuquerque, NM 87104. ✆ **800/237-2133** (reservations only) or 505/843-6300. Fax 505/842-8426. www.hotelabq.com. 188 units. $119–$219 double; $149–$350 junior suite. Children stay free in parent's room. AE, DC, DISC, MC, V. Free parking. **Amenities:** 2 restaurants; lounge; concierge; exercise room; Jacuzzi; outdoor pool (summer only); room service. *In room:* A/C, TV, hair dryer, Wi-Fi.

Hotel Andaluz ★★★ 👜 Built in 1939 by Conrad Hilton as the La Posada de Albuquerque, this hotel recently received a $30-million makeover and the new name Andaluz. The hotel at the center of downtown is listed on the National Register of Historic Places and is eco-friendly, with solar hot water and use of earth-friendly paint, varnishes, and carpeting. The lobby, a center of activities many nights when live music plays, offers a sophisticated ambience utilizing Moroccan and Spanish architectural elements around a central fountain. The elegance carries into the guest rooms decorated in warm earth tones. They have fine linens, granite counter tops, and views of the city and mountains. The hotel caters to business and leisure travelers with kiosks on the mezzanine that offer descriptions to and ticket sales for cultural events in the area. Andaluz also has an excellent restaurant and nightclub.

125 2nd St. NW, at Copper Ave., Albuquerque, NM 87102. (✆ **877/987-9090** or 505/242-9090. Fax 505/923-9015. www.hotelandaluz.com. 107 units. $119–$229 double; $450 suite. AE, DISC, MC, V. Self-parking $10/day, valet parking $16/day. **Amenities:** Restaurant; lounge; nightclub; concierge; exercise room; room service. *In room:* A/C, TV, hair dryer, MP3 docking station, Wi-Fi.

Hyatt Regency Albuquerque ★★ If you're looking for luxury and want to be right downtown, this is the place to stay. This $60-million hotel, which opened in 1990 and was remodeled in 2008, offers an elegant stay. The lobby features a palm-shaded fountain beneath a pyramidal skylight, and throughout the hotel's public areas is an extensive art collection, including original Frederic Remington sculptures. The spacious guest rooms enhance the feeling of richness with cushy bedding, warm colors, and views of the mountains. The hotel has a number of shops. McGrath's serves three meals daily in a setting of forest-green upholstery and black-cherry furniture.

330 Tijeras Ave. NW, Albuquerque, NM 87102. ✆ **800/233-1234** or 505/842-1234. Fax 505/843-2710. www.hyatt.com. 395 units. $159–$225 double; $400–$800 suite. AE, DC, DISC, MC, V. Self-parking $12,

Central Albuquerque Accommodations

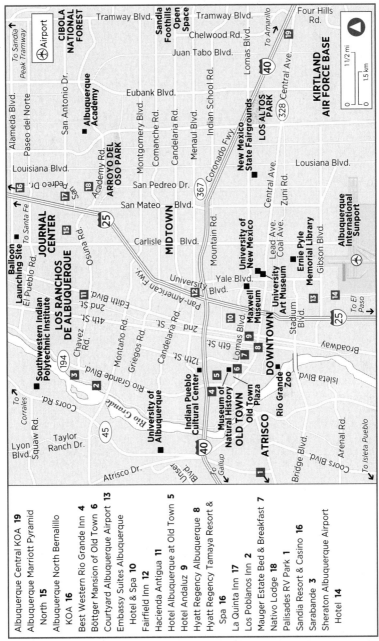

Albuquerque Central KOA **19**
Albuquerque Marriott Pyramid
North **15**
Albuquerque North Bernalillo
KOA **16**
Best Western Rio Grande Inn **4**
Böttger Mansion of Old Town **6**
Courtyard Albuquerque Airport **13**
Embassy Suites Albuquerque
Hotel & Spa **10**
Fairfield Inn **12**
Hacienda Antigua **11**
Hotel Albuquerque at Old Town **5**
Hotel Andaluz **9**
Hyatt Regency Albuquerque **8**
Hyatt Regency Tamaya Resort &
Spa **16**
La Quinta Inn **17**
Los Poblanos Inn **2**
Mauger Estate Bed & Breakfast **7**
Nativo Lodge **18**
Palisades RV Park **1**
Sandia Resort & Casino **16**
Sarabande **3**
Sheraton Albuquerque Airport
Hotel **14**

valet $16. **Amenities:** Restaurant; bar; concierge; health club; outdoor pool; room service; sauna. *In room:* A/C, TV, hair dryer, MP3 docking station, Wi-Fi ($10/day).

Nativo Lodge ★ This full-service hotel provides comfortable rooms with a Native American theme, utilizing high-tech elements as well. It's part of the Heritage Hotels & Resorts group, which, in recent years, has renovated a number of New Mexico hotels such as the Hotel Encanto in Las Cruces and Hotel Albuquerque at Old Town. The five-story building, renovated in 2004, has tan walls throughout the two-tiered lobby and standard-size guest rooms. The rooms are tastefully decorated with Native American geometric patterns, creating a cozy feel, with comfortable beds and good linens, a desk, and small balcony. The bathrooms are small but functional. Be sure to request a room well away from the lounge area, which can be noisy on weekend nights. The service is thoughtful and efficient. This is a good home base for the Balloon Fiesta, as well as to explore the city. The property even has a tepee used for special events.

6000 Pan American Fwy. NE, Albuquerque, NM 87109. ✆ **888/628-4861** or 505/798-4300. Fax 505/798-4305. www.nativolodge.com. $119–$129 double. AE, DC, DISC, MC, V. Free parking. **Amenities:** Restaurant; lounge; exercise room; Jacuzzi; indoor/outdoor pool; room service; sauna. *In room:* A/C, TV, fridge (in suites), hair dryer, Wi-Fi.

Sandia Resort & Casino ★★★ On the Sandia Reservation at the north end of town in a grand nine-story pueblo-style structure, this resort offers plenty of fun activities in a scenic setting. The hotel has spectacular views of the Sandia Mountains and the Albuquerque skyline. The lobby, constructed in a majestic mission church style, offers space for lounging, and just off it, a casino with 1,800 slots, Vegas-style gambling, and all the blinking lights that a gambler could want. The spacious rooms, decorated in an elegant Native American motif, have very comfortable beds, a lounge chair, desk, and louvered blackout blinds, as well as many amenities. The bathrooms are large, with Italian tile throughout, and robes. The suites are even more spacious. The Green Reed Spa offers a full range of treatments, and the Scott Miller–designed 18-hole golf course wraps around the hotel, giving a sense of lush green to the desert. The Bien Shur restaurant (p. 258) on the ninth floor is one of the city's finest dining experiences. Be aware that this resort best serves active people who like to play into the night. If you're looking for a more relaxing stay, you might choose the Hyatt Tamaya.

30 Rainbow Rd. NE, Albuquerque, NM 87113. ✆ **877/272-9199** reservations, 800/526-9366 or 505/798-3930. Fax 505/796-7606. 228 units. www.sandiaresort.com. $139–$299 double; $319–$389 1-bedroom suite; $699 2-bedroom suite. AE, DC, DISC, MC, V. Free valet parking. **Amenities:** 3 restaurants; lounge; free airport transfers; concierge; exercise room; golf course; Jacuzzi; large outdoor pool (weather permitting); room service; spa. *In room:* A/C, TV, hair dryer, Wi-Fi.

MODERATE

Best Western Rio Grande Inn ★ ☺ A 10-minute walk from Old Town, this well-cared for hotel offers comfortable accommodations at a reasonable price. It sits close to Interstate 40, so be sure to request a south-facing room, which will be quieter. The medium-size rooms are accessed off of interior corridors and have earthtone upholstery and walls, a desk, and comfortable chair. With a restaurant on-site and a fenced pool, this is a good option for families.

1015 Rio Grande Blvd. NW, Albuquerque, NM, 87104. ✆ **800/959-4726** or 505/843-9500. Fax 505/843-9238. www.riograndeinn.com. $89–$129 double. AE, DISC, MC, V. Free parking. Pets welcome ($25 one-time fee). **Amenities:** Restaurant; free airport transfer; exercise room, Jacuzzi, outdoor pool (heated year-round). *In room:* A/C, TV, hair dryer, Wi-Fi.

Courtyard Albuquerque Airport ★ ☺ If you want to be near the airport but have good access to the Interstate 25 and Albuquerque's attractions, this is a good choice. Opened in 1990, this four-story member of the Marriott family is built around an attractively landscaped courtyard. Families appreciate the security system—key cards must be used to access the hotel between 11pm and 6am—though most of the hotel's clients are business travelers. The units are roomy and comfortable, with walnut furniture and firm beds. Ask for a balcony room on the courtyard.

1920 Yale Blvd. SE, Albuquerque, NM 87106. ✆ **800/321-2211** or 505/843-6600. Fax 505/843-8740. www.marriott.com. 150 units. Mon–Thurs $139 double; Fri–Sun $89–$99 double. AE, DC, DISC, MC, V. Free parking. **Amenities:** Restaurant; lounge; exercise room; Jacuzzi; indoor pool. *In room:* A/C, TV, hair dryer, high-speed Internet.

Sheraton Albuquerque Airport Hotel ★★ This 15-story hotel right at the airport provides spacious rooms with a touch of elegance. The lobby, grill, and lounge areas employ a lot of sandstone, wood, copper, and tile to lend an Anasazi feel, which carries into the rooms, each with a broad view from a balcony. A recent remodel brought new, comfortable mattresses and bright contemporary furnishings. Air travelers enjoy this hotel's location, but because it has good access to freeways and excellent views, it could also be a wise choice for a few days of browsing around Albuquerque. Of course, you will hear some jet noise. The Rojo Grill serves a variety of American and Southwestern dishes.

2910 Yale Blvd. SE, Albuquerque, NM 87106. ✆ **505/843-7000.** Fax 505/246-8188. www.albuquerque grandairporthotel.com. 276 units. $79–$176 double. AE, DC, DISC, MC, V. Free parking. Pets welcome. **Amenities:** Restaurant; lounge; concierge; outdoor pool (summer only). *In room:* A/C, TV, fridge, hair dryer, Wi-Fi.

INEXPENSIVE

Fairfield Inn ✦ Owned by Marriott, this hotel has exceptionally clean rooms and easy access to freeways that can quickly get you to Old Town, downtown, or the Heights. Ask for an east-facing room to avoid the noise and a view of the highway. Rooms are medium size, as are the bathrooms. Each has a balcony or terrace. You probably couldn't get more for your money (in a chain hotel) anywhere else.

1760 Menaul Blvd. NE, Albuquerque, NM 87102. ✆ **800/228-2800** or 505/889-4000. Fax 505/872-3094. www.fairfieldinn.com. 188 units. $99 double. Children 18 and under stay free in parent's room. Free continental breakfast. AE, DC, DISC, MC, V. Free parking. **Amenities:** Health club; Jacuzzi; indoor/outdoor pool; sauna. *In room:* A/C, TV, Wi-Fi.

La Quinta Inn La Quinta offers reliable, clean rooms at a decent price. Rooms are tastefully decorated, fairly spacious, and comfortable, each with a table and chairs and a shower-only bathroom big enough to move around in. Each king room has a recliner, and two-room suites are available. If you're headed to the Balloon Fiesta, this is a good choice because it's not far from the launch site, though you'll have to reserve as much as a year in advance.

There's another La Quinta near the airport (2116 Yale Blvd. SE); you can make reservations for either branch at the toll-free number.

5241 San Antonio Dr. NE, Albuquerque, NM 87109. ✆ **800/753-3757** or 505/821-9000. Fax 505/821-2399. www.lq.com. 130 units. $72–$79 double (higher during Balloon Fiesta). Children stay free in parent's room. AE, DC, DISC, MC, V. Free parking. Pets welcome. **Amenities:** Outdoor pool (heated May–Oct). *In room:* A/C, TV, hair dryer, Wi-Fi.

Bed & Breakfasts

Böttger Mansion of Old Town ★ Decorated with a mixture antiques and contemporary furnishings, this 1910 historic inn situated right in Old Town offers a sweet taste of a past era. Currently the innkeepers are in the process of retheming the rooms to bring more Albuquerque history into the guests' stay. This includes one room with railroad and another with Route 66 memorabilia. All rooms are medium size and have excellent beds; most have small bathrooms. The rooms facing south let in the most sun but pick up a bit of street noise from nearby Central Avenue and a nearby elementary school. The school quiets down at night, but light sleepers might want a room at the back of the inn to avoid street noise. A guest computer and printer are available in the main living room. Breakfast, such as green-chile polenta quiche with a blueberry muffin, is served in the sunroom. All day, treats are available from the guest snack bar (try the chocolate cookies with a little chile in them). During warm months, the patio is lovely.

110 San Felipe NW, Albuquerque, NM 87104. ℂ **800/758-3639** or 505/243-3639. www.bottger.com. 7 units. $115–$179 double. Rates include full breakfast and snack bar. AE, DISC, MC, V. *In room:* A/C, TV, hair dryer, Wi-Fi.

Hacienda Antigua ★★ 🏚 This adobe home built in 1790 was once the first stagecoach stop out of Old Town in Albuquerque. Now, it's one of Albuquerque's more elegant inns. The artistically landscaped courtyard, with its large cottonwood tree and abundance of greenery, offers a welcome respite for tired travelers. The rooms are gracefully and comfortably furnished with antiques. My favorites all open onto the Great Room. La Capilla, the home's former chapel, has a serene and holy feel, and is furnished with a queen-size bed, a fireplace, and a carving of St. Francis (the patron saint of the garden). All the rooms are equipped with fireplaces. Two more modern rooms built in 2000 aren't quite as atmospheric as those in the main house. A gourmet breakfast, such as pecan waffles, is served in the garden during warm weather and by the fire in winter. The inn is a 15-minute drive from Old Town.

6708 Tierra Dr. NW, Albuquerque, NM 87107. ℂ **800/201-2986** or 505/345-5399. Fax 505/345-3855. www.haciendantigua.com. 8 units. $129–$209 double. Additional person $25. Rates include gourmet breakfast. AE, MC, V. Free parking. Pets welcome ($30 fee). **Amenities:** Concierge; Jacuzzi; outdoor pool. *In room:* A/C, fridge, hair dryer, Wi-Fi.

Los Poblanos Inn ★★ Nestled among century-old cottonwoods, this bed-and-breakfast sits on 25 acres of European-style gardens and peasantlike vegetable and lavender fields, providing one of the state's richest country living experiences. Notable architect John Gaw Meem built the structure, a 7-minute drive from Old Town, in the 1930s. Each of the six guest rooms, most arranged around a poetically planted courtyard with a fountain, has unique touches such as hand-carved doors, traditional tin fixtures, fireplaces, and views across the lushly landscaped grounds. The rooms vary in size. All are comfortable, tastefully decorated with good linens, and offer organic shampoo and soap scented with lavender from the inn's garden. At breakfast, you might feast on eggs Florentine made with eggs from the inn's chickens, spinach from the garden, and artisanal bread made locally, while watching peacocks preen outside the windows of the very Mexican-feeling, boldly decorated cantina. Light sleepers should be aware that the peacocks may caw at night. Fortunately, the inn provides earplugs.

4803 Rio Grande Blvd. NW, Albuquerque, NM 87107. ⓒ **866/344-9297** or 505/344-9297. Fax 505/342-1302. www.lospoblanos.com. 7 units. $130–$280 double. $25 additional person. Rates include full breakfast. AE, MC, V. Free parking. **Amenities:** Bike rentals; concierge; outdoor pool (summer only). *In room:* A/C, TV/DVD (some rooms), hair dryer, Wi-Fi.

Mauger Estate Bed & Breakfast ★ A restored Queen Anne–style home constructed in 1897, this former residence of wool baron William Mauger is listed on the National Register of Historic Places. Today, it is a wonderfully atmospheric bed-and-breakfast, with high ceilings and elegant decor. It's close to downtown and Old Town, just 5 blocks from the convention center, and only 5 miles from the airport, yet it sits off a side street that is very quiet. Some rooms feature period furnishings, while others have tasteful contemporary decor. The innkeeper here is dedicated to providing guests with a comfortable and personal stay. Treats of cheese, wine, and other beverages are offered in the evenings, and a full gourmet breakfast is served each morning in indoor and outdoor dining rooms.

701 Roma Ave. NW, Albuquerque, NM 87102. ⓒ **800/719-9189** or 505/242-8755. Fax 505/842-8835. www.maugerbb.com. 10 units. $99–$129 double. Additional person $15. Rates include full breakfast and evening refreshments. AE, DC, DISC, MC, V. Free parking. Dogs welcome with prior arrangement ($20 fee). *In room:* A/C, TV, fridge, hair dryer, Wi-Fi.

Sarabande ★ You'll find home-style comfort mixed with elegance at this bed-and-breakfast in the North Valley, a 10-minute drive from Old Town. Once you pass through the front gate and into the well-tended courtyard gardens with a fountain, you'll forget that you're staying on the fringes of a big city. With cut-glass windows, traditional antiques, and good bed linens, you'll be well pampered here. Innkeeper Janie Eggers has filled the home with fine art as well as comfortable modern furniture. The Rose Room has a Japanese soaking tub and kiva fireplace. The Iris Room has a king-size bed and stained-glass window depicting irises. Both rooms open onto a wisteria-shaded patio. The real gems here are two more Southwestern-style suites, each with *Saltillo* tile floors, a gas-burning fireplace, Jacuzzi tub, and private patio. Janie serves a full breakfast, including fresh fruit, baked goods, and an entree, either in the courtyard or the Southwest-style dining room.

5637 Rio Grande Blvd. NW, Albuquerque, NM 87107. ⓒ **888/506-4923** or 505/345-4923. Fax 505/341-0654. www.sarabandebb.com. 6 units. $89–$159 double. Rates include full breakfast. AE, DISC, MC, V. Free parking. **Amenities:** Jacuzzi; outdoor pool. *In room:* A/C, TV, Wi-Fi.

Near Albuquerque

Hyatt Regency Tamaya Resort and Spa ★★★ This is the spot for a get-away-from-it-all luxury vacation. Set in the hills above the lush Rio Grande Valley on the Santa Ana Pueblo, this pueblo-style resort offers a 16,000-square-foot full-service spa and fitness center, an 18-hole Twin Warriors Championship Golf Course designed by Gary Panks, and views of the Sandia Mountains. Rooms are spacious, with large tile bathrooms. Request one that faces the mountains for one of the state's more spectacular vistas. Other rooms look out across a large courtyard, where the pools and hot tub are. Though the resort is surrounded by acres of quiet countryside, it's only 20 minutes from Albuquerque and 50 minutes from Santa Fe. The concierge offers trips to attractions daily, as well as on-site activities such as hot-air balloon rides, horseback rides, and nature/cultural walks or carriage rides by the river. Plan at least one dinner at the innovative Corn Maiden (p. 260).

CRUISING corrales

If you'd like to travel along meadows and apple orchards into a place where life is a little slower and sweeter, head 20 minutes north of Albuquerque to the village of Corrales. Home to farmers, artists, and affluent landowners, this is a fun place to roam through shops and galleries, and, in the fall, sample vegetables from roadside vendors. Two excellent restaurants, both serving imaginative new American cuisine, sit on the main street. **Indigo Crow ★**, 4515 Corrales Rd. (© **505/898-7000;** www.indogocrowcafe.com), serves lunch and dinner Tuesday to Saturday 11:30am to 9pm, and brunch and dinner on Sunday 10am to 9pm. **Hannah & Nate's ★★**, 4512 Corrales Rd. (© **505/898-2370;** www.hannahandnates.com), serves delectable breakfasts, salads, and

sandwiches. It is open daily 7am to 2pm. If you'd like to stay in the village, contact the **Sandhill Crane Bed-and-Breakfast ★**, 389 Camino Hermosa (© **800/375-2445** or 505/898-2445; www.sandhill cranebandb.com).

The town also has a nature preserve and a historic church. In September, the Harvest Festival is well worth the trip. For more information about Corrales, contact Corrales Village (© **505/897-0502;** www.corrales-nm.org).

To get to the village, head north on either I-25 or Rio Grande Boulevard, turn west on Alameda Boulevard, cross the Rio Grande, and turn north on Corrales Road (NM 448). The village is just a few minutes up the road.

1300 Tuyuna Trail, Santa Ana Pueblo, NM 87004. © **800/554-9288** or 505/867-1234. www.tamaya. hyatt.com. 350 units. May–Oct $249–$459 double; Nov–Apr $153–$239 double. Suite rates available upon request. Inquire about spa, horseback riding, golf, and family packages. AE, DC, DISC, MC, V. Free parking. From I-25 take exit 242, following US 550 west to Tamaya Blvd.; drive 1½ miles to the resort. **Amenities:** 2 restaurants; 2 snack bars; lounge; children's programs; concierge; golf course; health club, Jacuzzi; 3 pools (heated year-round), room service; his/hers spa with steam room and sauna. *In room:* A/C, TV, fridge, hair dryer, Wi-Fi.

RV Parks

Albuquerque Central KOA   This RV park in the foothills east of Albuquerque is a good choice for those who want to be close to town. It offers some shade trees, lots of amenities, and convenient freeway access. Cabins are available.

12400 Skyline Rd. NE, Albuquerque, NM 87123. © **800/562-7781** or 505/296-2729. www.koa. com. $25–$30 tent site; $35–$65 RV site, depending on hookup; $45–$85 1-room cabin; $48–$95 2-room cabin. All prices valid for up to 2 people. Additional adult $5, child $3. AE, DISC, MC, V. Free parking. Pets welcome. **Amenities:** Bathhouse; bike rentals; fenced dog park; Jacuzzi; coin-op laundry; miniature golf; playground; outdoor pool; wheelchair-accessible restroom; Wi-Fi.

Albuquerque North Bernalillo KOA ★   More than 1,000 cottonwood and pine trees shade this park, and you'll see many flowers in the warm months. At the foot of the mountains, 14 miles from Albuquerque, this campground has plenty of amenities. Guests enjoy a free pancake breakfast daily and free outdoor movies. Reservations are recommended. Six camping cabins are also available.

555 Hill Rd., Bernalillo, NM 87004. © **800/562-3616** or 505/867-5227. www.koa.com. $21–$23 tent site; $30–$39 RV site, depending on hookup; $38 1-bedroom cabin; $48 2-bedroom cabin. Rates include pancake breakfast and are valid for up to 2 people. Additional person $3. Children 6 and under

free with parent. AE, DISC, MC, V. Free parking. Pets welcome. **Amenities:** Restaurant; coin-op laundry; playground; outdoor pool (summer only); store; Wi-Fi.

Palisades RV Park Sitting out on the barren west mesa, this RV park has nice views of the Sandia Mountains and is the closest RV park to Old Town and the Biological Park (10-min. drive; p. 269); however, it is also in a fairly desolate setting, with only a few trees about. In midsummer, it's hot.

9201 Central Ave. NW, Albuquerque, NM 87121. ⓒ **888/922-9595** or 505/831-5000. Fax 505/352-9599. www.palisadesrvpark.com. 110 sites. $27 per day; $128 per week; $335 per month plus electricity. MC, V. Free parking. Pets welcome. **Amenities:** Bathhouse; coin-op laundry; propane; store; Wi-Fi.

WHERE TO DINE
Restaurants by Cuisine

AMERICAN

Flying Star Cafe ★ (University/Nob Hill, $, p. 260)

Range Café ★ (Bernalillo, $$, p. 262)

66 Diner (University/Nob Hill, $, p. 260)

BAKERY

Flying Star Cafe ★ (University/Nob Hill, $, p. 260)

DELI/CAFE

Flying Star Cafe ★ (University/Nob Hill, $, p. 260)

Gold Street Caffè ★★ (Downtown, $$, p. 256)

The Grove Café & Market ★★ (Downtown, $$, p. 256)

FRENCH

La Crêpe Michel ★★ (Old Town, $$, p. 254)

GREEK

Yanni's Mediterranean Grill and Opa Bar ★★ (Nob Hill, $$, p. 259)

ITALIAN

Farina Pizzeria & Wine Bar ★★ (Downtown, $$, p. 256)

Scalo ★★ (University/Nob Hill, $$, p. 259)

NEW AMERICAN

Artichoke Cafe ★★ (Downtown, $$$, p. 255)

Bien Shur ★★★ (Northeast Heights, $$$, p. 258)

Corn Maiden ★★ (Santa Ana Pueblo, $$$, p. 260)

Gold Street Caffè ★★ (Downtown, $$, p. 256)

Jennifer James 101 ★★★ (Northeast Heights, $$$, p. 258)

Lucia ★★ (Downtown, $$$, p. 255)

Prairie Star ★★ (Santa Ana Pueblo, $$$, p. 261)

Seasons Rotisserie & Grill ★★ (Old Town, $$$, p. 252)

Slate Street Café ★★ (Downtown, $$, p. 257)

Standard Diner ★★ (Downtown, $$, p. 257)

Terra ★ (Old Town, $$$, p. 252)

Zinc Wine Bar and Bistro ★★ (University/Nob Hill, $$$, p. 259)

NEW MEXICAN

Duran Central Pharmacy ★ (Old Town, $, p. 254)

Mary & Tito's Café ★★ (Downtown, $, p. 257)

KEY TO ABBREVIATIONS:
$$$$** = Very Expensive **$$$** = Expensive **$$** = Moderate **$ = Inexpensive

Range Café ★ (Bernalillo, $$, p. 262)
Sadie's ★ (Old Town, $, p. 254)
Sophia's Place ★★ (Old Town, $, p. 254)

STEAK/SEAFOOD

Bien Shur ★★★ (Northeast Heights,
$$$, p. 258)

Corn Maiden ★★ (Santa Ana Pueblo,
$$$, p. 260)
Scalo ★★ (University/Nob Hill, $$,
p. 259)
Seasons Rotisserie & Grill ★★ (Old
Town, $$$, p. 252)

In or Near Old Town
EXPENSIVE

Seasons Rotisserie & Grill ★★ NEW AMERICAN/STEAK/SEAFOOD Between
sunshine-colored walls and under an arched ceiling, this restaurant serves sophisti-
cated flavors just steps from Old Town. It's a sweet oasis at midday and a romantic spot
in the evening. The upstairs cantina bustles at sundown, with folks drinking margari-
tas. Service is excellent. At lunch you can't go wrong with the Angus burger with lemon
aioli and roasted poblano chiles, served with herb fries. For the lighter eater, a number
of salads head the menu. Dinner brings more sophisticated offerings. The grilled pork
chop with goat cheese and roasted potatoes is tasty, as is the hoisin-glazed Atlantic
salmon with jasmine rice. A full bar and an imaginative wine and beer list accompany
the menu. On Saturday and Sunday evenings in summer, live jazz is played.

2031 Mountain Rd. NW. ⓒ **505/766-5100.** Reservations recommended at dinner. Main courses $7–$14
lunch, $16–$40 dinner. AE, DC, DISC, MC, V. Mon–Fri 11:30am–2:30pm; daily 5–10:30pm. Cantina daily 4pm–
midnight (Mon–Thurs until 11pm).

Terra ★ NEW AMERICAN Those who live in Albuquerque's north valley are
overjoyed to have fine dining within their midst (at the end of Rio Grande Blvd.,
about 15 min. from Old Town). Owner/chef Peter Lukes combines thoughtful fla-
vors with imaginative presentation. The setting is comfortable, quiet, and relaxed.
An exposed kitchen allows diners to watch the chef in action. The menu changes
with the seasons. During lunch you can select from sandwiches, such as a BLT with
salmon and smoked bacon, as well as a variety of salads and pasta dishes, such as a
four-cheese and chicken ravioli served with baby spinach. Dinner might start with
griddled blue crab and corn cakes and move on to hazelnut-crusted tilapia with
spaghetti squash. Vegetarian entrees are available, as are beer and wine. For dessert,
try the warm chocolate Appaloosa cake.

1119 Alameda NW. ⓒ **505/792-1700.** www.terrabistro.com. Reservations recommended. Lunch $8–$14;
dinner $17–$30. AE, DISC, MC, V. Tues–Fri 11am–2pm; Tues–Sat 5:30pm–close.

GASTROBLOG

If you're looking for an in-depth look at
Albuquerque's restaurants, check out
Gil's Thrilling (and filling) Blog ★★ at
www.nmgastronome.com/blog. Food
critic and New Mexico native Gil Garduño
has dined at more than 1,000 restaurants
in northern New Mexico. In his blog he
provides in-depth accounts and ratings,
of the food and the experience of dining
at most of them. You may spend hours
reading up on his favorites, or just take a
quick peek to get a recommendation.

Central Albuquerque Dining

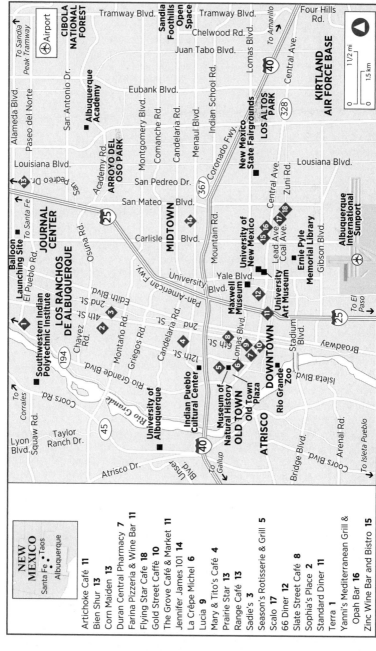

Artichoke Café **11**
Bien Shur **13**
Corn Maiden **13**
Duran Central Pharmacy **7**
Farina Pizzeria & Wine Bar **11**
Flying Star Café **18**
Gold Street Caffè **10**
The Grove Café & Market **11**
Jennifer James 101 **14**
La Crêpe Michel **6**
Lucia **9**
Mary & Tito's Café **4**
Prairie Star **13**
Range Café **13**
Sadie's **3**
Season's Rotisserie & Grill **5**
Scalo **17**
66 Diner **12**
Slate Street Café **8**
Sophia's Place **2**
Standard Diner **11**
Terra **1**
Yanni's Mediterranean Grill & Opah Bar **16**
Zinc Wine Bar and Bistro **15**

MODERATE

La Crêpe Michel ★★ FRENCH   Locals love this small cafe tucked away in a secluded walkway not far from the plaza, where the food is fun and imaginatively prepared. Run by chef Claudie Zamet-Wilcox from France, it has a cozy, informal European feel, with white table coverings and simple furnishings. Service is friendly and calm, which makes this a good place for a romantic meal. The *crêpe aux fruits de mer* (blend of sea scallops, bay scallops, and shrimp in a *velouté* sauce with mushrooms) is especially nice, as is the *crêpe à la volaille* (chunks of chicken in a cream sauce with mushrooms and Madeira wine). For a heartier meal, try one of the specials listed on the board on the wall, such as the beef filet or the *saumon au champagne* (filet of salmon with a white wine–and-cream sauce). For dessert, don't leave without having a *crêpe aux chocolat* (chocolate crepe).

400 San Felipe C2. ℂ **505/242-1251.** www.lacrepemichel.com. Main courses $7-$14 lunch, $10-$27 dinner. AE, DISC, MC, V. Tues-Sun 11:30am-2pm; Tues-Sat 6-9pm.

INEXPENSIVE

Duran Central Pharmacy ★ 👜 NEW MEXICAN   Sounds like an odd place to eat, I know. You could go to one of the touristy New Mexican restaurants in the middle of Old Town and have lots of atmosphere and mediocre food—or you could come here, where locals eat, and feast on better, more authentic fare. It's a few blocks up Central, east of Old Town. On your way through the pharmacy, you may want to stock up on specialty soaps; there's a pretty good variety here. The restaurant itself is plain, with a red-tile floor and small tables, as well as a counter, where you can eavesdrop on the chefs as they speak Spanish. For years, I used to come here for a bowl of green-chile stew and a homemade tortilla, which is still an excellent choice. Now I go for the full meals, such as the blue-corn enchilada plate or the huevos rancheros (eggs over corn tortillas, smothered with chile). The menu is short, but you can count on authentic northern New Mexican food.

1815 Central Ave. NW. ℂ **505/247-4141.** Menu items $6-$10. No credit cards. Mon-Fri 9am-6:20pm; Sat 9am-2pm.

Sadie's ★ ☺ NEW MEXICAN   Many New Mexicans lament the lost days when this restaurant was in a bowling alley. It's true that you can no longer hear the pins fall, and the main dining room is a little too big and the atmosphere a little too bright, but something is still drawing crowds: It's the food, with tasty sauces and large portions. I recommend the enchilada, either chicken or beef. The stuffed *sopaipilla* dinner is also delicious and is one of the signature dishes. All meals come with chips and salsa, beans, and *sopaipillas*. There's a full bar, with excellent margaritas (and TV screens for you sports lovers). A casual atmosphere where kids can be themselves makes this a nice spot for families.

6230 4th St. NW. ℂ **505/345-5339.** Main courses $8-$17. AE, DC, DISC, MC, V. Mon-Sat 11am-10pm; Sun 10am-9pm.

Sophia's Place ★★ 👜 NEW MEXICAN   Don't be daunted by the modest exterior of this bustling little cafe—it has very sophisticated and delectable flavors. Between sun-colored walls and vigas shining with multicolored Christmas lights, diners order at a counter and the food is brought to the table. It's tough to make suggestions because everything is delicious. Breakfast is served all day and includes stellar blue-corn pancakes and excellent huevos rancheros—two eggs on corn tortillas topped with meat or veggie chile and cheese and served with beans and potatoes. At lunch, the tacos with cod are some of the best I've had anywhere: soft corn tortillas with salsa crema, a side salad, beans, and rice. You can also order them with salmon or scallops. For dessert, try the pumpkin brownies. During warm months, diners enjoy sitting at picnic tables on the patio.

6313 4th St. NW ⓒ **505/345-3935.** Main courses $5–$12. AE, DISC, MC, V. Mon–Fri 7am–3pm; Sat–Sun 9am–2pm.

Downtown
EXPENSIVE

Artichoke Cafe ★★ NEW AMERICAN An art gallery as well as a restaurant, this popular spot has modern paintings and sculptures, offering bursts of color set against calm earth tones, a hint at the innovative dining experience offered here. Set in three rooms, this is a nice romantic place. The service is friendly and efficient. At lunch, a number of gourmet sandwiches top the menu along with salads. One of my favorites is the grilled Greek lamb salad, with tomatoes, capers, feta, and grilled eggplant. At dinner, you might start with roasted garlic with Montrachet goat cheese, and then move on to the house-made asparagus and mushroom ravioli in a fresh basil buerre blanc sauce or sea scallops wrapped in prosciutto served with green beans and small potatoes. A carefully selected beer and wine (*Wine Spectator* award-winning) list accompanies the menu. Recently the Artichoke has opened a wine bar on the premises, a fun, cozy spot to sample their wine list.

424 Central Ave. SE. ⓒ **505/243-0200.** www.artichokecafe.com. Reservations recommended. Main courses $9–$15 lunch, $18–$31 dinner. AE, DC, DISC, MC, V. Mon–Fri 11am–2pm; Sun–Mon 5:30–9pm; Tues–Sat 5:30–10pm.

Lucia ★★ NEW AMERICAN At the new Hotel Andaluz, this restaurant serves delectable meals in a warm, contemporary ambience. The place has high ceilings with hanging halogen lamps, lots of good wood, and an exhibition kitchen. Like the hotel, the menu here is inspired by Mediterranean flavors, using local and seasonal ingredients, when possible. At breakfast, you might try the lemon ricotta pancakes with maple syrup and at lunch a club with applewood-smoked bacon, egg, lettuce, tomato, and baby Gouda on sourdough bread. A vegetarian special tops the menu each day. Dinner might start with a beet-and–heirloom tomato salad with sherry-walnut dressing and herbed goat cheese and move on to—my favorite here—roasted butternut-squash ravioli with baby artichokes and a brown-butter sauce. Finish with mango-honey-lavender flan. A thoughtful international wine list accompanies the menu.

welcome TO EDO

Albuquerque's newest hot spot is east of downtown, thus termed EDo, around the area of Central Avenue SE. Renovation of some old buildings, including the brick Albuquerque High School campus into apartments, has brought new life to the area, and some great restaurants have joined the all-time favorite, the Artichoke Cafe. Look for the Grove and Standard Diner in EDo.

At Hotel Andaluz, 125 2nd St. NW, at Copper Ave. ✆ **505/923-9080.** www.hotelandaluz.com. Reservations recommended. Main courses $7–$15 breakfast, $9–$13 lunch, $10–$35 dinner. AE, DISC, MC, V. Mon–Sat 7–10:30am, 11am–2:30pm, and 5:30–10pm; Sun 9am–noon and 5:30–10pm. Free valet parking.

MODERATE

Farina Pizzeria & Wine Bar ★★ ITALIAN   This happening place serves memorable high-heat baked pizza and accompaniments. The contemporary setting has hardwood floors and aged-brick walls, along with retro-shiny tile work. In the evenings the place is so popular there is often a wait. Service is conscientious. You might start with an antipasto platter with artichoke hearts, and move onto a baby spinach salad. But you'll definitely want to save room for the pizza. Baked between 650 and 800 degrees, it has a flaky and crispy crust with a char that lends a smoky and caramelized taste. The toppings use local, seasonal ingredients, when possible. The *carne curate* has pepperoni, prosciutto, and salami, with tomato sauce and mozzarella, while the *formaggio della capra* has goat cheese, leeks, scallions, and pancetta. For dessert try the house-made gelato. An excellent selection of beers and wines accompanies the menu.

510 Central Ave. SE. ✆ **505/243-0130.** www.farinapizzeria.com. Pizzas $9–$14. AE, DISC, MC, V. Sun 5–9pm; Mon 11am–9pm; Tues–Fri 11am–10pm; Sat 4–10pm.

Gold Street Caffè ★★ NEW AMERICAN/CAFE   Opened in 1996, this hip little spot in the popular Gold Avenue district offers finely prepared food in a relaxed urban atmosphere. With its marble tabletops and hardwood floors, this place bustles at all hours. Service is courteous. Nice touches such as toast from Sage Bakehouse and upscale versions of classics greet you at breakfast. Try the Eggs Eleganza—two poached eggs atop toasted green chile brioche with local goat cheese and herbs. Lunch offers salads and sandwiches and some Mexican specialties, including fish tacos with black beans and coconut rice. The dinner menu is brief but good. You might have seafood stew or a grilled marinated chicken breast on spinach with raisins and pine nuts. An imaginative coffee, wine, and beer list accompanies the menu. Finish with a dessert special such as chocolate mousse pie.

218 Gold Ave. SW. ✆ **505/765-1633.** Reservations recommended at dinner. Breakfast $3–$13; lunch $7–$11; dinner $12–$20. AE, DISC, MC, V. Tues–Fri 7am–10pm; Sat 8am–10pm; Sun 8am–2pm; Mon 7am–2pm.

The Grove Café & Market ★★ 🍴 DELI/CAFE   Albuquerque's hippest new dining spot in the EDo district offers fresh breakfasts and lunches utilizing organic and locally grown produce in a fun and open space. Colorful nature paintings hang on sky blue walls, and a patio opens during warm months. Breakfast, served all day, offers creative twists on standards, such as French-style pancakes with fruit and crème fraiche, but the real winner here is the *croque madame*—Black Forest ham, tomato, and Gruyère cheese on rustic farm loaf, topped with a sunny-side-up egg. Lunch offers an array of salads and sandwiches. My favorites are the pressed ones such as the BLT, with applewood smoked bacon and guacamole on whole wheat. With cupcakes "in" these days, this place makes six flavors. My favorite is the strawberry cheesecake with mascarpone frosting. Wash it all down with latte or chai tea. This is also an excellent place to stock a picnic basket and purchase specialty teas and local truffles in the market portion of the restaurant.

600 Central Ave. SE (just west of I-25). ✆ **505/248-9800.** www.thegrovecafemarket.com. All main courses under $11. AE, MC, V. Tues–Sat 7am–4pm; Sun 8am–3pm.

Slate Street Café ★★ NEW AMERICAN   Set in an urban atmosphere with contemporary furnishings and red *bancos* along the walls, this restaurant serves what the owner calls "contemporary comfort food," meaning new variations on diner-style offerings. Though the ambience is a little sharp-edged for my taste, young people and business people enjoy its hardwood floors and moody lighting. The older set may find it too noisy for conversation. Owner Myra Ghattas, daughter of the Duran Central Pharmacy clan, spent years working for Hyatt away from home and returned to open this place. For breakfast she serves such fun food as a green eggs–and-ham omelet, which really has normal eggs with green chile mixed in. A favorite for lunch and dinner is the meatloaf wrapped in prosciutto with porcini gravy and "smashed potatoes." Not a diner-food fan? Try the grilled sesame ahi tuna, seared to perfection. Upstairs, the Wine Loft offers a fun and "very approachable" wine list and a bar menu that echoes that of the restaurant.

515 Slate St. NW (1 block north of Lomas btw. 5th and 6th sts.). ⓒ **505/243-2210.** www.slatestreetcafe. com. Reservations recommended. Main courses $5–$12 breakfast, $6–$15 lunch, $9–$26 dinner. AE, DISC, MC, V. Mon–Fri 7:30am–3pm; Tues–Thurs 5–9pm; Fri–Sat 5–10pm. Wine Loft Tues–Sat 4–10pm.

Standard Diner ★★ ☺ NEW AMERICAN   Set in a restored 1938 Texaco station, this restaurant serves fun takes on diner-style fare in a cheery Art Deco ambience. In 2009, the Standard was featured on the Food Network's *Diners, Drive-ins and Dives*. Comfy booths lining the walls and chrome-edged tables set the scene in two dining rooms, while a bar at the kitchen dresses the third. A casual patio opens during the warm months. All their bread is house made, including the biscuit under their eggs Benedict, one of my favorite dishes, served all day. Lunch and dinner offer a variety of salads, the most popular a Caesar with tempura-battered lobster. Burgers in many varieties are also a hit here, as is the mac and cheese, with bacon and herbed breadcrumbs. All desserts are house made, including their sorbet and ice cream. Such treats as banana cream pie and cherry strudel are favorites. Friendly and efficient service and a good beer and wine list enhance the experience. Kids will like the relaxed atmosphere, burgers, and mac and cheese.

320 Central Ave. SE. ⓒ **505/243-1440.** www.standarddiner.com. Reservations recommended on Fri–Sat night. Main courses $7–$11 brunch, $7–$17 lunch and dinner. AE, DISC, MC, V. Mon–Thurs 11am–9:30pm; Fri–Sat 11am–10:30pm; Sun 9am–9pm.

INEXPENSIVE

Mary & Tito's Café ★★ 🍴 NEW MEXICAN   In a modest setting with arched windows, a tile floor, and turquoise booths, this cafe has been serving some of the region's best New Mexican food for 48 years. It's so good that it received the James Beard Foundation's American Classic Restaurant award in 2010, a real surprise for the humble owner, Mary Gonzales, who, along with many family members, runs the cafe. The focus here is on the chile, made fresh and extremely flavorful. Their signature dish, *carne adovada* (pork simmered in red chile) is cooked for 5 hours and served with beans, rice, and a tortilla. On a recent visit, I enjoyed the blue-corn chicken enchiladas with red and green chile, served with beans, rice, and tortillas. Stuffed *sopaipillas* are also a big hit here, as is the combination plate, with beef tacos, a *relleno*, and cheese enchiladas. What's most unique about any of these dishes is that they are absolutely smothered with the best chile you've ever eaten, with only a minimum of extras such as cheese and sour cream to dilute the flavor. For dessert, the Mexican wedding cake is moist and delectable.

FAMILY-FRIENDLY RESTAURANTS

Flying Star Cafe (p. 260) With a huge selection, a relaxed atmosphere, and a number of locations, the whole family can enjoy this place.

Range Café (p. 262) The fun and funky decor and Taos Cow Ice Cream make this a good spot for kids.

Standard Diner (p. 257) Set in a renovated 1938 Texaco station, this upscale diner serves mac and cheese

and other Route 66 favorites for the young-at-heart.

Sadie's (p. 254) Kids like the quesadillas, tacos, and *sopaipillas* drizzled with honey; parents like the casual atmosphere where kid noise isn't scorned.

66 Diner (p. 260) A full range of burgers and treats such as root beer floats and hot fudge sundaes will make any youngster happy.

2711 4th St. NW. Ⓒ︎ **505/344-6266.** Main courses $5.50–$8.50. MC, V. Mon–Thurs 9am–6pm; Fri–Sat 9am–8pm.

Northeast Heights
EXPENSIVE

Bien Shur ★★★ NEW AMERICAN/STEAK/SEAFOOD   Set on the top floor of the Sandia Resort & Casino, this fine dining restaurant offers impressive views and delicious food, with a hint of Native America. With big windows facing east and west, you can see the mountains and the city while eating—this, accented by high ceilings and elegant Native American motif decor. Plan your meal at sunset for the most stunning effect. Service is excellent. You might start with escargot bourguignon and/or a marinated heirloom tomato salad with aged balsamic vinegar and fresh basil. For entrees, the grilled half rack of lamb is excellent, as is the chargrilled buffalo tenderloin, both served with a choice of sauces including roasted garlic, horseradish, or green-peppercorn demi-glace. Some good fish dishes dress the menu as well. My favorite dessert here is a Southwestern take on pecan pie—made with *piñon* nuts! The wine list is eclectic, with old- and new-world flavors—quite price approachable. The lounge and patio bar carry the same elegance and views and offer a grill and taco bar menu.

30 Rainbow Rd. NE, at Sandia Resort & Casino. Ⓒ︎ **800/526-9366.** www.sandiaresort.com. Reservations recommended. Main courses $24–$70. AE, DC, DISC, MC, V. Tues–Thurs 5–10pm; Fri–Sat 5–11pm.

Jennifer James 101 ★★★ 🍴 NEW AMERICAN   This restaurant's namesake may be Albuquerque's most notable chef. Unfortunately, she doesn't seem to have much longevity with her eateries. I hope this one will last. It's a comfortable place to spend an evening relishing delightful flavors. The setting is contemporary, with hardwood floors, drum-shaped light fixtures, and an exhibition kitchen in back. The food, too, hearkens back to elemental flavors, which is why she named the restaurant "101." But, really, nothing about this place is simple. James uses local, seasonal ingredients in completely imaginative ways, and the service is knowledgeable and efficient. The short menu features appetizers such as an arugula salad with dried apricots and hazelnut vinaigrette. For an entree, I've enjoyed almond-crusted halibut over basmati rice with a light curry sauce and French-style carrots. A dessert of hot milk cake with strawberries and cream is the best version of the traditional straw-berry shortcake I've had. A select wine and beer list accompanies the menu.

4615-A Menaul Blvd. NE. (C) **505/884-3860.** www.jenniferjames101.com. Reservations highly recom-mended. Main courses $16–$25. AE, DISC, MC, V. Tues–Sat 5–10pm.

University & Nob Hill

EXPENSIVE

Zinc Wine Bar and Bistro ★★ NEW AMERICAN   In a moody, urban atmo-sphere with wood floors and a high ceiling, this Nob Hill in-place serves imaginative food, using meticulously prepared seasonal ingredients. The bi-level dining room with well-spaced tables can get crowded and noisy at peak hours (especially under the balcony, so avoid sitting there then). Service is congenial but inconsistent. The lunch menu offers a variety of salads and sandwiches, as well as inventive dishes. One of my favorites is the mango-glazed chicken breast stir-fry. At dinner, the wild Alaskan halibut is tasty, as is the vegetarian crostada (also served at lunch), which is a baked pastry filled with vegetables and cheese. Sunday brunch is also offered, with items such as green-chile eggs benedict. An extensive wine list accompanies the menu, or you may simply opt for a martini from the full bar. In the lower level, a lounge serves less for-mally in a wine cellar atmosphere with live music playing 2 to 3 nights a week.

3009 Central Ave. NE. (C) **505/254-9462.** www.zincabq.com. Reservations recommended. Main courses $8–$14 lunch, $17–$27 dinner. AE, DC, DISC, MC, V. Tues–Fri and Sun 11am–2:30pm; Mon–Thurs 5–10pm; Fri–Sun 5–11pm. Wine bar Mon–Sat 5pm–1am, with food served till midnight.

MODERATE

Scalo ★★ ITALIAN/STEAK/SEAFOOD   This Nob Hill restaurant is a local favor-ite, so it's usually crowded, a good sign of the food's quality. The place has a simple, bistro-style elegance, with white-linen-clothed tables indoors, plus outdoor tables in a covered, temperature-controlled patio. Service is decent. The kitchen, which makes its own pasta and breads, offers an international menu with excellent selections for lunch and dinner. Seasonal menus focus on New Mexico–grown produce. At lunch you can select from salads, wood-fired pizzas, and panini. Their *panini con salsiccia* has sausage, caramelized onions, and mozzarella. The varied dinner menu offers soups, salads, pizza, pasta, and meat and fish entrees. The *bianchi e neri al capesante* has black and white linguine, shrimp, salmon, and peas in a cream sauce. Dessert specials change daily. The wine list won a *Wine Spectator* award; you can sample 30 wines by the glass, or you may order from the full bar.

3500 Central Ave. SE. (C) **505/255-8781.** www.scalonobhill.com. Reservations recommended. Main courses $6–$10 lunch, $8–$29 dinner. AE, DC, DISC, MC, V. Daily 11am–2:30pm; Fri–Sat 5–11pm; Sun 5–9pm. Limited bar menu daily 2:30–5pm.

Yanni's Mediterranean Grill and Opa Bar ★★ GREEK   With bright blue and white decor, Athenian-style pillars, and Mediterranean paintings on the walls, this is a great place for a festive meal. Locals crowd the cafe and patio with big windows look-ing out on Central Avenue. Service is friendly, though overworked during peak hours. All food is made fresh, with specials daily. You might start with jumbo sea scallops seared and served with grilled tomato, and then move on to one of the excellent spe-cials such as wild opah (a white fish) roasted with oranges, or, my favorite, oven-roasted lamb. The menu hosts a variety of pasta dishes and, of course, moussaka.

Entrees come with a salad, bread, vegetable, and a potato or rice side. The Greek potatoes seasoned with olive oil, garlic, and oregano are yummy. For dessert, try the tiramisu or baklava sundae. An international wine list featuring Greek offerings and a full bar accompany the menu. And the attached Opa! Bar provides live entertainment on weekends.

3109 Central Ave. NE. ℂ **505/268-9250.** www.yannisandopabar.com. Reservations recommended. Main courses $7–$14 lunch, $13–$27 dinner. AE, DISC, MC, V. Mon–Thurs 11am–10pm; Fri–Sat 11am–11pm; Sun noon–9pm.

INEXPENSIVE

Flying Star Cafe ★ ☺ AMERICAN/CAFE/BAKERY The Flying Star Cafe makes good on its promise of uptown food with down-home ingredients. It's a fun and friendly place with excellent contemporary international food. But beware: During mealtime, the university location on Central Avenue gets packed and rowdy. The selections range broadly, all made with local and organic produce, when possible. You can choose from 16 different breakfast options to homemade soups and salads to sandwiches and pasta (and pizza at the Juan Tabo and Rio Grande locations). Try the Rancher's Melt (New Zealand sirloin sautéed with green chile, provolone, and horseradish on sourdough) or the Buddha's Bowl (sautéed vegetables in ginger sauce with tofu over jasmine rice). Flying Star also has locations at 4501 Juan Tabo Blvd. NE (ℂ **505/275-8311**), 8001 Menaul Blvd. NE (ℂ **505/293-6911**), and 4026 Rio Grande Blvd. NW (ℂ **505/344-6714**). They don't serve alcohol, but they do brew up plenty of espresso and cappuccino. Kids enjoy the relaxed atmosphere and their own selections from the menu. Though hours vary for each location, they are all open daily for breakfast, lunch, and dinner.

3416 Central Ave. SE. ℂ **505/255-6633.** www.flyingstarcafe.com. All menu items under $15. AE, DISC, MC, V. Daily 6am–11:30pm.

66 Diner ☺ AMERICAN Like a trip back in time to the days when Martin Milner and George Maharis got "their kicks on Route 66," this thoroughly 1950s-style diner comes complete with Seeburg jukebox and full-service soda fountain. The white caps make great green-chile cheeseburgers, along with meatloaf sandwiches, grilled liver and onions, and chicken-fried steaks. Ham-and-egg and pancake breakfasts are served on weekends. Beer and wine are available. Comfy booths and their own menu will please the kids.

1405 Central Ave. NE. ℂ **505/247-1421.** www.66diner.com. Menu items $4–$10. AE, DC, DISC, MC, V. Mon–Fri 11am–11pm; Sat 8am–11pm; Sun 8am–10pm.

Outside Albuquerque

EXPENSIVE

Corn Maiden ★★ NEW AMERICAN/STEAK/SEAFOOD Plan a sunset dinner at this restaurant at the Hyatt Tamaya, north of town. You'll feast not only on delicious innovative cuisine, but also on one of the best views in New Mexico. Set in the Rio Grande valley, with banks of windows looking out on the Sandia Mountains, this restaurant has a comfortably subdued decor wrapped around an open kitchen. The menu changes seasonally, and the offerings will likely please conventional as well as adventurous palates. Served with your bread is a tasty Southwestern tapenade made with nopales cactus. For an appetizer, you might try the smoked duck–and-endive salad. For an entree, the big favorite is the rotisserie—an interesting

route 66 REVISITED: REDISCOVERING NEW MEXICO'S STRETCH OF THE MOTHER ROAD

As the old Bobby Troupe hit suggests: Get your kicks on Route 66. The highway that once stretched from Chicago to California was hailed as the road to freedom. During the Great Depression, it was the way west for farmers escaping Dust Bowl poverty out on the plains. If you found yourself in a rut in the late 1940s and 1950s, all you had to do was hop in the car and head west on Route 66.

Of course, the road existed long before it gained such widespread fascination. Built in the late 1920s and paved in 1937, it was the lifeblood of communities in eight states. Nowadays, however, US 66 is as elusive as the fantasies that once carried hundreds of thousands west in search of a better life. Replaced by other roads, covered up by interstates (mostly I-40), and just plain out of use, Route 66 still exists in New Mexico, but you'll have to do a little searching and take some extra time to find it.

Motorists driving west from Texas can take a spin (make that a slow spin) on a 20-mile gravel stretch of the original highway running from Glenrio (Texas) to San Jon. From San Jon to Tucumcari, you can enjoy nearly 24 continuous paved miles of vintage 66. In Tucumcari,

the historic route slices through the center of town along what is now Tucumcari Boulevard. Santa Rosa's main street, Historic Route 66, is that city's 4-mile claim to the Mother Road. In Albuquerque, US 66 follows Central Avenue for 18 miles, from the 1936 Expo New Mexico fairgrounds, past original 1930s motels and the historic Nob Hill district, on west through downtown.

One of the best spots to pretend you're a 1950s road warrior crossing the desert—whizzing past rattlesnakes, tepees, and tumbleweeds—is along NM 124, which winds 25 miles from Mesita to Acoma in northwestern New Mexico. You can next pick up old Route 66 in Grants, along the 6-mile Santa Fe Avenue. In Gallup, a 9-mile segment of US 66 is lined with restaurants and hotels reminiscent of the city's days as a Western film capital from 1929 to 1964. Just outside Gallup, the historic route continues west to the Arizona border as NM 118.

For more information about Route 66, contact the **Grants/Cíbola County Chamber of Commerce** (© **505/287-4802; www.grants.org**) or the **New Mexico Department of Tourism** (© **505/827-7400; www.newmexico.org**).

---

combination of meats and seafood. You'll also find an excellent Colorado rack of lamb crusted with pistachios and Dijon. Dessert brings a dazzling display of confections as lively to look at as to taste. Wine lovers have their pick of a broad range of labels.

In the Hyatt Regency Tamaya Resort and Spa, 1300 Tuyana Trail, Santa Ana Pueblo. © **505/771-6037.** www.tamaya.hyatt.com. Reservations recommended. Main courses $30–$49. AE, DC, DISC, MC, V. Tues–Thurs 5:30–9pm; Fri–Sat 5:30–10pm. From I-25 take exit 242, following US 550 west to Tamaya Blvd.; drive 1½ miles to the resort.

Prairie Star ★★ NEW AMERICAN   On the Santa Ana Pueblo, about 20 minutes north of Albuquerque, and set in a sprawling adobe home with a marvelous view across the high plains and the Santa Ana Golf Course, this restaurant offers an interesting blend of old and new, both in terms of atmosphere and flavor. It was built in the 1940s in Mission architectural style. Exposed vigas and full *latilla* ceilings, as well as hand-carved fireplaces and *bancos,* complement the thick adobe walls. Recently a wine bar has been added. Diners can start with oven-roasted crab cakes with roasted pepper ketchup and fennel relish. For an entrée, a good choice is the grilled bison strip loin with mashed potatoes and sautéed vegetables. A recent *Albuquerque Journal* review named it one of the best steakhouse "meat and potatoes" plates in the area. An extensive wine list (*Wine Spectator* award–winning) with more than 30 flavors by the glass tops out the menu, as do special desserts, which vary nightly.

288 Prairie Star Rd., Santa Ana Pueblo. ⓒ 505/867-3327. www.santaanagolf.com. Reservations recommended. Main courses $19–$35. AE, DC, DISC, MC, V. Tues–Sun 5:30–9pm.

MODERATE

Range Café ★ ☺ NEW MEXICAN/AMERICAN   This cafe on the main drag of Bernalillo, about 20 minutes north of Albuquerque, is a perfect place to stop on your way to or from town. Housed in what was once an old drugstore, the restaurant has a pressed-tin ceiling and is decorated with western touches, such as cowboy boots and whimsical art. The food ranges from enchiladas and burritos to chicken-fried steak to more elegantly prepared meals. For breakfast, try the pancakes or the breakfast burrito. For lunch or dinner, I recommend Tom's meatloaf, served with roasted-garlic mashed potatoes, mushroom gravy, and sautéed vegetables. For dinner, you might try pan-seared scallops with roasted poblano corn salsa, green beans and *arroz verde.* Taos Cow ice cream is the order for dessert, or try the baked goods and specialty drinks from the full bar. In the same locale, the Range has opened the Lizard Rodeo Lounge, a hoppin' place with Wild West decor that offers live music many nights a week. There's also a retail space that sells local art and New Mexico wines. Two other branches of the restaurant in Albuquerque have similar food offerings (4200 Wyoming Blvd. NE, ⓒ **505/293-2633;** and 2200 Menaul Blvd. NE, ⓒ **505/888-1660**).

925 Camino del Pueblo (P.O. Box 1780), Bernalillo. ⓒ **505/867-1700.** www.rangecafe.com. Breakfast and lunch $7–$18; dinner $10–$19. AE, DISC, MC, V. Summer daily 7:30am–9:30pm (Fri–Sat till 10pm); winter daily 7:30am–9pm (Fri–Sat till 9:30pm). Closed Thanksgiving, Christmas.

WHAT TO SEE & DO

Albuquerque's original town site, known today as Old Town, is the central point of interest for visitors. Here, grouped around the plaza, are the venerable Church of San Felipe de Neri and numerous restaurants, art galleries, and crafts shops. Several important museums are close by. Within a few blocks are the 25,000-square-foot Albuquerque Aquarium and the 50-acre Rio Grande Botanic Garden (near Central Ave. and Tingley Dr. NW), both well worth a visit.

But don't get stuck in Old Town. Elsewhere, you'll find the Sandia Peak Tramway, the new Balloon Museum, and a number of natural attractions. Within day-trip range are several pueblos and significant monuments (see "Exploring Nearby Pueblos & Monuments," later in this chapter).

The Top Attractions

Albuquerque Museum of Art and History ★ ☺   Take an interesting journey into New Mexico's present and past in this museum on the outskirts of Old Town. Most notable for me here are works from the museum's art collection, which

Central Albuquerque Attractions

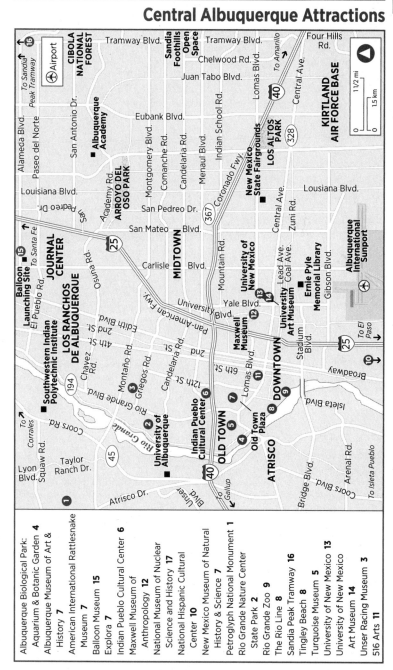

Albuquerque Biological Park:
Aquarium & Botanic Garden **4**

Albuquerque Museum of Art &
History **7**

American International Rattlesnake
Museum **7**

Balloon Museum **15**

Explora **7**

Indian Pueblo Cultural Center **6**

Maxwell Museum of
Anthropology **12**

National Museum of Nuclear
Science and History **17**

National Hispanic Cultural
Center **10**

New Mexico Museum of Natural
History & Science **7**

Petroglyph National Monument **1**

Rio Grande Nature Center
State Park **2**

Rio Grande Zoo **9**

The Rio Line **8**

Sandia Peak Tramway **16**

Tingley Beach **8**

Turquoise Museum **5**

University of New Mexico **13**

University of New Mexico
Art Museum **14**

Unser Racing Museum **3**

516 Arts **11**

includes large canvases by Fritz Scholder, Peter Hurd, Ernest Blumenshein, and Georgia O'Keeffe, as well as contemporary woodwork by Luis Tapia. Downstairs you'll take a trip through history, represented by an impressive collection of Spanish colonial artifacts. Displays here include Don Quixote–style helmets, swords, and horse armor, a 19th-century house compound and chapel, and gear used by *vaqueros*, the original cowboys who came to the area in the 16th century. In an old-style theater, two films on Albuquerque history are shown. An Old Town walking tour originates here at 11am Tuesday to Sunday during spring, summer, and fall. A gift shop sells books and jewelry, and a cafe serves upscale sandwiches and soups. Plan to spend 1 to 2 hours here

2000 Mountain Rd. NW. ⓒ **505/243-7255.** www.cabq.gov/museum. Admission $4 adults, $2 seniors 65 and older, $1 children 4-12. Tues–Sun 9am–5pm. Closed major holidays.

Balloon Museum ★★ ☺   The Anderson-Abruzzo Albuquerque International Balloon Museum holds special significance for me, as my parents owned part of the first hot-air balloon in Albuquerque over 30 years ago. Today, with the Albuquerque International Balloon Fiesta drawing hundreds of brilliantly colored and imaginatively shaped balloons to the city each October (p. 35), this museum's time has come. It tells the history of ballooning, from the first flight in France in 1783, with a rooster, sheep, and duck as passengers, to the use of balloons in military, science, and aerospace research. Most poignant are displays of Albuquerque balloonists Maxie Anderson and Ben Abruzzo, who, with Larry Newman, completed the first manned crossing of the Atlantic Ocean in 1978. Originals and replicas of various historic crafts dot the three-story-tall space, and windows look out at the Sandia Mountains and Rio Grande Valley. Kids will enjoy the flight simulator, which tests their ability to fly and land a balloon on target. Plan on spending at least an hour here.

9201 Balloon Museum Dr. NE. ⓒ **505/768-6020.** www.cabq.gov/balloon.com. Admission $4 adults, $2 seniors 65 and older, $1 children 4-12, free for children 3 and under. Tues–Sun 9am–5pm. Closed New Year's Day, Thanksgiving, Christmas, city holidays.

Indian Pueblo Cultural Center ★ ☺   Owned and operated as a nonprofit organization by the 19 pueblos of New Mexico, this is a fine place to begin an exploration of Native American culture. About a mile northeast of Old Town, this museum—modeled after Pueblo Bonito, a spectacular 9th-century ruin in Chaco Culture National Historic Park—consists of several parts.

You'll want to spend 1 to 2 hours here. Begin above ground, where you'll find changing shows of contemporary Puebloan arts and crafts. Next, head to the basement, where a permanent exhibit depicts the evolution of the various pueblos, from prehistory to present, and includes displays of the distinctive handicrafts of each community. Note especially how pottery differs in concept and design from pueblo to pueblo. In the main building is an enormous (10,000-sq.-ft.) **gift shop** featuring fine pottery, rugs, sand paintings, *katsinas*, drums, and jewelry, among other things. Southwestern clothing and souvenirs are also available. Prices here are quite reasonable.

Throughout the year, Native American dancers perform in an outdoor arena surrounded by original murals. Dances are performed Saturday and Sunday at noon in winter, and Saturday and Sunday at 11am and 2pm in spring. In summer, dances are scheduled at 2pm on Thursday and Friday, and 11am and 2pm Saturday. Often, artisans demonstrate their crafts as well. During certain weeks of the year, such as the Balloon Fiesta, dances are performed daily.

The restaurant serves traditional Native American foods. It's a good place for some Indian fry bread and a bowl of *posole.*

2401 12th St. NW. ☏ **866/855-7902** or 505/843-7270. www.indianpueblo.org. Admission $6 adults, $5.50 seniors, $3 students, free for children 4 and under. AE, DISC, MC, V. Daily 9am–5pm; restaurant Mon-Thurs 8am–8:30pm, Fri–Sat 8am–9pm, Sun 8am–4pm. Closed New Year's Day, July 4, Labor Day, Thanksgiving, Christmas.

National Hispanic Cultural Center ★ In the historic Barelas neighborhood on the Camino Real, this gem of Albuquerque museums offers a rich cultural journey through hundreds of years of history and across the globe. It explores Hispanic arts and lifestyles with visual arts, drama, music, dance, and other programs. I most enjoy the 11,000-square-foot gallery space, which exhibits exciting contemporary and traditional works, as well as changing exhibits. A restaurant offers New Mexican and American food for breakfast and lunch. It's a good spot to sample authentic regional dishes such as tacos, enchiladas, and the rich custard dessert called flan. The shop offers a broad range of fun gifts from Latin America and New Mexico. Plan to spend 1 to 2 hours here, or watch for events and come in conjunction with them.

1701 4th St. SW (corner of 4th St. and Av. Cesar Chavez). ☏ **505/246-2261.** Fax 505/246-2613. www.nhccnm.org. Admission Tues–Sat $3 adults, $2 seniors 60 and over, free for children 16 and under; Sun free for all ages. AE, DISC, MC, V. Tues–Sun 10am–5pm. Restaurant Tues–Fri 9am–3pm; Sat 8am–3pm; Sun 9am–3pm. Closed New Year's Day, Memorial Day, Labor Day, Christmas.

Old Town ★★ A maze of cobbled courtyard walkways leads to hidden patios and gardens, where many of Old Town's 150 galleries and shops are located. Adobe buildings, many refurbished in the pueblo revival style of the 1950s, are grouped around the tree-shaded plaza, created in 1780. Pueblo and Navajo artisans often display their pottery, blankets, and silver jewelry on the sidewalks lining the plaza.

The buildings of Old Town once served as mercantile shops, grocery stores, and government offices, but the importance of Old Town as Albuquerque's commercial center declined after 1880, when the railroad came through 1¼ miles east of the plaza and businesses relocated to be closer to the trains. Old Town clung to its historical and sentimental roots, but the quarter fell into disrepair until the 1930s and 1940s, when artisans and other shop owners rediscovered it and the tourism industry burgeoned.

When Albuquerque was established in 1706, the first building erected by the settlers was the **Church of San Felipe de Neri,** which faces the plaza on its north side. It's a cozy church with wonderful stained-glass windows and vivid *retablos* (religious paintings). This house of worship has been in almost continuous use for nearly 300 years.

Though you'll wade through a few trinket and T-shirt shops on the plaza, don't be fooled: Old Town is an excellent place to shop. Look for good buys from the Native Americans selling jewelry on the plaza, especially silver bracelets and strung turquoise. If you want to take something fun home and spend very little, buy a dyed corn necklace. Your best bet when wandering around Old Town is to peek into shops, but there are a few places in which you'll definitely want to spend time. See "Shopping," later in this chapter, for a list of recommendations. An excellent Old Town historic walking tour originates at the Albuquerque Museum of Art and History (see above) at 11am Tuesday to Sunday during spring, summer, and fall.

Plan to spend 2 to 3 hours strolling around.

DOWNTOWN ARTS HUB

Set in a bright and airy exhibition space, **516 Arts ★**, 516 Central Ave. SW (ⓒ **505/242-1445;** www.516arts. org), presents museum-style art exhibitions, poetry events, live performances, gallery talks, and educational programs. The art is high quality, eclectic, and often a bit bizarre for my tastes, but hey, I'm just a Santa Fe girl. Past events included the national exhibit *Trappings: Stories of Women, Power and Clothing* and poetry readings by Jimmy Santiago Baca and Erika Sanchez. It's open Tuesday to Saturday noon to 5pm.

Northeast of Central Ave. and Rio Grande Blvd. NW. Old Town Visitor Center: 303 Romero St. NW, Albuquerque, NM 87104 (across the street from the Church of San Felipe de Neri). ⓒ **505/243-3215.** Visitor Center daily 10am–6pm summer; daily 10am–4:30pm rest of the year.

Sandia Peak Tramway ★★ ☺   This fun and exciting half-day or evening outing allows incredible views of the Albuquerque landscape and wildlife. The Sandia Peak Tram is a "jigback"; in other words, as one car approaches the top, the other nears the bottom. The two pass halfway through the trip, in the midst of a 1½-mile "clear span" of unsupported cable between the second tower and the upper terminal.

Several hiking trails are available on Sandia Peak, and one of them—La Luz Trail—takes you on a steep and rigorous trek from the base to the summit. The views in all directions are extraordinary. ***Note:*** The trails on Sandia may not be suitable for children. If you'd like to enjoy a meal during your trip, you can eat lunch (salads, burgers, and pasta dishes) or dinner (steaks, seafood, and pasta) at the **High Finance Restaurant and Tavern** at the top of the tram. Special tram rates apply with dinner reservations. Be aware that the tram does not operate on very windy days.

10 Tramway Loop NE. ⓒ **505/856-7325.** Fax 505/856-6335. www.sandiapeak.com. Admission $18 adults, $15 seniors and ages 13–20, $10 children 5–12, free for children 5 and under. Memorial Day to Labor Day daily 9am–9pm; ski season, spring, and fall Wed–Mon 9am–8pm, Tues 5–8pm. Closed 2 weeks each spring and fall for maintenance; check the website for details. Parking $1 daily. AE, DISC, MC, V. To reach the base of the tram, take I-25 north to Tramway Rd. (exit 234), then proceed east about 5 miles on Tramway Rd. (NM 556); or take I-40 to Tramway Blvd., exit 167 (NM 556), and head north 8½ miles.

Other Attractions

National Museum of Nuclear Science & History ★ ☺   Set in a new 30,000-square-foot building with 12 acres of exterior space, this museum offers the next-best introduction to the nuclear age after the Bradbury Science Museum in Los Alamos, making for an interesting 1- to 2-hour perusal. It traces the history of nuclear-weapons development, beginning with the top-secret Manhattan Project of the 1940s, and continues with explanations of nuclear use in power, medicine, and energy. The displays utilize interactive and touch-screen devices—one even calculates your exposure to radiation. There's also a kid's area that explores the science of Albert Einstein. You'll find full-scale casings of the "Fat Man" and "Little Boy" bombs, as well as a running roster of films exploring the atomic age.

601 Eubank SE (at Southern). ⓒ **505/245-2137.** Fax 505/242-4537. www.atomicmuseum.com. Admission $8 adults, $7 seniors, $7 children 6–17, free for children 5 and under. Children 11 and under

not admitted without adult. Group rates available. Daily 9am–5pm. Closed New Year's Day, Easter, Thanksgiving, Christmas.

Petroglyph National Monument ★★ ☺ These lava flows were once a hunting and gathering area for prehistoric Native Americans, who left a chronicle of their beliefs etched on the dark basalt boulders. Some 25,000 petroglyphs provide a nice outdoor adventure after a morning in a museum. You'll want to stop at the visitor center to get a map and check out the interactive computer. From there, you can drive north to the Boca Negra area, where you'll have a choice of three trails. Take the Mesa Point Trail (30 min.) that climbs quickly up the side of a hill, offering many petroglyph sightings as well as an outstanding view of the Sandia Mountains. If you're traveling with your dog, you can bring her along on the Rinconada Trail. Hikers can have fun searching the rocks for more petroglyphs; there are many yet to be found. This trail (a few miles south of the visitor center) runs for miles around a huge *rincon* (corner) at the base of the lava flow. Camping is not permitted in the park; it's strictly for day use, with picnic areas, drinking water, and restrooms provided.

6001 Unser Blvd. NW (3 miles north of I-40 at Unser and Western Trail). ℂ **505/899-0205.** Fax 505/899-0207. www.nps.gov/petr. Admission $1 per vehicle Mon–Fri, $2 Sat–Sun. DISC, MC, V. Visitor Center and Boca Negra area daily 8am–5pm. Closed New Year's Day, Thanksgiving, Christmas.

Turquoise Museum ☺ Don't be put off by the setting of this little gem of a museum in a strip mall west of Old Town. For those with curiosity, it's a real find that's been featured in *Smithsonian Magazine* and on *60 Minutes.* The passion of father and son Joe P. Lowry and Joe Dan Lowry, it contains "the world's largest collection of turquoise"—from 60 mines around the world. You start through a tunnel, where turquoise is embedded in the walls much like a mine, and move on to exhibits that present the blue stone's geology, history, and mythology. You'll see maps showing where turquoise is mined, ranging from Egypt to Kingman, Arizona, and find out how to determine whether the turquoise you're hoping to buy is quality or not. There's also a real lapidary shop; jewelry made there is sold in a gift shop that's open until 5pm. Plan to spend about a half-hour here.

2107 Central Ave. NW. ℂ **505/247-8650.** www.turquoisemuseum.com. Admission $4 adults, $3 children 7–12 and seniors 60 and over, free for children 6 and under, $10 family rate. AE, DISC, MC, V. Mon–Fri 9:30am–5pm; Sat 9:30am–4pm.

University of New Mexico The state's largest institution of higher learning stretches across an attractive 70-acre campus about 2 miles east of downtown Albuquerque, north of Central Avenue and east of University Boulevard. The five campus museums, none of which charges admission, are constructed (like other UNM buildings) in a modified pueblo style. Popejoy Hall, in the southcentral part of the campus, hosts many performing-arts presentations, including those of the New Mexico Symphony Orchestra; other public events are held in nearby Keller Hall and Woodward Hall.

I've found the best way to see the museums and campus is on a walking tour, which can make for a nice 2- to 3-hour morning or afternoon outing. Begin on the west side of campus at the Maxwell Museum of Anthropology. You'll find parking meters there, as well as Maxwell Museum parking, for which you can get a permit inside.

The **Maxwell Museum of Anthropology,** situated on the west side of the campus on Redondo Drive, south of Las Lomas Road (ℂ **505/277-4405;** www.unm.edu/maxwell), is an internationally acclaimed repository of Southwestern anthropological

TAKING HOME A southwest KITCHEN

If you've fallen in love with New Mexican and Southwestern cooking during your stay (or if you did even before you arrived), you might like to sign up for cooking classes with Jane Butel, a leading Southwest cooking authority, author of 19 cookbooks, and host of the national TV show *Jane Butel's Southwestern Kitchen.* At **Jane Butel Cooking School ★**, 2655 Pan American NE, Ste. F (**©** **800/473-8226** or 505/243-2622; www.janebutelcooking.com), you'll learn

the history and techniques of Southwestern cuisine and have ample opportunity for hands-on preparation. If you choose the weeklong session, you'll start by learning about chiles and move on to native breads and dishes, appetizers, beverages, and desserts. Weekend sessions and special vegetarian sessions are also available, as are some sessions that include "culinary tours." Call or visit Jane's website for current schedules and fees.

finds. What's really intriguing here is not just the ancient pottery, tools, and yucca weavings, but the anthropological context within which these items are set. You'll see a reconstruction of an archaeological site, complete with string markers, brushes, and field notes, as well as microscope lenses you can examine to see how archaeologists perform temper analysis to find out where pots were made, and pollen analysis to help reconstruct past environments. There are two permanent exhibits: *Ancestors,* which looks at human evolution, and *People of the Southwest,* a look at the history of the Southwest from 10,000 years ago to the 16th century from an archaeological perspective. It's open Tuesday to Saturday 10am to 4pm; the museum is closed Sundays, Mondays, and holidays. From the Maxwell, walk east into the campus until you come to the Duck Pond and pass Mitchell Hall; then turn south (right) and walk down a lane until you reach Northrup Hall.

In **Northrup Hall** (**©** **505/277-4204**), about halfway between the Maxwell Museum and Popejoy Hall in the southern part of the campus, the adjacent **Geology Museum** (**©** **505/277-4204**) and **Meteorite Museum** (**©** **505/277-1644**) cover the gamut of recorded time from dinosaur bones to moon rocks. Within the Geology Museum, you'll see stones that create spectacular works of art, from black-on-white orbicular granite to brilliant blue dioptase. In the Meteorite Museum, 550 meteorite specimens comprise the sixth-largest collection in the United States. You'll see and touch a sink-size piece of a meteorite that weighs as much as a car, as well as samples of the many variations of stones that fall from the sky. Both museums are open Monday to Friday 9am to 4pm.

From here, you walk east, straight through a mall that takes you by the art building to the Fine Arts Center. The **University of New Mexico Art Museum** (**©** **505/277-4001;** http://unmartmuseum.unm.edu) is located here, just north of Central Avenue and Cornell Street. The museum features changing exhibitions of 19th- and 20th-century art. Its permanent collection includes old masters paintings and sculpture, significant New Mexico artists, Spanish-colonial artwork, the Tamarind Lithography Archives, and one of the largest university-owned photography collections in the country. This is my favorite part. You'll see modern and contemporary works, and some striking images that you'll remember for years. It's open Tuesday to Friday 10am to 4pm, and Sat and Sun 1 to 4pm; the museum is closed holidays. A gift shop offers a variety of gifts and posters. Admission is free, with a suggested donation of $5.

By now you'll probably want a break. Across the mall to the north is the Student Union Building, where you can get treats ranging from muffins to pizza. Campus maps can be obtained here, along with directions. Touring these museums takes a full morning or afternoon.

1 University Hill NE (north of Central Ave.). © **505/277-0111.** www.unm.edu.

Unser Racing Museum　This museum honors the Unser family, pioneers of auto racing. Four generations of the Albuquerque family have won the pinnacle event, the Indianapolis 500, nine times. Designed in the shape of a racing wheel, the museum is organized into a number of spokes that present the Unser history, along with looks at many aspects of racing, including classic cars that ran in the Pike's Peak Race. Interactive exhibits provide a personal history told through the voices of the giants of auto racing. The facility also houses an art museum and library. Be aware that the price is pretty steep for what this museum offers. Plan to spend an hour here.

1776 Montano Rd. NW. © **505/341-1776.** Admission $10 adults, $6 seniors and military, free for children 15 and under. AE, DISC, MC, V. Daily 10am–4pm. Closed Easter, Thanksgiving, Christmas.

ESPECIALLY FOR KIDS

Albuquerque Biological Park: Aquarium and Botanic Garden ★★ ☺　For those of us born and raised in the desert, this attraction quenches years of soul thirst. The self-guided aquarium tour begins with a number of films, including a 9-minute one that describes the course of the Rio Grande from its origin to the Gulf Coast. Then, you'll move on to the ray pool, and next the eel tank—an arched aquarium you get to walk under. A colorful coral-reef exhibit comes next. Finally, culminating the show is a 285,000-gallon shark tank.

The Botanic Garden offers an excellent place to stroll through fragrant flowers with a few treats for kids as well. You'll pass through a number of gardens en route to a 10,000-square-foot conservatory, housing a desert collection and a Mediterranean collection. Beyond that, you can see a *curandera* (herb doctor) garden, with medicinal plants, and the Rio Grande Heritage Farm, with corrals, a vineyard, and orchard. Allow at least 2 hours to see both parks. There is a cafe on the premises. May to September, the PNM Butterfly Pavilion fills with the colors of several hundred North American butterflies.

2601 Central Ave. NW. © **505/764-6200.** www.cabq.gov/biopark. Admission $7 adults ($12 with Rio Grande Zoo admission), $3 seniors 65 and over and children 3–12 ($5 with Rio Grande Zoo admission). Ticket sales stop a half-hour before closing. MC, V. Daily 9am–5pm; (June–Aug Sat–Sun until 6pm). Closed New Year's Day, Thanksgiving, Christmas.

American International Rattlesnake Museum ★ 🎁 ☺　This unique museum, just off Old Town Plaza, has living specimens of common, uncommon, and very rare rattlesnakes of North, Central, and South America in naturally landscaped habitats. Oddities such as albino and patternless rattlesnakes are included, as is a display popular with youngsters: baby rattlesnakes. More than 30 species can be seen, followed by a 7-minute film on this contributor to the ecological balance of our hemisphere. Throughout the museum are rattlesnake artifacts from early American history, Native American culture, medicine, the arts, and advertising. You'll also find a gift shop that

IN SEARCH OF disneyland

If you want to occupy the kids for a day, there's a fun option, though don't expect Disneyland. **Cliff's Amusement Park,** 4800 Osuna Rd. NE (✆ **505/881-9373;** www.cliffs.net), has roller coasters, including the daring Galaxy, and a waterpark with some fun get-wet rides. Gate entrance is $2.50; ride passes run $20 for kids 48 inches tall and under and $25 for those over 48 inches; individual ride tickets are $2 to $6; and the Water Monkeys Adventure is $8.50.

specializes in Native American jewelry, T-shirts, and other memorabilia related to the natural world and the Southwest, all with an emphasis on rattlesnakes.

202 San Felipe St. NW. ✆ **505/242-6569.** www.rattlesnakes.com. Admission $5 adults, $4 seniors, $3 children. AE, DISC, MC, V. June–Aug Mon–Sat 10am–6pm, Sun 1–5pm; Sept–May Mon–Fri 11:30am–5:30pm, Sat 10am–6pm, Sun 1–5pm.

Explora ★ ☺ As a center for lifelong learning, Explora houses more than 250 hands-on exhibits in science, technology, and art. Visitors of all ages make their way through the mazelike museum exploring topics as diverse as water, the Rio Grande, light and optics, biological perception, and energy. The exhibits utilize technology that is creatively accessible to the public. My favorite is the Laminar Flow Fountain in which water leaps across spaces, seeming to come alive. Little kids especially enjoy the arts-and-crafts workshop where they can make art to take home. You could spend an hour and a half to a full day here.

1701 Mountain Rd. NW. ✆ **505/224-8300.** Fax 505/224-8325. www.explora.us. Admission $7 ages 12–64, $5 seniors 65 and over, $3 children 1–11. Mon–Sat 10am–6pm; Sun noon–6pm.

New Mexico Museum of Natural History and Science ★★ ☺ A trip through this museum will take you through 12 billion years of natural history, from the formation of the universe to the present day. You'll stroll through the "Age Jurassic Super Giants" display, where you'll find dinosaur skeletons cast from the real bones and see the latest display "Triassic: Dawn of the Dinosaur." You can ride the Evolator (kids love this!), a simulated time-travel experience that moves and rumbles, taking you 1¼ miles down through 38 million years of history. Soon, you'll find yourself in the age of the mammoths and moving through the Ice Age. Other stops along the way include the Naturalist Center, where kids can peek through microscopes and make their own bear or raccoon footprints in sand, and FossilWorks, where paleontologists work behind glass to excavate the bones of a seismosaurus. Be sure to check out the museum's planetarium. Those exhibits, as well as the DynaTheater, which surrounds you with images and sound, cost an additional fee. A gift shop on the ground floor sells imaginative nature games and other curios. This museum has good access for people with disabilities. Plan to spend 1 to 2 hours here, more if you take in extra attractions.

1801 Mountain Rd. NW. ✆ **505/841-2800.** www.nmnaturalhistory.org. Admission $7 adults, $6 seniors, $4 children 3–12, free for children 2 and under. DynaTheater, planetarium, and Virtual Voyages cost extra, with prices in the $7 range for adults and $4 range for children. Discount ticket combinations are available. Daily 9am–5pm. Closed on nonholiday Mon in Jan and Sept, New Year's Day, Thanksgiving, Christmas.

Rio Grande Nature Center State Park ★ ☺ This center, just a few miles north of Old Town, spans 270 acres of riverside forest and meadows that include stands of 100-year-old cottonwoods and a 3-acre pond. On the Rio Grande Flyway, an important migratory route for many birds, it's an excellent place to see sandhill cranes, Canadian geese, and quail—more than 260 bird species have made this their temporary or permanent home. In a protected area where dogs aren't allowed (you can bring dogs on most of the 2 miles of trails), you'll find exhibits of native grasses, wildflowers, and herbs. Inside a building built half above and half below ground, you can sit next to the pond in a glassed-in viewing area and comfortably watch ducks and other birds in their avian antics. There are 21 self-guided interpretive exhibits as well as photo exhibits, a library, a small nature store, and a children's resource room. On Saturday mornings, you can join a guided bird walk. Other weekend programs are available for adults and children, including nature photography, bird- and wildflower-identification classes, and twilight hikes. Call for a schedule.

2901 Candelaria Rd. NW. © **505/344-7240.** Fax 505/344-4505. www.nmparks.com. Admission $3 per vehicle. No credit cards (cash and checks only). Daily 10am–5pm; store Mon–Fri 11am–3pm, Sat-Sun 10am–4pm. Closed New Year's Day, Thanksgiving, Christmas.

Rio Grande Zoo ★ ☺ Some 250 species live on 64 acres of riverside bosque here among ancient cottonwoods. Open-moat exhibits with animals in naturalized habitats are a treat for zoogoers. Major exhibits include polar bears, giraffes, sea lions (with underwater viewing), the cat walk, the bird show, and ape country, with gorillas and orangutans. The zoo has an especially fine collection of elephants, koalas, polar bears, reptiles, and native Southwestern species. The Thunderbird Express Train operates in a nonstop loop around the zoo, except on Mondays. As well, the Rio Line operates between the zoo and the Albuquerque Biological Park (p. 269). There are numerous snack bars on the zoo grounds, and La Ventana Gift Shop carries film and souvenirs. Check out the seal and sea lion feeding at daily 10:30am and 3:30pm, the polar bear feeding at 2:30 daily, and the summer Zoo Music Concert Series.

903 10th St. SW. © **505/764-6200.** www.cabq.gov/biopark/zoo. Admission $7 adults ($12 with Aquarium and Botanic Garden admission), $3 seniors and children 3–12 ($5 with Aquarium and Botanic Garden admission), free for children 2 and under. MC, V. Daily 9am–5pm (summer weekends Sat-Sun 6pm). Closed New Year's Day, Thanksgiving, Christmas.

The Rio Line ★ ☺ This miniature train travels between the Tingley Train Station, the Albuquerque Biological Park, and the Rio Grande Zoo, stopping at each facility, with tickets available at each as well. Conductors give an interpretive tour and answer your questions as you ride. A round-trip journey lasts approximately 1 hour. This is a fun trip for families. *Note:* If you purchase a "combo ticket" for the Biological Park and Rio Grande Zoo, you get free between all stations. Also, during summer weekends, because of the high volume of visitors, only those with combo tickets can ride the Rio Line.

903 10th St. SW (station at Tingley Beach on Tingley Dr.) © **505/768-2000.** www.cabq.gov/biopark/trains.html. Train ride $2 adult, $1 children 3–12. MC, V. The train operates Tues–Sun approximately 10am–3:45pm. The last trains leave the Aquarium/Garden Station and the Asia Station at the zoo at 3:45pm, and the Tingley Station at 3pm.

ORGANIZED TOURS

Bus, Car & Trolley Tours

ABQ Trolly Company ★   A great way to get acquainted with the city, this open-air trolley tour takes visitors to 11 sights in 66 minutes. It starts in Old Town, heads up Route 66 to the Nob Hill shopping district, past the University of New Mexico, to the historic Barelas neighborhood, and to Tingley Beach.

Departs from 303 Romero St. NW in Old Town. ✆ **505/240-8000.** www.abqtrolley.com. $25 adults, $20 seniors 65 and older and students, $13 children 12 and under. AE, DISC, MC, V. Operates 2-4 times daily Tues-Sun Apr-Oct.

OUTDOOR ACTIVITIES

Ballooning

Visitors have a choice of several hot-air balloon operators; rates start at about $160 per person per hour. Call **Rainbow Ryders,** 5601 Eagle Rock Ave. NE (✆ **505/823-1111;** www.rainbowryders.com), or **World Balloon Corporation,** 1103 La Poblana NW (✆ **505/293-6800;** www.worldballoon.com).

If you'd rather just watch, go to the annual **Albuquerque International Balloon Fiesta** ★★★, which is held the first through second weekends of October (see "The Most Unforgettable Northern New Mexico Experiences," in chapter 1, and "Northern New Mexico Calendar of Events," in chapter 3, for details).

Biking

Albuquerque is a major bicycling hub in the summer, both for road racers and for mountain bikers. For an excellent map of Albuquerque bicycle routes, call the **Albuquerque Parks & Recreation Department** at ✆ **505/768-5300.** You can also find links to many recreation opportunities for adults and kids at **www.cabq.gov/visiting.html**. A great place to bike is **Sandia Peak** (✆ **505/242-9133;** www.sandiapeak.com) in Cíbola National Forest. You can't take your bike on the tram, but chairlift no. 1 is available for up- or downhill transportation with a bike. Bike rentals are available at the top and bottom of the chairlift. They cost $40 for adult bikes and $30 for junior ones. The lift costs $16 and runs on Saturday and Sunday, with Friday added in July and August, though you'll want to call to be sure. Helmets are mandatory. Bike maps are available; the clearly marked trails range from easy to very difficult.

Down in the valley, there's a **bosque trail** that runs along the Rio Grande, accessed through the Rio Grande Nature Center (see "Especially for Kids," above). To the east, the **Foothills Trail** runs along the base of the mountains. It's a fun, 7-mile-long trail that offers excellent views. Access it by driving east from downtown on Montgomery Boulevard, past the intersection with Tramway Boulevard. Go left on Glenwood Hills Drive and head north about a half-mile before turning right onto a short road that leads to the Embudito trail head.

Northeast Cyclery, 8305 Menaul Blvd. NE (✆ **505/299-1210**), rents bikes at the rate of $25 per day for front-suspension mountain bikes and $35 per day for road bikes. Multiday discounts are available. Unfortunately, the shop doesn't rent children's bikes. Rentals come with helmets.

GOLF ON THE SANTA FE TRAIL

Those golfers traveling through Albuquerque and northward will appreciate the nine respected courses that have teamed together to offer customized golf packages, including accommodations. **Golf on the Santa Fe Trail** (📞 **866/465-3660;** www.santafe trailgolf.com) includes such prestigious courses as the **Black Mesa Golf Club,** just north of Albuquerque at Santa Ana Pueblo (📞 **505/747-8946;** www. blackmesagolfclub.com), one of the state's premier golf settings since opening in 2003; and **Towa Golf Resort,** north of Santa Fe at Pojoaque Pueblo (📞 **877/465-3489;** www.golf newmexico.com), where 9 of the 18 holes were designed by Hale Irwin. To explore the other courses involved, check out their website.

Bird-Watching

Bosque del Apache National Wildlife Refuge ★★ (📞 505/835-1828; www. fws.gov/southwest/refuges/newmex/bosque/index.html) is a haven for migratory waterfowl such as snow geese and cranes. It's 90 miles south of Albuquerque on I-25, and it's well worth the drive. You'll find 7,000 acres of carefully managed riparian habitat, which include marshlands, meadows, agricultural fields, and old-growth cottonwood forests lining the Rio Grande. Particularly if you're here from November through March, the experience is thrilling, not only because of the variety of birds—more than 300 species—but also for the sheer numbers of them. Huge clouds of snow geese and sandhill cranes take flight at dawn and dusk, the air filling with the sounds of their calls and wing flaps. In early December, the refuge may harbor as many as 45,000 snow geese, 57,000 ducks of many different species, and 18,000 sandhill cranes. There are also plenty of raptors about, including numerous red-tailed hawks and northern harriers (or marsh hawks), Cooper's hawks and kestrels, and even bald and golden eagles. The refuge has a 15-mile auto-tour loop, which you should drive very slowly. Closer to town, check out the **Rio Grande Nature Center State Park** (see "Especially for Kids," above).

Fishing

Albuquerque's most notable fishing spot is **Tingley Beach** (📞 505/764-6281; www. cabq.gov/biopark/tingley), stocked weekly with trout, bass, and catfish. It's open daily and is free. To access Tingley from Rio Grande Boulevard, head west to Tingley Drive (Pkwy.) and turn south. Another option is **Shady Lakes** (📞 505/898-2568). Nestled among cottonwood trees, it's near I-25 on Albuquerque's north side. The most common catches are rainbow trout, black bass, bluegill, and channel catfish. To reach Shady Lakes, take I-25 north to the Tramway exit. Follow Tramway Road west for a mile and then go right on NM 313 for one-half mile. **Sandia Lakes Recreational Area** (📞 505/771-5190; www.sandiapueblo.nsn.us), also on NM 313, is another popular fishing spot. There is a bait and tackle shop there.

Golf

There are quite a few public courses in the Albuquerque area. The **Championship Golf Course at the University of New Mexico,** 3601 University Blvd. SE (✆ **505/277-4546;** www.unmgolf.com), is one of the best in the Southwest and was rated one of the country's top-25 public links by *Golf Digest.* **Desert Greens Golf Course,** 10035 Country Club Lane NW (✆ **505/898-7001;** www.desert greensgolf.com), is a popular 18-hole golf course on the west side of town.

Other Albuquerque courses to check with for tee times are **Ladera,** 3401 Ladera Dr. NW (✆ **505/836-4449**); **Los Altos,** 9717 Copper Ave. NE (✆ **505/298-1897;** www.cabq.gov/golf/los-altos); **Puerto del Sol,** 1800 Girard Blvd. SE (✆ **505/265-5636;** www.cabq.gov/golf/puerto-del-sol); **Arroyo del Oso,** 7001 Osuna Rd. NE (✆ **505/884-7505;** www.cabq.gov/golf/arroyo-del-oso); and **Sandia Golf Club** (✆ **505/798-3990;** www.sandiagolf.com), located at Sandia Resort and Casino on the north end of town.

If you're willing to drive a short distance just outside Albuquerque, you can play at the **Santa Ana Golf Club at Santa Ana Pueblo,** 288 Prairie Star Rd., Bernalillo, NM 87004 (✆ **505/867-9464;** www.santaanagolf.com), which was rated by the *New York Times* as one of the best public golf courses in the country. Club rentals are available (call for information). In addition, **Isleta Pueblo,** 4001 NM 47 (✆ **866/475-3822;** www.isletapueblo.com), south of Albuquerque, has an 18-hole course.

Trail Closures

The drought that has spread across the Southwest in recent years has caused the U.S. Forest Service to close trails in many New Mexico mountains during the summer in order to reduce fire hazard. Before you head out in this area, contact the **Sandia Ranger Station** (✆ **505/346-3900;** www.fs.fed.us/r3/cibola).

Hiking

The 1½-million-acre **Cíbola National Forest** offers ample hiking opportunities. Within town, the best hike is the **Embudito Trail,** which heads up into the foothills, with spectacular views down across Albuquerque. The 5.5-mile one-way hike is moderate to difficult. Allow 1 to 8 hours, depending on how far you want to go. Access it by driving east from downtown on Montgomery Boulevard past the intersection with Tramway Boulevard. Go left on Glenwood Hills Drive and head north about a half mile before turning right onto a short road that leads to the trail head. The premier Sandia Mountain hike is **La Luz Trail,** a very strenuous journey from the Sandia foothills to the top of the Crest. It's a 15-mile round-trip jaunt, and it's half that if you take the Sandia Peak Tramway (see "The Top Attractions," earlier in this chapter) either up or down. Allow a full day for this hike. Access is off Tramway Boulevard and Forest Service Road 333. For more details contact **Sandia Ranger Station,** NM 337 south toward Tijeras (✆ **505/346-3900;** www.fs.fed.us/r3/cibola).

Horseback Riding

Sometimes I just have to get in a saddle and eat some trail dust. If you get similar hankerings, call the **Hyatt Regency Tamaya Resort and Spa,** 1300 Tuyuna Trail, Santa Ana Pueblo (✆ **505/771-6060;** www.tamaya.hyatt.com). The resort offers 2½-hour-long rides near the Rio Grande for $75 per person. Children must be over 7 years

GETTING PAMPERED: THE spa SCENE

If you're looking to get pampered, you have a few options. **Mark Prado Salon & Spa** (*C* **505/298-2983** all locations) offers treatments at four locations: 1100 Juan Tabo Blvd. NE; 8001 Wyoming Blvd. NE; 3500 Central Ave. SE 7-B; and Cottonwood Mall, 10,000 Coors Blvd. NE.

Albuquerque's top-two luxurious spa experiences are at the **Hyatt Regency Tamaya Resort & Spa,** 1300 Tuyuna Trail, Santa Ana Pueblo (*C* **505/867-1234;** www.tamaya.hyatt.com), and the **Sandia Resort & Casino,** 30 Rainbow Rd. NE (*C* **800/526-9366** or 505/796-7500; www.sandiacasino.com). Each offers a broad array of treatments, as well as a sauna and a steam room, in refined atmospheres. The Tamaya is 15 minutes north of Albuquerque, near the village of Bernalillo, while the Sandia is on the north end of town, off Tramway Boulevard.

of age and over 4 feet tall. The resort is about 15 miles north of Albuquerque. From I-25 take exit 242, following US 550 west to Tamaya Boulevard, and drive 1½ miles to the resort.

Skiing

The **Sandia Peak Ski Area** is a good place for family skiing. There are plenty of beginner and intermediate runs. (If you're looking for more challenge or more variety, you'd better head north to Santa Fe or Taos.) The ski area has twin base-to-summit chairlifts to its upper slopes at 10,360 feet and a 1,700-foot vertical drop. There are 30 runs (35% beginner, 55% intermediate, 10% advanced) above the day lodge and ski-rental shop. Four chairs and two Pomas accommodate 3,400 skiers an hour. All-day lift tickets are $50 for adults, $40 for ages 13 to 20, and $40 for children ages 6 to 12 and seniors 62 to 71; free for children 46 inches tall or less in ski boots and seniors ages 72 and over. Rental packages are available. The season runs mid-December to mid-March. Contact the ski area, 10 Tramway Loop NE (*C* **505/242-9052;** www.sandiapeak.com), for more information, or call the hot line for ski conditions (*C* **505/857-8977**).

Cross-country skiers can enjoy the trails of the Sandia Wilderness from the ski area, or they can go an hour north to the remote Jemez Wilderness and its hot springs.

Tennis

Albuquerque has 29 public parks with tennis courts. Because of the city's size, your best bet is to call the **Albuquerque Convention and Visitors Bureau** (*C* **800/284-2282;** www.itsatrip.org) to find out which park is closest to your hotel.

SPECTATOR SPORTS

Baseball

The **Albuquerque Isotopes** play 72 home games as part of the Pacific Coast League in Isotopes Park. Tickets range in price from $6 to $24. For information, contact *C* **505/924-2255** (www.albuquerquebaseball.com). Isotopes Park is at 1601 Avenida

Cesar Chavez SE. Take I-25 south of town to Avenida Cesar Chavez and go east; the stadium is at the intersection of Avenida Cesar Chavez and University Boulevard.

Basketball

The University of New Mexico team, **the Lobos,** plays an average of 16 home games from late November to early March. Capacity crowds cheer the team at the 17,121-seat University Arena (fondly called "the Pit") at University and Stadium boulevards. For tickets and information, call ✆ **505/925-5626** (www.golobos.com).

Football

The **UNM Lobos** football team plays a September-to-November season—usually with five home games—at the 30,000-seat University of New Mexico Stadium, opposite both Albuquerque Sports Stadium and University Arena at University and Stadium boulevards. For tickets and information, call ✆ **505/925-5626** (www. golobos.com).

Horse Racing

The **Downs at Albuquerque Racetrack and Casino,** Expo New Mexico fair-grounds (✆ **505/266-5555** for post times; www.abqdowns.com) is near Lomas and Louisiana boulevards NE. Racing and betting—on thoroughbreds and quarter horses—take place mid-August through mid-November (including the New Mexico State Fair in Sept). The Downs has a glass-enclosed grandstand and exclusive club seating. General admission is free. Simulcast racing happens daily year-round, except Christmas. The 340-slot casino is open daily 10am to 2am, with drinks and dining in the Jockey Club.

SHOPPING

Visitors seeking regional specialties will find many **local artists** and **galleries** of interest in Albuquerque, although not as many as in Santa Fe and Taos. The galleries and regional fashion designers around the plaza in Old Town comprise a kind of a shopping center for travelers, with more than 40 merchants represented. The Sandia Pueblo runs its own **crafts market** at the reservation, off I-25 at Tramway Road, just beyond Albuquerque's northern city limits.

Albuquerque has three of the largest **shopping malls** in New Mexico, two within 2 blocks of each other on Louisiana Boulevard just north of I-40—Coronado Center and Winrock Center. The other is the Cottonwood Mall on the west mesa, at 10,000 Coors Blvd. NW (✆ **505/899-7467**). But the city's best mall is the **ABQ Uptown ★★** at Louisiana Boulevard NE and Indian School Road NE (✆ **505/883-7676;** www. abquptown.com), an outdoor mall with such anchors as Williams Sonoma, Pottery Barn, Sharper Image, Chicos, and Ann Taylor.

Business hours vary, but shops are generally open Monday to Saturday 10am to 6pm; many have extended hours; some have reduced hours; and a few, especially in shopping malls or during the high tourist season, are open on Sunday.

Best Buys

The best buys in Albuquerque are Southwestern regional items, including **arts and crafts** of all kinds—traditional Native American and Hispanic as well as contemporary works. In local Native American art, look for silver and turquoise jewelry, pottery, weavings, baskets, sand paintings, and Hopi *katsina* dolls. Hispanic folk art—handcrafted furniture, tinwork and *retablos,* and religious paintings—is worth seeking out. The best contemporary art is in paintings, sculpture, jewelry, ceramics, and fiber art, including weaving.

Other items of potential interest are Southwestern fashions, gourmet foods, and unique local Native American and Hispanic creations.

By far, the most **galleries** are in Old Town; others are spread around the city, with smaller groupings in the university district and the northeast heights. Consult the brochure published by the **Albuquerque Gallery Association,** *A Select Guide to Albuquerque Galleries,* or Wingspread Communications' annual *The Collector's Guide to Albuquerque,* widely distributed at shops. Once a month, usually from 5 to 9pm on the third Friday, the **Albuquerque Art Business Association** (✆ **505/244-0362;** www.artscrawlabq.org for information) sponsors an ArtsCrawl to dozens of galleries and studios. It's a great way to meet the artists.

You'll find some interesting shops in the Nob Hill area, which is just west of the University of New Mexico and has an Art Deco feel.

Following are some shopping recommendations for the greater Albuquerque area.

Arts & Crafts

Amapola Gallery ★ Fifty artists and craftspeople show their talents at this lovely cooperative gallery upstairs in the historic 1849 Romero House. You'll find pottery, paintings, textiles, carvings, baskets, jewelry, and other items. 205 Romero St. ✆ **505/242-4311.** www.amapolagallery.com.

Andrews Pueblo Pottery ★ Carrying Pueblo pottery ranging from the black firings of San Ildefonso to the sand-colored Acoma, this gallery is a place for rich perusing as well as serious buying. Also of note here are Zuni stone fetishes and Hopi *katsinas.* 303 N. Romero NW, Old Town. ✆ **877/606-0543.** www.andrewspp.com.

Bien Mur Indian Market Center ★ Sandia Pueblo's crafts market, on the reservation, sells turquoise and silver jewelry, pottery, baskets, *katsina* dolls, hand-woven rugs, sand paintings, and other arts and crafts. The market is open Monday through Saturday from 9:30am to 5:30pm and Sunday from 11am to 5:30pm. I-25 at Tramway Rd. NE. ✆ **800/365-5400** or 505/821-5400. www.sandiapueblo.nsn.us/bienmur.html.

Dartmouth Street Gallery ★ This gallery features tapestries by Nancy Kozikowski and a variety of work by 40 other contemporary artists, most from New Mexico. 510 14th St. SW. ✆ **800/474-7751** or 505/266-7751. www.dsg-art.com.

Gallery One This gallery features folk art, jewelry, contemporary crafts, cards and paper, and natural-fiber clothing. In the Nob Hill Shopping Center, 3500 Central Ave. SE. ✆ **505/268-7449.**

Hispaniae in Old Town ★ 🎒 Day of the Dead people and Frida Kahlo faces greet you at this wild shop with everything from kitschy Mexican tableware to fine Oaxacan woodcarvings. 410 Romero St. NW, Old Town. ✆ **505/244-1533.** www.hispaniae.com.

La Casita de Kaleidoscopes ★ This shop carries kaleidoscopes in a dizzying array (some 500) of styles, from egg- and tepee-shaped to fountains to little paper ones, with over 60 artists represented. 326-D San Felipe NW, in the Poco a Poco Patio in Old Town. ✆ **505/247-4242.** www.casitascopes.com.

Mariposa Gallery ★★ ✦ Eclectic contemporary art, jewelry, blown glass, and sculpture fill this Nob Hill shop, with prices that even a travel writer can afford. In the Nob Hill Shopping Center, 3500 Central Ave. SE. © **505/268-6828.** www.mariposa-gallery.com.

Ortega's Indian Arts and Crafts An institution in Gallup, adjacent to the Navajo Reservation, Ortega's now has this Albuquerque store. It sells, repairs, and appraises silver and turquoise jewelry. 6600 Menaul Blvd. NE, no. 359. © **505/-881-1231.**

The Pueblo Loft (at Gallery One) Owner Kitty Trask takes pride in the fact that all items featured at the Pueblo Loft are crafted by Native Americans. For almost 22 years, her slogan has been "Every purchase is an American Indian work of art." In the Nob Hill Shopping Center, 3500 Central Ave. SE. © **505/268-8764.**

Skip Maisel's ✦ If you want a real bargain in Native American arts and crafts, this is the place to shop. You'll find a broad range of quality and price here in goods such as pottery, weavings, and *katsinas*. Be sure to check out the 1933 murals by notable Navajo painter Harrison Begay and Pueblo painter Pablita Velarde, which adorn the outside of the store. 510 Central Ave. SW. © **505/242-6526.**

Tanner Chaney Galleries ★ In business since 1875, this gallery has fine Native American jewelry, pottery, rugs, and more. Most of these items are purchased directly from the artists who make them by hand. 323 Romero NW St., no. 4, Old Town. © **800/444-2242** or 505/247-2242. www.tannerchaney.com.

Weyrich Gallery (Rare Vision Art Galerie) Contemporary paintings, sculpture, textiles, jewelry, and ceramics by regional and nonregional artists are exhibited at this spacious midtown gallery. 2935-D Louisiana Blvd. at Candelaria Rd. © **866/372-1042** or 505/883-7410. www.weyrichgallery.com.

Wright's Collection of Indian Art This gallery, first opened in 1907, features a free private museum and carries fine handmade Native American arts and crafts, both contemporary and traditional. 1100 San Mateo Blvd. NE. © **505/266-0120.** www.wrightsgallery.com.

Books

Barnes & Noble On the west side, just north of Cottonwood Mall, this huge bookstore offers plenty of browsing room and a Starbucks Cafe for lounging. The store is known for its large children's section and weekly story-time readings. 3701 Ellison Dr. NW, no. A. © **505/792-4234.** Or at the Coronado Center, 6600 Menaul Blvd. NE. © 505/883-8200. www.barnesandnoble.com.

Bookworks ★ Selling both new and used books, Bookworks has one of the most complete Southwestern nonfiction and fiction sections in the region. A good place to linger, the store has a coffee bar and an area for readings. It also carries CDs, cassettes, and books on tape. 4022 Rio Grande Blvd. NW. © **505/344-8139.** www.bkwrks.com.

Borders This branch of the popular chain provides a broad range of books, music, and videos, and hosts in-store appearances by authors, musicians, and artists. Uptown Center, 2240 Q St. NE. © **505/884-7711.** www.borders.com.

Page One ★ This popular local bookstore offers a broad range of new and used books, DVDs, and CDs and often hosts readings by authors. Check out their website to find out the schedule. 11018 Montgomery NE. & **800/521-4122** or 505/294-2026. www.page1 book.com.

A TASTE OF THE grape

In addition to New Mexico's many enchanting sights, wineries drape the state, providing an excellent way to taste some of the 400-year-old growing tradition. Call to find out about their wine-tasting hours. Two Albuquerque wineries just a short, scenic drive from Old Town include **Anderson Valley Vineyards,** 4920 Rio Grande Blvd. NW, Albuquerque, NM 87107 (✆ **505/344-7266**); and **Casa Rondeña Winery,** 733 Chavez Rd., Los Ranchos de Albuquerque, NM 87107 (✆ **800/706-1699;** www.casarondena. com). **Sandia Shadows Vineyard and Winery,** 11704 Coronado NE, Albuquerque, NM 87122 (✆ **505/856-1006;** www.vivanewmexico.com/nm/wines. central.sandia.html) and **Gruet Winery,** 8400 Pan-American Hwy. NE, Albuquerque, NM 87113 (✆ **505/821-0055;** www.gruetwinery.com), are in the northeast heights.

Food

The Candy Lady Having made chocolate for more than 30 years, the Candy Lady is especially known for 21 varieties of fudge, including jalapeño flavor. The chile-*piñon* brittle has a nice zing. 524 Romero St. NW, Old Town. ✆ **800/214-7731** or 505/243-6239. www.thecandylady.com.

Rocky Mountain Chocolate Factory Old-fashioned candy is made right before your eyes. All chocolates are handmade. 380 Coronado Center. ✆ **888/525-2462.** www.rmcf.com.

Fashion

Albuquerque Pendleton ★ Cuddle up in a large selection of blankets and shawls, and haul them away in a handbag. 1100 San Mateo NE Blvd., Stes. 2 and 4. ✆ **505/255-6444.**

Gertrude Zachary ★★ This large well of imagination has beaded velvet scarves and elaborate antique furniture, but the real buy here is jewelry, ranging from traditional Native American bracelets and necklaces to wildly kitschy butterfly concho belts. Purses, beaded lamps—this place has anything that a contemporary gal could want. 3300 Central Ave. SE (in the Nob Hill area at Wellsley). ✆ **505/766-4700.** www.gertrudezachary.com.

Vintage Cowgirl 🎁 This shop arose out of history. JoAn Winkler's grandmother and mother were once part of "Pawnee Bill's Wild West Show." JoAn started by selling their old costumes and continued buying and selling embroidered blouses and jackets, hand-painted skirts, and silk cowgirl scarves called "wild rags," as well as boots and tees. 206 San Felipe NW. ✆ **505/247-2466.**

Gifts/Souvenirs

Jackalope International ★★ Wandering through this vast shopping area is like an adventure to another land—to many lands, really. You'll find Mexican *trasteros* (armoires) next to Balinese puppets. The store sells sculpture, pottery, and Christmas ornaments as well. 6400 San Mateo Blvd. ✆ **505/349-0955.** Also at 834 US 550 in Bernalillo. ✆ 505/867-9813. www.jackalope.com.

All That Glitters Is on Gold

For years, downtown Albuquerque has been reinventing itself and nowhere is the luster more brilliant than on Gold Avenue. A funky boutique street, it's the home of many unique shops and restaurants, well worth a morning or afternoon perusal. Look for "fine, fun, and funky" functional art at Patrician **Design,** 216 Gold Ave. SW (© **505/242-7646;** www.patriciandesign.com). Down the street, step into **Ooh! Aah! Jewelry,** 110 Amherst SE (© **505/242-7101;** www.oohaahjewelry.com), to find a wide selection of contemporary jewelry and handbags. If you work up an appetite, head to Gold Street Caffè (p. 256)

Home Furnishings

Ernest Thompson Furniture ★ Original-design, handcrafted furniture is exhibited in the factory showroom. Thompson is a fifth-generation furniture maker who still uses traditional production techniques. 4531 Osuna Rd. NE (¼ block west of I-25 and ½ block north on Osuna Rd.). © **800/568-2344** or 505/344-1994. www.ernestthompson.com.

El Paso Import Company ★ Advertising "unique furnishings from around the world," this place in the Nob Hill Shopping Center is packed with all manner of tables, *trasteros,* and chairs, most with aged and chipped paint for those who love the worn look. It's a fun place to browse even if you don't buy. 3500 Central SE, Nob Hill. © **888/999-3773.** www.elpasoimportco.com.

Strictly Southwestern You'll find nice, solid pine and oak Southwestern-style furniture here. Lighting, art, pottery, and other interior items are also available. 1321 Eubank Blvd. NE. © **800/336-7838.** www.strictlysouthwestern.com.

Markets

Flea Market Every Saturday and Sunday, year-round, the fairgrounds host this market from 7am to 6pm. It's a great place to browse for turquoise and silver jewelry and locally made crafts, as well as newly manufactured inexpensive goods such as socks and T-shirts. The place takes on a fair atmosphere, with the smell of cotton candy filling the air. There's no admission charge. Expo New Mexico fairgrounds. For information, call the Albuquerque Convention and Visitors Bureau, © **800/284-2282.** www.exponm.com/en/fleamarket.com.

ALBUQUERQUE AFTER DARK

Albuquerque has an active performing-arts and nightlife scene, as befits a city of half a million people. As also befits this area, the performing arts are multicultural, with Hispanic and (to a lesser extent) Native American productions sharing stage space with Anglo works, including theater, opera, symphony, and dance. Albuquerque also attracts many national touring companies. Nightclubs cover the gamut, with rock, jazz, and country predominant.

Complete information on all major cultural events can be obtained from the **Albuquerque Convention and Visitors Bureau** (© **800/284-2282;** staffed Mon–Fri 9am–5pm, with recorded information after hours). Current listings appear in the two daily newspapers; detailed weekend arts calendars can be found in Friday's *Journal*. The monthly *On the Scene* also carries entertainment listings.

Tickets for nearly all major entertainment and sporting events can be obtained from **Ticketmaster,** 4004 Carlisle Blvd. NE (© **800/745-3000**). Discount tickets are often available for midweek and matinee performances; check with individual theater or concert hall box offices.

The Performing Arts
CLASSICAL MUSIC

New Mexico Ballet Company   Founded in 1972, the state's oldest ballet company holds most of its performances at Popejoy Hall. Typically there's a fall production such as *Dracula,* a holiday one such as *The Nutcracker* or *A Christmas Carol,* and a contemporary spring production. 4200 Wyoming Blvd. NE, Ste. B2, Albuquerque, NM 87154-1518. © **505/292-4245.** www.newmexicoballet.org. Tickets $15–$40, depending on the performance and venue.

New Mexico Symphony Orchestra ★   My first introduction to symphony was with the NMSO. Although I was so young that I didn't quite understand the novelty of hearing live symphony, I loved picking out the distinct sounds and following as they melded together. The NMSO first played in 1932 (long before I attended, thank you) and has continued as a strong cultural force throughout the state. The symphony performs classics and pops, as well as family and neighborhood concerts. It plays for more than 20,000 grade-school students and visits communities throughout the state in its annual tour program. Concert venues are generally Popejoy Hall on the University of New Mexico campus, the National Hispanic Cultural Center, and the Rio Grande Zoo, all of which are accessible to people with disabilities. Guillermo Figueroa is the music director and conductor. I recommend going to one of the outdoor concerts at the band shell at the Rio Grande Zoo. 4407 Menaul Blvd. NE. © **800/251-6676** for tickets and information, or 505/881-9590. www.nmso.org. Ticket prices vary with concert; call for details.

Theater

Albuquerque Little Theatre   The Albuquerque Little Theatre has been offering a variety of productions ranging from comedies to dramas to musicals since 1930. Eight plays are presented here annually during a July-to-June season. Located across

---

THE MAJOR concert & performance HALLS

- **Journal Pavilion,** 5601 University Blvd. NE (© **505/452-5100**).
- **Keller Hall,** University of New Mexico, Cornell Street at Redondo Drive South NE (© **505/277-4569**).
- **KiMo Theatre** ★★, 423 Central Ave. NW (© **505/768-3544**). Take a self-guided tour of this historic 1927 theater to see elaborate

corbels and mosaic tile work in Pueblo Deco style. It's open Tuesday to Friday 8:30am to 4:30pm and Saturday 11am to 5pm.
- **Popejoy Hall,** University of New Mexico, Cornell Street at Redondo Drive South NE (© **505/277-3824**).
- **South Broadway Cultural Center,** 1025 Broadway Blvd. SE (© **505/848-1320**).

from Old Town, the theater offers plenty of free parking. 224 San Pasquale Ave. SW. ✆ **505/242-4750.** www.albuquerquelittletheatre.org. Tickets $22; $10 for student rush-tickets purchased 30 min. before showtime; $20 seniors. Box office Mon–Fri 11am–5:30pm.

Call after 10 Musical Theatre Southwest   From February to January, this theater presents six major Broadway musicals, in addition to several smaller productions, at various locations. Most productions are staged for three consecutive weekends, including some Sunday matinees. 6427 Linn St. NE. ✆ **505/265-9119.** www.musicaltheatresw. com. Tickets $15–$30 adults; students and seniors receive a $2 discount.

Vortex Theatre ★   A 35-year-old community theater known for its innovative productions, the Vortex is Albuquerque's "Off-Broadway" theater, presenting a range of plays from classic to original. You'll see such plays as *I Hate Hamlet* by Paul Rudnik and *Death & the Maiden* by Ariel Dorfman. Performances take place on Friday and Saturday at 8pm and on Sunday at 6pm. The black-box theater seats 90. 2004½ Central Ave. SE. ✆ **505/247-8600.** www.vortexabq.org. All tickets $15; student rush 5 min. prior $10.

The Club & Music Scene
ROCK/JAZZ

Burt's Tiki Lounge   This club won the weekly paper *Alibi*'s award for the best variety of drinks. The club offers live music Monday to Saturday 8pm to 2am and charges no cover. 313 Gold Ave. ✆ **505/247-2878.** www.burtstikilounge.com.

Graham Central Station   In the northeast heights, this huge club offers four disparate scenes: a country-and-western dance floor, a disco floor, a Latin floor, and a karaoke bar. It's open Wednesday to Saturday to 2am. 4770 Montgomery Blvd. (near San Mateo). ✆ **505/883-3041.** wwwgrahamcentralstation.com.

Ibiza ★★   At Hotel Andaluz, this glossy rooftop hotspot with a Mediterranean ambience features city views, a broad patio, and DJ or live music. It's a great place to dance. Happy hour is Wednesday to Friday 5 to 8pm; the club is open Wednesday to Saturday 9pm to 1:30am with a $10 cover. 125 2nd St. NW. ✆ **505/243-9090.** www. hotelandaluz.com.

Kelly's BYOB ★   Near the university, Kelly's is a local brewpub, set in a renovated auto-body shop. The place has tasty pub fare, excellent brew specials, and live music for special events. 3222 Central SE. ✆ **505/262-2739.** www.kellysbrewpub.com.

Nob Hill Bar & Grill   The college and post-college crowd flocks this restaurant to savor a broad selection of beers, tequilas, and whiskeys and nosh on Kobe beef burgers and fish tacos. 3128 Central Ave. SE. ✆ **505/266-4455.** www.upscalejoint.com.

One Up Elevated Lounge ★   In a contemporary setting with city views and cushy couches, this spot serves up something new nightly. Dance music ranges from salsa to R&B to rock, with food and drink specials to compliment the mood. Check out their website to see what's happening that week. 301 Central NW, 2nd floor. ✆ **505/242-1966.** www.oneupabq.com.

O'Niell's Pub   A favorite club in the University of New Mexico area, this Irish bar serves up good pub fare as well as live local music on Saturday nights and Celtic and bluegrass on Sunday evenings. 4310 Central SE. ✆ **505/255-6782.** www.oniells.com.

Q Bar ★   With sophisticated decor—lots of plush couches and comfy chairs in bright tones—this lounge in the Hotel Albuquerque at Old Town offers innovative cuisine, often live entertainment, and a dance floor. On weekend nights, it's packed with 20- and 30-somethings. It's open Tuesday to Saturday 4pm to 1am. 800 Rio Grande Blvd. NW. ⓒ **505/843-6300.**

More Entertainment

Albuquerque's best nighttime attraction is the **Sandia Peak Tramway,** from which you can enjoy a view nonpareil of the Rio Grande Valley and the city lights.

The best place to catch foreign films, art films, and limited-release productions is the **Guild Cinema,** 3405 Central Ave. NE (ⓒ **505/255-1848**). For film classics, check out the **Southwest Film Center,** on the UNM campus (ⓒ **505/277-5608**), which has double features, changing nightly (when classes are in session). In addition, Albuquerque has a number of first-run movie theaters whose numbers you can find in the local telephone directory.

Many travelers like to include a little dice-throw and slot-machine play in their trip to New Mexico. Those who do are in luck, with the expansive **Sandia Resort & Casino,** north of I-25 and a quarter mile east on Tramway Boulevard (ⓒ **800/526-9366;** www.sandiacasino.com). The $80-million structure sits on Sandia Pueblo land and has outstanding views of the Sandia Mountains. Built in pueblo architectural style, the graceful casino has a 3,650-seat outdoor amphitheater, three restaurants (see p. 258 for a review of the excellent **Bien Shur**), a lounge, more than 1,800 slot and video poker machines, the largest poker room in the state, and blackjack, roulette, and craps tables. It's open from 8am to 4am Sunday to Wednesday and 24 hours Thursday to Saturday. Fifteen minutes south of town, the **Hard Rock Hotel & Casino Albuquerque,** 11000 Broadway SE (ⓒ **877/747-5382** or 505/724-3800; www.hardrock casinoabq.com), is a luxurious, air-conditioned casino (featuring blackjack, poker, slots, bingo, and keno) with a full-service restaurant, nonsmoking section, and free bus transportation on request. It's open Thursday to Saturday 24 hours, Sunday to Wednesday 9am to 5pm.

EXPLORING NEARBY PUEBLOS & MONUMENTS

Ten Native American pueblos are within an hour's drive of central Albuquerque. One national and two state monuments preserve another five ancient pueblo ruins.

Pueblo Etiquette

When you visit pueblos, it's important to observe certain rules of etiquette: Remember to respect the pueblos as people's homes; don't peek into doors and windows or climb on top of the buildings. Stay out of cemeteries and ceremonial rooms (such as kivas), since these are sacred grounds. Don't speak during dances or ceremonies or applaud after their conclusion; silence is mandatory. Most pueblos require a permit to carry a camera or to sketch or paint on location. Several pueblos prohibit photography at any time, and many artists don't permit you to photograph their work.

The active pueblos nearby include Acoma, Cochiti, Isleta, Jemez, Laguna, Sandia, San Felipe, Santa Ana, Santo Domingo, and Zia. Of these, Acoma is the most prominent.

Acoma Pueblo ★★★

This spectacular "Sky City," a walled adobe village perched high atop a sheer rock mesa 365 feet above the 6,600-foot valley floor, is believed to have been inhabited at least since the 11th century—the longest continuously occupied community in the United States. Native legend claims that it has been inhabited since before the time of Christ. Both the pueblo and **San Estevan del Rey Mission** are National Historic Landmarks. In 2006, the Sky City Cultural Center and Haak'u Museum opened below Acoma, showcasing pottery, textiles, baskets, and other art from the tribe.

The Keresan-speaking Acoma (*Ack*-oo-mah) Pueblo boasts 6,005 inhabitants, but only about 50 people reside year-round on the 70-acre mesa top. They make their living from tourists who come to see the village, the large church containing examples of Spanish colonial art, and to purchase the pueblo's thin-walled white pottery with polychrome designs.

To reach Acoma from Albuquerque, drive west on I-40 approximately 52 miles to the Acoma–Sky City exit, then travel about 12 miles southwest.

You absolutely cannot wander freely around Acoma Pueblo, but you can start your tour at the 40,000-square-foot museum, which gives a good look into this culture, and peruse the gallery, offering art and crafts for sale. You can have a meal at the Yaak'a Café. Then board the **tour bus,** which climbs through a rock garden of 50-foot sandstone monoliths and past precipitously dangling outhouses to the mesa's summit. There's no running water or electricity in this medieval-looking village; a small reservoir collects rainwater for most purposes, but drinking water is transported up from below. Wood-hole ladders and mica windows are prevalent among the 300-odd adobe structures. As you tour the village, you'll have many opportunities to buy pottery and other pueblo treasures. Pottery is expensive here, but you're not going to find it any cheaper anywhere else, and you'll be guaranteed that it's authentic if you buy it directly from the crafts-person. Along the way, be sure to sample some Indian fry bread topped with honey.

The annual **San Esteban del Rey feast day** is September 2, when the pueblo's patron saint is honored with an 8am Mass, a procession, an afternoon corn dance, and an arts-and-crafts fair, which includes homemade games of chance and food stalls. (A popular item is the only-in-New Mexico snack "Kool-Aid and pickles"). A Governor's Feast is held annually in February, and 4 days of Christmas festivals run from December 25 to 28. Still cameras are allowed for a $10 fee, and guided tours do not operate on the mesa during feast days. You are not permitted to take photos of the cemetery or inside the mission church. Cameras are not permitted in the pueblo on feast days.

Contact **Sky City Cultural Center and Pueblo of Acoma** (© 888/747-0181; www.acomaskycity.org). Admission for the tour is $20 for adults, $15 for seniors (60 and over) and military, $10 for children 6 to 17, and free for children 5 and under, with discounts for students and Native American visitors. The tours run daily in the summer 9am to 5pm, and daily in spring, fall, and winter 10am to 3pm. The 1-hour, 20-minute tours begin every 45 minutes, depending on the demand. The pueblo is closed to visitors on Easter weekend (some years), June 24 and 29, July 10 to 13, the first or second weekend in October, and the first Saturday in December. It's best to call ahead to make sure that the tour is available when you're visiting.

Albuquerque & Environs

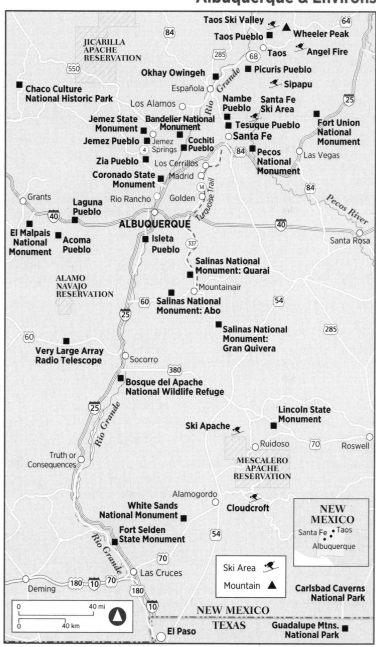

Taos Ski Valley
Taos Pueblo
Wheeler Peak
84
Taos
Angel Fire
285
68
JICARILLA
APACHE
RESERVATION
Okhay Owingeh
Picuris Pueblo
550
Española
Sipapu
Chaco Culture
National Historic Park
Los Alamos
Nambe
Pueblo
Santa Fe
Ski Area
25
Jemez State
Monument
Bandelier National
Monument
Tesuque Pueblo
Fort Union
National
Monument
Jemez Pueblo
Jemez
Springs
Cochiti
Pueblo
Santa Fe
4
Zia Pueblo
Los Cerrillos
Pecos
National
Monument
Las Vegas
84
Coronado State
Monument
Madrid
14
Grants
Laguna
Pueblo
Rio Rancho
Golden
84
40
ALBUQUERQUE
40
Santa Rosa
El Malpais
National
Monument
Acoma
Pueblo
Isleta
Pueblo
337
Salinas National
Monument: Quarai
ALAMO
NAVAJO
RESERVATION
Mountainair
60
Salinas National
Monument: Abo
54
25
60
Salinas National
Monument:
Gran Quivera
285
Very Large Array
Radio Telescope
Socorro
380
Bosque del Apache
National Wildlife Refuge
25
Lincoln State
Monument
Ski Apache
Truth or
Consequences
Ruidoso
70
Roswell
MESCALERO
APACHE
RESERVATION
Alamogordo
White Sands
National Monument
Cloudcroft
NEW
MEXICO
Santa Fe
Taos
Fort Selden
State Monument
54
Albuquerque
70
Rio Grande
Las Cruces
Ski Area
Deming
180
10
70
Mountain
Carlsbad Caverns
National Park
180
10
0   40 mi
0   40 km
NEW MEXICO
El Paso
TEXAS
Guadalupe Mtns.
National Park

A RENOVATED relic

In Mountainair, the **Shaffer Hotel and Restaurant** ★, 103 W. Main St. (☏ **888/595-2888** or 505/847-2888; www.shaffer hotel.com), offers a fun glimpse into the past. Renovated by Joel Marks, who stumbled on the place while riding his Harley through the Manzano Mountains, it has a stone fireplace and molded tin ceiling, as well as original Tiffany stained-glass windows. The attached restaurant is even more remarkable, with bright Southwest Art Deco murals on the ceiling, and chandeliers sporting Native American symbols. Diners enjoy huevos rancheros and breakfast burritos. Built in the 1920s by blacksmith Clem "Pop" Shaffer, it also has a curios shop named after the founder, selling turquoise jewelry, dreamcatchers, and *katsinas*. The hotel includes 19 rooms, some with shared bath. The rooms are fairly basic, but will serve those who like frontier-style antique hotels. Prices range from $28 to $89.

Coronado State Monument ★   When Spanish explorer Francisco Vásquez de Coronado traveled through this region in 1540–41 while searching for the Seven Cities of Cíbola, he wintered at a village on the west bank of the Rio Grande—probably one of the ruins of the ancient Anasazi Pueblo known as Kuaua. Those excavated ruins have been preserved in this state monument.

Hundreds of rooms can be seen, and a kiva has been restored so that visitors can descend a ladder into the enclosed space, once the site of sacred rites. Unique multicolored murals, depicting human and animal forms, were found on successive layers of wall plaster in this and other kivas here; some examples are displayed in the monument's small archaeological museum.

485 Kuaua Rd., Bernalillo. ☏ **505/867-5351.** www.nmmonuments.org. Admission $3 adults, free for children 16 and under. Wed–Mon 8:30am–5pm. Closed New Year's Day, Easter, Thanksgiving, Christmas. Located 20 miles north of Albuquerque; take I-25 to Bernalillo and US 550 west for 1¾ miles.

Salinas Pueblo Missions National Monument ★ 🏛   These rarely visited ruins provide a unique glimpse into history. The Spanish conquistadors' Salinas Jurisdiction, on the east side of the Manzano Mountains (southeast of Albuquerque), was an important 17th-century trade center because of the salt extracted by the Native Americans from the salt lakes. Franciscan priests, utilizing native labor, constructed missions of Abo red sandstone and blue-gray limestone for the native converts. The ruins of some of the most durable missions—along with evidence of preexisting Anasazi and Mogollon cultures—are the highlights of a visit here. The monument consists of three separate units: the ruins of Abo, Quarai, and Gran Quivira. They are situated around the quiet town of Mountainair, 75 miles southeast of Albuquerque at the junction of US 60 and NM 55.

Abo (☏ **505/847-2400**) boasts the 40-foot-high ruins of the **Mission of San Gregorio de Abo,** a rare example of medieval architecture in the United States. **Quarai** (☏ **505/847-2290**) preserves the largely intact remains of the **Mission of La Purísima Concepción de Cuarac** (1630). Its vast size, 100 feet long and 40 feet high, contrasts with the modest size of the pueblo mounds. A small museum in the visitor center has a scale model of the original church, along with a selection of artifacts found at the site. **Gran Quivira** (© **505/847-2770**) once had a population of 1,500. The pueblo has 300 rooms and 7 kivas. Rooms dating back to 1300 can be seen. There are indications that an older village, dating to 800, may have previously stood here. Ruins of two churches (one almost 140 ft. long) and a convent have been preserved. The visitor center includes a museum with many artifacts from the site and shows a 40-minute movie about the excavation of some 200 rooms, plus a short video of the pueblo's history. All three pueblos and the churches that were constructed above them are believed to have been abandoned in the 1670s.

Self-guided tour pamphlets can be obtained at the units' respective visitor centers and at the **Salinas Pueblo Missions National Monument Visitor Center** in Mountainair, on US 60, 1 block west of the intersection of US 60 and NM 55. The visitor center offers an audiovisual presentation on the region's history, a bookstore, and an art exhibit.

P.O. Box 517, Mountainair. © **505/847-2585.** www.nps.gov/sapu. Free admission. Sites summer daily 9am–6pm (till 5pm rest of year). Visitor center in Mountainair daily 8am–5pm. Closed New Year's Day, Thanksgiving, Christmas. Abo is 9 miles west of Mountainair on US 60. Quarai is 8 miles north of Mountainair on NM 55. Gran Quivira is 25 miles south of Mountainair on NM 55. All roads are paved.

Jemez Springs

Getting to this village along the Jemez River is half the fun. You'll drive the **Jemez Mountain Trail** ★ into the Jemez Mountains, a trip that can provide a relaxing retreat and/or an exhilarating adventure. In the area are historic sites and relaxing hot springs, as well as excellent stream fishing, hiking, and cross-country skiing. You may want to combine a drive through this area with a visit to Los Alamos and Bandelier National Monument (see chapter 11).

North of town you'll come to the **Soda Dam,** a strange and beautiful mineral mass formed by travertine deposits—minerals that precipitate out of geothermal springs. Considered a sacred site by Native Americans, it has a gushing waterfall and caves. During the warm months it's a popular swimming hole.

Jemez State Monument ★   A stop at this small monument takes you on a journey through the history of the Jemez people. The journey begins in the museum,

TRADITIONAL NATIVE AMERICAN
bread baking

While visiting the pueblos in New Mexico, you'll probably notice outdoor ovens (they look a bit like giant ant hills), known as *hornos,* which Native Americans have used to bake bread for hundreds of years. For Native Americans, making bread is a tradition that links them directly to their ancestors. Usually in the evening, the bread dough (made of white flour, lard, salt, yeast, and water) is made and kneaded, the loaves are shaped, and in the morning placed in the oven heated by a wood fire. They bake for about an hour. If you would like to try a traditional loaf, you can buy one at the **Indian Pueblo Cultural Center** in Albuquerque (see "What to See & Do," earlier in the chapter), among other places.

Historic Culture with a Hint of Honey

Jemez Pueblo, home to more than 3,000, no longer welcomes visitors except on selected days. However, visitors can get a taste of the Jemez culture at the **Walatowa Visitor Center,** on NM 4, 8 miles north of the junction with US 550 (⟨𝒞⟩ **575/834-7235;** www.jemezpueblo. org). A museum presents the history of the Jemez people and displays pottery and drums. A gift shop sells mostly fake Native American art, but also a few real pieces from the pueblo. The shop also offers information about hiking and scenic tour routes. While in the area, you may encounter Jemez people sitting under *ramadas* (thatch-roofed lean-tos) and selling home-baked bread, cookies, and pies. If you're lucky, they may also be making fry bread, which you can smother with honey for one of New Mexico's more delectable treats. The center is open Tuesday to Saturday 10am to 5pm, Sunday noon to 5pm.

which tells the tale of Giusewa, "place of boiling waters," the original Tewa name of the area. Then it moves out into the mission ruins, whose story is told on small plaques that juxtapose the first impressions of the missionaries against the reality of the Jemez life. The missionaries saw the Jemez people as barbaric and set out to settle them. Part of the process involved hauling up river stones and erecting 6-foot-thick walls of the Mission of San José de los Jemez (founded in 1621) in the early 17th century. Excavations in 1921–22 and 1935–37 unearthed this massive complex through which you may wander. You enter through a broad doorway to a room that once held elaborate fresco paintings, the room tapering back to the nave, with a giant bell tower above.

18160 NM 4 (P.O. Box 143), Jemez Springs. ⟨𝒞⟩ **505/829-3530.** www.nmmonuments.org. Admission $3 adults, free for children 17 and under. Wed–Mon 8:30am–5pm. Closed New Year's Day, Easter, Thanksgiving, Christmas. From Albuquerque, take NM 550 (NM 44) to NM 4 and then continue on NM 4 for about 18 miles.

WHERE TO STAY & DINE

Cañon del Rio Retreat & Spa ★   Set above a cottonwood-shaded arch of the Jemez River, the adobe-style Cañon del Rio offers comfortable rooms around a courtyard, each named after a Native American tribe. Each has a sliding glass door that opens out to a patio where there's a (not very clean) fountain. Located a short walk from the river, guests can fish if they'd like. The lap-pool, heated in summers, offers sunbathing or swimming. The beds are comfortable, and the baths very functional. The Great Room has a cozy, welcoming feel, with a big-screen TV, as well as a large table where breakfast (such as blue-corn blueberry pancakes) is served family style. An elegant new spa offers a variety of treatments.

16445 NM 4, Jemez Springs, NM 87025. ⟨𝒞⟩ **505/829-4377.** www.canondelrio.com. 6 units. $119–$200 double, depending on the season. Rates include full gourmet breakfast. AE, DISC, MC, V. **Amenities:** Jacuzzi; outdoor pool; spa. *In room:* A/C, hair dryer, Wi-Fi.

Dragonfly Cottage ★★ ☺   This sophisticated little house set above the Jemez River provides a nice retreat. It has two bedrooms and one bath, sun-colored walls, and a vaulted ceiling in the living room. A very refined place, it has a fireplace and a deck with views of the red-rock canyon walls, and a grill. The full kitchen makes this a nice choice for families. Breakfast is served at the Highway 4 Coffee House up the street. Two-night minimum stay required.

15975 NM 4 (south of mile marker 16), Jemez Springs, NM 87025. © **575/829-3410.** www.deserrwillowbandb.com. $149–$169 cottage. MC, V. Rates include full breakfast. Pets accepted with prior arrangement. *In room:* A/C, TV, hair dryer, kitchen.

Highway 4 Coffee House ★ This little cafe serves the best coffee in Jemez Springs, along with a variety of treats baked in-house. You can choose items that range from chocolate éclairs to quiches to panini sandwiches. The cafe has a country kitchen atmosphere with wooden tables and checker-painted floors. You can order drinks ranging from lattes to chai teas. On Wednesday evenings in winter they serve a yummy, informal fixed-price dinner—a great way to meet locals.

17502 NM 4, Jemez Springs, NM 87025. © **575/829-4655.** All menu items under $10; Wed dinner under $15. MC, V. Mon–Wed and Fri 6:30am–3pm; Sat-Sun 7:30am–4pm.

The Laughing Lizard Inn & Cafe ★ AMERICAN This is the kind of small-town cafe that doesn't have to try to have a personality. It already has thick adobe walls, wood floors, and a wood-burning stove for its innate charm. Added touches are the brightly painted walls and funky old tables. The menu is eclectic—most dishes have a bit of an imaginative flair. The burritos come in a variety of types, such as fresh spinach with black beans, mushrooms, jack cheese, salsa, and guacamole.

 SAMPLING NATURE'S nectars

The waters running through the Jemez area are high in mineral content. In fact, the manager of **Jemez Springs Bath House,** 62 NM 4, on the Jemez Springs Plaza (© **575/829-3303;** www.jemezspringsbathhouse.com), says they are so healing, more than once she's had to run after visitors who walked off without their canes. This bathhouse was one of the first structures to be built in what is now Jemez Springs. Built in the 1870s of river rock and mud, it has thick walls and a richly herbal scent. You soak in individual tubs in either the men's side or the women's side. In back are a series of massage rooms, where the spa offers a full range of treatments. In front is a gift shop packed with interesting soaps and soulful gifts. Jemez Springs Bath House is open daily 10am to 8pm.

Another option in town is the **Giggling Springs ★** (© **575/829-9175;** www.gigglingsprings.com), across the street from the Laughing Lizard. A small outdoor pool, surrounded by sandstone and funky art, highlights this place. The Jemez River acts as a cold plunge. It's open Wednesday to Sunday 11am to 8pm, with an abbreviated schedule in winter. Reservations recommended.

At **Ponderosa Valley Vineyard & Winery,** 3171 NM 290, Ponderosa, NM 87044 (© **800/946-3657** or 575/834-7487; www.ponderosawinery.com), 3 miles off NM 4 south of Jemez Springs, you'll find a quaint country store with some of New Mexico's best wines. The vintners preside over a small curved bar and will pour you delectable tastes while telling stories of the history of wine in New Mexico and of the Jemez area, where they have lived and grown grapes for more than 3 decades. A 10- to 15-minute tour will take you through the cellar and production buildings. You'll likely want to take a bottle with you. They range in price from $12 to $30.

The homemade pizzas, made with blue-corn crusts, feature ingredients such as pesto, sun-dried tomatoes, and feta, or more basic ones with red sauce as well. Beer and wine are served, and there are daily dessert treats such as *piñon* pie, chocolate mousse, and berry cobbler. The staff is friendly and accommodating. A small inn attached to the cafe provides inexpensive rooms that are clean but a bit timeworn.

17526 NM 4, Jemez Springs, NM 87025. ℂ **575/829-3108.** www.thelaughinglizard.com. Main courses $5–$10 lunch, and $6–$18 dinner. DISC, MC, V. Wed–Sat 8am–7:45pm; Sun 8am–4:45pm.

The Turquoise Trail ★★

Known as "the Turquoise Trail," NM 14 begins about 16 miles east of downtown Albuquerque, at I-40's Cedar Crest exit, and winds some 46 miles to Santa Fe along the east side of the Sandia Mountains. This state-designated scenic and historic route traverses the revived ghost towns of Golden, Madrid, and Cerrillos, where gold, silver, coal, and turquoise were once mined in great quantities. Modern-day settlers, mostly artists and craftspeople, have brought a renewed frontier spirit to the old mining towns.

SANDIA CREST   As you start along the Turquoise Trail, you may want to turn left onto Sandia Crest Road and drive about 5 minutes to the **Tinkertown Museum ★**, 121 Sandia Crest Rd. (ℂ **505/281-5233;** www.tinkertown.com). The creation of Ross Ward, who took 40 years to carve, collect, and construct the place, it is mostly a miniatures museum, featuring dollhouse-type exhibits of a mining town, a circus, and other venues, with push buttons to make the little characters move. The building itself is constructed of glass bottles, wagon wheels, and horseshoes, among other ingredients. Great fun for the kids here. It's open daily from April to October from 9am to 6pm. Adults $3, children 4 to 16 $1.

GOLDEN   Golden is approximately 10 miles north of the Sandia Park junction on NM 14. Its sagging houses, with their missing boards and the wind whistling through the broken eaves, make it a purist's ghost town. There's a general store widely known for its large selection of well-priced jewelry, and across the street, a bottle seller's "glass garden." Be sure to slow down and look for the village church, a great photo opportunity, on the east side of the road. Nearby are the ruins of a pueblo called **Paako,** abandoned around 1670.

MADRID   Madrid (pronounced "*Mah*-drid") is about 12 miles north of Golden. This town and neighboring Cerrillos were in a fabled turquoise-mining area dating back to prehistory. Gold and silver mines followed, and when they faltered, there was coal. The Turquoise Trail towns supplied fuel for the locomotives of the Santa Fe Railroad until the 1950s, when the railroad converted to diesel fuel. Madrid used to produce 100,000 tons of coal a year and was a true "company town," but the mine closed in 1956. Today, this is a village of artists and craftspeople seemingly stuck in the 1960s: Its funky, ramshackle houses have many counterculture residents who operate several crafts stores and galleries.

The **Old Coal Mine Museum and Old West Saloon** (ℂ **505/438-3780**) invites visitors to peek into a mine that was saved when the town was abandoned. You can see the old mine's offices, steam engines, machines, and tools. It's open daily; admission is $5 for adults, $3 for seniors, and free for children 5 and under.

Next door, the **Mine Shaft Tavern** (ℂ **505/473-0743**) continues its colorful career by offering a variety of burgers (try the green-chile cheeseburger) and presenting

Mining Town Art Walk

Once a fabled mining town, Madrid has become a notable arts village, a great place to wander on a sunny day. Start on the south end of town at **Al Leedom Studio,** 2485 NM 14 (*©* **505/473-2054;** www.alleedom.com), where the studio's namesake sells inventive glassware made in New Mexico from recycled glass. Around the corner, step into the **Painted Horse Gallery,** 2850 NM 14 (*©* **505/473-5900;** www.loonesome dovey.com), an intimate place showing modern landscape paintings by Dean Dovey, as well as jewelry and gifts. Just down the street, **Jezebel,** 2860 NM 14 (*©* **505/471-3795;** www.jezebelgallery. com), has lamps with dazzling slumped-glass shades. The shop also has a soda fountain selling Starbucks Coffee, breakfast items, and burgers.

Next door, **Indigo Gallery** ★, 2584 NM 14 (*©* **505/438-6202;** www.indigo gallery.com), represents 20 artists who live in New Mexico, their colorful work ranging from realism to abstract. Stop for coffee and pastries at **Java Junction,** 2855 NM 14 (*©* **505/438-2772;** www.java-junction.com), where you'll want to gawk over their vast hot sauce collection, including brands named "Scorned Woman," "Cowboy Cayenne," and "Original Death Sauce." If you'd like to stay the night, inquire about their Victorian suite upstairs. On the north end of town, check out **Seppanen & Daughters Fine Textiles** ★, 2879 NM 14 (*©* **505/424-7470;** www.finetextiles. com), a quaint house draped floor to ceiling with weavings from lands as near as Navajo and as distant as Tibet.

live music Saturday nights and Sunday afternoons; it's open for meals in summer Monday to Thursday 11am to 6pm and Friday to Sunday 11:30am to 7:30pm. In winter, meals are served Monday to Thursday from noon to 4pm and Friday to Sunday noon to 8pm. The bar is open in summer Sunday to Thursday 11am to 11pm and Friday to Saturday 11am to 1am. In winter the bar is open from Sunday to Thursday noon to 10pm and Friday to Saturday noon to 1am. Next door is the **Madrid Engine House Theater** (*©* **505/438-3780**), offering melodrama during the summer. Its back doors open out so a steam locomotive can take center stage.

A healthier dining option than the Mine Shaft is **Mama Lisa's Ghost Town Kitchen** ★, 2859 NM 14 (*©* **505/471-5769**). You'll find salads, sandwiches, and New Mexican specialties, all prepared with fresh ingredients. During the summer, it's open Friday to Sunday from 11am to 4:30pm. In winter, it's open intermittently, so call ahead.

CERRILLOS & GALISTEO   Cerrillos, about 3 miles north of Madrid, is a village of dirt roads that sprawls along Galisteo Creek. It appears to have changed very little since it was founded during a lead strike in 1879; the old hotel, the saloon, and even the sheriff's office look very much like parts of an Old West movie set. You may want to stop in at **Casa Grande Trading Post,** 17 Waldo St. (*©* **505/438-3008;** www. casagrandetradingpost.com.), a shop that was featured on PBS's *Antiques Roadshow.* You'll find lots of jewelry and rocks, as well as the **Cerrillos Turquoise Mining Museum,** full of artifacts from this region's mining era.

A good horseback-riding outfitter in the Galisteo Basin is **Broken Saddle Riding Company.** A 1¼-hour ride is $55 a person, a 2-hour ride is $80, a 3-hour ride is $100, and the 1½-hour sunset ride is $75. Riders are grouped according to skill level. For more information, call ✆ **505/424-7774** and listen to the recorded message, or go to www.brokensaddle.com.

If you're getting hungry on the outskirts of Santa Fe, stop by the **San Marcos Café ★**, 3877 NM 14, near Lone Butte (✆ **505/471-9298**). Set next to a feed store in a curvaceous old adobe with wood-plank floors and lots of Southwest ambience, this cafe serves creative fare such as cinnamon rolls and their special Eggs San Marcos—tortillas stuffed with scrambled eggs and topped with guacamole, pinto beans, Jack cheese, and red chile. The cafe is open daily 8am to 2pm (stops serving at 1:50pm).

FAST FACTS

FAST FACTS: NORTHERN NEW MEXICO

Area Codes   The telephone area code for northwestern New Mexico, including Albuquerque and Santa Fe, is **505.** For the rest of the state, including Taos, the code is **575.**

Business Hours   **Offices** and **stores** are generally open Monday to Friday 9am to 5pm, with many stores also open Friday night, Saturday, and Sunday. Most **banks** are open Monday to Thursday 9am to 5pm and Friday 9am to 6pm. Some may also be open Saturday morning. Most branches have ATMs available 24 hours. Call establishments for specific hours.

Cellphones (Mobile Phones)   See "Staying Connected," p. 46.

Drinking Laws   The legal age for purchase and consumption of alcoholic beverages is 21; proof of age is required and often requested at bars, nightclubs, and restaurants, so it's always a good idea to bring ID when you go out.

Bars may remain open until 2am Monday to Saturday and until midnight on Sunday. Wine, beer, and spirits are sold at licensed supermarkets and liquor stores, but there are no package sales on election days until after 7pm, and on Sundays before noon. It is illegal to transport liquor through most Native American reservations.

Do not carry open containers of alcohol in your car or any public area that isn't zoned for alcohol consumption. The police can fine you on the spot. Don't even think about driving while intoxicated.

Driving Rules   See "Getting There & Around," in chapter 3.

Electricity   Like Canada, the United States uses 110 to 120 volts AC (60 cycles), compared to 220 to 240 volts AC (50 cycles) in most of Europe, Australia, and New Zealand. Downward converters that change 220 to 240 volts to 110 to 120 volts are difficult to find in the United States, so bring one with you.

Embassies & Consulates   All embassies are in the nation's capital, Washington, D.C. Some consulates are in major U.S. cities, and most nations have a mission to the United Nations in New York City. If your country isn't listed below, call for directory information in Washington, D.C. (📞 **202/555-1212**) or check **www.embassy.org/embassies**.

The embassy of **Australia** is at 1601 Massachusetts Ave. NW, Washington, DC 20036 (📞 **202/797-3000;** http://australia.visahq.com). Consulates are in New York, Honolulu, Houston, Los Angeles, and San Francisco.

The embassy of **Canada** is at 501 Pennsylvania Ave. NW, Washington, DC 20001 (📞 **202/682-1740;** www.canadainternational.gc.ca/washington). Other Canadian consulates are in Buffalo (New York), Detroit, Los Angeles, New York, and Seattle.

The embassy of **Ireland** is at 2234 Massachusetts Ave. NW, Washington, DC 20008 (① **202/462-3939;** www.embassyofireland.org). Irish consulates are in Boston, Chicago, New York, San Francisco, and other cities. See website for complete listing.

The embassy of **New Zealand** is at 37 Observatory Circle NW, Washington, DC 20008 (① **202/328-4800;** www.nzembassy.com). New Zealand consulates are in Los Angeles, Salt Lake City, San Francisco, and Seattle.

The embassy of the **United Kingdom** is at 3100 Massachusetts Ave. NW, Washington, DC 20008 (① **202/588-6500;** www.ukinusa.fco.gov.uk). Other British consulates are in Atlanta, Boston, Chicago, Cleveland, Houston, Los Angeles, New York, San Francisco, and Seattle.

Emergencies In case of emergency, dial ① **911.** For more specific information, see "Fast Facts," in chapters 5, 12, and 16.

Gasoline (Petrol) At press time, the cost of gasoline in the U.S. (also known as gas, but never petrol) is abnormally high. In New Mexico, prices run a little above the national average. Taxes are already included in the printed price. One U.S. gallon equals 3.8 liters or .85 imperial gallons.

Holidays Banks, government offices, post offices, and many stores, restaurants, and museums are closed on the following legal national holidays: January 1 (New Year's Day), the third Monday in January (Martin Luther King, Jr., Day), the third Monday in February (Presidents' Day), the last Monday in May (Memorial Day), July 4 (Independence Day), the first Monday in September (Labor Day), the second Monday in October (Columbus Day), November 11 (Veterans' Day/Armistice Day), the fourth Thursday in November (Thanksgiving Day), and December 25 (Christmas). The Tuesday after the first Monday in November is Election Day, a federal government holiday in presidential-election years (held every 4 years, and next in 2012). For more information on holidays see "Calendar of Events," in chapter 3.

Insurance In these uncertain times, travel insurance is always a good idea, but if you find that option costly, here is something to consider: In this region the weather and political climate are fairly reliable, so your trip won't likely be interrupted by those conditions. For information on traveler's insurance, trip cancellation insurance, and medical insurance while traveling, please visit www.frommers.com/tips.

Internet Access See "Staying Connected," in chapter 3.

Legal Aid If you are "pulled over" for a minor infraction (such as speeding), never attempt to pay the fine directly to a police officer; this could be construed as attempted bribery, a much more serious crime. Pay fines by mail, or directly into the hands of the clerk of the court. If accused of a more serious offense, say and do nothing before consulting a lawyer. Here the burden is on the state to prove a person's guilt beyond a reasonable doubt, and everyone has the right to remain silent, whether he or she is suspected of a crime or actually arrested. Once arrested, a person can make one telephone call to a party of his or her choice. The international visitor should call his or her embassy or consulate.

Mail At press time, domestic postage rates were 28¢ for a postcard and 44¢ for a letter. For international mail, a first-class letter of up to 1 ounce costs 98¢ (75¢ to Canada and 79¢ to Mexico); a first-class postcard costs the same as a letter. For more information go to **www.usps.com**.

If you aren't sure what your address will be in the United States, mail can be sent to you, in your name, c/o General Delivery at the main post office of the city or region where you expect to be. (Call ① **800/275-8777** for information on the nearest post office.) The addressee must pick up mail in person and must produce proof of identity (driver's license, passport, etc.). Most post offices will hold mail for up to 1 month, and are open Monday to Friday from 8am to 6pm, and Saturday from 9am to 3pm.

Always include zip codes when mailing items in the U.S. If you don't know your zip code, visit **www.usps.com/zip4**.

Newspapers & Magazines See "Staying Connected," in chapter 3.

Passports See "Embassies & Consulates," above, for whom to contact if you lose your passport while traveling in the U.S. For other information, contact the following agencies:

For Residents of Australia Contact the Australian Passport Information Service at ℂ 131-232, or visit www.passports.gov.au.

For Residents of Canada Contact the central **Passport Office,** Department of Foreign Affairs and International Trade, Ottawa, ON K1A 0G3 (ℂ **800/567-6868;** www.ppt.gc.ca).

For Residents of Ireland Contact the **Passport Office,** Setanta Centre, Molesworth Street, Dublin 2 (ℂ **01/671-1633;** www.foreignaffairs.gov.ie).

For Residents of New Zealand Contact the **Passports Office,** Department of Internal Affairs, 47 Boulcott St., Wellington, 6011 (ℂ **0800/225-050** in New Zealand or 04/474-8100; www.passports.govt.nz).

For Residents of the United Kingdom Visit your nearest passport office, major post office, or travel agency, or contact the **Identity and Passport Service (IPS),** 89 Eccleston Sq., London, SW1V 1PN (ℂ **0300/222-0000;** www.ips.gov.uk).

For Residents of the United States To find your regional passport office, check the U.S. State Department website (www.travel.state.gov/passport) or call the **National Passport Information Center** (ℂ 877/487-2778) for automated information.

Police In case of emergencies, dial ℂ **911.** For local police stations, see "Fast Facts," in chapters 5, 12, and 16.

Smoking New Mexico recently outlawed smoking at indoor public places, including restaurants and nightclubs. Some hotels offer rooms that allow smoking, though the number of these is dwindling.

Taxes Please see "Fast Facts," in chapters 5, 12, and 16, for specifics about city taxes. The United States has no value-added tax (VAT) or other indirect tax at the national level. Every state, county, and city may levy its own local tax on all purchases, including hotel and restaurant checks and airline tickets. These taxes will not appear on price tags.

Telephones See "Staying Connected," in chapter 3.

Time New Mexico is on **Mountain Standard Time,** 1 hour ahead of the West Coast and 2 hours behind the East Coast. When it's 10am in Santa Fe, it's noon in New York, 11am in Chicago, and 9am in San Francisco.

Daylight saving time (summer time) is in effect from 1am on the second Sunday in March to 1am on the first Sunday in November, except in Arizona, Hawaii, the U.S. Virgin Islands, and Puerto Rico. Daylight saving time moves the clock 1 hour ahead of standard time.

Tipping In hotels, tip **bellhops** at least $1 per bag ($2–$3 if you have a lot of luggage) and tip the **chamber staff** $1 to $2 per day (more if you've left a big mess for him or her to clean up). Tip the **doorman** or **concierge** only if he or she has provided you with some specific service (for example, calling a cab for you or obtaining difficult-to-get theater tickets). Tip the **valet-parking attendant** $1 every time you get your car.

In restaurants, bars, and nightclubs, tip **service staff** and **bartenders** 15% to 20% of the check, tip **checkroom attendants** $1 per garment, and tip **valet-parking attendants** $1 per vehicle.

As for other service personnel, tip **cab drivers** 15% of the fare; tip **skycaps** at airports at least $1 per bag ($2–$3 if you have a lot of luggage); and tip **hairdressers** and **barbers** 15% to 20%.

Toilets   You won't find public toilets or restrooms on the streets in most U.S. cities, but they can be found in hotel lobbies, bars, restaurants, museums, department stores, railway and bus stations, and service stations. Large hotels and fast-food restaurants are often the best bet for clean facilities. Restaurants and bars in resorts or heavily visited areas may reserve their restrooms for patrons.

Visas   For information about U.S. visas, go to **www.travel.state.gov** and click on "Visas." Or go to one of the following websites:

Australian citizens can obtain up-to-date visa information from the **U.S. Embassy Canberra,** Moonah Place, Yarralumla, ACT 2600 (✆ **02/6214-5600**) or by checking the U.S. Diplomatic Mission's website at **http://canberra.usembassy.gov**.

British subjects can obtain up-to-date visa information by calling the **U.S. Embassy Visa Information Line** (✆ **0891/200-290**), or by visiting the "Visas" section of the American Embassy London's website at **www.usembassy.org.uk**.

Irish citizens can obtain up-to-date visa information through the **U.S. Embassy Dublin,** 42 Elgin Rd., Ballsbridge, Dublin 4 (✆ **353/1-668-8777; http://dublin.usembassy.gov**).

Citizens of **New Zealand** can obtain up-to-date visa information by contacting the **U.S. Embassy New Zealand,** 29 Fitzherbert Terrace, Thorndon, Wellington (✆ **644/472-2068; http://newzealand.usembassy.gov**).

Visitor Information   Numerous agencies can assist you with planning your trip. The Visitors Information Center for the **New Mexico Department of Tourism** is located at 491 Old Santa Fe Trail, Santa Fe, NM 87501 (✆ **800/733-6396** or 505/827-7400). You can also find general New Mexico information on the Department of Tourism's website at **www.newmexico.org**. Santa Fe, Taos, and Albuquerque each have their own information service for visitors (see the "Orientation" sections in chapters 5, 12, and 16, respectively).

A valuable resource for information on outdoor recreation is the **Public Lands Information Center,** on the south side of town at 301 Dinosaur Trail, Santa Fe, NM 87508 (✆ **877/276-9404** or 505/954-2002; www.publiclands.org). Here, adventurers can find out what's available on lands administered by the National Forest Service, the Bureau of Land Management, the Fish and Wildlife Service, the National Park Service, the New Mexico Department of Game and Fish (which sells hunting and fishing licenses), and the New Mexico State Parks Division. The New Mexico Department of Tourism will send you a free state map if you call **800/733-6396** or 505/827-7400. Or, check out **www.mapquest.com**.

Water   All municipal water in the region is potable.

Wi-Fi   See "Staying Connected," in chapter 3.

AIRLINE WEBSITES

MAJOR AIRLINES

American Airlines & American Eagle
www.aa.com

Continental Airlines
www.continental.com

Delta Air Lines
www.delta.com

United Airlines
www.united.com

US Airways
www.usairways.com

BUDGET AIRLINES

Frontier Airlines
www.frontierairlines.com

Southwest Airlines
www.southwest.com

Index

See also Accommodations and
Restaurant indexes, below.

General Index

A

AAA (American Automobile
Association), 63
Abbey, Edward, 26
Abiquiu, 100, 173
Abiquiu Reservoir, 181
Abo, 286
ABQ Health Partners (Santa Fe),
68
ABQ Ride (Albuquerque), 240,
241, 243
ABQ Trolly Company
(Albuquerque), 272
ABQ Uptown (Albuquerque),
276
Absolute Nirvana Spa & Gardens
(Santa Fe), 138
Academic and cultural trips, 45
Accessibility, 39, 42–43
Access New Mexico, 42
Accommodation Hot Line (Santa
Fe), 70
Accommodations, 47–48. *See
also* Accommodations Index
　Albuquerque, 243–251
　best, 4–5
　Chama, 178–179
　Chimayo, 168
　Española area, 173–174
　Jemez Springs, 288–289
　Pojoaque Pueblo, 158–159
　responsible tourism and, 44
　Santa Fe. *See* Santa Fe,
　　accommodations
　Taos. *See* Taos,
　　accommodations
Acoma Pueblo, 284–287
Act I Gallery (Taos), 227
Adams, Ansel, 181
Adieb Khadoure Fine Art (Santa
Fe), 140
Adobe Bar (Taos), 232
Adolph Bandelier House (Santa
Fe), 130
Adventure and wellness trips,
45–46
Airports, 37–38
Alamo (Albuquerque), 241
Albuquerque, 15–16, 238–292
　accommodations, 243–251
　business hours, 241
　currency exchange, 242
　doctors, 242
　downtown, 238
　　restaurants, 255–258
　emergencies, 242
　getting around, 241

hospitals, 242
hot lines, 242
Internet access, 242
layout of, 240–241
library, 242
lost property, 242
maps, 241
nearby pueblos and
　monuments, 283–292
nightlife, 280–283
Old Town. *See* Old Town
outdoor activities, 272–275
parking, 241
pharmacies, 242
police, 242
post offices, 242
radio stations, 242
restaurants, 251–262
shopping, 276–280
sights and attractions, 262–
　272
spectator sports, 275–276
taxes, 242
television, 243
time zone, 243
transit information, 243
visitor information, 240
weather forecasts, 243
Albuquerque Art Business
Association, 277
Albuquerque Biological Park:
Aquarium and Botanic Garden,
269
Albuquerque Central KOA, 250
Albuquerque Convention and
Visitors Bureau, 240
Albuquerque Gallery
Association, 277
Albuquerque International
Balloon Fiesta, 35, 272
Albuquerque International
Sunport, 37–38, 240
Albuquerque Isotopes, 275–276
Albuquerque Journal, 242
Albuquerque Little Theatre, 281–
282
Albuquerque Museum of Art and
History, 262, 264
Albuquerque North Bernalillo
KOA, 250–251
Albuquerque Parks & Recreation
Department, 272
Albuquerque Pendleton, 279
Alcalde, 171
Alibi (Albuquerque), 242
Al Leedom Studio (Madrid), 291
Alley Cantina (Taos), 232
All Santa Fe Reservations, 70
Altermann Galleries (Santa Fe),
143
Amapola Gallery (Albuquerque),
277
American Automobile
Association (AAA), 63
American Eagle, 38, 62
American Indian Week
(Albuquerque), 32

American International
Rattlesnake Museum
(Albuquerque), 269–270
Amole Canyon, 220
Amtrak, 38, 39
Anaconda Bar (Taos), 232
Anaya, Rudolfo, 26
Ancestral Puebloans (Anasazi),
10, 16
　Anasazi Restaurant & Bar
　(Santa Fe), 128
Anderson Valley Vineyards
(Albuquerque), 279
Andrea Fisher Fine Pottery
(Santa Fe), 142
Andrew Smith Gallery (Santa
Fe), 143
Andrews Pueblo Pottery
(Albuquerque), 277
Angel Fire Resort, 219–220, 236–
237
Angel Fire Resort Golf Course,
223
Architecture, 21–23
Area codes, 293
Arroyo de los Chamisos Trail
(Santa Fe), 120
Arroyo del Oso (Albuquerque),
274
Arroyo Hondo, 234
Arroyo Seco, 224, 227
Arroyo Seco Mercantile, 227
Art, 20–21
The Art Center at Fuller Lodge
(Los Alamos), 164
Art classes, Taos, 217
Artemisia (Taos), 229
Art galleries. *See also* Arts and
crafts
　Albuquerque, 277–278
　Chama, 179
　Cordova, 168–169
　Los Alamos, 164
　Los Ojos, 180
　Madrid, 291
　Santa Fe, 140–144
　Taos, 227–228
　Truchas, 169
Arthur Boyle House (Santa Fe),
130
Art museums
　Albuquerque
　　Albuquerque Museum of
　　Art and History, 262,
　　264
　　University of New Mexico
　　Art Museum, 268–269
　Santa Fe
　　Georgia O'Keeffe
　　Museum, 110
　　Indian Arts Research
　　Center, 113, 116
　　Institute of American
　　Indian Arts Museum,
　　116
　　Museum of Indian Arts &
　　Culture, 116–117

Accommodations

Restaurants